ZAGAT

New Jersey
Restaurants
2012/13

LOCAL EDITORS
Mary Ann Castronovo Fusco and Pat Tanner
STAFF EDITOR
Yoji Yamaguchi with Curt Gathje

Published and distributed by
Zagat Survey, LLC
76 Ninth Avenue
New York, NY 10011
T: 212.977.6000
E: newjersey@zagat.com
www.zagat.com

ACKNOWLEDGMENTS

We thank Mike Lima and Rosie Saferstein, as well as the following members of our staff: Caitlin Miehl (editor), Anna Hyclak (editor), Brian Albert, Sean Beachell, Katie Carroll, Maryanne Bertollo, Reni Chin, Larry Cohn, Nicole Diaz, Jeff Freier, Alison Gainor, Matthew Hamm, Kelly Dobkin, Justin Hartung, Marc Henson, Ryutaro Ishikane, Natalie Lebert, Mike Liao, Vivian Ma, James Mulcahy, Polina Paley, Amanda Spurlock, Chris Walsh, Jacqueline Wasilczyk, Sharon Yates, Anna Zappia and Kyle Zolner.

The reviews in this guide are based on public opinion surveys. The ratings reflect the average scores given by the survey participants who voted on each establishment. The text is based on quotes from, or paraphrasings of, the surveyors' comments. Phone numbers, addresses and other factual data were correct to the best of our knowledge when published in this guide.

Contents

Ratings & Symbols

	Name	Symbols	Cuisine	Zagat Ratings			
Zagat Top Spot				FOOD	DECOR	SERVICE	COST

Area, Address & Contact

Z Tim & Nina's ◑ *Pizza*   ∇ 23 | 9 | 13 | $15

Atlantic City | 5678 Pacific Ave. (Atlantic Ave.) | 609-555-1212 | www.zagat.com

Review, surveyor comments in quotes

"Miles from the boardwalk but still not far enough away", this "never-closing" AC "eyesore" "single-handedly" started the "saltwater-taffy pizza craze" that's "sweeping the casino capital" like "a run of bad luck"; don't forget to "visit the all-you-can-stomach buffet" – "it's to die for" (or from) – but don't look for ambiance because "T & N don't know from design", or service, for that matter, which is not that surprising, given the "giveaway" prices.

Ratings

Food, Decor & **Service** are rated on a 30-point scale.

0 – 9	poor to fair
10 – 15	fair to good
16 – 19	good to very good
20 – 25	very good to excellent
26 – 30	extraordinary to perfection
∇	low response	less reliable

Cost

The price of dinner with a drink and tip; lunch is usually 25% to 30% less. For unrated **newcomers** or **write-ins,** the price range is as follows:

I	$25 and below	E	$41 to $65
M	$26 to $40	VE	$66 or above

Symbols

Z	highest ratings, popularity and importance
◑	serves after 11 PM
S M	closed on Sunday or Monday
⊄	no credit cards accepted

About This Survey

This **2012/13 New Jersey Restaurants Survey** is an update reflecting significant developments since our last Survey was published. It covers 1,135 restaurants in the state, including 89 important additions. We've also indicated new addresses, phone numbers and other major changes. Like all our guides, this one is based on input from avid local diners – 6,909 all told. Our editors have synopsized this feedback, including representative comments (in quotation marks within each review). To read full surveyor comments – and share your own opinions – visit **zagat.com,** where you will also find the latest restaurant news, special events, deals, reservations, menus, photos and lots more, **all for free.**

ABOUT ZAGAT: In 1979, we started asking friends to rate and review restaurants purely for fun. The term "user-generated content" had yet to be coined. That hobby grew into Zagat Survey; 33 years later, we have over 375,000 surveyors and cover airlines, bars, dining, fast food, entertaining, golf, hotels, movies, music, resorts, shopping, spas, theater and tourist attractions in over 100 countries. Along the way, we evolved from being a print publisher to a digital content provider, e.g. **zagat.com** and Zagat mobile apps (for Android, iPad, iPhone, BlackBerry, Windows Phone 7 and Palm webOS). We also produce marketing tools for a wide range of blue-chip corporate clients. And you can find us on Google+ and just about any other social media network.

UNDERLYING PREMISES: Three simple ideas underlie our ratings and reviews. First, we believe that the collective opinions of large numbers of consumers are more accurate than those of any single person. (Consider that our surveyors bring some 998,000 annual meals' worth of experience to this survey, visiting restaurants regularly year-round, anonymously – and on their own dime.) Second, food quality is only part of the equation when choosing a restaurant, thus we ask our surveyors to rate food, decor and service separately and then estimate the cost of a meal. Third, since people need reliable information in an easy-to-digest format, we strive to be concise and we offer our content on every platform – print, online and mobile.

THANKS: We're grateful to our local editors, Mary Ann Castronovo Fusco, a freelance editor and contributor to *New Jersey Monthly*, and Pat Tanner, a restaurant critic for *New Jersey Monthly,* food blogger for DineWithPat.com and food columnist for *The Princeton Packet* and *U.S. 1.* We also sincerely thank the thousands of people who participated in this survey – this guide is really "theirs."

JOIN IN: To improve our guides, we solicit your comments – positive or negative; it's vital that we hear your opinions. Just contact us at **nina-tim@zagat.com.** We also invite you to join our surveys at **zagat.com.** Do so and you'll receive a choice of rewards in exchange.

New York, NY
May 9, 2012

Nina and Tim Zagat

What's New

Although the economy appears to have finally turned the corner, many people are still struggling. Witness the efforts of native rocker Jon Bon Jovi, who opened the nonprofit **JBJ Soul Kitchen** in Red Bank, where diners pay what they can afford or do volunteer work to settle their tabs. The past year also saw an influx of affordable eateries geared toward these still-uncertain times. That being said, a number of high-end debuts reflect optimism about the restaurant scene.

MAKING LEMONADE: Even as eateries continue to be shuttered, established Jersey chefs are stepping in with new ventures to take their place. Zod Arifai (Montclair's **Blu** and **Next Door**) now dishes up his popular Med-inspired New American fare at the revamped **Daryl** in New Brunswick, while Ryan DePersio, who made his name at **Fascino** (Montclair) and **Bar Cara** (Bloomfield), oversees the Eclectic **Nico** at NJPAC in Newark, which replaced Theater Square Grill. Others are reinventing their own restaurants, such as Thomas Ciszak, whose former **Copeland** in Morristown became the American **Blue Morel,** and star chef Michael White, the owner of NYC's No. 1 Italian, **Marea,** who converted his Bernardsville property, **Due Terre,** into **Osteria Morini,** an offshoot of his famed SoHo Italian.

CASINO ROYALES: Much of the higher-end action has been taking place at the casinos. Luke Palladino opened a grander spin-off of his eponymous Northfield Italian inside Harrah's in nearby Atlantic City, while Chris Scarduzio, who teamed with Georges Perrier at Caesars' **Mia,** has added a namesake steakhouse, **Scarduzio's,** at the Showboat. Michel Richard is just one of several nationally acclaimed chefs opening restaurants in the Revel Casino in 2012. Set to open at press time are Richard's American **O Bistro & Wine Bar** and **The Breakfast Room** and Robert Wiedmaier's Belgian gastropub, **Mussel Bar.** Not far behind are **Central Michel Richard,** three by Jose Garces (**Amada, Village Whiskey, Distrito**), Iron Chef alum Marc Forgione's **American Cut** steakhouse, **Azure** by Alain Allegretti and a branch of the NY cafe **Lugo.**

 GARDEN STATE: The locavore movement continues to gain traction, with Jersey eateries at every price point touting ingredients served within hours of being picked, often from the restaurants' on-site gardens or from dedicated plots at nearby farms. Some even maintain their own farms, such as the Kingston Italian **Eno Terra,** the New American **Ninety Acres at Natirar** in Peapack and New American newcomer **Ursino** in Union. More and more diners consider this so important that a majority says it's willing to pay more for such ingredients.

New Jersey
May 9, 2012

Mary Ann Castronovo Fusco
Pat Tanner

Most Popular

Plotted on the map at the back of this book.

1. Nicholas | *American*
2. Cheesecake Factory | *American*
3. River Palm | *Steak*
4. Cafe Panache | *Eclectic*
5. Highlawn Pavilion | *American*
6. Five Guys | *Burgers*
7. Ruth's Chris | *Steak*
8. P.F. Chang's | *Chinese*
9. Scalini Fedeli | *Italian*
10. Saddle River Inn | *Amer./French*
11. Cafe Matisse | *Eclectic*
12. Amanda's | *American*
13. Serenade | *French*
14. Bernards Inn | *American*
15. Legal Sea Foods | *Seafood*
16. Frog and the Peach | *American*
17. Latour | *French*
18. CulinAriane | *American*
19. Lorena's | *French*
20. Varka | *Greek/Seafood*
21. Origin | *French/Thai*
22. Pluckemin Inn | *American*
23. Moonstruck | *American/Med.*
24. Fascino | *Italian*
25. Avenue | *French*
26. Baumgart's Café | *Amer./Asian*
27. Morton's Steak | *Steak*
28. Ninety Acres | *American*
29. Il Mondo Vecchio | *Italian*
30. David Burke | *American*
31. Osteria Giotto | *Italian*
32. Fornos of Spain | *Spanish*
33. Chef's Table | *French*
34. Blue Point | *Seafood*
35. Park & Orchard | *Eclectic*
36. Basilico | *Italian*
37. Chart House | *Seafood*
38. McCormick/Schmick's | *Seafood*
39. Huntley Taverne | *American*
40. Bay Ave. Trattoria | *Amer./Italian*
41. A Toute Heure | *American*
42. Chef Vola's | *Italian*
43. Rat's | *French*
44. Arthur's Tavern | *Steak*
45. 410 Bank St. | *Carib./Creole*
46. Elements | *American*
47. Manor | *American*
48. Buddakan | *Asian*
49. It's Greek To Me | *Greek*
50. Due Mari | *Italian*

Many of the above restaurants are among New Jersey's most expensive, but if popularity were calibrated to price, a number of other restaurants would surely join their ranks. To illustrate this, we have added two pages of Best Buys starting on page 16.

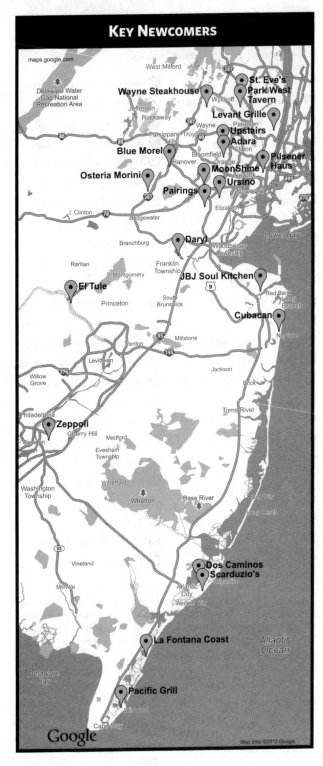

KEY NEWCOMERS

maps.google.com

West Milford

Delaware Water
Gap National
Recreation Area

Wayne Steakhouse
Wyckoff

St. Eve's
Park West
Tavern

Jefferson
Rockaway

Wayne

Levant Grille

Parsippany-Troy
Hills

Paterson

Upstairs
Adara

Blue Morel

Bloomfield
Hanover

Clinton

MoonShine

Orange
Newark

Pilsener
Haus

Osteria Morini

Pairings

Ursino

New York

Clinton

Bridgewater

Elizabeth

Lower Bay

Branchburg

Daryl

Woodbridge
Township

Raritan

Franklin
Township

JBJ Soul Kitchen

Montgomery

El Tule

Princeton

South
Brunswick

Red Bank
Long
Branch

Cubacan

Neptune

Trenton

Millstone

Levittown

Jackson

Brick

Willow
Grove

Toms River

Philadelphia

Zeppoli
Cherry Hill

Medford

Camden

Evesham
Township

Washington
Township

Waterford

Wharton

Bass River

Surf City
Long Beach

Vineland

Millville

Dos Caminos
Scarduzio's

Atlantic
City
Ventnor City

Brigantine

Atlantic
Ocean

Delaware
Bay

La Fontana Coast

Pacific Grill

Wildwood

Cape May

Google

Map data ©2012 Google

Vote at zagat.com

Key Newcomers

Our editors' picks among this year's arrivals. See full list at p. 213.

Adara | *Amer.* | Molecular gastronomy at a spendy Montclair BYO

Blue Morel | *Amer.* | Seasonal fare, sushi and wine bar in Morristown

Cubacan | *Cuban* | South Beach meets Asbury Park in upscale-casual digs

Daryl | *Amer.* | Pricey American in New Brunswick's Heldrich Hotel

Dos Caminos | *Mexican* | Large upscale cantina in AC's Harrah's Casino

El Tule | *Mexican/ Peruvian* | Cozy midpriced BYO in Lambertville

JBJ Soul Kitchen | *Amer.* | Bon Jovi's pay-what-you-can Red Bank eatery

La Fontana Coast | *Italian* | Expensive seasonal BYO in Sea Isle City

Levant Grille | *Med.* | Turkish and Persian dishes rule at this Englewood BYO

MoonShine | *American* | Comfort fare in a supper-club setting in Millburn

Osteria Morini | *Italian* | Bernardsville satellite of the high-end SoHo eatery

Pacific Grill | *American* | Pricey seasonal sibling of Cape May's Union Park

Pairings | *Amer.* | New American plus global flavors at this Cranford BYO

Park West Tavern | *American* | Park Steakhouse's pricey sibling in Ridgewood

Pilsener Haus | *Austrian/Hungarian* | Midpriced Hoboken beer garden

Scarduzio's | *Japanese/Steak* | Upscale steak and sushi at AC's Showboat

St. Eve's | *American* | Moderately priced Ho-Ho-Kus BYO

Upstairs | *Amer.* | Pricey small and large plates in modern Montclair digs

Ursino | *American* | High-style design meets farm-to-table fare in Union

Wayne Steakhouse | *Steak* | High-end Wayne surf 'n' turfer

Zeppoli | *Italian* | Collingswood BYO from chef Joseph Baldino (ex Vetri)

On the Horizon: Veteran restaurateurs Jeanne & Frank Cretella (**Liberty House** in Jersey City, **Stone House at Stirling Ridge** in Warren) purchased the shuttered **Ryland Inn** and are planning a mid-2012 reopening of that legendary Whitehouse property.

Top Food

29	Nicholas | *American*
28	Shumi | *Japanese*
	Sapori | *Italian*
	Washington Inn | *American*
	Lorena's | *French*
	Chef's Table | *French*
	Bay Ave. Tratt. | *Amer./Italian*
	Saddle River Inn | *Amer./French*
27	CulinAriane | *American*
	Little Café | *Eclectic*
	Scalini Fedeli | *Italian*
	Serenade | *French*
	Picnic | *American*
	Drew's Bayshore | *American*
	Sagami | *Japanese*
	Restaurant Latour | *American*
	Andre's | *American*
	Dino & Harry's | *Steak*
	Cafe Matisse | *Eclectic*
	Whispers | *American*
	Milford Oyster | *Seafood*
	DeLorenzo's Pies | *Pizza*
	Old Homestead | *Steak*
	Cafe Panache | *Eclectic*
	Bernards Inn | *American*
	Stage Left | *American*

	Le Rendez-Vous | *French*
	Il Mulino NY | *Italian*
	Yellow Fin | *American*
26	Belford Bistro | *American*
	Latour | *French*
	A Toute Heure | *American*
	Piccola Italia | *Italian*
	Elements | *American*
	Yumi | *Asian*
	Ebbitt Room | *American*
	Chef Vola's | *Italian*
	Rosemary & Sage | *American*
	White House | *Sandwiches*
	Perryville Inn | *American*
	Porto Leggero* | *Italian*
	Augustino's | *Italian*
	Girasole | *Italian*
	410 Bank St. | *Carib./Creole*
	Hamilton's | *Mediterranean*
	Nomad Pizza | *Pizza*
	Dock's Oyster | *Seafood*
	Amanda's | *American*
	Black Duck | *Eclectic*
	Blue Bottle | *American*
	Il Fiore* | *Italian*
	Cucharamama | *S American*

BY CUISINE

AMERICAN (NEW)

29	Nicholas
28	Bay Ave. Trattoria
	Saddle River Inn
27	CulinAriane
	Picnic

AMERICAN (TRAD.)

28	Washington Inn
26	Perryville Inn
24	Manor
	Meil's
	Ram's Head Inn

BURGERS

23	White Manna
22	Barnacle Bill's
21	Bobby's Burger
	Five Guys
19	Elevation Burger

CHINESE

26	Wonder Seafood
25	West Lake Seafood
	Meemah
24	Chef Jon's
	Joe's Peking

COFFEE SHOP/DINER

24	Mustache Bill's
22	Skylark
19	Ponzio's
	Mastoris
18	Tick Tock Diner

CUBAN

25	La Isla
23	Rebecca's
22	Martino's
	Casona
21	Cuba Libre

---

* Indicates a tie with restaurant above; excludes places with low votes, unless otherwise indicated

Vote at zagat.com

ECLECTIC
27 Little Café
Cafe Matisse
Cafe Panache
26 Black Duck
25 Labrador

FRENCH
28 Lorena's
Saddle River Inn
27 Serenade
26 Latour
Chez Catherine

FRENCH (BISTRO)
28 Chef's Table
27 Le Rendez-Vous
25 Le Fandy
24 Sophie's Bistro
23 Madame Claude

GREEK
26 Varka
25 Taverna Mykonos
24 Limani
23 Axia Taverna
Pithari Taverna

INDIAN
24 Saffron
Mehndi
23 Cinnamon
Moghul
Chand Palace

ITALIAN
28 Sapori
Bay Ave. Trattoria
27 Scalini Fedeli
Il Mulino NY
26 Piccola Italia
Chef Vola's
Porto Leggero
Augustino's
Girasole
Il Fiore
Mia

JAPANESE
28 Shumi
27 Sagami
25 Taka
Sakura-Bana
Fuji

MEDITERRANEAN
26 Hamilton's
25 Moonstruck
Sage

23 Sofia
Vine

MEXICAN
25 La Esperanza
24 Tortilla Press
Taqueria
El Mesón Café
Casa Maya

MIDDLE EASTERN
23 Silk Road
22 Pamir
Ibby's Falafel
Bosphorus
Norma's

PIZZA
27 DeLorenzo's Pies
26 Nomad Pizza
25 Grimaldi's Pizza
Napoli's Pizza
Conte's

SEAFOOD
27 Milford Oyster
26 Dock's Oyster
SeaBlue
Blue Point
25 Navesink Fishery

SOUTH AMERICAN/ PAN-LATIN
26 Cucharamama
23 Casa Solar
Zafra
22 Brasilia
20 Rio Rodizio

SPANISH/PORTUGUESE
24 Fernandes Steak
Spain
Fornos of Spain
Casa Vasca
23 Bistro Olé

STEAKHOUSES
27 Dino & Harry's
Old Homestead
26 Steakhouse 85
Capital Grille
Roots Steak

THAI
26 Siri's
25 Origin
Sri Thai
24 Pad Thai
Siam Garden

BY SPECIAL FEATURE

BREAKFAST

24 Hobby's Deli
Meil's
23 Zafra
Mad Batter
22 Toast

BRUNCH

26 Elements
Amanda's
25 Anthony David's
Verjus
24 Tortilla Press

CHILD-FRIENDLY

22 Skylark
21 Hot Dog Johnny's
Surf Taco
20 Pop Shop
19 Baumgart's Café
Cheesecake Factory

HOTEL DINING

27 Restaurant Latour
Crystal Springs Resort
Whispers
Hewitt Wellington
Old Homestead
Borgata
Il Mulino NY
Trump Taj Mahal
26 Ebbitt Room
Virginia Hotel

OFFBEAT

26 Chef Vola's
Augustino's
25 Manon
Trinity
Meemah

PEOPLE-WATCHING

27 Dino & Harry's
Bernards Inn
26 Cucharamama
Mia
Buddakan

POWER SCENES

27 Scalini Fedeli
Serenade
Old Homestead
26 Porto Leggero
Rist. da Benito

QUICK BITES

27 DeLorenzo's Pies
25 Napoli's Pizza
24 Tortilla Press
Taqueria
Hobby's Deli

QUIET CONVERSATION

28 Chef's Table
Saddle River Inn
27 Restaurant Latour
Whispers
26 Elements

SINGLES SCENES

26 Cucharamama
Mia
Buddakan
Atlantic B&G
25 Tomatoes

SPECIAL OCCASION

29 Nicholas
28 Washington Inn
Chef's Table
Saddle River Inn
27 CulinAriane

TRENDY

28 Lorena's
27 Picnic
Drew's Bayshore
Dino & Harry's
Cafe Matisse

WINNING WINE LISTS

29 Nicholas
28 Washington Inn
27 Scalini Fedeli
Serenade
Restaurant Latour

BY LOCATION

Top Decor

28	Ninety Acres		Ram's Head Inn
	Highlawn Pavilion		Manor
	Stone House		Catherine Lombardi
	Rat's		Chart House
27	Peter Shields	25	SeaBlue
	Nicholas		Waterside
	Buddakan		Porto Leggero
	Avenue		Grato
26	Bernards Inn		Grand Cafe
	Washington Inn		Eno Terra
	Restaurant Latour		Elements
	Chakra		Izakaya
	Ebbitt Room		Scalini Fedeli
	Gables		Hotoke
	Pluckemin Inn		Raven & Peach*
	Cafe Madison		Molly Pitcher
	Red Square		Seasons 52
	Serenade		Amanda's
	Capriccio		Moonstruck
	Cafe Matisse		Peacock Inn

OUTDOORS

Alice's		Rat's	
Avenue		Sirena	
Maritime Parc		Sofia	
Moonstruck		Stone House	
Ninety Acres		Waterside	

ROMANCE

Bernards Inn		Pluckemin Inn	
Chakra		Restaurant Latour	
Ebbitt Room		Scarborough Fair	
Esty Street		Sergeantsville Inn	
Peacock Inn		Whispers	

ROOMS

Buddakan		Nicholas	
Cafe Matisse		Ninety Acres	
Chelsea Prime		Peter Shields	
Elements		Porto Leggero	
Harvest Bistro		Stony Hill Inn	

VIEWS

Atlantic B&G		Le Jardin	
Avenue		Liberty House	
Café Gallery		Stella Marina	
Chophouse		Vu	
Highlawn Pavilion		Walpack Inn	

Vote at zagat.com

Top Service

28	Nicholas	Ikko
27	Lorena's	Chef's Table
	Washington Inn	Andre's
	Restaurant Latour	
26	Milford Oyster	**25** Capital Grille
	Whispers	Resto
	Bernards Inn	Highlawn Pavilion
	Picnic	Pluckemin Inn
	Sapori*	Manor
	Scalini Fedeli	Mattar's Bistro
	Cafe Matisse	Ram's Head Inn
	Saddle River Inn	La Spiaggia
	Capriccio	Chez Catherine
	Peter Shields	Il Capriccio
	Serenade	Grand Cafe
	Stage Left	Cafe Panache
	Old Homestead	CulinAriane
	Porto Leggero	Elements
	Ebbitt Room	Amanda's
	Rist. da Benito	Steakhouse 85
		SeaBlue

Best Buys

Everyone loves a bargain, and New Jersey offers plenty of them. All-you-can-eat options are mostly for lunch and/or brunch. For prix fixe menus, call ahead for availability.

ALL YOU CAN EAT

27 Bernards Inn
25 Madeleine's
24 Saffron
   Fernandes Steak
   Manor
   Mehndi
23 Cinnamon
   Moghul
   Chand Palace
   Black Forest Inn
22 KC Prime
   Mantra
   Brasilia
   Rod's Steak

BYO

28 Shumi
   Sapori
   Lorena's
   Chef's Table
   Bay Ave. Trattoria
   Saddle River Inn
   La Locanda
27 CulinAriane
   Little Café
   Picnic
   Drew's Bayshore
   Sagami
   Oliver a Bistro
   Cafe Matisse

EARLY-BIRD ($40 AND UNDER)

28 Washington Inn ($24)
26 Perryville Inn ($18)
   Amanda's ($16)
   Black Duck ($22)
   Cucharamama ($20)
   Peter Shields ($40)
25 Giumarello's ($13)
   Harvest Moon ($27)
24 Tortilla Press ($17)
   La Spiaggia ($18)
   Merion Inn ($17)
23 Elements Café ($15)
   Axelsson's ($22)
22 Avenue ($30)

FAMILY-STYLE

26 Piccola Italia
   Chef Vola's
24 Mesob
   Pad Thai
   Trattoria Mediterranea
23 E & V
22 Spanish Tavern
21 GoodFellas
   Carmine's
20 Gaetano's
   P.F. Chang's
   Maggiano's
18 Cassie's

PRIX FIXE LUNCH (UNDER $30)

26 Belford Bistro ($11)
   Latour ($25)
   Perryville Inn ($20)
   Girasole ($15)
   Frog and the Peach ($25)
25 Madeleine's ($22)
   Sumo ($10)
   Esty Street ($19)
   Le Fandy ($21)
24 Wasabi ($10)
   Eno Terra ($24)
   Village Green ($20)
23 Mikado ($9)
21 Panico's ($15)

PRIX FIXE DINNER ($50 AND UNDER)

28 Sapori ($45)
27 Drew's Bayshore ($27)
   Oliver a Bistro ($35)
   Andre's ($50)
   Dream Cuisine ($45)
26 Latour ($40)
   Frog and the Peach ($35)
25 Madeleine's ($33)
   Filomena Italiana ($15)▽
   Steve & Cookie's ($24)
   David Burke ($35)
   Fuji ($50)
   Ruth's Chris ($43)
23 Chophouse ($35)

BEST BUYS: BANG FOR THE BUCK

In order of Bang for the Buck rating.

1. Hot Dog Johnny's
2. White Manna
3. White Mana
4. Five Guys
5. Surf Taco
6. Jimmy Buff's
7. Hiram's Roadstand
8. Mustache Bill's
9. Ibby's Falafel
10. Elevation Burger
11. Smashburger
12. Benny Tudino's
13. Tito's Burritos
14. White House
15. WindMill
16. Baja Fresh
17. Pop Shop
18. Taqueria
19. Rutt's Hut
20. Bobby's Burger
21. Rolling Pin
22. DeLorenzo's Pies
23. DeLorenzo's Pizza
24. Holsten's
25. Nomad Pizza
26. Napoli's Pizza
27. Tony Luke's
28. Tacconelli's Pizza
29. Richard's
30. Grimaldi's Pizza
31. Java Moon
32. Pop's Garage
33. Conte's
34. Toast
35. Hobby's Deli
36. Fedora Café
37. El Azteca
38. Brooklyn's Pizza
39. Nana's Deli
40. Kibitz Room

BEST BUYS: OTHER GOOD VALUES

Aleppo
Allen's Clam Bar
Avenue Bistro Pub
Blue Fish Grill
Casa Maya
Cassie's
Chef Jon's
Country Pancake
Cubby's BBQ
DiPalma Bros.
El Cid
Eppes Essen
Fishery
Fortune Cookie
Freshwaters
Gianna's
Greek Taverna
Hummus Elite
India/Hudson
Je's
Kairo Kafe
Karma Kafe
Kaya's Kitchen
La Esperanza
La Griglia
Little Food
Lotus Cafe
Market Roost
Minado
Norma's
Rumba Cubana
Sakura Spring
Sanducci's Trattoria
Settimo Cielo
Skylark
Somsak
Tiger Noodles
Très Yan & Wu
Vincentown Diner
West Lake Seafood

RESTAURANT DIRECTORY

	FOOD	DECOR	SERVICE	COST

Aamantran ⓜ *Indian*
▽ 21 | 15 | 20 | $26

Toms River | Victoria Plaza | 1594 Rte. 9 S. (Church Rd.) | 732-341-5424
In Hindi, the name means 'invitation' and this Indian BYO in a Toms River strip mall draws diners with its clay ovens, Bollywood soundtrack and "large selection" of "very good" vittles; "friendly" staffers willing to "answer any questions" and "inspiring" lunch buffets add to its appeal.

Aangan *Indian*
23 | 18 | 20 | $26

Freehold Township | A&M Plaza | 3475 Rte. 9 N. (Three Brooks Rd.) | 732-761-2900 | www.aanganfreehold.com
The menu consists of "all the favorite" if "usual" Indian choices, but the "top-flight" chow is always "fresh" at this "spacious" BYO in Freehold's A&M Plaza; daily lunch buffets and dinner buffets on Sundays and Thursdays keep the costs "reasonable" and make this one a "worthwhile" option.

Aby's *Mexican*
20 | 11 | 18 | $23

Matawan | 141 Main St. (Little St.) | 732-583-9119
Proponents praise the "fresh", "simple" Mexican food "done well" at this "humble" "neighborhood" BYO in Downtown Matawan; sure, the interior's strictly "bare-bones" and the service "inconsistent", but the portions are "generous", the prices "comfortable" and there's a guitarist on Saturday nights in the summer.

Acacia ⓜ *American*
23 | 21 | 22 | $50

Lawrenceville | 2637 Main St. (bet. Craven Ln. & Phillips Ave.) | 609-895-9885 | www.acaciacuisine.com
This "pleasant" "local favorite" serves an "interesting menu" of "delicious" modern American food in a "lovely" setting "right on Main Street in the quiet town of Lawrenceville"; some find it "a bit pricey", but loyalists say this "high-quality" spot is "worth every penny" – and the BYO policy makes the tabs "slightly less painful."

Acquaviva delle Fonti ⓜ *Italian*
22 | 21 | 23 | $45

Westfield | 115 Elm St. (bet. Broad & Orchard Sts.) | 908-301-0700 | www.acquaviva-dellefonti.com
"Dependably delicious", this "upbeat", "upscale" Westfield Italian set in a former bank building offers a Med-accented menu and features "relaxing" courtyard seating, "outstanding" service and alfresco music; though it can be "a bit loud" and you may have to wait, "even with a reservation", overall it's a "thoroughly enjoyable experience."

NEW Adara ⓈⓂ *American*
- | - | - | E

Montclair | 77 Walnut St. (Grove St.) | 973-783-0462 | www.restaurantadara.com
At this Montclair BYO American, chef-owner Tre Ghosal (ex Nouveau Sushi) conjures molecular magic that's showcased on à la carte, three-course prix fixe and (reservation-only) multicourse 'tour' menus, plus a minibar option that comes with a mocktail; modern art graces the earth-toned, minimalist space that formerly housed Passionné; P.S. the name means 'caring' in Sanskrit.

Adega Grill *Portuguese/Spanish*   22 | 22 | 22 | $43

Newark | 130-132 Ferry St. (bet. Madison & Monroe Sts.) |
973-589-8830 | www.adegagrill.com

"Superior seafood" and "imaginative", "authentic" Portuguese
dishes make this "inviting" Newark Iberian "one of the better ones in
the Ironbound"; "fancy wine cellar" decor (complete with faux
grapevines) lends an "upscale" vibe, while "efficient" service and
free parking around the corner ice the cake.

Ah'Pizz *Pizza*   22 | 15 | 18 | $23

Montclair | 7 N. Willow St. (Glen Ridge Ave.) | 973-783-9200 |
www.ahpizznj.com

"Quality Neapolitan pizza comes to NJ" via the "authentic" "hand-
made" pies emanating from the wood-burning brick oven of this
"off-the-beaten-track" Montclair BYO; "big-time" prices for the
genre and a "casual" (verging on "spartan") setting come with the
territory, but most find it "well worth seeking out" – despite no reservations and no phone orders accepted.

Ajihei Ⓜ *Japanese*   25 | 11 | 15 | $33

Princeton | 11 Chambers St., downstairs (Nassau St.) |
609-252-1158

Loyal advocates of this "sublime" Japanese BYO in Princeton consider chef Koji Kitamura's "impeccably fresh" sushi some of the best
"outside of NY", and though service is "grumpy" and the decor "un-
remarkable", it's usually "difficult to get into"; P.S. no reservations
are accepted, and because of its "tiny" dimensions, only groups of
four or less are seated.

Akai Lounge *Japanese*   24 | 19 | 21 | $41

Englewood | 11 N. Dean St. (Palisade Ave.) | 201-541-0086
Some of the "best sushi outside Japan" nets "wow" responses at this
"chic" Japanese near Englewood PAC that's a magnet for a "young-
ish" crowd and *Real Housewives* types; "great" entrees, "gracious"
service and "creative" drinks all earn kudos, though "steep price
tags" come with the territory.

Akbar *Indian*   20 | 19 | 18 | $30

Edison | 21 Cortland St. (Patrick Ave.) | 732-632-8822 |
www.akbarrestaurant.com

This three-room, 500-seat Edison Indian offers "classic" cooking
that's "consistently good" (albeit "a little bit pricey") served by an
"accommodating" crew in a "Bollywood"-esque setting; though
weekend dining skews "loud", the "fair-priced" all-you-can-eat buffet lunch makes the din easier to swallow.

Alchemist & Barrister *American*   16 | 16 | 18 | $36

Princeton | 28 Witherspoon St. (Nassau St.) | 609-924-5555 |
www.theaandb.com

Regulars stick to the "cozy bar" and "enclosed patio" at this "old-
line" "stalwart" in the heart of Princeton rather than its just "serviceable" dining rooms; though the "reliable" burgers and brews trump

the "fancier entrees" on the Traditional American menu, it's still a no-brainer for "parents weekends" given that "great location."

Aldo & Gianni ⊠ *Italian* | 21 | 15 | 20 | $41 |

Montvale | A&P Shopping Ctr. | 108 Chestnut Ridge Rd. (Grand Ave.) | 201-391-6866 | www.aldoandgianni.com

"Excellent", "old-school" cooking and "solicitous" service make this "popular" Montvale strip-mall Italian a "neighborhood standby"; the intimate setting can be "noisy" and the "traditional" cooking supplies "no surprises", but at least the pricing is "fair"; P.S. a recent redo may not be reflected in the Decor score.

Aleppo *Syrian* | - | - | - | I |

Paterson | 939 Main St. (Montclair Ave.) | 973-977-2244

Syrian takes on Middle Eastern classics abound at this modest venue in Paterson, where the flavorful food features ingredients like cherry juice, pomegranate syrup and the renowned red pepper from which the restaurant takes its name; alcohol is not allowed on premises.

Ali Baba *Mideastern* | 19 | 11 | 18 | $23 |

Hoboken | 912 Washington St. (bet. 9th & 10th Sts.) | 201-653-5319

"Going strong since the '80s", this "casual" Hoboken BYO is known for its "wonderful" Mideastern cooking, "plentiful" portions and "fair prices"; but even though the atmosphere is "hospitable", it could definitely "use some sprucing up", hence its reputation as a "favorite take-out spot."

Alice's *American* | 21 | 20 | 19 | $37 |

Lake Hopatcong | 24 Nolans Point Park Rd. (Nolans Point Rd.) | 973-663-9600 | www.alicesrestaurantnj.com

"Innovative" chef David Drake works "magic" with everything from "fine fare to comfort food" at this "worthwhile" New American, where the "weathered" room opens onto a deck boasting "picturesque" views of Lake Hopatcong; the "fun bar scene" can make it "a bit loud", but "attentive" service and "affordable" tabs help to distract; P.S. breakfast is served on Saturday and Sunday.

Aligado *Thai* | ▽ 24 | 16 | 20 | $26 |

Hazlet | 2780 Rte. 35 (Miller Ave.) | 732-888-7568

Chef-owner George Zhenz is "always around" at this BYO "hidden gem" secreted in a "trailerlike building" on Route 35 in Hazlet; "to-die-for" sushi, "tasty" Thai food" and "friendly" service make the "tired" decor easier to overlook.

A Little Bit of Cuba Dos Ⓜ *Cuban* | 19 | - | 20 | $28 |

Freehold | 2 E. Main St. (South St.) | 732-577-8506 | www.alittlebitofcubados.com

Locals consider this Cuban BYO in Freehold authentic enough to make them "want to visit Havana", while "nice" staffers, a "fun" atmosphere and "real-deal" cooking make "loud" live music on Saturdays more tolerable; it moved from its former strip-mall digs to its current storefront location post-Survey.

	FOOD	DECOR	SERVICE	COST

Allen's Clam Bar Ⓜ *Seafood*   ▽ 22 | 11 | 21 | $21

New Gretna | 5650 Rte. 9 (bet. Frenchs Ln. & Rte. 679) | 609-296-4106
"Clams!" – think half-shell, steamed, Casino – keep locals coming back
to this "popular", no-frills BYO in New Gretna that also slings "basic
fried seafood"; there's "not much decor" and it's "always jammed in
the summer", but at least service is "fast" and the price is right.

Alps Bistro Ⓜ *German*   - | - | - | M

Allentown | 4 S. Main St. (Church Rd.) | 609-223-0335
The eight tables at this modest BYO German in Allentown fill up
fast, thanks to its reliable, affordable wursts, schnitzels and stru-
dels, as well as Eastern European faves such as kielbasa and chicken
paprikash, which are served by friendly owners in a homey space
adorned with children's artwork; open for lunch daily, it serves dinner Thursdays–Saturdays and breakfast on weekends.

ⓩ Amanda's *American*   26 | 25 | 25 | $49

Hoboken | 908 Washington St. (bet. 9th & 10th Sts.) | 201-798-0101 |
www.amandasrestaurant.com
Dining doesn't get much more "civilized" than at this "serene"
Hoboken "class act", a "special place" offering a "delectable"
American menu served in a "romantic", circa-1895 brownstone; the
early-bird dinner is a "real steal", Sunday brunch is "fab" and the
service "makes you feel special" – in short, this "quality" experience
"does everything right"; P.S. there's validated parking in a nearby
lot, but not for early birds.

A Mano *Pizza*   22 | 18 | 19 | $25

Ridgewood | 24 Franklin Ave. (Chestnut St.) | 201-493-2000 |
www.amanopizza.com
"Napoli comes to Ridgewood" via this "crowd-pleasing" pizzeria
that's been officially certified for its "authentic-to-a-fault" Neapolitan
pies crafted in "gander"-worthy wood-fired ovens (the name translates as 'by hand'); the "high quality" is reflected in the "high-end"
tabs, though it is a BYO with a vino license.

Amarone *Italian*   21 | 16 | 22 | $41

Teaneck | 63 Cedar Ln. (Broad St.) | 201-833-1897 |
www.amaroneristorante.net
The "consistently good" Italian fare is "prepared however you want
it" at this "neighborhood favorite" set in a "cozy" former carriage
house in Teaneck; "outstanding" service makes you "feel welcome",
but some say the menu is getting "tired", ditto the "uninspired" decor.

Amelia's Bistro *American*   19 | 18 | 19 | $32

Jersey City | 187 Warren St. (bet. Essex & Morris Sts.) | 201-332-2200 |
www.ameliasbistro.com
A "prime spot for Paulus Hook people-watching", this New American
"neighborhood go-to" in Jersey City offers "dependable" comfort
food in a "relaxed yet upscale" atmosphere that's "great for a casual
night out"; but even though its brunch is "awesome", service and decor "leave a bit to be desired."

	FOOD	DECOR	SERVICE	COST

Amici Milano *Italian* | 22 | 16 | 21 | $34 |

Trenton | 600 Chestnut Ave. (Roebling Ave.) | 609-396-6300 |
www.amicimilano.com

Appreciated for "keepin' it real in the 'burg", this "old-school" Italian in Trenton's Chambersburg maintains its "reputation for quality" even though old-timers insist it "used to be better"; still, the "friendly" servers remain "on point" and the "not-too-fancy" digs are "nice enough for an evening out", especially with live piano and song some evenings.

Amiya *Indian* | 19 | 16 | 17 | $31 |

Jersey City | Harborside Financial Ctr. | 160 Greene St.
(Christopher Columbus Dr.) | 201-433-8000 | www.amiyarestaurant.com

"Tasty" Indian cuisine at a "reasonable" price point is served in a "sophisticated" setting at this "creative" Jersey City venue set in the Harborside Financial Center; though some surveyors are "underwhelmed", alfresco tables, validated parking and an all-you-can-eat lunch buffet help sweeten the deal.

Andreotti's Viennese Café *Italian* | - | - | - | E |

Cherry Hill | Pine Tree Plaza | 1442 Marlton Pike E. (Covered Bridge Rd.) | 856-795-0172 | www.andreottis.com

The name notwithstanding, this upscale Cherry Hill eatery serves a menu of French-accented Italian cuisine, including small plates and tasting-menu options, in a dining room decorated with turn-of-the-century posters; there's also a bakery and a wine boutique, where wine dinners and tastings are held.

▣ Andre's ⑧Ⓜ *American* | 27 | 21 | 26 | $51 |

Newton | 188 Spring St. (bet. Adams & Jefferson Sts.) | 973-300-4192 |
www.andresrestaurant.com

Chef-owner Andre de Waal's "inventive" seasonal American cooking paired with "terrific" vinos make this "charming", tin-ceilinged storefront a bona fide "destination" in Newton (it also features an on-site wine boutique); throw in "hospitable" service and a "romantic" mood, and the result is a dining experience that's "top-notch on every level"; P.S. open Wednesday–Saturday only.

Angelo's Fairmount Tavern *Italian* | 21 | 15 | 20 | $33 |

Atlantic City | 2300 Fairmount Ave. (Mississippi Ave.) | 609-344-2439 |
www.angelosfairmounttavern.com

For a "respite" from Atlantic City's "huge casino restaurants", insiders eschew the boardwalk for this "old-fashioned" Italian, now in its eighth decade, where the Mancuso family "makes you feel at home" with "mama's-in-the-kitchen" "red-gravy" cooking and "no-nonsense" service; despite "kitschy decor" and a no-reservations policy, most agree everything's "still solid" here.

Animo Juice *Mexican* | - | - | - | I |

Haddonfield | 113 Kings Hwy. (bet. Mechanic & Tanner Sts.) |
856-427-9070 | www.animojuice.com

Organic and non-GMO ingredients are emphasized on the menu of this Haddonfield Mexican juice and burrito bar, which also serves a

	FOOD	DECOR	SERVICE	COST

limited selection of soups, salads and snacks; the setting is fairly basic, but so are the prices.

Anjelica's ⓜ *Italian*   24 | 17 | 20 | $44

Sea Bright | 1070 Ocean Ave. (bet. Peninsula Ave. & River St.) | 732-842-2800 | www.anjelicas.com

An "angel must be in the kitchen" of this "bustling" Southern Italian BYO in Sea Bright, a "real find" on the Jersey Shore, where the "heavenly" food and "skilled service" offset the "raucous atmosphere", "tight tables" and "long waits", even with reservations.

Anna's Italian Kitchen ⓜ *Italian*   23 | 17 | 21 | $43

Middletown | Fountain Ridge Shopping Ctr. | 1686 Rte. 35 S. (Old Country Rd.) | 732-275-9142 | www.annasitaliankitchen.com

"Hands-on" chef Anna Perri produces "fine Italian food" (think "unmatchable" gnocchi, "excellent" linguini) at this "tasty" BYO parked in an "obscure strip mall" on Route 35 in Middletown; too bad about the "blah" decor and somewhat "expensive" pricing, but at least the service is "lovely."

𝗡𝗘𝗪 Anna's Ristorante *Italian*   - | - | - | M

Summit | 67 Union Pl. (bet. Beechwood Rd. & Maple St.) | 908-273-4448 | www.annasristorante.com

Sunny Tuscan-orange walls, a brick oven and a roster of comforting Italian standards are the order of the day at this casual BYO in the former space of Brix 67 near the train station in Summit; the menu also features healthy and gluten-free choices.

Anthony David's *Italian*   25 | 19 | 21 | $45

Hoboken | 953 Bloomfield St. (10th St.) | 201-222-8399 | www.anthonydavids.com

Chef-owner Anthony Pino's "welcoming" Italian BYO in Hoboken serves "inspired" brunches and dinners in a variety of settings: a "beautiful" storefront gourmet shop, a "romantic" back room or on alfresco sidewalk tables "away from the bustle of Washington Street"; despite "cramped" digs and "painful" weekend waits, many find it "worthy of repeat visits."

Anthony's ⓜ *Italian*   24 | 19 | 21 | $36

Haddon Heights | 512 Station Ave. (bet. Atlantic Ave. & White Horse Pike) | 856-310-7766 | www.anthonyscuisine.com

Anthony Iannone's "upscale" BYO in "quaint little" Haddon Heights offers a "not-standard" Italian menu featuring "lovely twists on the classics" served "with style" in three "intimate" dining rooms; "tasty" signature dishes like the Crab Tomasso "take you back to another world and time."

Antonia's by the Park *Italian*   ▽ 20 | 18 | 20 | $46

North Bergen | 9011 Palisade Ave. (Woodcliff Ave.) | 201-868-0750 | www.antoniasbythepark.com

"Tasty" if "not creative", the "simple", "homestyle" fare at this casual North Bergen Italian near North Hudson Park is "reasonably priced";

| | FOOD | DECOR | SERVICE | COST |

though service can be "slow" and the weekend music "overwhelming", a "friendly" mood and easy parking make it a "nice local" option.

Anton's at the Swan ☒ *American* | 22 | 21 | 22 | $49 |

Lambertville | Swan Hotel | 43 S. Main St. (Swan St.) | 609-397-1960 | www.antons-at-the-swan.com

"Tucked away" in Lambertville's historic Swan Hotel, this "romantic" New American "charmer" also earns kudos for chef-owner Chris Connor's "consistently good" seasonal menu in the dining room – and more "casual" offerings in the "coziest bar around"; "top-notch" service and a pretty patio seal its rep as a "special-occasion place."

Aozora *French/Japanese* | 24 | 19 | 20 | $44 |

Montclair | 407 Bloomfield Ave. (Seymour St.) | 973-233-9400 | www.aozorafusion.com

Admirers "aodore" chef-owner Nelson Yip's "artful" sushi at this "pleasing", "pricey" Montclair BYO offering "excellent" French-Japanese fusion fare that lives up to "NYC standards"; though some find the service "inconsistent" and the "Zen-like" decor "ho-hum", it morphs into a "madhouse" on weekends for a reason.

NEW Aqua Blu Kitchen & Cocktails *American* | - | - | - | E |

Toms River | 3410 Rte. 37 E. (Bridge St.) | 732-270-1180 | www.aquablukitchen.com

A sprawling space boasting multiple dining rooms, two bars and a lounge suits the wide range of New American offerings (from crudo to sliders) at this spendy Toms River eatery located at the foot of the bridge that leads to Seaside; sunset views from the outdoor patio and live music on weekends are added attractions.

Ariana *Afghan* | ▽ 18 | 14 | 21 | $25 |

Voorhees | Eagle Plaza Shopping Ctr. | 700 Haddonfield Berlin Rd. (White Horse Rd.) | 856-784-1100 | www.restaurantariana.com

Bringing "something different" to Voorhees, this Afghani BYO offers "flavorful stews" and "scrumptious skewers" in a "suburban", "family-friendly" strip-mall setting; everything is cooked to order by owner Kadir Sultani and his family, so it can be "as spicy as you like."

Ariel's *Eclectic* | ▽ 20 | 16 | 17 | $33 |

Englewood | 18 Engle St. (bet. Demarest & Palisade Aves.) | 201-569-1202 | www.arielskosher.com

At this "quality" kosher BYO in Englewood, the "interesting" Eclectic offerings range from pasta and pizza to seafood and desserts like beignets and chocolate soufflés; too bad the service varies as well, from "good" to "slow."

Armando's *Italian* | 19 | 17 | 19 | $42 |

Fort Lee | 144 Main St. (Parker Ave.) | 201-461-4220 | www.armandos.net

"Hearty portions" of "well-prepared", "old-school" Italian food draw "lotsa locals" to this Fort Lee "institution" near the GW Bridge; maybe the menu "could use some new additions" and the decor a "face-lift", but at least the pricing's "affordable" and the service "attentive."

	FOOD	DECOR	SERVICE	COST

Armando's Tuscan Grill *Italian*   20 | 17 | 16 | $35

River Vale | 688 Westwood Ave. (Peters Pl.) | 201-722-5820 |
www.armandostuscangrill.com

This "casual" Italian BYO set in a River Vale shopping center (and sibling of Armando's in Fort Lee) is known for its "excellent" pizza, pasta, veal and beef entrees, all prepared in an open kitchen; it's just the ticket for a "quick meal with the family", although service at this "work in progress" still "needs a lot of work."

Aroma Royal Thai *Thai*   22 | 21 | 22 | $27

Franklin Park | 3175 Rte. 27 (Delar Pkwy.) | 732-422-9300

"Solid" Thai food, "well prepared" and "well priced" – and served by "nice", "friendly" folks – distinguishes this "small" BYO from its numerous strip-mall competitors along Route 27 in Franklin Park; "pretty" decor adds to its allure.

Arthur's Steakhouse & Pub *Steak*   19 | 12 | 17 | $32

North Brunswick | 644 Georges Rd. (Ashland Pl.) | 732-828-1117 |
www.arthurssteakhouse.org

Fans of this "fun", "roll-up-your-sleeves" North Brunswick chop shop keep coming back for its "huge" steaks, "awesome" ribs and "juicy" burgers; though critics say both the quality and the decor have gone "downhill", thankfully the prices are "rock-bottom", especially for early-birds.

Arthur's Tavern *Steak*   20 | 14 | 17 | $31

Hoboken | 237 Washington St. (3rd St.) | 201-656-5009
Morris Plains | 700 Speedwell Ave. (Littleton Rd.) | 973-455-9705
www.arthurstavern.com

"Mighty" steaks, "excellent" burgers and "cheap" tabs lure "carnivores on a budget" to these "loud", "checkered-tablecloth" steakhouses in Hoboken and Morris Plains; despite "rush-you-through-your-meal" service, "frayed-around-the-edges" decor and "challenging" weekend waits (they don't take reservations), those looking for a "lively" time have no complaints.

Arturo's Ⓜ *Italian*   23 | 20 | 21 | $48

Midland Park | 41 Central Ave. (bet. Greenwood & Madison Aves.) |
201-444-2466 | www.arturos-restaurant.com

"Classic" Southern Italiana is "done very well" at this "formal" Midland Park "place to be seen" that's a magnet for "forty- and fifty-something" types; kudos go to the "tasty" chow and "throwback" mood (think "Sinatra in the background"), leaving the "relatively high cost" as the only sticking point.

Arturo's *Pizza*   24 | 14 | 20 | $26

Maplewood | 180 Maplewood Ave. (Baker St.) | 973-378-5800 |
www.arturosnj.com

"Heavenly" thin-crust brick-oven pizza is the bread and butter of this "tiny" Maplewood BYO, but on Saturday nights chef Dan Richer provides a "city experience in the suburbs" with his "amazing" (reservation-only) prix fixe Italian meals made from the "freshest local ingredients"; true, the decor's "nothing special" and the dimensions "cramped", but "family-friendly" service and "affordable" tabs seal the deal.

Arugula *Italian* — | — | — | E

Sewell | 373 Egg Harbor Rd. (bet. Greentree & Trent Rds.) | 856-589-0475 | www.arugularestaurant.net
At their high-end Sewell eatery, chefs Nicholas Tomasetto and Stefano Gervasi create modern takes on traditional Italian cuisine, which are served in a flamboyantly colorful space; BYO and an early-bird prix fixe make it more affordable.

Assaggini di Roma *Italian* ∇ 24 | 16 | 21 | $38

Newark | 134 Clifford St. (bet. Adams & Van Buren Sts.) | 973-466-3344
"One of the few Italian restaurants" in Newark's Ironbound district, this "old-school" joint features a "large menu" of "delicious" dishes served in an atmosphere with a "real family feel"; granted, the room's "not pretty", but a "knowledgeable" staff and a vocalist on some nights help distract.

Assembly Steak House *Steak* 16 | 18 | 17 | $52

Englewood Cliffs | 495 Sylvan Ave. (Palisade Ave.) | 201-568-2616 | www.assemblysteakhouse.com
Area execs assemble at this "old-style suburban" steakhouse in Englewood Cliffs, which is a no-brainer for a "business lunch" given its convenient location; too bad the "average" offerings come at "above-average" prices, but at least there's a "liberal buy-back policy" at the "busy" bar.

A Tavola Ⓜ *Italian* 20 | 14 | 18 | $33

Old Bridge | Deep Run Shopping Ctr. | 3314 Rte. 9 S. (Ferry Rd.) | 732-607-1120 | www.atavola1.com
"Solid" Italian cooking with a "creative streak" draws patrons to this "friendly", "neighborhood" BYO in an Old Bridge strip mall; there's "not much atmosphere" and the open kitchen makes for "a lot of noise", but the staff "treats you like family" and special events pair dinner with entertainment.

Athenian Garden Ⓜ *Greek* 23 | 15 | 19 | $28

Galloway Township | 619 S. New York Rd. (bet. Brook Ln. & Holly Brook Rd.) | 609-748-1818 | www.athenian-garden.com
"Bringing Greece to Galloway", this "family-run" Hellenic BYO serves a "reasonably priced" "quality" menu in a "tucked-away" setting that's a 15-minute drive from Atlantic City; the "plain" decor is trumped by a "homey" ambiance and "welcoming" staffers.

Atlantic Bar & Grill Ⓜ *American/Seafood* 26 | 22 | 23 | $51

South Seaside Park | Central & 24th Aves. (J St.) | 732-854-1588 | www.atlanticbarandgrillnj.com
Views of "crashing waves" and "dune grass blowing in the breeze" supply the atmosphere at this oceanside American seafooder in South Seaside Park where the "delectable" cooking is a match for the "majestic" vistas from its floor-to-ceiling windows; just

ignore the "seedy" exterior and get there "early" – "long waits" are the norm here.

☑ A Toute Heure Ⓜ *American*   26 | 19 | 24 | $46

Cranford | 232 Centennial Ave. (Elm St.) | 908-276-6600 |
www.atouteheure.com

Showcasing "local, seasonal ingredients", this "farm-to-table" Cranford BYO features a "delectable" American menu with French and Spanish accents served by a "charming" crew; maybe the seating is "tight" and reservations "tough" (it's "easier to get into a White House state dinner"), but that's because this "tucked-away treasure" is such a "big-league" hit.

Augustino's ☒♈ *Italian*   26 | 18 | 22 | $46

Hoboken | 1104 Washington St. (bet. 11th & 12th Sts.) | 201-420-0104
Reservations are an "absolute must" at this "unique" 33-seater, "Hoboken's answer to Rao's", where "perfect" Southern Italian dishes at "reasonable" tabs are served by "snarky", "salty" waitresses who are "as fresh as the seafood"; sure, it's "cash-only" and the mood strictly "dine-and-dash", but if nothing else, "it's an experience."

Aunt Berta's Kitchen Ⓜ *Soul Food/Southern*   – | – | – | M

Oaklyn | 639 White Horse Pike (Greenwood Ave.) | 856-858-7009 |
www.auntbertaskitchen.com

Healthy versions of Cajun-accented Southern comfort food are the forte of this midpriced soul food specialist in Oaklyn, which offers family-style platters, weekend brunch and a Sunday supper special.

☑ Avenue *French*   22 | 27 | 21 | $52

Long Branch | Pier Vill. | 23 Ocean Ave. (bet. Chelsea Ave. & Laird St.) |
732-759-2900 | www.leclubavenue.com

"Unusually sophisticated for the Jersey Shore", this "gorgeous" French brasserie in Long Branch's Pier Village boasts "delicious" food, "stylish" decor, "sweeping" ocean views and a "scene-and-a-half" vibe, stoked by a "beautiful", "dressed-up" crowd; "pretty-penny" pricing and "attitude" from the otherwise "professional" staff come with the territory.

Avenue Bistro Pub *American*   19 | 16 | 20 | $34

Verona | 558 Bloomfield Ave. (bet. Gould St. & Park Pl.) | 973-239-7444 |
www.avenuebistropub.com

"Interesting" American comfort food arrives in "pleasant" environs at this "simple" spot in Verona where the "under-$20 wine selections help keep the bill down"; it's a "nice place to drop in for a drink" during the midday happy hour, and there's "great" outside seating to boot.

Avon Pavilion *American*   19 | 18 | 20 | $30

Avon-by-the-Sea | 600 Ocean Ave. (bet. Norwood & Woodland Aves.) |
732-775-1043 | www.avonpavilion.com

Aka the "Av Pav", this seasonal boardwalk BYO in Avon is best known for its "awesome" ocean panoramas, "summer breezes" and "upbeat" "college-kid servers"; given that the "basic" American food on offer is "nothing extraordinary", its "main asset is the location."

	FOOD	DECOR	SERVICE	COST

Axelsson's Blue Claw *Seafood*   23 | 21 | 23 | $48

Cape May | 991 Ocean Dr. (Rte. 109) | 609-884-5878 |
www.blueclawrestaurant.com

"Off the beaten path" in the Cape May boatyard, this seasonal sea-fooder supplies "quality" dinners served by an "exceptionally nice" team in a "linen-tablecloth" setting; though the food's "not haute cuisine", it's "reliable" enough and certainly "fresh" – local fishermen "deliver their catch" right outside the door.

Axia Taverna *Greek*   23 | 23 | 22 | $50

Tenafly | 18 Piermont Rd. (bet. Central Ave. & Jay St.) | 201-569-5999 |
www.axiataverna.com

"Modern takes" on classic Greek dishes are served at this "stylish" Tenafly duplex where the menu options are "satisfying" albeit "expensive" and include "fabulous fish", "excellent" mezedes (small plates) and "sophisticated" desserts; the "contemporary", stone-lined setting can be "noisy", but in warm weather it's "delightful" when they roll up the former garage doors fronting the building.

Azúcar Ⓜ *Cuban*   20 | 19 | 19 | $39

Jersey City | 495 Washington Blvd. (bet. 14th St. & Newport Pkwy.) |
201-222-0090 | www.azucarcubancuisine.com

A "little bit of Cuba" lands in Jersey City via this "cool" Cubano whose "authentic" offerings are even more "delicious" when washed down with a "great mojito"; the "sexy" double-decker setting includes a clubby upstairs cigar lounge, and late-night it morphs into a "lively", "salsa"-friendly scene.

Babylon *Mediterranean*   21 | 16 | 22 | $31

River Edge | 606 Kinderkamack Rd. (Monroe Ave.) | 201-646-0005 |
www.babylonrest.com

"Hearty" Med fare with a pronounced Turkish accent is served with "family warmth" at this airy River Edge venue; though the decor strikes some as "cold", folks are glad it's "back to being BYO" again.

Backyards Bistro *American*   ∇ 18 | 7 | 15 | $22

Hoboken | 732 Jefferson St. (8th St.) | 201-222-2660

Dishes from a "big menu" are purveyed in "tiny" digs at this "nice" American BYO in Hoboken where the "filling", "home-cooked" dishes are "surprisingly good" ("two words: pretzel bread"); but since the joint is so "cramped" with "no decor to speak of", many go the "take-out" route.

Bahama Breeze *Caribbean*   17 | 20 | 19 | $27

Wayne | Wayne Towne Ctr. | 101 Rte. 23 (North Leg) |
973-237-0412

NEW Woodbridge | 520 Woodbridge Center Dr. (bet. Main St. & Rte. 1) | 732-726-8951

Cherry Hill | Cherry Hill Mall | 2000 Rte. 38 (Haddonfield Rd.) |
856-317-8317

www.bahamabreeze.com

This "fairly standard" chain serves "not bad" "quasi-Caribbean" chow for a "decent price"; ok, they're "far from fine dining", but the "beachy" settings are "enjoyable" enough when accompanied by a "silly, sugary" cocktail.

Bahrs Landing *Seafood*

17 | 16 | 18 | $38

Highlands | 2 Bay Ave. (Highland Ave.) | 732-872-1245 | www.bahrslanding.com

This "nothing-fancy" seafooder overlooking Sandy Hook Bay has been a Highlands "classic" since 1917; fans say its "simple" traditional fare – especially the lobster – "couldn't get any fresher", though critics contend the "just ok" grub and "welcome-to-1960" decor "could use more spice."

NEW Baia *Italian*

- | - | - | E

Somers Point | 998 Bay Ave. (Goll Ave.) | 609-926-9611 | www.baiarestaurant.com

Views of Great Egg Harbor Bay and boats pulling up to the dock next to its multilevel decks are part of the attraction of this sprawling Somers Point seasonal; three bars, live entertainment and an upscale, traditional Italian menu with an emphasis on seafood complete the picture.

Baja *Mexican*

18 | 14 | 17 | $29

Hoboken | 104 14th St. (Washington St.) | 201-653-0610
Jersey City | 117 Montgomery St. (bet. Marin Blvd. & Warren St.) | 201-915-0062
www.bajamexicancuisine.com

"Muy bueno", "inexpensive" Mexican grub in "portions large enough to share" keep the traffic brisk at these "loud" and "lively" cantinas in Hoboken and Jersey City; cynics shrug that they're "run-of-the-mill", but "amazing" margaritas, a vast tequila selection and "friendly" bartenders compensate.

Baja Fresh Mexican Grill *Mexican*

17 | 11 | 15 | $12

East Rutherford | 93 Rte. 17 S. (bet. Paterson Ave. & Stanley St.) | 201-507-1644
Wayne | 1600 Rte. 23 N. (Packanack Lake Rd.) | 973-872-2555
East Brunswick | 683 Rte. 18 (Kendall Rd.) | 732-967-0505
East Hanover | East Hanover Plaza | 136 Rte. 10 (Ramada Dr.) | 973-952-0080
South Plainfield | 6400 Hadley Rd. (Stelton Rd.) | 908-756-4141
Watchung | 1595 Rte. 22 W. (Raymond Ave.) | 908-322-0202
Union Township | 2311 Rte. 66 (Neptune Blvd.) | Ocean Township | 732-493-5300
Cherry Hill | Garden State Park | 2000 Rte. 70 W. (Bet. Garden State Blvd. & Haddonfield Rd.) | 856-488-9703
Mount Laurel | Centerton Sq. | 10A Centerton Rd. (Union Mill Rd.) | 856-802-0892
Voorhees | Echelon Village Plaza | 1120 White Horse Rd. (Bibbs Rd.) | 856-784-5955
www.bajafresh.com
Additional locations throughout New Jersey

Somewhat "upscale fast food" that's "relatively healthy" and "as fresh as the name implies" is the concept at this Mexican chain that may not be "what you get in Mexico" but is "tasty" all the same;

it also appeals to "budget-minded" types since it's "hard to beat for the price."

Bamboo Leaf Ⓜ *Thai/Vietnamese* | 22 | 16 | 19 | $29 |

Bradley Beach | 724 Main St. (McCabe Ave.) | 732-774-1661
Howell | Howell Ctr. | 2450 Rte. 9 S. (White St.) | 732-761-3939

They "try really hard" at these bamboo-bedecked Southeast Asian BYOs to produce "reasonably authentic" food – Thai and Vietnamese in Bradley Beach and strictly Siamese in the Howell Center; at both locations, service is "efficient", the decor "lackluster" and the price tags "low."

Bangkok Garden *Thai* | 23 | 14 | 20 | $27 |

Hackensack | 261 Main St. (bet. Camden & Salem Sts.) | 201-487-2620 | www.bangkokgarden-nj.com

Bang for the buck is the order of the day at this "excellent" Hackensack Thai "seafood specialist" that lures in Bergen County "courthouse employees" with "inexpensive" lunch deals; don't mind the "no-frills" storefront setting: "sweet service" and a "relaxed" mood compensate.

Bar Cara Ⓜ *Italian* | 20 | 20 | 19 | $39 |

Bloomfield | 1099 Broad St. (bet. Highfield Rd. & Watchung Ave.) | 973-893-3681 | www.bar-cara.com

Don't expect typical red sauce at this "Manhattan-style" Bloomfield Italian, a "chic" sibling of Montclair's Fascino from "whiz kid" chef Ryan DePersio; though there's applause for the "fantastic" cooking and "happening" vibe, fence-sitters find the cuisine "not as good as the flagship" and say service "needs a little fine-tuning."

Barnacle Bill's ● *Burgers* | 22 | 16 | 19 | $28 |

Rumson | 1 First St. (River Rd.) | 732-747-8396 | www.barnaclebillsrumson.com

"Mouthwatering" burgers are the star of the show at this "fun" Rumson "dump" on the Navesink River, a "super-casual" place where patrons "watch Sunday football" and toss their "peanut shells on the floor"; despite a "noisy" sound level, "corny nautical decor" and "slow" service, it's usually a "mob scene", so "plan on waiting."

Barnsboro Inn *American* | ▽ 22 | 21 | 20 | $38 |

Sewell | 699 Main St. (Center St.) | 856-468-3557 | www.barnsboroinn.com

A "cozy historic" tavern in South Jersey around since 1776, this "nicely updated" Sewell charmer serves an "uncomplicated" American menu that's both classic (prime rib, crab imperial) and updated (ahi tuna with black sesame seeds); you can "actually have a conversation" here, and there's plenty of time to do so since the "pace is slow."

Barone's Tuscan Grille *Italian* | 22 | 19 | 22 | $33 |

Moorestown | 280 Young Ave. (Main St.) | 856-234-7900 | www.baronerestaurants.com

Tuscan Pizza Kitchen *Italian*

Moorestown | 200 Young Ave. (bet. Centerton Rd. & County Rd. 537) | 856-234-7080 | www.baronerestaurants.com

(continued)

Villa Barone   *Italian*

Collingswood | 753 Haddon Ave. (bet. Frazer & Washington Aves.) | 856-858-2999 | www.villabaronesite.com
Maple Shade | 112 W. Main St. (bet. Lippincott & Terrace Aves.) | 856-779-0100 | www.baronerestaurants.com

"Carb lovers" tout these South Jersey BYOs offering "consistent" "red-gravy" cooking; sure, they're "not fancy", but prices are "reasonable", portions are "generous" and the overall word is "satisfying."

Barrels   *Italian*   `21` `14` `19` `$31`

Linwood | 199 New Rd. (Central Ave.) | 609-926-9900 Ⓢ
Margate | 9 S. Granville Ave. (bet. Atlantic & Ventnor Aves.) | 609-823-4400
www.barrelsfoods.com

These "reasonably priced" "homestyle" Italians in the Shore towns of Linwood and Margate are quintessential "neighborhood" BYOs with "classic" *cucina* and "neighborhood" vibes; since there's "no atmosphere" in evidence, many opt for "takeout."

⚡ Basilico   *Italian*   `23` `21` `21` `$45`

Millburn | 324 Millburn Ave. (bet. Main St. & Whittingham Terrace) | 973-379-7020 | www.basilicomillburn.com

A "consistent winner", this "sophisticated", "pricey" Italian BYO "convenient to the Paper Mill Playhouse" is Millburn's "shining star", a "New Yorkey" kind of place serving "top-notch" pastas, "high-quality" entrees and "amazing" desserts; the "modern" digs can be "somewhat noisy", so regulars show up midweek and request seating in the "quaint" garden, weather permitting.

Basil T's   *American/Italian*   `20` `20` `20` `$37`

Red Bank | 183 Riverside Ave. (Maple Ave.) | 732-842-5990 | www.basilt.com

Red Bank's "popular" brewpub is known for its "sociable" atmosphere – especially in the "lively" bar – along with "solid" Italian-American comfort vittles washed down with "great" house beers; the "super-friendly" staff is a plus, but many report it's "too pricey for what it is."

⚡ Baumgart's Café   *American/Asian*   `19` `14` `18` `$27`

Edgewater | City Pl. | 59 The Promenade (River Rd.) | 201-313-3889
Englewood | 45 E. Palisade Ave. (bet. Dean St. & Grand Ave.) | 201-569-6267
Livingston | Livingston Town Ctr. | 4175 Town Center Way (Livingston Ave.) | 973-422-0955
Ridgewood | 158 Franklin Ave. (Walnut St.) | 201-612-5688
www.baumgartscafe.com

Despite the "schizophrenic" Asian-American menu (with everything from "Chinese food to ice cream") and '50s "soda-fountain" decor, this "bustling" quartet draws "crowds" mainly because of its "bargain" tabs (all are BYOs save for the Edgewater outlet); "fast turnaround" makes up for the "loud" acoustics and "glorified diner" vibe.

	FOOD	DECOR	SERVICE	COST

Ⓩ Bay Avenue
Trattoria Ⓜ *American/Italian* — 28 | 13 | 23 | $44

Highlands | 122 Bay Ave. (Cornwell St.) | 732-872-9800 | www.bayavetrattoria.com

"Creative chef" Joe Romanowski and "fabulous host" Maggie Lubcke supply the "magic" at this "unassuming" Italian-American BYO in Highlands where "divinely prepared" dishes and "tiny" dimensions make reservations "a must any night of the week"; though the decor is "nonexistent", few notice since the "emphasis is on the food" here.

Bazzarelli *Italian* — 19 | 17 | 20 | $32

Moonachie | 117 Moonachie Rd. (Joseph St.) | 201-641-4010 | www.bazzarellirestaurant.com

Perfect "before the Meadowlands", this "casual", "family-run" Moonachie Italian scores points with "large platters" of "tasty" "homestyle" standards, including a particularly "delicious" pizza; "friendly" staffers and "reasonable" rates help explain why it's been in business since 1971.

Ⓩ Belford Bistro *American* — 26 | 19 | 23 | $45

Belford | 870 Main St. (Maple Ave.) | 732-495-8151 | www.belfordbistro.com

"Shore foodies" head for an "out-of-the-way" Belford strip mall to sample the New American "culinary artistry" of chefs Kurt Bomberger and Crista Trovato at this "intimate", "NYC-quality" BYO; the staff "knows their food", weekday bargain prix fixes bring costs down and, no surprise, it's "harder to get into than in the past."

NEW Bell & Whistle Ⓢ Ⓜ *American/Southern* — – | – | – | M

Hopewell | 9 E. Broad St. (Blackwell Ave.) | 609-466-7800 | www.bell-whistle.com

Well-priced American comfort food with a twist is the draw at this Hopewell entry whose name reflects the nearby church bell and fire-house 'whistle'; copper and stone figure in the striking modern setting outfitted with skylights, a vaulted ceiling and a patio, and you can BYO or choose from a list featuring Hopewell Valley bottles.

Bella Sogno Ⓜ *Italian* — 21 | 18 | 18 | $34

Bradley Beach | 600 Main St. (Brinley Ave.) | 732-869-0700 | www.bellasognorestaurant.com

It may be parked on a "side street" in Bradley Beach, but the Italian cooking is decidedly "Main Street" at this "reliable" Shore BYO where the prices are "reasonable" and "reservations should be made in advance."

Bell's Mansion *American* — 15 | 19 | 16 | $38

Stanhope | 11 Main St. (Rte. 183) | 973-426-9977 | www.bellsmansion.com

Set in an early-19th-century mansion in Stanhope, this "respectable" American earns kudos for its "romantic" air and unusual history (it's said to be "haunted" by two ghosts); too bad the food can be "hit-or-miss", ditto the "inconsistent" service.

Bell's Tavern ⌷ *American/Italian* | 20 | 14 | 20 | $29

Lambertville | 183 N. Union St. (bet. Buttonwood & Elm Sts.) | 609-397-2226 | www.bellstavern.com

Lambertville locals consider this tourist-free, "no-reservations" joint their equivalent of "*Cheers*", a "not-so-well-kept secret" that's been purveying "consistent", "down-home" Italian-American fare since 1938; despite the "cash-only" policy, be prepared for a "crush" of folks.

Belmont Tavern ⌷ *Italian* | 23 | 8 | 15 | $34
(aka Stretches)

Belleville | 12 Bloomfield Ave. (Belmont Ave.) | 973-759-9609

This Belleville Italian is like "stepping back in time" with its "old-school" cooking, "cast-of-characters" crowd and "cash-only" policy; ignoring the "gritty" neighborhood, "barroom" decor and "feisty" service, regulars eschew a menu and order its "famous Chicken Savoy."

Benihana *Japanese* | 18 | 18 | 19 | $38

Short Hills | 840 Morris Tpke. (South Terrace) | 973-467-9550

Edison | 60 Parsonage Rd. (bet. Mason St. & Oakwood Ave.) | 732-744-0660

Toms River | Ocean County Mall | 1201 Hooper Ave. (Oak Ave.) | 732-736-7071

Pennsauken | 5255 Rte. 70 (McClellan Ave.) | 856-665-6320

www.benihana.com

At these links in the "original" teppanyaki chain, "swift knives" and "decent showmanship" from the chefs make for "entertaining" meals with the kids, even if the flavors can be "hit-or-miss"; there's "no intimate dining here", but then again the "distracting" "floor show" can be a "good thing" "if you don't like the person you're with."

Benito's Ⓜ *Italian* | 23 | 20 | 23 | $50

Chester | 44 Main St. (bet. Perry & Warren Sts.) | 908-879-1887 | www.benitostrattoria.com

Off the beaten track in Chester, this BYO Italian "mainstay" is a real "crowd-pleaser" thanks to "reliable, old-fashioned" cooking and "old-line" service; while aesthetes say the "homey" decor "could use a good redo", the "friendly" atmosphere is fine as is.

Benny Tudino's ●⌷ *Pizza* | 22 | 6 | 14 | $12

Hoboken | 622 Washington St. (bet. 6th & 7th Sts.) | 201-792-4132

"Ridiculously large, hanging-off-the-plate" slices are the calling cards of this longtime, "high-volume" Hoboken pizzeria where patrons exit "bigger in the belly" but "not lighter in the wallet"; voters split on the quality – "classic NY taste" vs. "bigger doesn't always mean better" – though there's consensus on the lack of decor and service; P.S. no credit cards accepted.

Berkeley Restaurant & ▽ 20 | 12 | 18 | $28
Fish Market *Seafood*

South Seaside Park | Central & 24th Aves. (J St.) | 732-793-0400 | www.berkeleyrestaurantandfishmarket.com

This "typical" seasonal seafooder in South Seaside Park has been reeling in "quality" fin fare since 1925, and dishing it out in "sizable" portions for "reasonable" tabs; 360-degree views of Barnegat Bay from the top floor and "obliging" staff distract from the lack of decor.

☑ Bernards Inn *American*   27 | 26 | 26 | $67

Bernardsville | 27 Mine Brook Rd. (Quimby Ln.) | 908-766-0002 | www.bernardsinn.com

"One of NJ's best", this "blue-blood" Bernardsville New American – a "real special-occasion place" set in a historic, circa-1907 inn – pairs chef Corey Heyer's "top-of-the-line" seasonal cuisine with a "deep" wine list, "spectacular" desserts and "old-world" service; it's "tough on the wallet", but the menu in the "fun" bar area is "more accessible."

Berta's Chateau *Italian*   22 | 17 | 22 | $52

Wanaque | 7 Grove St. (Prospect St.) | 973-835-0992 | www.bertaschateau.com

Celebrating Italy's Piedmont region, this Wanaque "wonder" pairs chef-owner Peter Bernstein's "classic" cooking with an "unbeatable" wine list, served by a staff that's "never far from your table"; critics call the decor "tired" and the extensive menu "confusing", but concede that it's been around since 1927 for a reason.

Beyti Kebab *Turkish*   21 | 11 | 18 | $29

Union City | 4105 Park Ave. (bet. 41st & 42nd Sts.) | 201-865-6281 | www.beytigrill.com

"Authentic" Turkish cooking turns up at this "reasonably priced" Union City BYO that also incorporates a market and a butcher shop into its "modest" storefront setting; ok, the decor may be "plain", but no one notices when the "fun" Saturday night belly dancer and live musicians shake things up.

Biagio's *Italian*   17 | 16 | 17 | $31

Paramus | 299 Paramus Rd. (bet. Century & Dunkerhook Rds.) | 201-652-0201 | www.biagios.com

A "reliable" nexus for business or family dining, this "unpretentious" Paramus Italian proffers an "extensive" menu of "traditional" "red-sauce" dishes as well as "great" thin-crust pizza; naysayers find both the food and service "inconsistent", preferring the "lively" "young bar scene" instead.

Bibi'z ● *American*   - | - | - | M

Westwood | 284 Center Ave. (bet. Irvington St. & Westwood Ave.) | 201-722-8600 | www.bibizlounge.com

There's a think-globally-eat-locally philosophy in play at this casual yet elegant Westwood New American that focuses on grass-fed beef, sustainable seafood and regional produce (similarly, the water is filtered on-site and the wine list includes organic options); live entertainment keeps the mood upbeat until the midnight closing time.

Bicycle Club *American*   14 | 14 | 14 | $32

Englewood Cliffs | 487 Sylvan Ave. (Dillingham Pl.) | 201-894-0880 | www.thebicycleclub.com

"Afterthought" food arrives in a "no-personality" setting at this Englewood Cliffs American founded in '69 but revamped in '09; even though it's "not as good" since it shifted gears, the "big bar scene" makes it a better "pickup joint" than restaurant.

NEW Biddy O'Malley's *American/Pub Food*   — | — | — | M

Northvale | 191 Paris Ave. (Walnut St.) | 201-564-7893 | www.biddyomalleys.com

New American pub fare with an Irish lilt plays no second fiddle to the extensive beer list at this midpriced Northvale public house that features sustainable seafood and Balthazar bread on its menu; bright colors, a fireplace and original artwork create a warm, cheery tableau, while happy-hour specials keep all eyes smiling.

Bienvenue Ⓜ *French*   22 | 19 | 21 | $48

Red Bank | 7 E. Front St. (Wharf Ave.) | 732-936-0640 | www.bienvenuerestaurant.com

For a "bit of the Left Bank" in Red Bank, try this "sweet", "petite" bistro that charms fans with its "classic" French cooking, "comfortable" cafe decor and "attentive" staffers; prices skew "high", but $30 prix fixe dinners Tuesdays–Thursdays and a BYO policy "help keep the final tab within reason."

Big Ed's BBQ *BBQ*   18 | 11 | 17 | $25

Matawan | 305 Rte. 34 N. (Disbrow Rd.) | 732-583-2626 | www.bigedsbbq.com

Sports fans and BBQ lovers "pig out" on the "down-home" eats at this "messy", "busy" Matawan 'cue shack, beloved for its "bargain" all-you-can-eat ribs (which are either "delicious" or "run-of-the-mill", depending on who's talking); "outdated" Western-themed furnishings and "sticky" housekeeping come with the territory.

Bin 14 *Italian*   22 | 22 | 20 | $41

Hoboken | 1314 Washington St. (bet. 13th & 14th Sts.) | 201-963-9463 | www.bin14.com

"Young, lively" types match "fantastic" vinos with "innovative" Italian small plates at this "trendy little" Hoboken wine bar via Anthony Pino, the chef of nearby Anthony David's; granted, the "prices add up quickly" and it can be one "tough reservation", but most agree it doesn't get much more "sophisticated" in these parts.

Bistro at Red Bank *Eclectic*   21 | 19 | 20 | $39

Red Bank | 14 Broad St. (bet. Front & Mechanic Sts.) | 732-530-5553 | www.thebistroatredbank.com

There's "something for everyone" at this Red Bank "fixture" featuring everything from pizza to sushi to its "legendary" crackling calamari salad on its "interesting" Eclectic menu; other assets include "helpful" personnel, a "cozy" setting and "fun" people-watching from sidewalk seats; P.S. NJ wines are on offer, but they "don't mind if you BYO."

Bistro di Marino Ⓜ *Italian*   22 | 17 | 20 | $36

Collingswood | 492 Haddon Ave. (Crestmont Terrace) | 856-858-1700 | www.bistrodimarino.com

Gnocchi – equally "enjoyable" as an appetizer or entree – is the specialty of this Italian BYO named after chef James Marino, whose "outstanding" cooking trumps the "plain" digs; the pricing's a "good value for Collingswood", and there's jazz on the courtyard on Thursdays.

Bistro 55 *American*
19 | 20 | 20 | $40

Rochelle Park | 55 Rte. 17 S. (bet. Becker & Grove Aves.) | 201-845-3737 | www.southcitygroup.net

"Comfort food" gets a "gourmet" spin at this "cool" Rochelle Park American (part of the South City Group), where chef Ken Trickilo pairs "inventive" grub with a "wide selection" of "outstanding" craft beers; though some shrug it's "expensive for what it is", that's not impeding its "very active" "white-collar" bar scene.

Bistro Olé Ⓜ *Portuguese/Spanish*
23 | 19 | 22 | $40

Asbury Park | 230 Main St. (Mattison Ave.) | 732-897-0048 | www.bistroole.com

Pucker up for "kisses" from "outrageous" owner Rico Rivera at this "splashy" Iberian BYO in Asbury Park, known for its "ample portions" of "captivating" seafood and paella as well as "amazing sangria" made from the wine you bring along; some say the place is "not what it used to be", yet there are always "long lines" on summer weekends – primarily due to the "no-reservations" rule.

Blackbird Dining
Establishment Ⓜ *French/Italian*
24 | 17 | 22 | $43

Collingswood | 714 Haddon Ave. (bet. Collings & Irvin Aves.) | 856-854-3444 | www.blackbirdnj.com

"Delicious" modern French-Italian food served by an "eager" team makes this Collingswood BYO "one of the gems of South Jersey"; while it's "high"-priced for the area, "cutting-edge cuisine" is the payoff; P.S. its more casual sibling, West Side Gravy, shares the space.

Black Duck on Sunset *Eclectic*
26 | 22 | 24 | $47

West Cape May | 1 Sunset Blvd. (B'way) | 609-898-0100 | www.blackduckonsunset.com

"First-class" cooking draws diners to this "out-of-the-way" Eclectic in West Cape May, where regulars recommend you "definitely have the duck"; "efficient" service, a money-saving BYO policy and a "laid-back" setting in an "old Victorian" house add to its appeal.

Black-Eyed Susans Café Ⓜ⇗ *American*
– | – | – | E

Harvey Cedars | 7801 Long Beach Blvd. (78th St.) | 609-494-4990 | www.blackeyedsusanscafe.com

By day a coffeehouse, this seasonal, cash-only BYO in Harvey Cedars morphs into a fine-dining destination after dark with the addition of white linens and candlelight; the farm-to-table American menu comes via husband-and-wife team Christopher Sanchez and Ashley Pellagrino, popular LBI chefs and caterers.

Black Forest Inn *Continental/German*
23 | 22 | 21 | $44

Stanhope | 249 Rte. 206 N. (I-80, exit 25) | 973-347-3344 | www.blackforestinn.com

"You won't leave hungry" from this "meat-and-potatoes" German-Continental in Stanhope where the hearty cooking is "rich" and even tastier come "Oktoberfest"; *ja,* it's "pricey" and modernists find the setting a bit "tired", but overall it's "dependable" for the genre.

Black Horse Tavern *American* | 18 | 19 | 20 | $37 |

Mendham | 1 W. Main St. (Hilltop Rd.) | 973-543-7300 | www.blackhorsenj.com

This "venerable" Mendham country inn, set in a Colonial farmhouse, features "loud, family-friendly" dining in its "barn"-like pub as well as a "more formal" affair in its "pricier" tavern; either way, expect "solid", if "predictable", American eats and a "Wasp-heaven" crowd.

Black Trumpet *American* | 24 | 22 | 23 | $52 |

Spring Lake | Grand Victorian Hotel | 1505 Ocean Ave. (bet. Madison & Newark Aves.) | 732-449-4700 | www.theblacktrumpet.com

Set in Spring Lake's oceanfront Grand Victorian Hotel, this "true-find" New American purveys a "superb" menu of "creative" selections, served in a "lovely" dining room or "splendid" porch; a BYO policy and "unobtrusive" service make the "upmarket" tabs easier to digest.

NEW Blind Boar ● *BBQ* | - | - | - | M |

Norwood | 595 Broadway (Livingston) | 201-784-6900 | www.theblindboar.com

Pitmaster Jay Lippin fires up savory BBQ combos and comfort-food faves in a family-friendly Norwood setting, while specialty beers and panko-coated pickle chips stoke the sports crowd at the bar; quirky flea-market and estate-sale finds line the walls, but the real bargains are the $9.95 prix fixe lunch, weeknight $15.95 prix fixe dinner and $19.95 all-you-can-eat ribs on Tuesday nights.

Blu ⓜ *American* | 25 | 17 | 21 | $46 |

Montclair | 554 Bloomfield Ave. (Maple Pl.) | 973-509-2202 | www.restaurantblu.com

For a taste of "NYC in Montclair", try this "trendy" American BYO where chef Zod Arifai's "fanciful" cooking is "done to perfection" and served in "intimate" environs; maybe the decor could stand some "sprucing up" (ditto the sometimes "chilly" service), but in the end the "cuisine makes the experience worthwhile" here; P.S. adjacent sibling Next Door serves a similar menu at a more relaxed price.

Blue Bottle Cafe 🄴ⓜ *American* | 26 | 18 | 23 | $49 |

Hopewell | 101 E. Broad St. (Elm St.) | 609-333-1710 | www.thebluebottlecafe.com

Every dish "pops" at Aaron and Rory Philipson's New American BYO, a Hopewell "hot spot" hidden behind a "diner"-like exterior and comprised of three "intimate" (read: "crowded") rooms; its "loyal following" applauds the "masterful preparation" and "terrific" service, not the "tough reservations" and "limited parking."

Blue Danube *E Euro.* | ▽ 22 | 15 | 20 | $32 |

Trenton | 538 Adeline St. (Elm St.) | 609-393-6133 | www.bluedanuberestaurant.net

Eastern European "soul food" fills out the menu of this "neighborhood" nexus in Trenton hailed for its "hearty" fare; regulars relish the "generous" sampler platters of schnitzel and stuffed cabbage, presented in a setting that's "stuffy" but "charming in a Transylvanian way."

Blue Fish Grill Ⓜ *Seafood* | 21 | 16 | 19 | $28 |

Flemington | 9 Central Ave. (Mine St.) | 908-237-4528 | www.thebluefishgrill.com

Although located near the Flemington outlets, this "informal" BYO seafooder exudes a "slice-of-the-Shore" vibe with its "picnic-table" seating and "honest, not fancy" food; no reservations are accepted, but "timely" service from an "efficient" crew ratchets up the "friendly" feel.

NEW Blue Morel *American* | - | - | - | E |
(fka Copeland)

Morristown | Westin Governor Morris | 2 Whippany Rd. (Lindsley Dr.) | 973-451-2619 | www.bluemorel.com

Executive chef Kevin Takafuji executes a high-end menu featuring culinary director Thomas Ciszak's signature sushi and raw bar offerings plus farm-to-table New American dishes at this sleek eatery-cum-wine bar (complete with private 18-seat wine room) in Morristown's Westin Governor Morris; it's pricey, but the expansive Sunday brunch buffet and weekday express-lunch specials may appeal to the budget-minded.

Blue Pig Tavern *American* | 21 | 20 | 20 | $42 |

Cape May | Congress Hall Hotel | 251 Beach Ave. (bet. Congress & Perry Sts.) | 609-884-8421 | www.congresshall.com

"Delicious" breakfasts and breezy patio seating are among the "best features" of this "quaint" tavern nestled inside Cape May's "historic" Congress Hall Hotel; "terrific" Traditional American eats and "old seaside" decor distract from the "no-bargain" pricing.

Blueplate *American* | - | - | - | M |

Mullica Hill | 47 S. Main St. (High St.) | 856-478-2112 | www.blueplatenj.com

By day, it's a "humble", "diner-esque" affair that lives up to its name with "homey" counter-service breakfasts and lunches, but after dark this Mullica Hill BYO morphs into a "more upscale" experience with "imaginative" American dinners; at all hours, the crowd's a mix of locals and antiques shoppers.

🅩 Blue Point Grill *Seafood* | 26 | 16 | 22 | $43 |

Princeton | 258 Nassau St. (Pine St.) | 609-921-1211 | www.bluepointgrill.com

The "Shore comes to Nassau Street" at this "heart-of-Princeton" BYO vending an "extensive" selection of fresh seafood, "simply" and "perfectly" prepared; "knowledgeable" service and a "lovely sidewalk patio" embellish the overall "fun" mood, and regulars are thrilled that it's "finally taking reservations."

Bobby Chez Ⓜ *Seafood* | 24 | 11 | 18 | $23 |

Margate | 8007 Ventnor Ave. (Gladstone Ave.) | 609-487-1922

(continued)

Bobby Chez

Mays Landing | Shoppes at English Creek | 6041 Black Horse Pike (Cape May Ave.) | 609-646-4555

Cherry Hill | Tuscany Mktpl. | 1990 Rte. 70 E. (Old Orchard Rd.) | 856-751-7575

Collingswood | 33 W. Collings Ave. (Haddon Ave.) | 856-869-8000

Mount Laurel | Centerton Sq. | 32 Centerton Rd. (Marter Ave.) | 856-234-4146

Sewell | 100 Hurffville Crosskeys Rd. (Glassboro Cross Keys Rd.) | 856-262-1001

www.bobbychezcrabcakes.com

Famed for its "can't-be-beat" crab cakes (not to mention "rockin'" rotisserie chicken and lobster mashed potatoes), this "minimally decorated" chainlet is mainly for "takeout" given its "no-atmosphere" settings; P.S. the food arrives partially cooked accompanied by an "idiot-proof guide" on how to reheat the grub "in your own oven."

Bobby Flay Steak Ⓜ *Steak* 25 | 25 | 24 | $65

Atlantic City | Borgata Hotel, Casino & Spa | 1 Borgata Way (Huron Ave.) | 609-317-1000 | www.bobbyflaysteak.com

Bobby Flay, the "god of grilling", proves that he "sure knows how to grill a steak" at this "outstanding" chop shop set inside Atlantic City's Borgata Hotel; a "superb" wine list and a "lavishly decorated" setting by David Rockwell embellish the overall "luscious" feel, but don't forget to bring all your credit cards – this one's priced for "high rollers."

Bobby's Burger Palace *Burgers* 21 | 15 | 17 | $17

Paramus | Bergen Town Ctr. | 610 Bergen Town Ctr. (Rte. 4) | 201-368-7001

Eatontown | Monmouth Mall | 180 Rte. 35 (Wyckoff Rd.) | 732-544-0200

🆕 **Cherry Hill** | Cherry Hill Mall | 2000 Rte. 38 (Haddonfield Rd.) | 856-382-7462

www.bobbysburgerpalace.com

"Very good" – "not outstanding" – hamburgers are upstaged by "killer" sweet potato fries and "sinful" shakes at this fast-food chainlet from top toque Bobby Flay; the "retro-diner" settings may be too "stark" for some, but the "crunchified" burgers (with potato chips atop the patties) are "a must"; the Cherry Hill location opened post-Survey.

🆕 Bombay Bistro Ⓜ *Indian* - | - | - | M
(fka Dabbawalla)

Summit | 427 Springfield Ave. (bet. Maple St. & Woodland Ave.) | 908-918-0330 | www.thebombaybistro.net

The owners of Summit's Dabbawalla changed the name, decor, menu and even staff for this new incarnation of their casual Indian BYO; the menu features traditional offerings such as chicken tikka masala and lamb rogan josh plus contemporary inventions such as roti quesadilla and a beef burger with masala potatoes.

	FOOD	DECOR	SERVICE	COST

Bonefish Grill *Seafood* | 21 | 19 | 20 | $35 |

Paramus | 601 From Rd. (bet. Mack Centre Dr. & Ring Rd.) | 201-261-2355
East Brunswick | 335 Rte. 18 (Highland St.) | 732-390-0838
Green Brook | 215 Rte. 22 E. (bet. Washington Ave. & Warrenville Rd.) | 732-926-8060
Iselin | 625 US Hwy. 1 (bet. Gill Ln. & Green St.) | 732-634-7379
Pine Brook | 28 Rte. 46 (Hook Mountain Rd.) | 973-227-2443
Brick | 179 Van Zile Rd. (Rte. 70) | 732-785-2725
NEW **Red Bank** | 447 Rte. 35 (Navesink River Rd.) | 732-530-4284
Egg Harbor Township | 3121 Fire Rd. (Tilton Rd.) | 609-646-2828
Deptford | 1709 Deptford Center Rd. (Almonessen Rd.) | 856-848-6261
Marlton | 500 Rte. 73 N. (bet. Baker Blvd. & Lincoln Dr.) | 856-396-3122
www.bonefishgrill.com

The majority have "no bones" to pick with this "midlevel" Outback offshoot and "forget it's a chain", thanks to "fresh" fin fare and "friendly" service (management "clearly sends" the staff to "Server U") in "warm" environs; though some report "crowded", "chaotic" scenes on weekends, for most it remains a solid option "without going broke" for nights you "don't feel like cooking."

Bosphorus *Turkish* | 22 | 11 | 19 | $25 |

Lake Hiawatha | 32 N. Beverwyck Rd. (bet. Lake Shore Dr. & Vail Rd.) | 973-335-9690 | www.bosphorusrestaurantnj.com

There's "excellent value" on the menu of this Lake Hiawatha Turkish BYO where the "surprisingly good-quality" food and "reasonable" tabs earn it "local-find" status; though the storefront setting gets "no stars for decor", at least the staff is "friendly" and "helpful."

Bottagra Ⓜ *Italian* | 20 | 23 | 19 | $48 |

Hawthorne | 80 Wagaraw Rd. (Goffle Rd.) | 973-423-4433 | www.bottagra.com

The Revolutionary-era DeGray house – "in the middle of nowhere" in Hawthorne – has been remodeled into a "gorgeous" Tuscan villa at this modern Italian that lures a "young crowd" with its "wonderful" cooking and "big, brassy" mood; maybe the service "could be more attentive", but most feel they "know what they're doing" here.

Boulevard Five 72 *American* | 25 | 23 | 22 | $57 |

Kenilworth | 572 Kenilworth Blvd. (24th St.) | 908-709-1200 | www.boulevardfive72.net

"NYC chic" comes to Kenilworth via this "sophisticated" New American from chef Scott Snyder, whose flavors "jump off the plate"; a "beautiful" setting, "engaging" staffers and "hear-yourself-talk" acoustics compensate for the "not-inexpensive" tabs.

Braddock's Ⓜ *American* | 19 | 22 | 21 | $45 |

Medford | 39 S. Main St. (Union St.) | 609-654-1604 | www.braddocks.com

This "charming", circa-1823 Medford establishment offers "old-school" American food and grog in two distinctive settings: a casual downstairs pub and a more formal upstairs dining room; "warm Colonial decor" and "attentive" service reflect its "quaint" appeal, though the "pricey" tariffs are a touch more modern.

	FOOD	DECOR	SERVICE	COST

Brandl ☑ *American* — 24 | 18 | 20 | $49

Belmar | 703 Belmar Plaza (bet. 8th & 9th Aves.) | 732-280-7501 |
www.brandlrestaurant.com

Chef Chris Brandl demonstrates his "enormous skill" at this "unpretentious" New American BYO "hidden" in a Shore strip mall; true, it's "somewhat pricey for Belmar" and the "downscale" decor and "not-that-great" service "could be better", yet most feel this "little gem" has "special occasion" written all over it.

Brasilia Grill *Brazilian* — 22 | 16 | 20 | $32

Newark | 132 Ferry St. (bet. Madison & Monroe Sts.) | 973-465-1227
Newark | 99 Monroe St. (bet. Ferry & Lafayette Sts.) | 973-589-8682
www.brasiliagrill.net

All-you-can-eat mavens dig into the "endless supply" of "outstanding" grilled meats at these Brazilian churrascarias in the Ironbound that are a "quick walk" from Newark's Penn Station; insiders advise you "take it slow in the beginning" – they "bring the good stuff last."

Brass Rail *American* — 19 | 19 | 18 | $38

Hoboken | 135 Washington St. (2nd St.) | 201-659-7074 |
www.thebrassrailnj.com

Hoboken locals "unwind" at this "longtime" duplex featuring a "lively" bar scene on the ground floor and slightly more "elegant" dining above; the "not-fancy" American eats are "good" and "affordable" enough to seduce a "younger crowd", especially for the "fun" weekend brunch.

NEW Breakfast Room *American* — - | - | - | M

Atlantic City | Revel | 500 Boardwalk (Metropolitan Ave.) |
855-348-0500 | www.revelresorts.com

Atlantic City high rollers can ante up for a full American breakfast or grab-and-go options such as pastries from renowned chef Michel Richard at his midpriced AM-only spot at Revel; expect his signature whimsical touch in everything from French toast crème brûlée to filet mignon.

Brennen's Steakhouse *Steak* — 23 | 20 | 21 | $48

Neptune City | 62 W. Sylvania Ave. (Merritt Ave.) |
732-774-5040

"Early-bird deals" are part of the "fantastic value" that's the lure at this "on-the-money" Neptune chophouse, where the "basic" menu aspires to "NY quality"; "cordial" employees and live piano music "make for a good time", though the "healthy bar scene" adds some "noise" to the otherwise "comfortable" surroundings.

Brick City Bar & Grill *Pub Food* — 18 | 21 | 16 | $31

Newark | 35 Edison Pl. (bet. Broad & Mulberry Sts.) | 973-596-0004 |
www.brickcitybar.com

This "handsome" sports pub near Newark's Prudential Center slings "decent" enough comfort grub ferried by a "slow" but "hot"-looking staff; given the "loud din", critics say it's "better as a bar", though it's a no-brainer for a pre- or post-game "bite and a beer."

	FOOD	DECOR	SERVICE	COST

NEW Brick Lane Curry House *Indian*

- | - | - | M

Ridgewood | 34 Franklin Ave. (Chestnut St.) | 201-670-7311
Upper Montclair | 540 Valley Rd. (Wildwood Ave.) |
973-509-2100
www.bricklanecurryhouse.com

The incendiary British-style Indian curries served at these casual, midpriced links of a Manhattan-based chain bring the heat to Ridgewood and Upper Montclair; the scorching 10-chile phall will test your mettle, but milder options abound, along with soothing lassis to tame the fire, while economical lunch specials and BYO help you avoid burning a hole in your wallet.

Brickwall Tavern ◑ *Pub Food*

18 | 17 | 18 | $26

Asbury Park | 522 Cookman Ave. (Bangs Ave.) | 732-774-1264 |
www.brickwalltavern.com

"Fun" times trump the "better-than-average" American pub grub on offer at this "noisy" Asbury Park "staple" that's probably more "sports bar" than restaurant; still, fans say the "easygoing" atmosphere, "inexpensive" tabs and "live music" make it a "great place to chill."

Brioso *Italian*

24 | 19 | 20 | $41

Marlboro | Willow Pointe Shopping Ctr. | 184 Rte. 9 (Willow Ln.) |
732-617-1700 | www.briosoristorante.com

A "sleeper on Route 9", this "festive" BYO in a Marlboro strip mall serves "beautifully prepared" Italian dishes for "reasonable Central NJ prices"; sure, its numerous regulars may receive "extra special care", but the staff makes all comers "feel welcome and at home."

Brio Tuscan Grille *Italian*

19 | 22 | 20 | $33

Cherry Hill | Towne Place at Garden State Park | 901 Haddonfield Rd.
(Graham Ave.) | 856-910-8166
NEW Marlton | Promenade at Sagemore | 500 Rte. 73 S. (bet. Brick Rd. &
Marlton Pkwy.) | 856-983-0277
www.brioitalian.com

"Comfortable", "family-friendly" "surroundings" and "humongous portions" of "nicely presented" "traditional" Italian fare win fans for this "surprisingly non-kitschy" Cherry Hill link; a few purists dismiss it as "corporate" and "bland", and others warn it "can be very noisy" ("especially on weekends"), but most agree it's on the "nicer side of chains" and the prices are "reasonable"; the Marlton location opened post-Survey.

Brooklyn's Coal-Burning Brick-Oven Pizzeria ⊅ *Pizza*

22 | 12 | 16 | $20

Edgewater | Edgewater Commons Shopping Ctr. | 443 River Rd.
(Old River Rd.) | 201-945-9096
Hackensack | 161 Hackensack Ave. (Devoe Pl.) | 201-342-2727
Ridgewood | 15 Oak St. (Ridgewood Ave.) | 201-493-7600

These Bergen County pizzerias turn out thin-crust pies so "finger-licking" good that fans are willing to overlook the "no-slice", "no-delivery", "no-reservations" and no-plastic policies – even "underwhelming" service and "spartan" decor don't keep them from being "good family" choices; P.S. Edgewater and Ridgewood are BYOs, Hackensack serves beer and wine.

Brothers Moon ⓜ *American*   23 | 17 | 22 | $42

Hopewell | 7 W. Broad St. (Greenwood Ave.) | 609-333-1330 | www.brothersmoon.com

Locals and locavores alike are over the moon about this Hopewell "neighborhood" BYO, where "caring" chef Will Mooney "keeps close to the farm" – and the seasons – with his "inventive" New American recipes; "polite" servers help "make the meal enjoyable", but the "funky", former deli setting (that still offers takeout) "could stand refurbishing."

Bruschetta ⓢ *Italian*   21 | 20 | 20 | $42

Fairfield | 292 Passaic Ave. (Pier Ln.) | 973-227-6164 | www.bruschettarestaurantonline.com

"Solid" Northern Italian dishes fill out the menu of this "refined" Fairfield venue that sports a "pretty" bar area and a nightly piano player; midweek specials and coupon deals ensure that it's "always busy" with an "older crowd", while a "willing" staff augments the "relaxing" mood.

NEW Bucu *Bakery/Burgers*   - | - | - | I

Paramus | 65 Rte. 4 W. (Spring Valley Rd.) | 347-470-2828 | www.eatbucu.com

Beaucoup de flavor and calories await at this burger bar–cum–bakery located on the shopping-mall-halla of Paramus' Route 4, offering hamburgers (choose a combo or build your own), hand-cut fries, hot dogs and more, plus cupcakes and cookies baked on the premises and Max & Mina's ice cream from the milk bar; expect quasi–table service (you order at the counter) in the high-ceilinged storefront with banquettes and a long communal table.

Ⓩ Buddakan *Asian*   26 | 27 | 23 | $53

Atlantic City | Pier Shops at Caesars | 1 Atlantic Ocean (Arkansas Ave.) | 609-674-0100 | www.buddakanac.com

Stephen Starr's "phenomenal" Pan-Asian "scene" in AC's Pier at Caesars (a spin-off of the Philly and Manhattan outposts) offers "beautifully realized" fusion specialties in an "over-the-top" setting complete with a "giant" gilded Buddha and "glorious" communal table; ok, it's "very pricey" and "very noisy", but all agree that it's a "true experience" and "excellent for a special occasion."

NEW Bushido Bar & Restaurant *Japanese*   - | - | - | M

Cliffside Park | 671 Palisades Ave. (bet. Columbia & Lawton Aves.) | 201-941-6600 | www.bushidobar.com

Sushi, sashimi and an array of cooked seafood and meats come izakaya-style (i.e. small plates) at this chic, cozy Cliffside Park Japanese, while exotic cocktails, microbrewed beers and sake bolster the minimalist boutique wine list; the sleek black-and-red interior is dominated by a multihued Chihuly-style blown-glass chandelier evoking a balloon drop.

	FOOD	DECOR	SERVICE	COST

BV Tuscany ⓜ *Italian*
▽ 23 | 21 | 24 | $41

Teaneck | 368 Cedar Ln. (Palisade Ave.) | 201-287-0404 |
www.bvtuscany.com

"Fabulous" Italian fare with "imaginative" Tuscan tweaks draws applause at this "quiet" Teaneck sleeper where the "accommodating" service matches the "comfy", "low-key" vibe; though the prices tend to be "upscale", "great" business-lunch specials lure bargain-hunters.

Cabin, The *American*
18 | 15 | 18 | $27

Howell | 984 Rte. 33 E. (Fairfield Rd.) | 732-462-3090 |
www.thecabinrestaurant.net

It's "always packed" at this "noisy", "blue-collar" American on Route 33 in Howell where the "unpretentious" tavern food comes at "good-bang-for-the-buck" prices; "rustic" log-cabin decor, "flirty" service and live weekend entertainment keep its "biker" fan base happy.

Cafe Arugula ⓜ *Italian*
21 | 16 | 20 | $39

South Orange | 59 S. Orange Ave. (Scotland Rd.) | 973-378-9099 |
www.cafearugulasouthorange.com

"Trustworthy" is the word on this Italian BYO "oldie but goodie" near Seton Hall in South Orange, where "huge" portions and "consistent" cooking make it a "never-fail" treat; the "dated" setting may be "a bit dark" and the pricing's "high for what it is", but there's nothing wrong with its "neighborhood feel"; P.S. "save room for the gelato."

Café Azzurro *Italian*
24 | 20 | 22 | $43

Peapack | 141 Main St. (bet. Todd & Willow Aves.) | 908-470-1470 |
www.cafeazzurronj.com

"Practically the only game in town", this "country-casual" Peapack BYO exudes "small-town" charm with its "excellent" Italian meals and "eager-to-please", "easy-on-the-eyes" staffers; a "wonderful" patio and "affordable" price points ice the cake.

Cafe Bello *Italian*
22 | 20 | 24 | $39

Bayonne | 1044 Ave. C (50th St.) | 201-437-7538 |
www.cafebellobayonne.com

This "popular neighborhood spot" is a "big hit in Bayonne", the "kind of place Frank Sinatra would go" thanks to its "delicious" Italian classics and "attentive" service; the "moderate prices" and those "friendly regulars at the bar" compensate for the "tough parking" situation.

Cafe Coloré ⓜ *Italian*
19 | 17 | 18 | $37

Freehold Township | Chadwick Sq. | 3333 Rte. 9 N. (Jackson Mills Rd.) |
732-462-2233 | www.cafecolorenj.com

Locals are "loyal" to this "basic" Italian BYO set in an "obscure" Freehold strip mall, citing "above-average" cooking and "friendly" service; still, a few find it "pricey" for what it is.

Cafe Emilia *Italian*
22 | 19 | 22 | $47

Bridgewater | 705 Rte. 202 N. (Allen Rd.) | 908-429-1410 |
www.cafeemilia.com

"Business" types on "expense accounts" patronize this "under-promoted" Bridgewater Italian where "dependable" food, "careful" service and "unassuming", "old-school" decor combine for a "consistent" dining experience; though some find it "unimaginative", others say it's "pleasant."

Café Gallery *Continental* | 20 | 23 | 21 | $39 |

Burlington | 219 High St. (Pearl St.) | 609-386-6150

There's art "on the plate" *and* "on the walls" at this longtime Continental "institution" where the "traditional" offerings are "well prepared", but the real draw is an "excellent" location on Burlington's High Street; "caring" service, a "lovely" garden and "magnificent" views of the Delaware River add to its allure.

Cafe Graziella *Italian* | 20 | 15 | 18 | $35 |

Hillsborough | Cost Cutters Shopping Ctr. | 390 Rte. 206 (Andria Ave.) | 908-281-0700 | www.cafegraziella.com

Set in a "nondescript" Hillsborough strip mall, this Italian BYO slings "above-average" "red-sauce" classics in "plentiful" portions; while the "dated" digs "could use some sprucing up", "reasonable" prices (helped by online coupons) make this one a relatively "good value."

Cafe Italiano *Italian* | 19 | 16 | 19 | $41 |

Englewood Cliffs | 14 Sylvan Ave. (bet. Irving & Washington Aves.) | 201-461-5041 | www.cafeitaliano.net

Former NYC mayor Jimmy Walker's summer home is the "historic setting" of this "reliable" Englewood Cliffs Italian serving "steady-as-she-goes" fare that appeals to the "early bird–special crowd"; somewhat "lackluster" service and "musky" decor detract, but swell "outdoor dining" and "fair prices" are reasons why it's "always busy."

Cafe Loren ⓜ *American* | ▽ 25 | 18 | 24 | $52 |

Avalon | 2288 Dune Dr. (23rd St.) | 609-967-8228 | www.cafeloren.com

This "upscale" Avalon BYO has been an "excellent" option for 30-plus years thanks to its "fabulous" American cooking and "lovely" service; despite "nondescript" decor and "pricey" tabs, devotees say it's an "excellent" alternative to the "crowded Cape May dining" scene.

⊠ Cafe Madison ⓈⓂ *American* | 22 | 26 | 22 | $45 |

Riverside | 33 Lafayette St. (Madison St.) | 856-764-4444 | www.cafemadison.com

"Hidden" in South Jersey's Riverside, this "boomers' beachhead" has "special occasion" written all over it thanks to its "delicious" seasonal Americana, "superior" service and "waterfall"-equipped barroom; though tabs skew "high-end", "Manhattan decor" and "first-rate" live entertainment help to distract.

⊠ Cafe Matisse ⓈⓂ *Eclectic* | 27 | 26 | 26 | $69 |

Rutherford | 167 Park Ave. (bet. Highland Cross & Park Pl.) | 201-935-2995 | www.cafematisse.com

"Stunning" says it all about this Rutherford "gem" where the "off-the-charts" Eclectic offerings are available only in three- or four-course grazing menus and served in a "romantic" room decorated with "Matisse prints" – or in an "utterly charming" back garden; the "stratospheric" prices are somewhat alleviated by the BYO policy (there's an on-site wine shop), but given the "stellar" service and "polished ambiance", it's "worth every penny and more."

Cafe Metro *Eclectic*   22 | 17 | 21 | $28

Denville | 60 Diamond Spring Rd. (bet. 1st Ave. & Orchard St.) | 973-625-1055 | www.thecafemetro.com

"Healthy cooking" is the thing at this Eclectic BYO in Denville that specializes in vegetarian and vegan dishes that make fans "feel good about eating"; local art on the walls enhances the "warm", "California" vibe, while alfresco dining on the porch is a big "plus."

🔲 Cafe Panache 🔲 *Eclectic*   27 | 23 | 25 | $59

Ramsey | 130 E. Main St. (bet. Island Ave. & Spruce St.) | 201-934-0030 | www.cafepanachenj.com

Chef-owner Kevin Kohler tantalizes the "sophisticated" set with an "exceptional" seasonal menu and "seamless" service at this "top-drawer" Eclectic BYO, the epitome of "big-ticket" dining in Ramsey; a "refreshingly elegant" setting and "friendly but formal" ambiance are further reasons why it can be "hard to get a reservation" at this "first-rate" "destination."

Caffe Aldo Lamberti *Italian*   24 | 23 | 24 | $50

Cherry Hill | 2011 Rte. 70 W. (Haddonfield Rd.) | 856-663-1747 | www.caffelamberti.com

"Fine dining" in Cherry Hill doesn't get much better than at this "up-upscale" Italian from the Lamberti family, an "all-time favorite" and perennial high scorer with "especially great" seafood, "professional" service and a wine bar stocked with a 1,000-label list; no surprise, "big-city prices" are part of the "elegant" experience.

Caffe Galleria *Eclectic*   ∇ 21 | - | 22 | $30

Lambertville | Lambertville House Hotel | 32 Bridge St. (Union St.) | 609-397-2400 | www.caffegalleria.com

"Vegetarians and omnivores" happily coexist at this Lambertville BYO, supplying a "something-for-everyone" selection of "healthy" Eclectic choices served by "nice folks"; it relocated from its former "hippie"-esque digs to the historic Lambertville House Hotel post-Survey.

Calandra's Mediterranean Grill *Mediterranean*   21 | 20 | 20 | $36

Fairfield | Hampton Inn & Suites | 118 Rte. 46 E. (bet. Plymouth St. & Tobia Pl.) | 973-575-6500 | www.calandras.net

"Excellent bread" from the off-site Calandra Bakery is the star of the show at this "respectable" Mediterranean in Fairfield's Hampton Inn, where the vibe is "comfortable" and "outdoor dining" is a plus; surveyors split on the service ("confident" vs. "unpolished"), but agree on the "affordable" tabs.

Campino Mercado *Portuguese*   ∇ 22 | 18 | 25 | $38

Newark | 70 Jabez St. (New York Ave.) | 973-589-4004 | www.campinomercado.com

"Big portions" of "reliable" Portuguese food come at wallet-friendly prices at this Newark Iberian in the Ironbound that aficionados call "one of the better" examples of the genre; similarly, murals of the homeland make for an ambiance that rises above that of the competition.

⚡ Capital Grille *Steak*
26 | 25 | 25 | $62

Paramus | Garden State Plaza | 1 Garden State Plaza (Roosevelt Ave.) | 201-845-7040
Cherry Hill | Cherry Hill Mall | 2000 Rte. 38 (Haddonfield Rd.) | 856-665-5252
www.thecapitalgrille.com

Sure, they're "part of a chain", but these "swank" "meat lover's paradises" in Paramus and Cherry Hill attract "well-heeled" "movers and shakers" jonesing for slabs of "superb beef" paired with "to-die-for sides"; expect an "extensive wine list", "clubby" atmospherics and service that "makes you feel like royalty", which you may have to be to afford the "prime prices."

⚡ Capriccio Ⓜ *Italian*
25 | 26 | 26 | $61

Atlantic City | Resorts Atlantic City Casino & Hotel | 1133 Boardwalk (North Carolina Ave.) | 609-340-6789 | www.resortsac.com

Diners "hit the jackpot" at this "outstanding" Italian in AC's Resorts Casino, where the winnings include "skillfully prepared", "osso good" dishes served by a "wonderful" team in a "stunning", "Gilded Age" setting replete with "fantastic ocean views"; but a post-Survey change in the hotel's ownership puts its ratings (and future) in question.

Capt'n Ed's Place *Seafood/Steak*
20 | 15 | 19 | $32

Point Pleasant | 1001 Arnold Ave. (Pine Bluff Ave.) | 732-892-4121 | www.captnedsplace.com

This "fun" BYO surf 'n' turf "haunt" down the Shore in Point Pleasant is best known for an "amusing" gimmick: "grilling your own" meats on a sizzling stone; small fry enjoy the tanks stocked with local fish – and their own menu – though grown-ups cite "long weekend waits."

Cara Mia *Italian*
- | - | - | E

Millburn | 194 Essex St. (bet. Lackawanna Pl. & Old Short Hills Rd.) | 973-379-8989 | www.caramiamillburn.com

Across from the Millburn train station and near the Paper Mill Playhouse, this family-run Italian BYO supplements its à la carte offerings with a selection of salads and grilled panini at lunch; exposed brick lends warmth to the dining room while French doors opening onto the sidewalk provide a breath of fresh air.

Carmine's *Italian*
21 | 20 | 20 | $41

Atlantic City | Quarter at the Tropicana | 2801 Pacific Ave. (Iowa Ave.) | 609-572-9300 | www.carminesnyc.com

"Best with a group", this "noisy" AC spin-off of the NYC original is known for "heavy-duty old-school" Italian chow served family-style on platters "humongous" enough to "feed the entire Soprano family"; sure, it's a "bit of a factory" and a "tourist trap", but it's a good place to "let your hair down" and priced fairly.

	FOOD	DECOR	SERVICE	COST

Casa Dante *Italian*
24 | 20 | 22 | $53

Jersey City | 737 Newark Ave. (bet. Kennedy Blvd. & Summit Ave.) | 201-795-2750 | www.casadante.com

"See and be seen" at this "old-time" Jersey City "political hangout", a "true institution" where the "old-school" Italian cooking is "done right" and it "always feels like 1975 – until the bill comes", that is; "solicitous" service from "ancient waiters" and "campy" weekend entertainment add to the "Sinatra"-esque vibe, though insiders say it "helps to be known" here.

Casa Giuseppe ⑤ *Italian*
22 | 18 | 24 | $44

Iselin | 487 Rte. 27 (Talmadge Ave.) | 732-283-9111 | www.casagiuseppe.com

"NY-style" service led by a "pampering" owner makes for "exceptional" dining at this Northern Italian storefront in Iselin, despite its "nondescript" exterior and location on "industrial" Route 27; the cuisine, while "not innovative", is "damned good" and manages to convey a "sense of Italy."

Casa Maya *Mexican*
24 | 17 | 20 | $25

Gillette | 615 Meyersville Rd. (Hickory Tavern Rd.) | 908-580-0799
High Bridge | 1 Main St. (Bridge St.) | 908-638-4032
www.casamayamexican.com

"Charmingly colorful", these Sonoran-style Mexican BYOs in High Bridge and Gillette do a "fantastic job" with "robust flavors" and "affordable" pricing, though the "kitschy", "hole-in-the-wall" decor is another story; the no-reservations policy can translate into "long lines", so regulars opt for "takeout."

Casa Solar Ⓜ *Pan-Latin*
23 | 18 | 19 | $39

Belmar | 1104 Main St. (bet. 11th & 12th Aves.) | 732-556-1144

A "delicious" mix of "unique" Pan-Latin flavors is yours at this "unpretentious" Belmar BYO that's perfect for those "willing to try something that they're unable to pronounce correctly"; too bad it "suffers in the service department", but otherwise it's a "solid" bet.

Casa Vasca *Spanish*
24 | 15 | 21 | $37

Newark | 141 Elm St. (Prospect St.) | 973-465-1350 | www.casavascarestaurant.com

"Prodigious quantities" of "excellent" Basque-accented cooking make this "homey" Newark Spaniard "one of the most reliable" in the Ironbound; although it's "a step off the beaten track" and reservations can "mean nothing", "truly affordable" tabs and a free attended parking lot are reasons why it's "often crowded" here.

Casona Ⓜ *Cuban*
22 | 20 | 20 | $35

Collingswood | 563 Haddon Ave. (Knight Ave.) | 856-854-5555 | www.mycasona.com

Collingswood's Restaurant Row is home to this "casual" Cuban BYO, an "unexpected find" with a "tasty" menu that includes an "outstanding" slow-roasted pork; set in a circa-1905 house done up in "faux Key West"–style (with a "Jersey flavor"), it's beloved for its "beautiful" wraparound porch that's enclosed during cold weather; P.S. the second and third floors are open for private parties.

Cassie's *Italian* | 18 | 14 | 17 | $27 |

Englewood | 18 S. Dean St. (bet. Englewood & Palisade Aves.) | 201-541-6760 | www.cassiespizzeria.com

"Family-style" dishes (including "reliably good" pizza from a coal-burning oven) and a "family-friendly" mood – i.e. "noisy" – make this Englewood Italian a "great place for the kids"; "generous portions", "economical" price points and casual outdoor seating reflect its "no-pretentions" vibe.

Cathay 22 *Chinese* | 22 | 17 | 19 | $33 |

Springfield | 124 Rte. 22 (bet. Hillside & Stern Aves.) | 973-467-8688 | www.cathay22.com

The "imaginative", "beautifully prepared" Sichuan fare at this "white-tablecloth" Springfield Chinese makes fans forgive its location on "dreary Route 22"; though the decor "needs updating" and service can range from "outstanding" to "spotty", modest pricing and "sophisticated execution" add some luster to this Asian "pearl."

❷ Catherine Lombardi *Italian* | 24 | 26 | 25 | $52 |

New Brunswick | 3 Livingston Ave., 2nd fl. (George St.) | 732-296-9463 | www.catherinelombardi.com

"Top notch" sums up the "exceptional dining experience" at this "highly regarded" upstairs sibling to New Brunswick's Stage Left, where "dynamite" Italian cooking, "gracious" service and "lavish", crimson-hued surroundings make for "special" evenings; still, critics say "top notch" also refers to the "inflated prices."

Cenzino 🅱 *Italian* | 24 | 20 | 24 | $48 |

Oakland | 589 Ramapo Valley Rd. (bet. Navajo Way & Thunderbird Dr.) | 201-337-6693 | www.cenzinos.com

"Fabulous" regional cooking and "excellent" service from a "tuxedo"-clad team make the "upscale" tabs understandable at this *"bellissimo"* Oakland Italian; weekends can be "crowded and noisy" (especially at the "busy bar"), but a "pleasant", omnipresent owner ensures that "warmth abounds."

❷ Chakra 🅱 *American* | 20 | 26 | 19 | $53 |

Paramus | 144 Rte. 4 (Arcadian Way) | 201-556-1530 | www.chakrarestaurant.com

"Slinky" atmospherics and an "awesome" pickup scene thrill "young" types at this "sexy" New American destination in Paramus; maybe the "creative", "pricey" eats are overwhelmed by the "warehouse acoustics" and "chic" *"Indiana Jones"* decor, but there's no doubt it's a "great place to make an impression"; it's now open for lunch on weekdays.

Chambers Walk Cafe 🅱 *American* | 21 | 17 | 19 | $31 |

Lawrenceville | 2667 Main St. (bet. Gordon & Phillips Aves.) | 609-896-5995 | www.chamberswalk.com

An "informal" setting is home to this "honest", "real-deal" BYO in Lawrenceville where "especially good" soups and salads are lunchtime "musts" and a "creative" New American bistro menu reigns at night; at any time, expect "welcoming" service from a "friendly team."

Chand Palace *Indian* | 23 | 15 | 19 | $23

Parsippany | 257 Littleton Rd. (Parsippany Rd.) | 973-334-5444
Piscataway | 1296 Centennial Ave. (bet. Stelton Rd. & Washington Ave.) | 732-465-1474
www.chandpalace.com

"Even meat lovers" relish the "flavorful" Indian vegetarian fare (along with "many" vegan options) at these BYO siblings in Parsippany and Piscataway; regulars tout the "outstanding" lunch and dinner buffets as a "good value", though prices are "reasonable" no matter what you order.

Chao Phaya *Thai* | 22 | 14 | 19 | $24

Somerset | Somerset Village Shopping Ctr. | 900 Easton Ave. (Foxwood Dr.) | 732-249-0110
Somerville | 9 Davenport St. (Main St.) | 908-231-0655
www.chaophayathaicuisine.com

When "you want it hot, they'll make it hot" at these Siamese twin BYOs in Somerset and Somerville, where the Thai food is "tasty" and the tabs "economical"; despite nondescript decor, the "quiet" settings are conducive to "peaceful meals" and the "helpful" staff "doesn't rush you."

Charley's Ocean Grill *American* | 18 | 19 | 19 | $37

Long Branch | 29 Avenel Blvd. (Ocean Ave.) | 732-222-4499 | www.charleysoceangrill.com

Bermuda fish chowder is a menu "knockout" at this "steady" North Shore American, parked a block from the ocean in Long Branch; "friendly" bars upstairs and down feature "great" views (and multiple TVs), and though some find this old salt "better" since it was remodeled, critics contend "it's not what it used to be."

Charrito's *Mexican* | 22 | 16 | 18 | $28

Hoboken | 1024 Washington St. (bet. 10th & 11th Sts.) | 201-659-2800
Hoboken | 121 Washington St. (bet. 1st & 2nd Sts.) | 201-418-8600
El Charro *Mexican*
Weehawken | 974 JFK Blvd. E. (bet. 47th & 48th Sts.) | 201-330-1130
www.loscharritos.com

Fans tip their sombreros to the "super-flavorful" Oaxacan cuisine served at these "reasonably priced" Mexican BYOs celebrated for their "awesome" tableside guacamole; "tight quarters" and "rushed" service are trumped by outdoor seating at the Hoboken outposts, while El Charro boasts a full liquor bar, outdoor seating and a drop-dead view of the NYC skyline.

Char Steak House *Steak* | 22 | 25 | 22 | $65

Raritan | 777 Rte. 202 N. (1st Ave.) | 908-707-1777 | www.charsteakhouse.com

"Formidable", "top-quality" chops are devoured by the "under-30 set" at this "über-trendy" steakhouse that's cloaked in mahogany, warmed by two fireplaces and "fashionable for Raritan"; given the "stunning" decor, "resortlike" patio and "active bar scene", the "NYC pricing" is a bit more understandable.

🔲 Chart House *Seafood* | 21 | 26 | 21 | $53 |

Weehawken | Lincoln Harbor | Pier D/T (Harbor Blvd.) | 201-348-6628
NEW Atlantic City | Golden Nugget Hotel & Casino | Brigantine Blvd. & Huron Ave. | 609-340-5030
www.chart-house.com

"Intoxicating" views of the NYC skyline make the "well-prepared" surf 'n' turf taste even better at this upscale chain seafooder in Weehawken (and its newer sibling in AC) that's "known more for its scenery" than its "consistent" cuisine; "attentive" service keeps it a "safe" bet, though some stern critics call it "average for the price"; the Golden Nugget location opened post-Survey.

Chateau of Spain *Spanish* ▽ | 23 | 17 | 19 | $30 |

Newark | 11 Franklin St. (bet. Broad & Mulberry Sts.) | 973-624-3346 | www.chateauofspain.com

Set in the Ironbound a few blocks from Newark's Prudential Center, this longtime Spaniard (since 1975) offers "very good" dishes served in "you-won't-leave-hungry" portions; a tile-floored, double-decker setting and "prompt", "courteous" service come with the territory.

🔲 Cheesecake Factory *American* | 19 | 19 | 18 | $30 |

Hackensack | Shops at Riverside | 197 Riverside Sq. (Hackensack Ave.) | 201-488-0330 ●
NEW Short Hills | Short Hills Mall | 1200 Morris Tpke. (John F. Kennedy Pkwy.) | 973-921-0930
Wayne | Willowbrook Mall | 1700 Willowbrook Blvd. (Rte. 46) | 973-890-1400
Bridgewater | Bridgewater Commons | 400 Commons Way (Rte. 206) | 908-252-0399
Edison | Menlo Park Mall | 455 Menlo Park Dr. (Rte. 1) | 732-494-7000
Freehold | Freehold Raceway Mall | 3710 Rte. 9 S. (bet. Rtes. 33 & 537) | 732-462-6544
Cherry Hill | Marketplace at Garden State Park | 931 Haddonfield Rd. (off Rte. 70) | 856-665-7550
www.thecheesecakefactory.com

There are "no surprises" in store at this "wildly popular" American chain, just "steady" food "turned up a notch" and served in "button-bursting portions" from a menu the size of "*War and Peace*"; though critics cite "long waits" and find the "decibels as high as the calorie count", many more call it a "failsafe" choice simply because "you know what you're getting" and it's "always good."

Chef Jon's *Chinese* | 24 | 15 | 20 | $25 |

Whippany | Pine Plaza Shopping Ctr. | 831 Rte. 10 (Jefferson Rd.) | 973-585-6258 | www.chefjons.com

"Vastly superior" Chinese food comes to Morris County via this "genuine" article improbably set in a Whippany shopping center on Route 10; chef Hua Zhang excels at the "adventurous" specialties of his native Shanghai, but even the more standard dishes receive raves – and the staff "really hustles" to boot; it's BYO.

	FOOD	DECOR	SERVICE	COST

☑ Chef's Table 🅜 French
28 | 19 | 26 | $52

Franklin Lakes | Franklin Square Shopping Ctr. | 754 Franklin Ave. (Harriet Pl.) | 201-891-6644

"Stellar" traditional French cuisine from chef Claude Baills and "impeccable service" overseen by his "gracious" wife lend "destination" status to this BYO bistro in a Franklin Lakes strip mall; insiders warn of "small" dimensions, "tight" seating and "tough" weekend reservations, but ultimately this place "still has it" – "why go to NYC?"

☑ Chef Vola's 🅜⇆ Italian
26 | 12 | 23 | $53

Atlantic City | 111 S. Albion Pl. (Pacific Ave.) | 609-345-2022 | www.chefvolas.com

"Difficult reservations" is putting it mildly at this "hidden" Italian BYO on an AC side street, where the "just-like-mama's" cooking enjoys a fervid "cult following" despite a cash-only policy, "low-ceilinged basement" setting and "tables closer than Siamese twins"; it's "no longer a secret" – "everybody knows the unlisted number" – and first-timers are willing to "sell their first-born" for a table.

Chelsea Prime Steak
▽ 24 | 27 | 23 | $65

Atlantic City | Chelsea Hotel | 111 S. Chelsea Ave., 5th fl. (Pacific Ave.) | 609-428-4545 | www.thechelsea-ac.com

Though the "A-plus" steaks are aged and the cocktails are "retro", the "crowd is 'now'" at this "beautiful" chop shop inside AC's boutique Chelsea Hotel; "lovely" service, "delicious" ocean views and sophisticated "black-and-white" decor right out of a 1940s "supper club" make the "expensive" tabs more understandable.

Chengdu 46 🅜 Chinese
24 | 18 | 22 | $40

Clifton | 1105 Rte. 46 E. (Van Houten Ave.) | 973-777-8855 | www.chengdu46.com

"Authentic" Sichuan flavors spice up the "gourmet" offerings at this "designer" Chinese parked in a Clifton strip mall; though the decor's getting "tired" and the tabs "steep" for the genre, fans say it's "worth the extra cost" for such a "high-class", "not-typical" experience.

☑ Chez Catherine 🅩🅜 French
26 | 23 | 25 | $66

Westfield | Best Western Westfield | 431 North Ave. W. (bet. Broad & Prospect Sts.) | 908-654-4011 | www.chezcatherine.com

The "owners' pride comes through on the plate" at this "as-good-as-advertised" Westfield "jewel" where "out-of-this-world" classic French cuisine arrives in an "unlikely" location (alongside a Best Western hotel); some protest "small portions" and "luxury" prices, but most purr this "formal" "class act" is nothing short of *"fantastique"*; P.S. dinner is prix fixe only, jackets suggested.

Chez Elena Wu Chinese/Japanese
22 | 18 | 20 | $30

Voorhees | Ritz Shopping Ctr. | 910 Haddonfield Berlin Rd. (bet. Laurel Oak Blvd. & White Horse Rd.) | 856-566-3222

Even though "Elena Wu no longer owns it", this "high-end" Voorhees BYO still purveys a "creative", French-accented Chinese-Japanese menu that includes some "surprisingly good" sushi; surveyors split on the decor ("comfortable" vs. "dull") but the "fast" service is fine as is.

Chickie & Pete's Cafe ● *Pub Food*   17 | 17 | 17 | $24

NEW **Wildwood** | Boardwalk (Cedar Ave.) | 609-770-8833 ●
Egg Harbor Township | 6055 Black Horse Pike (English Creek Ave.) | 609-272-1930 ●
Ocean City | Boardwalk (9th St.) | 609-545-8720 ⌧ Ⓜ
Bordentown | 183 Rte. 130 (Ward Ave.) | 609-298-9182 ●
www.chickiesandpetes.com

"Loud and friendly", these "basic" South Jersey outposts of the Philly-based sports bar chain serve "typical" pub grub along with their "claim to fame": "addictive" crab fries (think french fries with Old Bay seasoning); although there are "TVs aplenty", service can be "hard to find."

Chilangos *Mexican*   21 | 15 | 19 | $27

Highlands | 272 Bay Ave. (bet. Marina Bay Ct. & Sea Drift Ave.) | 732-708-0505

"Above-average" Mexican chow washed down with "yummy" margaritas is the draw at this "small", no-reservations storefront in Monmouth County's Highlands; though some find the experience "hit-or-miss", there's nothing wrong with the "friendly" service.

NEW Chinese Mirch Ⓜ *Asian*   - | - | - | M

North Brunswick | 2800 State Rd. 27 (Finnigans Ln.) | 732-951-8424 | www.chinesemirch.com

This affordable North Brunswick BYO offshoot of NYC's Curry Hill original offers its novel Chinese-Indian fusion fare in a simple but sleek, family-friendly setting; the name translates loosely as 'spicy Chinese', but the firepower can be fine-tuned to order.

Chophouse, The *Seafood/Steak*   23 | 24 | 23 | $55

Gibbsboro | 4 S. Lakeview Dr. (Clementon Rd.) | 856-566-7300 | www.thechophouse.us

Parked in "tiny" Gibbsboro in Camden County, this "fancy-night-out" surf 'n' turfer earns its chops with the "highest quality" cuts, "cooked properly" and served by an "attentive" team; "high-end" decor, an "amazing" lake view and an "extensive" wine list help to explain the "not-cheap" tabs.

Christie's Italian Seafood Grill *Italian*   26 | 19 | 24 | $42

Howell | Howell Ctr. | 2420 Rte. 9 S. (White St.) | 732-780-8310

"Close to perfection", this Howell strip-mall BYO lays out an "extensive" roster of consistently "superb" Italian dishes – not just seafood – abetted by "second-to-none" service; as it can be "noisy" during prime times, insiders "recommend going during the week."

Christopher *Eclectic*   - | - | - | M

Cherry Hill | 306 Kresson Rd. (Brace Rd.) | 856-354-1500 | www.christophercherryhill.com

Seafood-centric Eclectic fare with an Italian accent is the calling card of Christopher Bovino's Cherry Hill BYO, where dishes such as portobello mushrooms stuffed with jumbo lump crab cakes are served in a simple, casual setting that's comfortable for couples and families alike, the strip-mall location notwithstanding.

Ciao *Italian*
21 | 21 | 21 | $39

Basking Ridge | Riverwalk Village Ctr. | 665 Martinsville Rd. (Independence Blvd.) | 908-647-6007 | www.ciaorest.com

"Solid Italian fare", from seafood to coal-oven pizza, turns up at this "hopping" Basking Ridge bistro that's a "more casual" sibling of 3 West next door; "friendly" service and a "crackling" fireplace keep the mood "warm", while "pretty" decor and "moderate" costs make it a "popular" choice for everyone from "families" to "chic singles."

Cinnamon *Indian*
23 | 14 | 21 | $26

Morris Plains | 2920 Rte. 10 W. (bet. Parks & Powder Mill Rds.) | 973-734-0040 | www.cinnamonindianrestaurant.com

"Savory delicacies" are served by an "attentive" crew at this "flavorful" Indian BYO located in an "unassuming" Morris Plains strip mall; too bad there's "not much in the way of decor", but the "good-value" lunch buffet is "perfect for those that can't make a decision."

Circa Ⓜ *French*
∇ 17 | 21 | 19 | $45

High Bridge | 37 Main St. (McDonald St.) | 908-638-5560 | www.circa-restaurant.com

"Well-presented" small plates and "inventive" cocktails circulate in "comfy" environs at this "cool" French bistro in High Bridge; critics think the menu's "a little too limited" and fret the place has "gone flat", but at least the service remains "well versed."

Claude's *French*
∇ 27 | 22 | 26 | $51

North Wildwood | 100 Olde New Jersey Ave. (1st Ave.) | 609-522-0400 | www.claudesrestaurant.com

This "real surprise" ensconced in an "unlikely" North Wildwood address serves "fantastic" French bistro classics that transport Francophiles "back to St. Germain"; service that makes you "feel like family" pairs well with the "warm", "romantic" atmosphere; P.S. closed from October to mid-April.

Clementine's Café Ⓢ *Creole*
23 | 21 | 22 | $44

Avon-by-the-Sea | 306 Main St. (Lincoln Ave.) | 732-988-7979 | www.clementinesavon.com

"Think N'Awlins" and its "big" Creole flavors to get the gist of this "unique" little Avon BYO that's "like nothing else at the Shore" (for one thing, it's "one of the few to take reservations"); it's "decorated to the nines" with "kitschy" "knickknacks", although what's "colorful" for some is too "gaudy" for others.

Clydz ◗ *American*
22 | 17 | 20 | $42

New Brunswick | 55 Paterson St., downstairs (Spring St.) | 732-846-6521 | www.clydz.com

It's always game time at this "popular" New Brunswick New American where "adventuresome" meats (like elk and rattlesnake) are paired with "deadly" martinis poured at the "lively" bar; its subterranean, "low-ceilinged" setting has a "speakeasy" feel that appeals to everyone from jurors to collegians.

Coconut Bay Fusion Cuisine *Asian*   ▽ 22 | 18 | 21 | $27

Voorhees | Echelon Village Plaza | 1120 White Horse Rd.
(bet. Executive Dr. & Haddonfield Berlin Rds.) | 856-783-8878 |
www.coconutbayfusion.com

Many "interesting choices" fill out the menu of this Voorhees Pan-Asian BYO vending both standard and fusion dishes; fans report that everything is "fresh", "well prepared" and competently delivered, while night owls are pleased it's open relatively "late" (10 PM Sunday–Thursday, 11 PM Friday and Saturday).

Columbia Inn Ⓜ *Italian*   21 | 14 | 18 | $33

Montville | 29 Main Rd. (Morris Ave.) | 973-263-1300 |
www.thecolumbiainn.com

"Top-notch", thin-crust pizza is "*the* reason to go" to this "casual" Italian trattoria housed in Montville's former 19th-century town hall; naysayers natter about "dated" decor and "slow" service, but the $9.95 three-course lunch special keeps tabs and tongues in check.

Conte's *Pizza*   25 | 9 | 18 | $19

Princeton | 339 Witherspoon St. (Guyot Ave.) | 609-921-8041 |
www.contespizzaandbar.com

In a "town of institutions", this longtime Princeton pizzeria is a "charmingly decrepit" survivor, renowned for its "almost transparent" thin-crust pies and "Formica"-and-"linoleum" decor right out of an "Elks Club"; "no-frills" service comes with the territory and no matter when you show up, there's "always a wait."

Continental *Eclectic*   23 | 23 | 21 | $38

Atlantic City | Pier Shops at Caesars | 1 Atlantic Ocean (Arkansas Ave.) |
609-674-8300 | www.continentalac.com

Stephen Starr's "cool" Eclectic offers a "seriously good", globe-trotting small-plates menu (and "even better cocktails") delivered by a "young, enthusiastic" team; the sprawling, "retro-chic" setting in Atlantic City's Pier at Caesars trumps the Philadelphia original with "amazing" "midcentury modern decor" and really "great ocean views."

Copper Canyon *Southwestern*   23 | 21 | 18 | $47

Atlantic Highlands | Blue Bay Inn | 51 First Ave. (bet. Center Ave. &
Ocean Blvd.) | 732-291-8444 | www.thecoppercanyon.com

"Delicious" Southwestern chow is the calling card of this "pretty" spot inside Atlantic Highlands' Blue Bay Inn, where the fare can be paired with "smokin'" margaritas concocted from a deep tequila list; "noisy" sound levels and "unfriendly", "rush-you-out" service are downsides, but otherwise the dining here is "first-rate."

Copper Fish *American/Seafood*   ▽ 20 | 21 | 19 | $48

West Cape May | 416 Broadway (bet. Congress St. & Sunset Blvd.) |
609-898-1555

The "chef knows what he's doing" at this American seafooder that has recently relocated to the former Daniel's on Broadway digs in

West Cape May; though critics cite "overpricing", "underportioning" and "disorganized" service, loyalists insist "it has potential"; P.S. there are a limited number of NJ wines on offer, but they're happy to have you BYO.

Corso 98 *Italian*
22 | 19 | 22 | $44

Montclair | 98 Walnut St. (Willow St.) | 973-746-0789 | www.corso98.com
An "extended family feel" courtesy of a "personable" owner courses through this "cozy" Montclair storefront where the "rock-solid" cooking is "not your typical red-sauce Italian"; though "on the pricey side", it is a BYO that fans call hard to beat for a "quiet, pleasant" meal.

Costanera Ⓜ *Peruvian*
▽ 24 | 20 | 23 | $40

Montclair | 511 Bloomfield Ave. (bet. Fullerton Ave. & Park St.) | 973-337-8289 | www.costaneranj.com
"Gourmet" Peruvian fare turns up at this "fantastic" Montclair BYO where fans "can't say enough great things" about its "diverse", "beautifully presented" menu and "first-rate" service; throw in "original" decor and reasonable pricing, and it's easy to see why it's become one of the "most popular" "kids on the block."

Country Pancake House ⊅ *American*
19 | 9 | 15 | $18

Ridgewood | 140 E. Ridgewood Ave. (Walnut St.) | 201-444-8395 | www.countrypancakehouse.net
"Colossal", "Paul Bunyan"–size portions are the order of the day at this "ridiculously cheap" Ridgewood BYO serving "stomach-shattering" Traditional Americana (and breakfast all day) to a "faithful clientele"; sure, it's "cash-only", service is "unreliable" and the decor "dingy", but there's a reason why this place is "always packed."

Court Street *Continental*
22 | 18 | 20 | $34

Hoboken | 61 Sixth St. (bet. Hudson & Washington Sts.) | 201-795-4515 | www.courtstreet.com
All rise for "solid" Continental fare served in "classy yet casual" digs at this "affordable" Hoboken "standby" known for its "excellent" Sunday brunch and "especially good" early-bird; some jurors find the overall experience "unspectacular", but the ambiance is "pleasant" and, assuming you're legal, the "bar rocks."

Crab House *Seafood*
16 | 18 | 16 | $38

Edgewater | 541 River Rd. (Gorge Rd.) | 201-840-9311 | www.crabhouseseafood.com
A "glorious" view of Manhattan and the "mighty" Hudson River is the hook at this "moderately priced" Edgewater edition of the Florida seafood chain where the "so-so" cooking may display a "lack of subtlety"; "spotty" service adds to the "nothing-special" vibe, though fans say it works for "family celebrations" and "wowing out-of-towners."

Crab's Claw Inn *Seafood*
18 | 15 | 18 | $36

Lavallette | 601 Grand Central Ave. (President Ave.) | 732-793-4447 | www.thecrabsclaw.com
"Basic" Shore seafood is dished out at this "relaxed" Lavallette "standby" known for "good-not-great" eats accompanied by "plenty of

draft beer"; in the winter, it's a "destination for the retired crowd", but in season, "plan on a wait" – even though some say it's "past its prime."

Crab Trap *Seafood*   21 | 17 | 19 | $37

Somers Point | 2 Broadway (Somers Point Circle) | 609-927-7377 | www.thecrabtrap.com

"Old-school" fin fare arrives in a "classic" fish-shack setting at this "been-there-forever" seafooder in Somers Point that's a "senior hang-out" off season and a "tourist" magnet in summer; critics crab it could stand "a little updating" in the decor and service areas, but concede that the bar overlooking Great Egg Harbor is its "saving grace."

Cranbury Inn *American*   14 | 17 | 17 | $36

Cranbury | 21 S. Main St. (bet. Cranbury Station Rd. & Evans Dr.) | 609-655-5595 | www.thecranburyinn.com

"Nothing has changed" at this "historic", circa-1750 Cranbury tavern, where "hearty" albeit "middling" Traditional American fare is delivered in an "Early American" setting; most feel it's "down at the heels", with an "inconsistent" kitchen, "outdated" decor and service that "needs work", a shame since there's "so much potential" here.

Cross Culture *Indian*   - | - | - | M

Haddonfield | 208 Kings Hwy. E. (bet. Haddon Ave. & Mechanic St.) | 856-428-4343

At this moderately priced Haddonfield BYO, Indian staples such as chicken tikka masala are prepared at varying degrees of spiciness to suit all palates and served in a spacious, white-tablecloth setting.

Crown Palace *Chinese*   20 | 19 | 18 | $29

Marlboro | 8 N. Main St. (School Rd.) | 732-780-8882
Middletown | 1283 Rte. 35 (Kings Hwy.) | 732-615-9888
www.crownpalacerestaurant.com

Weekend brunches rolling out a "wide variety" of dim sum are the hook at this Monmouth County Chinese, though the everyday "cut-above" cooking keeps it "always busy"; the Marlboro branch boasts a "pretty little garden" with a koi pond, Middletown has a "spectacular" fish tank and both share "upscale" aspirations.

NEW Cubacan *Cuban*   - | - | - | M

Asbury Park | 800 Ocean Ave. (Asbury Ave.) | 732-774-3007 | www.cubacan.net

South Beach meets the Asbury Park boardwalk at this upscale Cuban serving small and large plates backed by midpriced Spanish and South American wines in an urban-chic setting featuring rosewood floors, mosaic tiles and white curtains with wrought-iron valances; ocean views and live bands on weekends complete the picture.

Cuba Libre *Cuban*   21 | 24 | 21 | $42

Atlantic City | Quarter at the Tropicana | 2801 Pacific Ave. (Iowa Ave.) | 609-348-6700 | www.cubalibrerestaurant.com

It's Havana by way of "Hollywood" at this "novel" Cuban inside AC's Tropicana, where "excellent" chow and "hospitable" service take a backseat to the "loud, bustling" scene and over-the-top decor (that in-

| | FOOD | DECOR | SERVICE | COST |

cludes a Soviet missile replica); even though it's a link of a national chain, fans of "something different" can't get enough of its "Latin flair."

Cuban Pete's *Cuban*
19 | **22** | **17** | **$31**

Montclair | 428 Bloomfield Ave. (Fullerton Ave.) | 973-746-1100 | www.cubanpetesrestaurant.com

"Like a night in old Havana", this "upbeat" Montclair "hot spot" vends a "quixotic" Cuban menu in a "colorful" Caribbean courtyard setting, but the cooking is undercut by "haphazard" service and "chaotic", "bring-a-megaphone" acoustics (think "bongo-drum serenades"); "reasonable" tabs and a BYO policy (though it also boasts a lineup of sangrias) supply the "value."

Cubanu *Cuban*
▽ **21** | **19** | **22** | **$31**

Rahway | 1467 Main St. (Lewis St.) | 732-499-7100 | www.cubanu.com

"Creative" twists on classic dishes make for "tasty" tapas and entrees at this Rahway Cuban lounge that's suitable for either a "romantic dinner" or "after-work outing"; though some say the portions are too "small" for the cost, service gets "high marks" and DJs plus dancing equal "fun, fun, fun."

Cubby's BBQ *BBQ*
19 | **10** | **15** | **$20**

Hackensack | 249 S. River St. (bet. Kennedy & Water Sts.) | 201-488-9389 | www.cubbysbarbeque.com

Everyone from "suits" to "truck drivers" queues up at this "no-pretenses" Hackensack roadhouse where "large" portions of "better-than-average" BBQ are slung at a "fair price"; there's "no decor to speak of" and service is "cafeteria-style", but "fast."

Cucharamama Ⓜ *S American*
26 | **22** | **22** | **$45**

Hoboken | 233 Clinton St. (3rd St.) | 201-420-1700 | www.cucharamama.com

"Unusual", "eye-opening" dishes and "fabulous" breads from a wood-fired oven are paired with "exotic" cocktails at this "exciting" Hoboken South American showcasing the "magic touch" of chef/food historian Maricel Presilla; though the quarters are "super-tight" and "prices can creep up", the "inviting" atmosphere and "top-notch" service make it an "amazing find."

Cucina Calandra *Italian*
21 | **19** | **20** | **$35**

Fairfield | Best Western Fairfield Executive Inn | 216-234 Rte. 46 E. (Horseneck Rd.) | 973-575-7720 | www.cucinacalandra.com

Another *bambino* of the namesake bakery family, this "quite good" Southern Italian inside Fairfield's Best Western is known for its "fabulous" bread (and the complimentary loaf offered as a parting gift is a "nice touch"); "ample portions", a "child-friendly" ambiance and cost-cutting "coupons" make it a natural for "families."

Cucina Rosa *Italian*
21 | **18** | **21** | **$39**

Cape May | Washington Street Mall | 301 Washington St. (Perry St.) | 609-898-9800 | www.cucinarosa.com

The aroma of "homemade red sauce" lures patrons into this "must-visit" Italian BYO "conveniently located" on Cape May's Washington

Street Mall; "reasonable" tabs, "pleasant" service and a patio with excellent people-watching opportunities ice the cake.

☑ CulinAriane ☒Ⓜ *American* | 27 | 20 | 25 | $58 |

Montclair | 33 Walnut St. (Pine St.) | 973-744-0533 | www.culinariane.com
"Labor-of-love" dining comes to Montclair via this "splendid" New American BYO where chef-owners Ariane and Michael Duarte approach culinary "perfection" with their "superb" menus and "gracious" service; granted, it's "expensive" and rather "tiny", but admirers say it's a bona fide "go-to" for a "special night out"; P.S. dinner only, Wednesday–Saturday.

Daddy O *American* | 19 | 22 | 19 | $46 |

Long Beach Township | Daddy O Hotel | 4401 Long Beach Blvd. (44th St.) | 609-494-1300 | www.daddyohotel.com
Rather "glitzy" for Long Beach, this "sleek" American brings a "W Hotel" vibe to the Jersey Shore with its "retro" "'60s" design, "NYC-cool" following and "top-shelf" bar scene; it's a "nice departure from the flip-flop crowds", even though its "haute cafeteria" offerings are "not cheap."

Da Filippo's ☒ *Italian/Seafood* | 24 | 18 | 23 | $43 |

Somerville | 132 E. Main St. (bet. Hamilton & Meadow Sts.) | 908-218-0110 | www.dafilippos.com
The "fish steals the show" at this Somerville storefront Italian, a "mom-and-pop" operation with "authentic Sicilian flair" on the plates and a "welcoming" vibe in the air; weekend "piano music" adds to the "charming" mood, but some find the pricing a bit "high" even though it's BYO.

Dai-Kichi *Japanese* | 23 | 16 | 21 | $35 |

Upper Montclair | 608 Valley Rd. (Bellevue Ave.) | 973-744-2954
"High-quality" sushi and "unique" rolls make this Upper Montclair Japanese a "local favorite", and it's recently added a second floor and acquired a liquor license (though you can still BYO for a "reasonable corkage fee"); "eager-to-please" staffers and outdoor garden seating complete the "reliable" picture.

D & L Barbecue Ⓜ *BBQ* ▽ | 24 | 10 | 16 | $30 |

Bradley Beach | 714 Main St. (bet. Lareine & McCabe Aves.) | 732-776-7488 | www.dlbbq.com
Having relocated from one seaside community (Asbury Park) to another (Bradley Beach), this "no-frills" BYO still slings "lip-smackin'" BBQ and "first-rate" mac 'n' cheese in a "no-atmosphere" setting; overall, it's a "solid" effort, save for the "slow" service.

Daniel's Bistro Ⓜ *Continental* | - | - | - | E |

Point Pleasant Beach | 115 Broadway (bet. Baltimore & Boston Aves.) | 732-899-5333
This BYO in Point Pleasant Beach plies a thoroughly modern Continental menu, with the surf options just as popular as the turf; though the room can be loud, early visitors report the meals proceed at a leisurely pace.

	FOOD	DECOR	SERVICE	COST

Danny's ● *Steak*
20 | 16 | 19 | $41

Red Bank | 11 Bridge Ave. (Front St.) | 732-741-6900 |
www.dannyssteakhouse.com

"Affable" owner Danny Murphy can often be found at this Red Bank
"mainstay" that's been in business since '69 serving "reliable"
steaks and seafood as well as some "excellent" sushi; though most
agree there's "nothing out of the ordinary" going on here, it is "close
to the theaters" and hosts a popular "neighborhood bar" scene.

Dante's Ristorante *Italian*
20 | 16 | 19 | $37

Mendham | 100 E. Main St. (Cold Hill Rd.) | 973-543-5401 |
www.dantenj.com

"Reliable and friendly", this Mendham BYO augments its "traditional"
Italian menu with "well-made" pizza, "amazing up-front nibbles" and
"specials for every taste"; regulars cite "attentive" service and "reasonable" tabs as reasons it's been on the scene since 1991.

NEW Daryl *American*
- | - | - | E

(fka Daryl Wine Bar)

New Brunswick | Heldrich Hotel | 302 George St. (New St.) |
732-253-7780 | www.darylrestaurant.com

Fans of Zod Arifai's popular Blu and Next Door in Montclair will welcome his New American cuisine at this recently reopened high-
design contemporary spot in New Brunswick's Heldrich Hotel; he's
kept the wine bar concept from its previous incarnation, offering
two-, four- and six-ounce pours and a supplemental list of 50 whites
and 50 reds under $50.

NEW Da's Kitchen *Thai*
- | - | - | I

Hopewell | 21 E. Broad St. (Seminary Ave.) | 609-466-8424 |
www.daskitchenhopewell.com

At her BYO Thai in Hopewell, veteran chef/co-owner Da Detoro, who
trained at the Royal Thai Culinary School and opened her first restaurant at 18, accommodates personal spice preferences and special
requests with ease as she prepares authentic dishes from an open
kitchen; photos and memorabilia from Thailand grace the storefront
setting, and there's sidewalk seating on the tree-lined street.

NEW Da Soli Ⓜ *Italian*
- | - | - | M

Haddonfield | Shops at 116 | 116 Kings Hwy. E. (Tanner St.) |
856-429-2399 | www.dasolirestaurant.com

Chef-owner Mark Berenato has gone *da solo* (on his own) with this
midpriced BYO Italian trattoria in a Haddonfield mini-mall; while the
decor of the two-story space is rustic Tuscan, his menu hails from all
over Italy, ranging from handmade pastas to supplì (risotto cro-
quettes stuffed with beef and mozzarella) to gelati made in-house.

Dauphin Grille *American*
∇ 22 | 23 | 23 | $45

Asbury Park | Berkeley Hotel | 1401 Ocean Ave. (6th Ave.) |
732-774-3474 | www.dauphingrille.com

The latest "winner" from Shore restaurateur Marilyn Schlossbach
(Labrador Lounge, etc.), this eatery in Asbury Park's restored Berkeley

Hotel features an "interesting" American menu with European accents; "inspired service", a "fun atmosphere" and a "beautiful" setting are reasons why it won't stay "off the radar" for long.

Davia *Italian*
20 | 16 | 21 | $32

Fair Lawn | 6-09 Fair Lawn Ave. (bet. River Rd. & 6th St.) | 201-797-6767 | www.daviarest.com

There's "value for the money" at this "cozy" Fair Lawn Italian, especially its four-course, $14 (cash-only) early-bird, one of the "best deals in town"; otherwise, expect an "older" crowd sampling "interesting" cooking in a setting that's "quiet enough for conversation."

◪ David Burke Fromagerie Ⓜ *American*
25 | 24 | 24 | $64

Rumson | 26 Ridge Rd. (Ave. of Two Rivers) | 732-842-8088 | www.fromagerierestaurant.com

Star chef Burke "got his start" at this "upper-crust" Rumson classic and his "modernized" revamp since taking over features "lighter" American "fare with flair" (including his signature angry lobster and cheesecake lollipops); though the crowd's as "Waspy" as ever, now its "intimate" rooms are "brighter" and the pricing so "expensive" that "budget-conscious foodies" reserve the experience for a "special occasion" – or go for "Tuesday burger night."

DeAnna's ⊠Ⓜ *Italian*
24 | 22 | 20 | $40

Lambertville | 54 N. Franklin St. (Coryell St.) | 609-397-8957 | www.deannasrestaurant.com

"Awesome homemade pasta" is the specialty of this "upscale" Italian in Lambertville with an "energetic" vibe and a "fun" bar scene; regulars tout the $20, three-course 'locals' menu' on Tuesdays and Wednesdays – and live music on Thursdays and Fridays.

Delicious Heights *American*
18 | 20 | 19 | $34

Berkeley Heights | 428 Springfield Ave. (Lone Pine Dr.) | 908-464-3287 | www.deliciousheights.com

Bringing some "energy" to "sleepy" Berkeley Heights, this strip-mall American features a "solid", "something-for-everyone" menu of comfort-food classics, but it's the "loud", "hopping scene" at the "cool", TV-laden bar that makes it a "young person" magnet.

DelMonico *Eclectic/Steak*
▽ 27 | 24 | 25 | $50

Cedar Grove | 505 Pompton Ave. (Cedar St.) | 973-433-0333 | www.villagerestaurantgroup.com

North Jersey restaurateur Bobby Wong (Mignon, Tina Louise) and actor James Gandolfini (*The Sopranos*) are the minds behind this sceney Cedar Grove eatery that transcends the steakhouse genre by offering an extensive, 'steak-and-beyond' menu with Asian and Italian options; slick red-and-black decor and smart service complete the ambitious picture.

DeLorenzo's Pizza ⊠ *Pizza*
24 | 11 | 18 | $17

Hamilton | Risoldi's Mkt. | 3100 Quakerbridge Rd. (Sloan Ave.) | 609-588-5630

(continued)

(continued)

DeLorenzo's Pizza
Trenton | 1007 Hamilton Ave. (bet. Ardmore & Fairmount Aves.) |
609-393-2952 Ⓜ⇄
www.delospizza.com
Debate rages on as to which progeny of the DeLorenzo pizzeria clan offers the superior pie, but fans say this BYO Trenton "fixture" turns out "authentic" – verging on "awesome" – pizzas, with "gruff" service, "no ambiance" and a cash-only policy included in the package; the outpost in Risoldi's Market opened post-Survey.

☑ DeLorenzo's Tomato Pies Ⓜ *Pizza*   27 | 15 | 18 | $19
Robbinsville | Washington Town Ctr. | 2350 Rte. 33
(Robbinsville Edinburg Rd.) | 609-341-8480 |
www.delorenzostomatopies.com
Though the Trenton original shuttered in 2012, this Robbinsville BYO still "lives up to its reputation" with "gold-standard" pizzas that some consider the "holy grail" of tomato pies; you can still bank on "indifferent" service, "long waits" and a no-rezzie policy.

Delta's Ⓜ *Southern*   22 | 23 | 21 | $41
New Brunswick | 19 Dennis St. (bet. Hiram Sq. & Richmond St.) |
732-249-1551 | www.deltasrestaurant.com
Transplanted Southerners get their fix of "stepped-up soul food" at this "cool" joint in Downtown New Brunswick where the "beautiful", 1850s-era setting features a long bar, gallery seating and Ansel Adams photos on the walls; live entertainment and "courteous" service are "added benefits."

Dimora *Italian*   24 | 21 | 21 | $57
Norwood | 100 Piermont Rd. (bet. Briarwood & Pierson Aves.) |
201-750-5000 | www.dimoraristorante.com
A "NYC wannabe with the food to back it up", this "all-around great" "back-road" Italian in Norwood is known for its "terrific" seafood, "wonderful" pastas and "treat-you-like-royalty" service; its "high-roller" following digs the "scene", the "table-hopping" and the "classy" milieu, and ignores the "expensive" tabs and "loud" sound level.

Dim Sum Dynasty *Chinese*   20 | 15 | 18 | $27
Ridgewood | 75 Franklin Ave. (Oak St.) | 201-652-0686 |
www.dimsumdynastynj.com
"Top-quality" Cantonese dim sum – served from "roving carts" during weekend brunch – brightens this "little piece of Chinatown in Ridgewood"; "plain" decor and "slow" service are trumped by "lots of variety" and a BYO policy that keeps prices in check.

Dinallo's *Italian*   22 | 15 | 21 | $44
River Edge | 259 Johnson Ave. (Madison St.) | 201-342-1233 |
www.dinallosrestaurant.com
Like a "time warp" to the "days of Frank Sinatra", this "red-sauce" Italian in River Edge purveys an "excellent", "homestyle" menu in a "casual" milieu; some say it "caters to regulars" and the "cougar"-esque "bar scene supersedes the food", but it's still "enjoyable."

☒ Dino & Harry's *Steak*   27 | 23 | 24 | $59

Hoboken | 163 14th St. (Garden St.) | 201-659-6202 |
www.dinoandharrys.com

"Phenomenal" chops "cooked just right" and "delicious" sides fill
out the menu of this "classic" Hoboken steakhouse set in a former 19th-century saloon (and *On the Waterfront* location) replete with vintage stained glass and a tin ceiling; "prompt"
service, "lovely" piano music and live jazz make the "over-the-top"
tabs easier to stomach.

Dino's *Italian*   22 | 21 | 23 | $44

Harrington Park | 12 Tappan Rd. (Schraalenburgh Rd.) | 201-767-4245 |
www.dinoshp.com

"Excellent" cuisine, "accommodating" service and a "tranquil",
"parklike" location make for "wonderful dining" at this Harrington
Park Italian; "fair prices" and a "nice bar area" complete the "comfortable" picture; P.S. closed Tuesdays.

DiPalma Brothers Ⓜ *Italian*   ▽ 21 | 17 | 18 | $35

North Bergen | 8728 Kennedy Blvd. (bet. 87th & 88th Sts.) |
201-868-3005 | www.dipalmabrothers.com

One part Italian restaurant, one part "antiques shop", this "unusual" North Bergen BYO offers "hearty" cooking in a "vintage"
room where the decor's for sale too; "problem parking" and the
no-reservations policy are trumped by its "modest" cost and
"family-friendly" reception.

Dish Ⓜ *American*   25 | 16 | 20 | $42

Red Bank | 13 White St. (Broad St.) | 732-345-7070 |
www.dishredbank.com

"Unexpected twists" on American comfort food fill out the menu of
this "delightful" BYO set in a "small" Red Bank storefront; an "efficient", "friendly" crew makes the "challenging" acoustics and "tight-
squeeze" seating ("keep your elbows close") more bearable.

Diving Horse *Seafood*   ▽ 24 | 20 | 21 | $50

Avalon | 2109 Dune Dr. (21st St.) | 609-368-5000 |
www.thedivinghorseavalon.com

Named for an early-20th-century boardwalk attraction, this sea-
food-focused Avalon BYO is a "great addition" to the Seven Mile
Island "scene", especially since both the staff and the fin fare are
"young" and "fresh"; the "charming", whitewashed-farmhouse setting also features breezy patio seating.

Dock's Oyster House *Seafood*   26 | 21 | 24 | $52

Atlantic City | 2405 Atlantic Ave. (Georgia Ave.) | 609-345-0092 |
www.docksoysterhouse.com

A "throwback to the *Boardwalk Empire*" era of AC, this circa-1897
seafood "icon" still scores high for its "fabulous" fin fare served by
an "outstanding" team in a "days-gone-by" setting; nightly piano
music and a "good" wine list help distract from the "noisy" decibels
and modern-day prices.

	FOOD	DECOR	SERVICE	COST

Dong Bang Grill ◑ *Korean*
▽ 22 | 14 | 18 | $40

Fort Lee | 1616 Palisade Ave. (Main St.) | 201-242-4485
"Tasty and enjoyable", this casual Fort Lee Korean vends "first-rate" BBQ accompanied by a "jaw-dropping assortment" of sides; though service wavers between "lacking" and "excellent", and tabs skew "a bit expensive" for the genre, overall it's "a lot of fun."

Don Pepe *Portuguese/Spanish*
22 | 16 | 20 | $41

Newark | 844 McCarter Hwy. (Raymond Blvd.) | 973-623-4662 | www.donpeperestaurant.com
Pine Brook | 18 Old Bloomfield Ave. (Changebridge Rd.) | 973-882-6757 | www.donpepeii.com
"Enormous" steaks and "lobsters that could be put on a leash" are washed down with "tasty" sangria at these "bustling" Iberians in Newark and Pine Brook famed for their "gigantic portions"; some pundits pout that "quality has declined" and call for a decor "make-over", but "easy parking" and "value" pricing win out.

Don Pepe's Steakhouse *Steak*
22 | 18 | 20 | $48

Pine Brook | 58 Rte. 46 W. (bet. Chapin & Van Winkle Rds.) | 973-808-5533 | www.donpepesteakhouse.com
Regulars "bring a backpack for the leftovers" at this "casual" Pine Brook steakhouse and seafooder where "filet mignons the size of footballs" "overflow the plates"; despite "long waits" and "noisy" sound levels, the "solid" cooking and "good" service make it a "reliable" dining option.

Don Quijote *Spanish*
18 | 14 | 17 | $35

Fairview | 344 Bergen Blvd. (Jersey Ave.) | 201-943-3133
There's "bang for your buck" galore at this "busy" Fairview Spaniard known for its "tasty" paella and "bargain twin lobster" early-bird (Monday–Friday); the decor may be "dreary" and the "Spanglish-speaking" service varies from "friendly" to "inattentive", but the weekend mariachi bands keep things lively.

NEW Dos Caminos *Mexican*
- | - | - | E

Atlantic City | Harrah's | 777 Harrah's Blvd. (Brigantine Blvd.) | 609-441-5747 | www.doscaminos.com
Steve Hanson's BR Guest group brings Mexican into the AC casino mix with this Harrah's outpost of the upscale Manhattan-based chain known for guac prepared tableside and standout margaritas; spectacular bay views and a cool contemporary design that includes leather walls are other draws.

Dream Cuisine Cafe 🅱🅼 *French*
▽ 27 | 17 | 21 | $42

Cherry Hill | Tuscany Mktpl. | 1990 Rte. 70 E. (Old Orchard Rd.) | 856-751-2800 | www.dreamcuisinecafe.net
"Hidden" in a Cherry Hill strip mall, this French BYO "sleeper" makes fans want to "linger" thanks to its "absolutely wonderful" Provençal cooking served by an "on-top-of-it" staff; an "intimate" setting, "leisurely" pacing and a "great price-to-quality ratio" seal the deal.

	FOOD	DECOR	SERVICE	COST

Z Drew's Bayshore Bistro M *American* | 27 | - | 23 | $42 |

Keyport | 28 E. Front St. (Division St.) | 732-739-9219 |
www.bayshorebistro.com

Admirers are "impressed" with the "remarkable" "craftsmanship"
and "honest cooking" of chef Andrew Araneo at this Keyport
American BYO that's renowned for its "heartfelt" Cajun-accented
eats with a decided "New Orleans kick", served by a "congenial"
staff; a 2011 relocation to larger, more upscale digs may help allevi-
ate the "wait" to get in.

NEW Duck King *Chinese* | - | - | - | M |

Edgewater | 880 River Rd. (Hilliard Ave.) | 201-945-8823

Authentic Beijing duck tops the bill at this Chinese in an Edgewater
strip mall that draws a diverse crowd with a moderately priced menu
of steamed seafood, Shanghainese noodles and Chinese-American
staples, all served in a casual space with large windows and mirrors
on the walls that give it a bright, airy feel; it serves only Tsingtao
beer, but you can BYO.

Due Mari *Italian* | 26 | 24 | 25 | $55 |

New Brunswick | 78 Albany St. (Neilson St.) | 732-296-1600 |
www.duemarinj.com

It "feels like Manhattan" at this "smart" New Brunswick Italian,
where the "exquisite" menu offers a mix of "serious" seafood and
"stellar" pastas; "suave" service burnishes the "sophisticated"
mood, while a "well-appointed" room with "nicely spaced tables"
makes it "conducive to good conversation."

E & V M⇗ *Italian* | 23 | 13 | 20 | $34 |

Paterson | 320 Chamberlain Ave. (bet. Preakness & Redwood Aves.) |
973-942-8080 | www.evrestaurant.com

"Groaning platters" of "old-school" Italian standards arrive in "not-
fancy" digs at this "word-of-mouth" place in Paterson; founded in
'67, it's "still going strong" thanks to "fast" service and "1970s pricing", though some gripe about the "cash-only" rule and "*molto*
waiting" on weekends.

East *Japanese* | 19 | 15 | 17 | $30 |

Teaneck | 1405 Teaneck Rd. (bet. Rte. 4 & Tryon Ave.) |
201-837-1260

Patrons praise the "nice variety" of fresh sushi plucked from a "con-
veyor belt" at this "long-established" Teaneck Japanese that also
provides "excellent" cooked dishes; though foes fret about "assembly-
line" quality and "dated" decor, most agree it's "quick, inexpensive"
and "fun" for the kiddies.

Z Ebbitt Room *American* | 26 | 26 | 26 | $65 |

Cape May | Virginia Hotel | 25 Jackson St. (bet. Beach Ave. &
Carpenter Ln.) | 609-884-5700 | www.virginiahotel.com

"Fine dining" doesn't get much better than this "real memory
maker" in Cape May's Virginia Hotel, where "heavenly" modern
Americana is ferried by an "attentive but not overbearing" staff in a

"relaxed", "romantic" atmosphere; though it all "comes at a price", it takes the Shore experience "to the next level"; a 2011 renovation may not be reflected in the Decor score.

Eccola *Italian*   23 | 19 | 21 | $41

Parsippany | 1082 Rte. 46 W. (Beverwyck Rd.) | 973-334-8211 | www.eccolarestaurantnj.com

"Imaginative" cooking lures locals to this "upbeat" Italian in a Parsippany strip mall, where "reasonable" tabs and an "eager-to-please staff" make it a longtime local "tradition"; since it's "always crowded" and "noisy", insiders "get there early."

Edo Sushi *Chinese/Japanese*   ∇ 20 | 13 | 19 | $27

Pennington | Pennington Shopping Ctr. | 25 Rte. 31 S. (bet. Delaware & Franklin Aves.) | 609-737-1190 | www.edosushiwok.com

"Sushi is the best bet" at this "modest" Chinese-Japanese hybrid in the "unassuming" Pennington Shopping Center; "great value" and "nice variety on the menu" make this BYO a "sure bet", even if the "pedestrian" decor could use an upgrade.

Edward's Steakhouse 🗷 *Steak*   23 | 18 | 22 | $58

Jersey City | 239 Marin Blvd. (York St.) | 201-761-0000 | www.edwardssteakhouse.com

Although housed in an "elegant" 1870s brownstone, this Jersey City chophouse stakes its reputation on "NY-quality" meats and sea-food, served to a "classy" crowd peppered with "local politicos" and "special-occasioners"; granted, it's "way expensive", but there's a bargain $30 prix fixe Monday–Wednesday nights.

Egan & Sons *Irish*   19 | 21 | 19 | $33

Montclair | 118 Walnut St. (Forest St.) | 973-744-1413 | www.egannsons.com
West Orange | 104 Harrison Ave. (bet. Cherry & Main Sts.) | 973-736-3355 | www.eganswestorange.com

There's "quite the bar scene" in progress at this Irish pub twosome in Montclair and West Orange, so the "tasty" chow plays second fiddle to the "strong" drinks and "eye-candy"-studded crowd; still, some say it's "not bad if you don't want to have a conversation with your dinner companion" given the "can't-hear-yourself-think" acoustics.

El Azteca *Mexican*   21 | 12 | 19 | $20

Mount Laurel | Ramblewood Shopping Ctr. | 1155 Rte. 73 N. (Church Rd.) | 856-914-9302 | www.elaztecaonline.com

Family-run and family-friendly, this Mount Laurel cantina special-izes in "down-home" Mexican "comfort food" that's really "fresh"; devotees ignore the "lack of decor" and report that the portion sizes are "great for the price"; P.S. BYO tequila and the "friendly" staff will concoct "tasty" margaritas.

El Caney 🗷 *Cuban*   - | - | - | I

Bergenfield | 49 W. Church St. (Washington Ave.) | 201-374-1107

Generous, family-style portions of authentic Cuban cooking at rock-bottom tabs draw crowds to this tiny Bergenfield joint that's recently moved across the street from its original, even tinier, location; given limited seating and ramshackle decor that lives up to the name (it translates as 'the hut'), most opt for takeout.

El Cid *Spanish*   22 | 16 | 20 | $45

Paramus | 205 Paramus Rd. (bet. Century Rd. & Rte. 4) | 201-843-0123

"Olympic portions" are the hook at this Paramus Spanish surf 'n' turfer where "brontosaurus-size" steaks and "feed-a-large-army" prime rib keep gluttons sated; ok, it's "not classy" and the atmosphere is "noisy and chaotic", but "once you start drinking the sangria, who cares?"

☑ Elements *American*   26 | 25 | 25 | $66

Princeton | 163 Bayard Ln. (bet. Birch & Leigh Aves.) | 609-924-0078 | www.elementsprinceton.com

Finally, there's a "restaurant worth bragging about in Princeton" thanks to this "original" New American showstopper helmed by toque Scott Anderson, whose "haute" menu focuses on "locally grown, sustainable products"; "understated" "modern" decor (reminiscent of "Fallingwater"), "well-versed" service and "inventive" cocktails distract from the "Manhattan prices" and strange location on a "busy curve" of Route 206.

Elements Asia *Asian*   23 | 20 | 20 | $33

Lawrenceville | Village Commons | 4110 Quakerbridge Rd. (Village Rd.) | 609-275-4988 | www.elementsasia.com

Parked in a Lawrenceville strip mall, this "steady" Asian fusion BYO is especially touted for its "sublime" sushi rolls, although its Chinese, Japanese and Thai dishes all "play well together"; opinion splits on a recent renovation that added hibachi tables – "improved" vs. "sterile" – but there's agreement on the "reasonable" tabs and "helpful" staffers.

Elements Café Ⓜ *American*   23 | 18 | 23 | $36

Haddon Heights | 517 Station Ave. (White Horse Pike) | 856-546-8840 | www.elementscafe.com

"Tempting" small plates make a "delicious" impression at this "quiet" American tapas BYO in suburban Haddon Heights in Camden County; it's "lots of fun", and though tabs can add up, the 'Last Chance Sunday Supper' (four courses, $24) is a notable value.

Elevation Burger *Burgers*   19 | 12 | 15 | $12

Montclair | Phoenix Bldg. | 367 Bloomfield Ave. (Willow St.) | 973-783-8000

Moorestown | Moorestown Mall | 400 Rte. 38 (bet. Lenola Rd. & Nixon Dr.) | 888-291-4620

www.elevationburger.com

This "new breed" national burger chain, with links in Montclair and Moorestown, takes the genre in a "green" direction via organic, grass-fed beef and fries cooked in olive oil; the "marketing pitch" is fast food you can "feel good about", and the "earnest" patties are appropriately "tasty" and "well intentioned."

	FOOD	DECOR	SERVICE	COST

El Familiar *Colombian/Mexican*

| | - | - | - | M |

Toms River | Stella Towne Ctr. | 1246 Rte. 166 (Hilltop Rd.) |
732-240-6613 | www.elfamiliar.com

This modest Toms River BYO offers a menu of both Mexican and
Colombian dishes; maybe it looks like *"abuelita's* living room" and
the staff can get "caught up in the soccer match", but at least its
"homemade" cooking is the "real" thing.

El Mesón Café *Mexican*

| | 24 | 16 | 22 | $26 |

Freehold | 40 W. Main St. (Throckmorton St.) | 732-308-9494
Parked on Freehold's Main Street, this "little" Mexican BYO-cum-
market slings "honest", "real-McCoy" chow at great "bang-for-the-
buck" rates; the "cheesy" setting is "pretty basic", but there's
outdoor seating and "polite", "efficient" service.

NEW El Tule Ⓜ *Mexican/Peruvian*

| | - | - | - | M |

Lambertville | 49 N. Main St. (Coryell St.) | 609-773-0007 |
www.eltulerestaurant.com

Weekend reservations are recommended at this midpriced BYO in
Downtown Lambertville that's already popular for fresh Mexican
fare as well as authentic dishes from the owners' native Peru; colorful
art brightens up the cozy space, which boasts a dog-friendly patio.

Elysian Café *French*

| | 21 | 21 | 21 | $36 |

Hoboken | 1001 Washington St. (10th St.) | 201-798-5898 |
www.elysiancafe.com

Home to the "most beautiful ceiling in Hoboken", this "classic"
French bistro set in a "beautifully restored" 1895 saloon serves an
"outstanding" menu that strikes all the "right notes" – "their reach
does not exceed their grasp"; fun fact: it's "named after Elysian
Fields", said to be the site of the first organized baseball game.

ⓩ Eno Terra *Italian*

| | 24 | 25 | 24 | $53 |

Kingston | 4484 Rte. 27 (Academy St.) | 609-497-1777 |
www.enoterra.com

"Locally grown food" fills out the menu of this "memorable",
"middle-of-nowhere" Kingston Italian where chef Chris Albrecht's
"gourmet" preparations are served by a "superb" team; sure, the
prices are "stiff", but the modern setting, carved out of a 1714-
vintage structure, is pretty "spectacular" looking.

Epernay Ⓜ *French*

| | 21 | 19 | 21 | $43 |

Montclair | 6 Park St. (Rte. 506) | 973-783-0447 | www.epernaynj.com
Everything's *"très français"* at this "homey" "little bit of Paris" in
Montclair that purveys traditional Gallic items like "delicious" mussels and "excellent" steak frites; a "hands-on" owner and "reasonable" tabs (it's BYO) make for "comfortable, no-surprises" dining.

Eppes Essen *Deli*

| | 20 | 10 | 15 | $24 |

Livingston | 105 E. Mt. Pleasant Ave. (Livingston Ave.) | 973-994-1120 |
www.eppesessen.com

"Ginormous" portions of "classic Jewish soul food" ("bring the
Maalox") are served at this 1957-vintage Livingston deli where the

	FOOD	DECOR	SERVICE	COST

kosher-style offerings split surveyors: "mouthwatering" vs. "mediocre"; "consistently slow" staffers and "boring" decor make takeout a sensible option.

Espo's ⊄ *Italian*

23	10	19	$27

Raritan | 10 Second St. (bet. Anderson & Thompson Sts.) | 908-685-9552
It's "old-school all the way" at this circa-1974 Raritan tavern, where the "incredible red sauce" is a standout on the otherwise "predictable" Southern Italian menu; alright, this "hole-in-the-wall" doesn't take plastic or rezzies, but locals say good "bang for the buck" makes it a "wonderful find."

Esposito's Park Cafe *American/Italian* (aka Park Cafe)

-	-	-	M

Cliffside Park | 790 Anderson Ave. (Columbia Ave.) | 201-313-2441 | www.espositosparkcafe.com
Neapolitan-style brick-oven pizza and a "fun vibe" draw locals to this Cliffside Park run by the Esposito family (Villa Amalfi); look for a casual Italian-American menu offering the usual suspects: burgers, sandwiches, and salads.

Esty Street *American*

25	24	23	$59

Park Ridge | 86 Spring Valley Rd. (Fremont Ave.) | 201-307-1515 | www.estystreet.com
"Beautifully renovated" with a luxe private-club feel, this "fancy" New American in Park Ridge follows through with "excellent", "creative" cooking that burnishes its "big-time atmosphere"; nitpickers protest "skimpy" portions and "Park Avenue" prices, but the "seasoned" service and "sophisticated" mood are fine as is.

Etc. Steakhouse *Kosher/Steak*

▽ 25	19	24	$48

Teaneck | 1409 Palisade Ave. (State St.) | 201-357-5677 | www.etcsteakhouse.com
The "unexpected" is par for the course at this Teaneck kosher steakhouse where meats and seafood get "innovative" treatment and the small 30-seat setting includes a pre-meal hand-washing station; though "prices are high", the staff "makes a real effort"; P.S. it's BYO, but wines must be kosher and mevushal.

Eurasian Eatery ☒ *Eclectic*

23	14	21	$25

Red Bank | 110 Monmouth St. (bet. Maple Ave. & Pearl St.) | 732-741-7071 | www.theeurasianeatery.com
Red Bank is the site of this "longtime", "family-run" BYO near the Count Basie Theater, featuring a "something-for-everyone" selection of "delicious" Eclectic vittles that includes some "unconventional" vegetarian choices; though the decor could stand an "update", there's nothing wrong with the "brisk, friendly" service.

Europa South ☒ *Portuguese/Spanish*

21	16	21	$39

Point Pleasant Beach | 521 Arnold Ave. (Rte. 35) | 732-295-1500 | www.europasouth.com
"Still going strong", this Point Pleasant Beach Iberian "institution" dishes out some of the "best" paella around, served by "warm" wait-

ers; the "dark" interior may be getting "a little tired", but stalwarts insist it's "been around forever" for a reason.

Far East Taste *Chinese/Thai*   23 | 6 | 21 | $20

Eatontown | 19 Main St. (Broad St.) | 732-389-9866 | www.fareasttaste.com

Both Chinese and Thai dishes are offered at this small, "off-the-beaten-path" BYO in Eatontown, where the "low-budget" grub and "prompt" service show remarkable "attention to detail"; the same can't be said about the "nonexistent" decor, however, so insiders say takeout is a "better option."

Farnsworth House ● *Continental*   22 | 17 | 21 | $35

Bordentown | 135 Farnsworth Ave. (Railroad Ave.) | 609-291-9232 | www.thefarnsworthhouse.com

Inhabiting a "beautiful" circa-1682 building, this longtime Bordentown "mainstay" offers "reliable" Continental fare served by "friendly" folks; the double-decker setting features a "casual" ground-floor bar and a "prettier" upstairs dining room, though aesthetes say the "old decor" is a tad tired.

☷ Fascino ☒ *Italian*   26 | 21 | 24 | $56

Montclair | 331 Bloomfield Ave. (bet. Grove & Willow Sts.) | 973-233-0350 | www.fascinorestaurant.com

"Something of a legend", this "classy", family-run BYO in "highly competitive Montclair" fascinates followers with chef Ryan DePersio's "inventive" Italian *cucina* and mom Cynthia's "divine" desserts; despite "limited parking", "hard-to-get" reservations and "expensive" pricing, many feel that this is "as sophisticated as it gets on the other side of the Hudson."

Federici's ⊟ *Pizza*   21 | 12 | 18 | $24

Freehold | 14 E. Main St. (South St.) | 732-462-1312 | www.federicis.com

"Family-owned and -operated" since 1921, this "old-established" Freehold pizzeria is famed for its "outstanding" thin-crust pies (the "other food is just ok") and "reasonable" tabs; "tacky" decor and a "cash-only" rule are trumped by "fun" alfresco seating – and the "occasional Bruce sighting."

Fedora Café Ⓜ *Eclectic*   20 | 17 | 17 | $21

Lawrenceville | 2633 Main St. (bet. Craven Ln. & Phillips Ave.) | 609-895-0844 | www.fedoracafe.webs.com

Popular with Lawrenceville locals and prep-school students, this "quirky" Eclectic BYO reminiscent of the "set of *Friends*" is a "comfy" hangout with a "coffee-shop vibe"; the "quick-bite" menu "never changes" and service runs "slow", but if nothing else, it's "economical."

Fernandes Steakhouse II *Portuguese/Spanish*   24 | 19 | 21 | $41

Newark | 152-158 Fleming Ave. (Chapel St.) | 973-589-4344 | www.fernandessteakhouse.com

An "endless parade" of "succulent" skewered meats thrills carnivores at this "off-the-beaten-path" Iberian-Brazilian rodizio in Newark's Ironbound; alright, it's habitually "crazy crowded" – "'noisy' is an understatement" here – but portions are "large", service is "friendly" and valuewise, "you get your money's worth in spades."

Ferry House *American/French* `- | - | - | E`

Princeton | 32 Witherspoon St. (Spring St.) | 609-924-2488 | www.theferryhouse.com

Back in business following a hiatus, this Downtown Princetonian via chef-owner Bobby Trigg offers the Franco-American cooking that made this BYO a local favorite; diehards are relieved that the signature firecracker shrimp is still on the menu.

Fiddleheads ⓜ *American* `23 | 16 | 23 | $39`

Jamesburg | 27 E. Railroad Ave. (Forsgate Dr.) | 732-521-0878 | www.fiddleheadsjamesburg.com

"Reservations are a must" at this "small" New American BYO in "historic" Jamesburg, a "neighborhood" storefront that's "usually filled with steady customers"; given the "interesting" menu, "personable" service and "reasonable" tabs, many feel it's "time to expand."

15 Fox Place ⓈⓂ *Italian* `23 | 22 | 25 | $70`

Jersey City | 15 Fox Pl. (bet. Giles & West Side Aves.) | 201-333-1476 | www.womcatering.com

You "feel like you're eating at grandma's" at this "cozy" Jersey City BYO serving "old-fashioned" Italian comfort food, and "way too much of it"; the "pricey", prix fixe-only menu means you "can't choose the selections", but different dining rooms supply "varied atmospheres" that work for "a crowd" or a "romantic dinner"; it's open for dinner Thursdays–Saturdays (reservations required) and its new alfresco-only adjunct, Kathryn's, serves dinner Mondays–Wednesdays.

55 Main Ⓢ *American* `22 | 18 | 20 | $41`

Flemington | 55 Main St. (Bloomfield Ave.) | 908-284-1551 | www.55main.com

"Accomplished" chef Jonas Gold serves up an "imaginative" menu at this "intimate", "trattorialike" New American in Downtown Flemington; though naysayers quibble it's "not as good as it used to be", supporters tout its "comfortable vibe" and "great location", adding that "BYO makes it more affordable."

Filomena Cucina Italiana *Italian* `∇ 25 | 20 | 22 | $48`

Clementon | 1380 Blackwood Clementon Rd. (bet. Laurel & Little Gloucester Rds.) | 856-784-6166 | www.filomenascucina.com

The specials are usually a "good bet" at this "nothing-fancy" Clementon Italian, one of three separately owned South Jersey offspring of the eponymous DiVentura family matriarch; "substantial portions", a "nice" bar and "friendly" service also earn kudos; P.S. there's live music Tuesday–Saturday.

Filomena Cucina Rustica *Italian* `∇ 18 | 19 | 20 | $39`

West Berlin | 13 Berlin Cross Keys Rd. (White Horse Pike) | 856-753-3540 | www.filomenasberlin.com

You'll find a "friendly crowd" at this "hangout" for West Berlin's "fortysomethings", along with a menu of Italian "standards" that includes a signature potato gnocchi made from Mama Filomena's own recipe; bargain-hunters tout its $20 early-bird, available from Monday to Thursday.

Filomena Lakeview *Italian* ∇ 23 | 21 | 22 | $39

Deptford | 1738 Cooper St. (Almonesson Rd.) | 856-228-4235 | www.filomenalakeview.com

After a renovation that added an upstairs patio, this "outstanding" Italian set in a restored Colonial-era inn in Deptford finally has a lake view; "tasty" cooking, "knowledgeable" staffers and "reasonable" prices for the quality are all part of the package, along with "great entertainment" on select evenings.

Fin M *Seafood* ∇ 25 | 25 | 22 | $68

Atlantic City | Tropicana Casino & Resort | 2831 Boardwalk (Iowa Ave.) | 800-345-8767 | www.tropicana.net

"Unbeatable ocean views" combine with an "expertly prepared" menu at this seafooder tethered to AC's Tropicana Hotel; though the fin fare's "fantastic", fans also plug its outdoor "boardwalk" seating and indoor sea-glass color scheme; sure, it all comes at an "expensive" price, but a 50-under-$50 wine list helps reel in costs.

Fin Raw Bar & Kitchen *Seafood* - | - | - | M

Montclair | 183 Glen Ridge Ave. (Forest St.) | 973-744-0068 | www.finrawbarandkitchen.com

An octet of oysters and daily display of sustainable whole fish and crustaceans prepared by chef Michael Juliano (ex South City Grill) lure finatics to this Montclair BYO seafooder (sibling of Salute down the street), which also serves steaks and other land-based offerings; the space is both rustic and chic, sporting burlap net lampshades and exposed beams juxtaposed with glittering tiles around the open kitchen.

Fiorino Ø *Italian* 24 | 22 | 23 | $52

Summit | 38 Maple St. (Springfield Ave.) | 908-277-1900 | www.fiorinoristorante.com

"Consistently scrumptious" in every way, this "special-occasion" Northern Italian is a destination for "high-end" dining with the "Summit elite" (and drinking with local "divorcées" at the "fun bar"); "fabulous" food, "charming" "continental" service and a "nicely decorated" setting are reasons why it's "packed every night."

Fire & Oak *American* 19 | 22 | 18 | $42

Jersey City | Westin Jersey City Newport Hotel | 479 Washington Blvd. (6th St.) | 201-610-9610
Montvale | Courtyard by Marriott | 100 Chestnut Ridge Rd. (Lake St.) | 201-307-1100
www.fireandoak.com

Perhaps best for the "atmosphere and the bar" scene, these hotel-based American grills in Jersey City and Montvale provide "above-average" fare in "dark", "Houston's-clone" settings; though service can be "all over the map", it's a hit with a "40s crowd" that digs the "surprisingly trendy" vibe.

	FOOD	DECOR	SERVICE	COST

NEW Firecreek *American* — | - | - | E

Voorhees | Voorhees Town Ctr. | 13109 Town Center Blvd.
(Echelon Rd.) | 856-344-7901 | www.firecreek-restaurant.com
Seasonal New American fare and live music top the bill at this new
Voorhees outpost of an upscale Downington, PA, eatery, while BYO
Sundays and monthly wine dinners sweeten the deal; an open
kitchen is a highlight of the airy space with exposed rafters and a
glass wall, and there's outdoor seating in the warmer months.

Fishery, The *Seafood* ∇ 20 | 13 | 16 | $20

South Amboy | 1812 Rte. 35 N. (Midland Ave.) | 732-721-9100
"Nothing smells fishy unless it's supposed to" at this way-casual
BYO seafood shack in South Amboy; clams, oysters on the half-shell
and "large" portions of "well-cooked" seafood (by the pound or plat-
ter) keep regulars angling for a table or grabbing takeout.

Z Five Guys *Burgers* 21 | 10 | 16 | $12

Hackensack | Home Depot Shopping Ctr. | 450 Hackensack Ave.
(Grand Ave.) | 201-343-5489
Millburn | Milburn Mall | 2933 Vauxhall Rd. (Valley St.) |
908-688-8877
Edison | Wick Shopping Plaza | 561 Rte. 1 (bet. Dey Pl. & Fulton St.) |
732-985-5977
Parsippany | Troy Hills Shopping Ctr. | 1103 Rte. 46 (Beverwyck Rd.) |
973-335-5454
Watchung | Blue Star Shopping Ctr. | 1701 Rte. 22 (Terrill Rd.) |
908-490-0370
Woodbridge | Woodbridge Center Mall | 250 Woodbridge Center Dr.
(Maple Hill Dr.) | 732-636-1377
Brick | Habitat Plaza | 588 Rte. 70 (Cedar Bridge Ave.) | 732-262-4040
Toms River | Orchards at Dover | 1311 Rte. 37 W. (bet. Bimini Dr. &
St. Catherine Blvd.) | 732-349-3600
Mount Ephraim | Audubon Shopping Ctr. | 130 Black Horse Pike
(Mt. Ephraim Ave.) | 856-672-0442
Voorhees | Eagle Plaza Shopping Ctr. | 700 Haddonfield Berlin Rd.
(White Horse Rd.) | 856-783-5588
www.fiveguys.com
Additional locations throughout New Jersey
"Juicy, greasy" burgers with "all the trimmings" "blow away" the
competition at this chain, a "presidential favorite" that's also prized
for its "farm-to-fryer" fries and "free peanuts while you wait";
maybe some "don't get the hype", but these "bare-bones" joints are
"taking the world by storm."

NEW 5 Seasons Bistro M *American* — | - | - | M

Ridgewood | 28 Oak St. (bet. Franklin & Ridgewood Aves.) |
201-857-5900 | www.5seasonsbistro.com
At their Ridgewood BYO, Laurie Cera and her son, Larry, offer New
American fare featuring locally sourced produce, as well as 'fifth-
season' greenhouse harvests, on monthly changing lunch, dinner
and Sunday brunch menus, plus desserts from Cera *fils* that take the
cake; though the ambiance in the bi-level space could be sunnier,
there's alfresco seating for 15 – in season, natch.

	FOOD	DECOR	SERVICE	COST

Fleming's Prime Steakhouse *Steak*   `23` `24` `23` `$60`

Edgewater | City Pl. | 90 The Promenade (bet. Gorge & River Rds.) |
201-313-9463
Marlton | 500 Rte. 73 N. (bet. Baker Blvd. & Lincoln Dr.) | 856-988-1351
www.flemingssteakhouse.com

"They know their meat" at these links of the nationwide steakhouse
chain where "well-aged" chops are ferried by a "professional" staff
in "clubby", "dark-wood" surroundings; "high" prices aside, it's "reliable" and "always hits the spot", though the unconvinced note
there's "nothing here you can't find anywhere else."

Flirt Sushi Lounge *Japanese*   `23` `21` `20` `$40`

Allendale | 140 W. Allendale Ave. (Myrtle Ave.) | 201-825-9004 |
www.flirtsushi.com

"Serious" sushi and "ingenious" rolls come with "naughty" names
(e.g. Pink Pussy Cat, Big Balls) at this "stylish", "seductive" Japanese
BYO in Allendale; the less enamored sigh the "playful" menu is "getting old", but many more find it a "fun" "date-night" option.

Fontana di Trevi Ⓜ *Italian*   `23` `18` `20` `$42`

Leonia | 248 Fort Lee Rd. (Broad Ave.) | 201-242-9040 |
www.fontanaditrevirestaurant.com

Ok, there are "no fountains" in sight, just "first-rate" food at this
"classy" Italian BYO transplanted to Leonia from Manhattan; a
"warm", "old-country" setting and "welcoming" vibe compensate
for the "not-abundant" portion sizes and rather "pricey" tabs.

Fornelletto Ⓢ Ⓜ *Italian*   `24` `24` `23` `$54`

Atlantic City | Borgata Hotel, Casino & Spa | 1 Borgata Way (Huron Ave.) |
609-317-1000 | www.theborgata.com

Chef Stephen Kalt assembles a "superb", "attractively presented"
modern Italian menu at this upscale-casual spot inside AC's Borgata
Hotel; the "charming wine-cellar" decor makes sense given the "extensive wine list", leaving "pricey" tabs and "noisy" acoustics as the
only sticking points.

ⓩ Fornos of Spain *Spanish*   `24` `18` `22` `$44`

Newark | 47 Ferry St. (Union St.) | 973-589-4767 |
www.fornosrestaurant.com

Brace yourself for "a ton" of Spanish surf 'n' turf served in "mega-
portions" and washed down with "delicious" sangria at this "bustling",
250-seat "warhorse" in Newark's Ironbound; though "service suffers
on busy nights" and the hacienda-style decor could stand a "redo", the
cooking here is "always consistent" and the free parking a "big plus."

Fortune Cookie *Chinese*   `▽` `21` `9` `18` `$22`

Bridgewater | 41 Old York Rd. (Oak St.) | 908-429-8886 |
www.fortunecookienj.com

"Not your typical Americanized Chinese" establishment, this "unusual" Bridgewater BYO specializes in "authentic Hunan" specialties that are "spicy" and served "steaming hot"; "adventuresome"
folks don't mind the "nondescript" decor and "language-barrier"
service when "dishes you can't find elsewhere" are the payoff.

| | FOOD | DECOR | SERVICE | COST |

410 Bank Street *Caribbean/Creole*
26 | 21 | 24 | $54

Cape May | 410 Bank St. (bet. Broad & Lafayette Sts.) | 609-884-2127 | www.410bankstreet.com

For most, the "creative" Caribbean-Creole cooking of chef Henry Sing Cheng served by a "cheery" team keeps this longtime Cape May "classic" an "absolute favorite"; sure, it's on the "expensive" side, seating is "tight" and the Victorian setting "not special", but devotees declare it "feels like Key West and tastes like New Orleans"; P.S. reservations are "a must", and you can "bring your best bottle" or opt for the NJ wines offered.

Franco's Metro *Italian*
∇ 19 | 13 | 17 | $33

Fort Lee | Plaza West Shopping Ctr. | 1475 Bergen Blvd. (Oakdene Ave.) | 201-461-6651 | www.francosmetro.com

"Simple" Italian cooking and "good" brick-oven pizza turn up at this longtime "neighborhood" joint parked in a Fort Lee strip mall; the "nondescript" location off Route 46 is "convenient" and the cooking "consistent" enough to make for a "better-than-average" experience.

Frankie Fed's Ⓜ *Italian*
21 | 10 | 19 | $25

Freehold Township | 831 Rte. 33 E. (Kozloski Rd.) | 732-294-1333 | www.frankiefeds.com

The Godfather Pizza is "to die for" at Frankie's all-in-the-Federici-family BYO in Freehold, where the entire thin-crust line is "addictive", the rest of the Italian menu just "fair"; ambiancewise, it's "not much to look at", though service is "pleasant" and the mood "comfortable" and "family-oriented."

Fredo's Italian Restaurant Ⓜ *Italian*
∇ 22 | 19 | 21 | $36

Freehold Township | A&M Plaza | 3475 Rte. 9 N. (Three Brooks Rd.) | 732-294-7400

There's "good value for your money" at this Freehold Township Italian set in a Route 9 strip mall, thanks to "tasty" food doled out in "large portions"; "friendly" service and BYO-assisted price tags keep the trade brisk.

Frenchtown Inn Ⓜ *Eclectic/French*
23 | 22 | 23 | $49

Frenchtown | 7 Bridge St. (Rte. 29) | 908-996-3300 | www.frenchtowninn.com

Offering four "charming" dining rooms, this "quaint" French-Eclectic is set in an "elegantly restored" 19th-century inn beside the Delaware River in "rural" Frenchtown; the "top-of-the-line" food is a match for the "romantic" ambiance, even if it's somewhat "pricey" and can be a "long ride" to get there; P.S. regulars make a beeline for the "delightful" porch.

Frescos *Italian/Mediterranean*
22 | 20 | 23 | $47

Cape May | 412 Bank St. (bet. Broad & Lafayette Sts.) | 609-884-0366 | www.frescoscapemay.com

Reservations are a must at this seasonal Med-Italian trattoria in "pricey Cape May", which "never disappoints" given its "flavor-rich" food and "above-and-beyond" service; like its sibling, 410 Bank, it's set in a "great old" Victorian house and offers local wines, though it's alright to BYO.

Fresco Steak & Seafood Grill *Seafood/Steak*

25 | 21 | 23 | $38

Milltown | Heritage Shopping Plaza | 210 Ryders Ln. (Tices Ln.) | 732-246-7616 | www.restaurantfresco.com

No wonder this "consistently fine" "great value" in Milltown is always "packed": its Italian-accented land-and-sea menu is "done right", the seafood is "fresh" and the staff "welcoming" – plus its "convenient" shopping-center location (with a wine shop "just a few steps away") makes BYO easy.

Freshwaters Southern Cuisine Ⓜ *Southern*

▽ 21 | 16 | 22 | $30

Plainfield | 1442 South Ave. (Terrill Rd.) | 908-561-9099 | www.myfreshwaters.com

"Outstanding", "affordable" soul food is offered at this Plainfield BYO where the "piping hot" Southern "home cookin'" includes all the genre staples along with some Cajun-Creole faves; a "welcoming" ambiance and "exceptional" artwork on the walls seal the deal.

🄳 Frog and the Peach *American*

26 | 23 | 24 | $62

New Brunswick | 29 Dennis St. (Hiram Sq.) | 732-846-3216 | www.frogandpeach.com

Bruce Lefebvre's "farm-fresh", "innovative" cuisine "aims to please – and succeeds" – at this "fine-dining" New Brunswick American with an "understated" design and "well-informed" staffers; though a few croak about "small", "expensive" portions, the bar menu is "surprisingly reasonable" and prix fixe options make for a "peachy" experience.

Fuji Ⓜ *Japanese*

25 | 22 | 23 | $43

Haddonfield | Shops at 116 | 116 Kings Hwy. E. (Tanner St.) | 856-354-8200 | www.fujirestaurant.com

Matt Ito slices some of the "best sushi in South Jersey" at this "creative" BYO that "brings Japan to Haddonfield" – and fans say it comes at "half the price" of what it would cost in NYC; a "pretty", "relaxing" setting and "wonderful" service complete the "outstanding" package.

Full Moon Café *Eclectic*

19 | 15 | 20 | $23

Lambertville | 23 Bridge St. (Union St.) | 609-397-1096 | www.cafefullmoon.com

"Above-average" breakfasts and lunches are served at this "hippie-cool" Eclectic "staple" in "charming Lambertville", where service comes "with a smile" and the artwork on the walls is for sale; it only serves dinner once a month (when there's a full moon, natch), but it's "cheery" and "affordable" all the time; P.S. closed Tuesdays.

🄳 Gables, The *Eclectic*

24 | 26 | 22 | $57

Beach Haven | Gables Inn | 212 Centre St. (bet. Bay & Beach Aves.) | 609-492-3553 | www.gableslbi.com

A "charming" Victorian B&B is home to this "impressive" Eclectic in Beach Haven on LBI, known for its "gourmet" meals, "sweet" setting

	FOOD	DECOR	SERVICE	COST

and "gorgeous front porch"; ok, it's "expensive" (though BYO is available), but a "romantic" mood and "accommodating" service make for "tried-and-true" "fine dining."

Gabriela's Ⓜ *Portuguese*

18	13	19	$34

Somerville | 42 W. Main St. (Division St.) | 908-526-7070 |
www.gabrielasrestaurant.com

Portugal is the port of call for this humble Somerville BYO serving a "homestyle" menu with an "emphasis on seafood" in a setting that "leaves a little to be desired"; although some critics "regret not driving to Newark", most call it "authentic" enough.

Gaetano's *Italian*

20	16	20	$36

Red Bank | 10 Wallace St. (Broad St.) | 732-741-1321 |
www.gaetanosredbank.com

"Satisfying meals" for a "satisfying price" are plated at this "dependable" Red Bank Italian that offers both BYO and wines from NJ's Westfall Winery; an on-site market and "casual" vibe offset the "plain" surroundings.

Gallagher's Steak House *Steak*

22	20	21	$56

Newark | Newark Liberty Int'l Airport | Terminal C |
973-286-0034
Atlantic City | Resorts Atlantic City Casino & Hotel |
1133 Boardwalk (North Carolina Ave.) | 609-340-6555 |
www.gallaghersresorts.com

"All the favorites" from the "traditional" NY chophouse chain - i.e. "good-quality" beef in "plentiful portions" - turn up at these knockoffs in Resorts AC and Newark International Airport; sure, you'll need to "bring your wallet" and purists sigh merely "average", but they're handy when the "jetway beckons" or just to "blow your jackpot winnings."

Gam Mee Ok ●ⓏⓂ *Korean*

▽ 21	16	15	$23

Fort Lee | 485 Main St. (Edwin Ave.) | 201-242-1333 |
www.gammeeok.com

It's all-Korean, all the time at this casual "24/7" Fort Lee outpost where the "signature" seolleongtang soup will "cure all that ails you" (just be aware that it's an "acquired taste"); granted, the staff could be "friendlier", but the kitchen's consistency is truly "amazing."

Garlic Rose Bistro *Eclectic*

20	15	20	$35

Cranford | 28 North Ave. W. (bet. Eastman St. & Union Ave.) |
908-276-5749
Madison | 41 Main St. (bet. Green Village Rd. & Waverly Pl.) |
973-822-1178
www.garlicrose.com

"Ward off vampires and have a great meal" at this Eclectic duo that draws "adventurous" types and "*Twilight*" fans since "everything on the menu is infused with garlic", right down to the ice cream; critics complain of "overkill", "blah" decor and "cramped" conditions, but ultimately most leave here "happy and smelly"; P.S. Madison is BYO, while Cranford has a "wallet-friendly wine list."

	FOOD	DECOR	SERVICE	COST

Gazelle Café ⓜ *American*
23 | 17 | 20 | $34

Ridgewood | 11 Godwin Ave. (Franklin Ave.) | 201-689-9689 |
www.gazellecafe.com

"Health-conscious" types tout this "cool" Ridgewood BYO for its "always fresh" American dishes prepared "in front of your eyes" in an "open kitchen with nothing to hide"; though it can get "noisy" at times, "accommodating" service and "reasonable" prices compensate.

GG's ⓔ *American*
▽ 25 | 21 | 24 | $51

Mount Laurel | DoubleTree Guest Suites Mount Laurel |
515 Fellowship Rd. (Rte. 73) | 856-222-0335 |
www.ggsrestaurant.com

Though it's "hard to find an excellent restaurant in a hotel", this New American tucked inside a Mount Laurel DoubleTree is a "hidden gem", with "excellent" contemporary cooking and a "nice setting"; nightly piano music (Tuesday–Saturday) and "great service" ice the cake; P.S. on Sundays it's open for hotel guests only.

Gianna's *Italian*
▽ 20 | 17 | 20 | $41

Carlstadt | 843 Washington Ave. (Moonachie Rd.) | 201-460-7997 |
www.giannas.biz

"Family-style" is the philosophy behind this "traditional" Carlstadt Italian in an industrial zone near the Meadowlands, where the "super-size" servings supply "lots of food" for the money; even if the decor could stand a "makeover", at least the staffers make everyone feel "welcome."

Girasole *Italian*
26 | 23 | 22 | $53

Atlantic City | Ocean Club Condos | 3108 Pacific Ave. (bet. Chelsea & Montpelier Aves.) | 609-345-5554 | www.girasoleac.com

Situated in a "nice spot" – a condo a block away from the Atlantic City boardwalk – this "superior" Italian boasts "refined", "old-fashioned" cooking served in a "cool", sunflower-themed setting festooned with "Versace decorations"; it feels as though it's "miles from the hustle and bustle of the casinos" and draws the "localin' crowd" unfazed by the "high prices" and service with "a little attitude."

Girasole *Italian*
26 | 20 | 23 | $44

Bound Brook | 502 W. Union Ave. (Thompson Ave.) | 732-469-1080 |
www.girasoleboundbrook.com

A "big reputation" makes for "hard-to-get weekend reservations" at this "family-run" Bound Brook BYO that's a "standout in a region full of Italian restaurants"; fans touting the "exceptional" cooking, "involved" owners and "beautiful decor" dub it a "local favorite" – and an automatic choice for "special occasions."

Giumarello's ⓜ *Italian*
25 | 22 | 23 | $49

Westmont | 329 Haddon Ave. (Maple Ave.) | 856-858-9400 |
www.giumarellos.com

This "upscale" Westmont Italian stands apart from the South Jersey pack thanks to its "fine" food and "make-you-feel-special" service; admirers also applaud its "quiet", "fireplace"-enhanced ambiance, though there's a "hopping" bar on premises that's popular in its own right for "delish" martinis and a "world-class" happy hour.

NEW GK's Red Dog Tavern at Rod's *Pub Food*

-	-	-	M

Morristown | Madison Hotel | 1 Convent Rd. (bet. Madison Ave. & Old Turnpike Rd.) | 973-539-6666 | www.gksreddog.com

Honoring Gerard Keller (founder of sibling Rod's Steak & Seafood Grille), this playful pub in Morristown's Madison Hotel appeals to all ages with a menu of grilled flatbreads, dry-aged steaks, a raw bar and fresh takes on classic bar fare (think lamb burgers and hand-made chili dogs), complemented by artisanal ales and a diverse wine list, plus specialty sodas and shakes; true to the name, pictures of dogs grace the casual space.

Gladstone Tavern *American*

21	22	20	$44

Gladstone | 273 Main St. (Pottersville Rd.) | 908-234-9055 | www.gladstonetavern.com

Gladstone's "horsey set" touts the "tasty" Americana served at this "upscale" tavern set in a "beautifully restored" 1847 farmhouse done up in "country chic"–style, with a "wonderful" patio and a "horse statue" on the porch; it's "romantic" inside, energetic at the bar and especially "nice in the winter when the fireplace is lit."

GoodFellas **⑤** *Italian*

21	18	20	$40

Garfield | 661 Midland Ave. (Plauderville Ave.) | 973-478-4000 | www.goodfellasnj.com

"Revisit *The Sopranos*" at this "dependable" Garfield Italian, where the "classic" cooking comes in "ample portions" for prices that "won't break the bank"; some fret it's "past its time", but "friendly" service by "real Italian waiters" keeps it a "local favorite."

Grabbe's **⑤Ⓜ** *Seafood*

-	-	-	M

Westville | 19 Delsea Dr. (B'way) | 856-456-3594 | www.crabs.net

They serve crabs (and everyone else) year-round at this Westville seafooder-cum–fish market, which offers a midpriced menu of fresh fin fare, plus a limited selection of sandwiches and burgers, in a utilitarian space.

Grain House *American*

19	20	20	$41

Basking Ridge | Olde Mill Inn | 225 Rte. 202 (I-287, exit 30B) | 908-221-1150 | www.oldemillinn.com

"Horsey" Basking Ridge is the site of this "atmospheric" eatery in the Olde Mill Inn, an "awesome", circa-1768 gristmill that now serves a "reliable, if not overly imaginative" American menu; the "rustic", "Colonial farmhouse" look matches the "convivial" mood, and there's also a "pubby" tavern across the hall.

Z Grand Cafe **⑤** *French*

25	25	25	$68

Morristown | 42 Washington St. (bet. Court St. & Schuyler Pl.) | 973-540-9444 | www.thegrandcafe.com

Appropriately "grand dining" is yours at this "old-fashioned" Morristown "bastion" where "glorious" French cuisine with Asian flourishes is served by a tuxedoed, "been-there-forever" staff; while cynics say that the "luxurious" scene recalls a "dowager's apartment" populated by "older folks" with "fat wallets", devotees declare that "classic never goes out of style."

◪ Grato *Italian*

| 22 | 25 | 22 | $46 |

Morris Plains | 2230 Rte. 10 W. (Tabor Rd.) | 973-267-4006 | www.gratorestaurant.com

For a "nice change from the run-of-the-mill", check out this "high-end" Morris Plains trattoria (and Tabor Road Tavern sibling) praised for its "excellent" *cucina* and "elegant-without-being-stuffy" mien; granted, it's "quite pricey", but the service is "refined" and the bar's a magnet for a "dressy, sophisticated crowd."

Greek Taverna *Greek*

| 20 | 16 | 19 | $33 |

Edgewater | City Pl. | 55 The Promenade (River Rd.) | 201-945-8998
Glen Rock | 175 Rock Rd. (Main St.) | 201-857-4528
Montclair | 292 Bloomfield Ave. (Gates Ave.) | 973-746-2280
www.greektavernausa.com

"Gargantuan portions" are the signature of this Hellenic trio that "tastes like Greece" even though the decor "feels like Epcot" and the crowds can make for "jet-runway" noise levels; the Edgewater and Montclair satellites are BYO, while Glen Rock has a full bar.

Grenville, The ⓜ *American*

| 17 | 22 | 20 | $45 |

Bay Head | Grenville Hotel | 345 Main Ave. (bet. Harris & Karge Sts.) | 732-892-3100 | www.thegrenville.com

"Charming" is the word for this "pretty place" inside an old Bay Head hotel with a "Victorian-Shore" feel and a "little-bit-of-heaven" veranda; too bad the "old-fashioned" Americana is only "fair", leaving many to say it "could be a gold mine, but really misses the mark."

Grimaldi's Pizza *Pizza*

| 25 | 14 | 18 | $21 |

Hoboken | 133 Clinton St. (2nd St.) | 201-792-0800
Hoboken | 411 Washington St. (bet. 4th & 5th Sts.) | 201-792-0010
Highlands | 123 Bay Ave. (bet. North & Spring Sts.) | 732-291-1711 ⌿
www.grimaldis.com

"Twentysomethings on shoestring budgets" who don't feel like "schlepping to the Brooklyn original" tout these "old-school" pizzerias in Hoboken and Highlands for their "exceptional" pies; all right, they "don't sell slices" and the decor is "typical pizza parlor", but devotees insist they're the "best in NJ, hands down."

Grissini *Italian*

| 22 | 21 | 21 | $60 |

Englewood Cliffs | 484 Sylvan Ave. (Palisade Ave.) | 201-568-3535 | www.grissinirestaurant.com

"Glitzy" is the word for this Englewood Cliffs Italian where the "NYC"-quality food plays second fiddle to the "rich", "jaded" crowd, "big bar scene" and a parking lot that looks like a "Bavarian car dealership"; no question, it's "expensive" and some say "regulars are treated better" than first-timers, but the place stays "crowded" for a reason.

	FOOD	DECOR	SERVICE	COST

Grub Hut *BBQ/Mexican* — 21 | 10 | 19 | $23

Manville | 307 N. Main St. (Knopf St.) | 908-203-8003 |
www.grubhutbbq.com

"More interesting than the name suggests", this "unique" Manville
BYO slings a "delicious", but "messy" mix of Mexican and BBQ; even
though there's "no decor" and service is "rough around the edges",
it's "totally fun" and worthy of donning your "dressy sweatpants."

Gusto Grill ● *American* — 19 | 17 | 20 | $29

East Brunswick | 1050 Rte. 18 N. (Rues Ln.) | 732-651-2737 |
www.gustogrill.com

There's "no need to go beyond burgers and salads" at this "noisy"
East Brunswick American, a "hybrid sports bar/family restaurant"
that's more about "watching the game" than dining; still, service is
"upbeat", the mood is "fun" and the price is right.

Hamilton & Ward *Steak* — ▽ 23 | 25 | 26 | $89

Paterson | 101 Ward St. (Hamilton St.) | 973-345-8444 |
www.hamiltonandward.com

A "high-end" steakhouse lands opposite the courthouse in Downtown
Paterson at this flashy "surprise", where the chops are "outstanding", if not the prices; the food arrives in a big wood- and leather-
lined setting and service is "excellent", starting with the "courteous"
valet-parking attendant who greets you at the entrance.

Hamilton's Grill Room *Mediterranean* — 26 | 22 | 24 | $52

Lambertville | 8 Coryell St. (bet. Lambert Ln. & Union St.) |
609-397-4343 | www.hamiltonsgrillroom.com

Chef Mark Miller prepares "incredible" Mediterranean meats and
seafood with "ingenuity, not insanity" at this "secluded" Lambertville
treasure tucked "off the tourist track" near the Delaware River Canal;
it's "very popular" thanks to its "inviting" decor, "leisurely pace" and
"casual outdoor seating", and although a BYO, you can always get a
drink at The Boathouse, the quirky bar across the courtyard.

Hanami *Chinese/Japanese* — 20 | 15 | 18 | $31

Cresskill | 41 Union Ave. (Piermont Rd.) | 201-567-8508
Westwood | 301 Center Ave. (Westwood Ave.) | 201-666-8508
www.hanamirestaurant.com

This Chinese-Japanese BYO duo offers a "nice variety" of "creditable"
fare – including sushi – in "comfortable" if "simple" digs; but although
the kitchen is "reliable", service varies from "helpful" to "brusque."

Harvest Bistro Ⓜ *American/French* — 21 | 24 | 20 | $52

Closter | 252 Schraalenburgh Rd. (Old Hook Rd.) | 201-750-9966 |
www.harvestbistro.com

There's a "bountiful harvest" in store at this "upscale" Closter bistro,
though the "ambitious" Franco-American cooking pales in compari-
son to its "gorgeous" "rustic" setting with soaring ceilings and the
"most beautiful fireplace in NJ"; service may skew "slow" and you'll
need a "fat wallet" when the check arrives, but a "lovely garden" and
"active bar scene" help to distract.

	FOOD	DECOR	SERVICE	COST

Harvest Moon Inn ⓜ *American* | 25 | 22 | 23 | $49 |

Ringoes | 1039 Old York Rd. (Rte. 202) | 908-806-6020 |
www.harvestmooninn.com

"Remarkable food" is served in a "classic" dining room (or more casual
tavern) at this "comfortable" New American housed in a Federal-style
building in "out-of-the-way" Ringoes; a few find it "a bit too expensive"
and say the "time-warp Colonial-floral" decor needs an update, but
overall this is "delightful adult" dining fit for "special occasions."

Harvey Cedars Shellfish Co. ⊅ *Seafood* | 23 | 11 | 17 | $31 |

Beach Haven | 506 Centre St. (Pennsylvania Ave.) | 609-492-2459
Harvey Cedars | 7904 Long Beach Blvd. (79th St.) | 609-494-7112
www.harveycedarsshellfishco.com

Embodying the "LBI experience", these summer "fish shacks" turn
out "basic", "extremely fresh" seafood in "wear-your-bathing-suit"
settings; the menus and service differ slightly – Beach Haven is nicknamed the 'Clam Bar' and comes with a side of manager "attitude" –
but both share BYO and cash-only policies.

Hat Tavern *American* | - | - | - | M |

Summit | Grand Summit Hotel | 570 Springfield Ave. (bet. Blackburn Rd. &
Tulip St.) | 908-273-7656 | www.hattavern.com

Summit's 19th-century Grand Summit Hotel is home to this
Traditional American tavern set in the former Hunt Club digs; look for
a variety of small plates and comfort fare made from locally sourced
ingredients, washed down with an extensive list of domestic ales.

Helmers' *German* | 19 | 16 | 18 | $35 |

Hoboken | 1036 Washington St. (11th St.) | 201-963-3333 |
www.helmersrestaurant.com

"Hearty" says it all about this circa-1936 Hoboken "institution" plying "traditional German" grub in a "relaxed" tavern atmosphere; an
"outstanding" beer list and "festive" times at Oktoberfest make up
for what critics call a general sense of "decline."

⚡ Highlawn Pavilion *American* | 25 | 28 | 25 | $64 |

West Orange | Eagle Rock Reservation | 1 Crest Dr. (Eagle Rock Ave.) |
973-731-3463 | www.highlawn.com

"Wondrous" views of the Manhattan skyline are accompanied by
"classically elegant" fare at this "stylish" New American on a West
Orange mountaintop that simply "screams special occasion"; "ex-
pert" service makes the "NYC prices" easier to swallow, though
"good value" at midday makes it "perfect" for a business lunch;
P.S. dress code is business casual, but "people still come dressed up."

High Street Grill *American* | ▽ 20 | 17 | 19 | $34 |

Mount Holly | 64 High St. (bet. Brainerd & Garden Sts.) | 609-265-9199 |
www.highstreetgrill.net

"Solid" contemporary American grub is paired with a "good selection" of craft beers at this double-decker joint in Mount Holly;
there's a brewpublike main floor as well as a white-tablecloth dining
room above, with competent service and casual pricing throughout.

	FOOD	DECOR	SERVICE	COST

Hiram's Roadstand ⑰ *Hot Dogs* | 21 | 7 | 15 | $12

Fort Lee | 1345 Palisade Ave. (Harmon Ave.) | 201-592-9602

"Passing mustard" since 1932, this "quintessential hot dog stand" in Fort Lee slings "sinfully good" deep-fried wieners in a "roadside" setting complete with outdoor picnic tables; "fill-and-spill" counter service and a no-plastic policy come with the territory.

Hobby's Delicatessen Ⓢ *Deli* | 24 | 10 | 19 | $20

Newark | 32 Branford Pl. (Halsey St.) | 973-623-0410 | www.hobbysdeli.com

Newark locals and "jury-duty escapees" relish the "hearty" fare served at this "classic" Jewish deli-cum-"time machine" near the Prudential Center; oy vey, it could "use a refresher" in the decor and service departments, yet diehards declare this "landmark" is still "worth patronizing"; P.S. breakfast and lunch only, plus dinner before Devils and Nets games.

Hoboken Bar & Grill *American* | 19 | 17 | 17 | $32

Hoboken | 230 Washington St. (3rd St.) | 201-222-6050 | www.hobokenbarandgrill.com

"Good" American bar-and-grill items are dispatched at this "well-priced" Hoboken spot best known for its "bar scene" and "rocking happy hour"; foes find it "as generic as its name", citing "typical" eats and a "rowdy" following.

Ho-Ho-Kus Inn & Tavern *American* | 21 | 23 | 21 | $48

Ho-Ho-Kus | 1 E. Franklin Tpke. (Sheridan Ave.) | 201-445-4115 | www.hohokusinn.com

There's plenty of "pizzazz" on the American menu of this "reborn" Ho-Ho-Kus "landmark" set in a historic, "lavishly restored" Dutch Colonial mansion where multiple dining rooms and outdoor areas offer dining options "from formal to relaxed"; the "cozy" tavern is the most "casual" enclave, but wherever you sit, expect slightly "higher-than-average" tabs befitting an "upscale" experience; P.S. BYO without corkage on Mondays.

Holsten's ◉ *American* | 16 | 12 | 16 | $15

Bloomfield | 1063 Broad St. (Watchung Ave.) | 973-338-7091 | www.holstens.com

The Sopranos filmed its "cliffhanger ending" at this Bloomfield ice cream parlor that now draws tourists seeking "final-episode" merch, but locals still turn up for its "limited menu" of "old-fashioned" Americana; cheap tabs and "what-you-see-is-what-you-get" decor are part of the "nostalgic" experience.

Homestead Inn *Italian* | 22 | 11 | 20 | $49

Trenton | 800 Kuser Rd. (bet. Barbara Dr. & Nottinghill Ln.) | 609-890-9851

With no menus, no listed prices and "no questions answered", this "quirky", 1939-vintage Trenton Italian is either "special" or "weird", depending on who's talking; its "old-school" "red-sauce" cooking and "who-cares?" decor are beloved by regulars, and some say it "helps" if you tag along with one of them.

	FOOD	DECOR	SERVICE	COST

Hot Dog Johnny's ⌦ *Hot Dogs* — 21 | 14 | 18 | $9
Buttzville | Rte. 46 (Rte. 31) | 908-453-2882 | www.hotdogjohnny.com
A "family tradition" since 1944, this cash-only Buttzville roadside wiener wonderland is a strictly "no-frills" affair vending "crunchy" hot dogs washed down with buttermilk and birch beer; an "awesome location on the Pequest River" makes it a natural for a "picnic", and there are bonus swings for the kiddies.

☑ Hotoke *Asian* — 20 | 25 | 19 | $44
New Brunswick | 350 George St. (Bayard St.) | 732-246-8999 | www.hotokerestaurant.com
"Jersey's version of Tao", this sizable Pan-Asian duplex is "so cool" that its "hip" following wonders if they're in Downtown New Brunswick or "Midtown Manhattan"; a "wonderfully varied" menu and "great drinks" (including a deep sake list) arrive in "loud", "loungey" digs equipped with a communal table and a large Buddha.

Hummus Elite *Mediterranean* — ∇ 21 | 13 | 19 | $15
Englewood | 39 E. Palisade Ave. (bet. Dean & Engle Sts.) | 201-569-5600 | www.hummuselite.com
"Israeli-style" recipes and "out-of-this-world" hummus fill out the menu of this casual Med BYO in Englewood; the setting's compact, but the value's "good" and the kosher fare a "vegetarian's delight."

Hunan Chinese Room *Chinese* — 20 | 17 | 18 | $28
Morris Plains | 255 Speedwell Ave. (Hanover Ave.) | 973-285-1117
Cantonese, Hunan and Sichuan dishes come "packed with flavor" at this Morris Plains "neighborhood haunt" that's "nicer looking on the inside" than the average for the genre; some find it "hit-or-miss", but most agree on the "gracious" owner and "extremely affordable" costs.

Hunan Spring *Chinese* — 18 | 11 | 16 | $24
Springfield | 288 Morris Ave. (Caldwell Pl.) | 973-379-4994 | www.hunanspringrestaurant.com
"Still going strong", this Springfield BYO vet vends "consistent", "no-surprises" Chinese standards that are "flavorful" and fairly priced; too bad about the "ordinary", "diner"-esque decor and so-so service, but takeout is always an option.

Hunan Taste *Chinese* — 24 | 24 | 22 | $32
Denville | 67 Bloomfield Ave. (Main St.) | 973-625-2782 | www.hunantaste.com
"Not your local Chinese take-out place", this "opulent" Denville venue purveys "beautifully displayed" Hunan, Mandarin and Sichuan specialties in an "extremely cool", "pagoda"-esque setting (complete with aquarium room dividers); "well-dressed" staffers provide "extra-nice" service, making the "extra cost" easier to understand.

Huntley Taverne *American* — 22 | 24 | 21 | $50
Summit | 3 Morris Ave. (Springfield Ave.) | 908-273-3166 | www.thehuntleytaverne.com
The "food rocks and the cocktails are well mixed" at this "bustling" Summit New American, a "fun place" to be "hip in the suburbs" with

a "wannabe-NYC" ambiance and "tons of singles"; two "welcoming" fireplaces and "upscale" Craftsman-style decor supply the "warm" glow, service is "reliable" and the pricing, no surprise, is "high-end."

Ibby's Falafel *Mideastern*

	22	9	17	$13

NEW Hoboken | 614 Washington St. (bet. 6th & 7th Sts.) | 201-610-1300
Jersey City | 303 Grove St. (bet. Mercer & Wayne Sts.) | 201-432-2400 ●
Freehold | 4 W. Main St. (Court St.) | 732-409-1234 ⊟
www.ibbysfalafel.com

"Cheap, quick and easy", these Mideastern "holes-in-the-wall" sling "outstanding" hummus, falafel and shawarma in "no-atmosphere" storefront settings, but given their "tiny" dimensions, regulars say "takeout" is the way to go; P.S. the Freehold outlet is cash-only.

Iberia Peninsula ● *Portuguese/Spanish*

	20	17	19	$37

Newark | 63-69 Ferry St. (bet. Prospect & Union Sts.) |
973-344-5611

Iberia Tavern ● Ⓜ *Portuguese/Spanish*

Newark | 80-84 Ferry St. (bet. Congress & Prospect Sts.) | 973-344-7603
iberiarestaurants.com

"Solid performers" in Newark's Ironbound, these "always packed" Iberian siblings draw crowds with their "celebratory" rodizio and "abundant" portions of seafood; ok, they're "rambunctious" and some sense a "food-clearance-sale" mood, but they're hard to beat for "value" since they churn out "more food than you can imagine"; P.S. on-site parking lots are a big plus.

I Gemelli *Italian*

	▽ 24	15	23	$41

South Hackensack | 268 Huyler St. (bet. Dinallo & Hoffman Sts.) |
201-487-4220 | www.igemelliristorante.com

Although this South Hackensack Italian may be "short on decor", fans say it's "large on food and service", with "excellent" grub and "accommodating" staffers; fans say there's a "real effort" being made to please patrons, starting with the BYO policy.

Ⓩ Ikko *Japanese*

	25	19	26	$29

Brick | Brick Plaza Mall | 107 Brick Plaza (bet. Cedar Bridge Ave. & Rte. 70) | 732-477-6077 | www.ikkosteakhouse.com

Everyone from sushi purists to finicky grandkids have a "fine time" at this "something-for-everybody" Japanese BYO in the Brick Plaza Mall; "entertaining" hibachi and sushi chefs whip up their "super-fresh" handiwork in a large, "pleasant" space, tended by "person-able", "extremely attentive" staffers.

Ⓩ Il Capriccio Ⓢ *Italian*

	25	25	25	$61

Whippany | 633 Rte. 10 (Whippany Rd.) | 973-884-9175 |
www.ilcapriccio.com

It's "old-school" all the way at this "stellar", jackets-suggested Whippany Italian where the food is "prepared to high standards", the mood is "quiet" and the service "impeccable"; though the "elegant" decor is a bit "over-the-top" for some (ditto the "steep" prices), overall it's "perfect for a romantic dinner or special occasion"; "live piano" music Wednesday–Saturday nights is a "wonderful" touch.

	FOOD	DECOR	SERVICE	COST

NEW Il Cinghiale Trattoria Ⓜ *Italian* — | — | — | M

Little Ferry | 201 Main St. (John St.) | 201-440-2272

Named for the wild boar that flavors its signature pappardelle, this warm, intimate Little Ferry Italian tames appetites with reasonably priced regional dishes from Piedmont, Tuscany and the chef-owner's native Sicily; distinctive housemade desserts and BYO add to the value.

Il Fiore *Italian* 26 | 17 | 22 | $33

Collingswood | 693-695 Haddon Ave. (Collings Ave.) | 856-833-0808

An *abbondanza* of "simple" but "excellent" dishes makes this Collingswood "gem" "what an Italian BYO should be", with "old-world" service and "incredibly reasonable" tabs icing the cake; no wonder fans overlook the "hectic", "no-atmosphere" room and timing that can be "a little off."

Il Michelangelo *Italian* 20 | 21 | 22 | $40

Boonton | 91 Elcock Ave. (Powerville Rd.) | 973-316-1111 | www.ilmichelangelo.com

"Delicious" meals are paired with "great wines" at this "charming family" Italian set in a 19th-century Boonton stagecoach inn; a facade face-lift has given dining on the porch new luster, while the "clubby" upstairs bar and "friendly", "professional" staff contribute to the "convivial" mood.

Z Il Mondo Vecchio Ⓢ *Italian* 26 | 20 | 22 | $52

Madison | 72 Main St. (Central Ave.) | 973-301-0024 | www.ilmondovecchio.com

A "more affordable" sibling of Michael Cetrulo's Scalini Fedeli in Chatham, this "Energizer Bunny" of a BYO in Madison keeps on going thanks to "fantastic" Italian cooking that seems to "get better with time"; alright, service can be "unpredictable" and it's so "tight" there's "not enough room to wear a sweater", but the hard-to-get prime-time reservations after 20 years attest to its "deserved popularity."

Z Il Mulino New York *Italian* 27 | 23 | 24 | $71

Atlantic City | Trump Taj Mahal | 1000 Boardwalk (Virginia Ave.) | 609-449-6006 | www.ilmulino.com

For an "impeccable" Italian meal on a "big night out" in AC, it "doesn't get any better" than this Taj Mahal facsimile of the legendary NY original; expect "insanely good" classic cooking, "white-glove" service from a tuxedoed team and a "beautiful", traditionally appointed setting – but since it's a definite "splurge", "bring the credit card with no balance."

Il Vecchio Cafe *Italian* 20 | 18 | 18 | $36

Caldwell | Calandra's Vill. | 234 Bloomfield Ave. (bet. Arlington & Forest Aves.) | 973-226-8889 | www.calandrasitalianvillage.com

The latest member of the Calandra family's ever-expanding empire, this Caldwell Italian turns out "heaping" dishes of "tasty" pasta in a "casual", brightly lit space with "family" appeal galore; grown-ups favor the "better deal" available during happy hour at the bar.

Il Villaggio ⊠ *Italian/Seafood*   24 | 23 | 24 | $47

Carlstadt | 651 Rte. 17 N. (Passaic Ave.) | 201-935-7733 | www.ilvillaggio.com

"Perfect for a special night out", this "fancy" Carlstadt Italian seafooder serves a "splendid" menu that includes an "extensive" list of specials; "impeccable" service and a "beautiful, grand" setting burnish the "romantic" mood, so even though it's "a bit pricey", it's "worth the extra euros."

IndeBlue Ⓜ *Indian*   ▽ 25 | 24 | 25 | $23

Collingswood | 619 Collings Ave. (White Horse Pike) | 856-854-4633 | www.indebluerestaurant.com

Collingswood locals like the "unique" cooking and "fair prices" at this "popular" Indian BYO from chef Rakesh Ramola (ex Philly's Tiffin); homemade breads straight out of a tandoor oven and plenty of vegetarian options keep it "popular" enough to warrant an expansion: it's just moved across the street to bigger digs.

India on the Hudson *Indian*   ▽ 21 | 14 | 19 | $29

Hoboken | 1210 Washington St. (bet. 12th & 13th Sts.) | 201-222-0101 | www.indiaonthehudson.com

"Authentic", "tasty" cooking comes in "pleasant", recently renovated digs at this Hoboken Northern Indian; some say the space is kind of "tight", but "modest" prices – especially those lunchtime "good deals" – keep the trade brisk.

Inlet Café *Seafood*   20 | 15 | 19 | $36

Highlands | 3 Cornwall St. (Shrewsbury Ave.) | 732-872-9764 | www.inletcafe.com

This second-generation seasonal seafooder, "right on the water" in Highlands, features "terrific" dockside views from its big outdoor deck overlooking Sandy Hook Bay; although it's a tad "pricey" for what it is, regulars say its "first-rate" fin fare and "fabulous summer atmosphere" are hard to beat.

In Napoli *Italian*   17 | 13 | 19 | $36

Fort Lee | 116 Main St. (Central Rd.) | 201-947-2500 | www.inapoli.com

"Nice for the price", this longtime Fort Lee Southern Italian near the George Washington Bridge offers "lots of food for the money" along with a "busy bar" that's a "good place to watch the game"; critics cite "dreary" looks and a "quantity-beats-quality" approach, calling it "consistently average."

Inn at Millrace Pond *American/Continental*   ▽ 23 | 25 | 23 | $45

Hope | Inn at Millrace Pond | 313 Johnsonburg Rd. (bet. Rtes. 519 & 611) | 908-459-4884 | www.innatmillracepond.com

Extolled for its "rustic beauty" and favored as a "romantic", "special-celebration" destination, this American-Continental set in an 18th-century Hope gristmill offers "excellent" food on its "gorgeous" main level as well as less pricey options in the downstairs tavern.

| | FOOD | DECOR | SERVICE | COST |

Inn at Sugar Hill ⓜ *American* ▽ 18 | 23 | 21 | $38

Mays Landing | 5704 Mays Landing-Somers Point Rd. (River Rd.) | 609-625-2226 | www.innatsugarhill.com

Sweet indeed are the fireplace-equipped Victorian dining rooms at this "quiet" Mays Landing inn that also boasts "can't-be-beat" veranda views of the Great Egg Harbor River; though the kitchen's Traditional American fare may lack consistency, the service is "top-notch."

Inn of the Hawke *American* 20 | 18 | 20 | $30

Lambertville | 74 S. Union St. (Mt. Hope St.) | 609-397-9555

The bar area at this "comfortable" Lambertville inn is a locals' "gathering spot", and may be more popular than the "nothing-fancy", faux-Colonial dining room offering "dependable" American comfort grub; "friendly" service and "moderate" prices complete the "relaxed" picture.

Irish Pub & Inn ⓞ⊟ *Pub Food* 18 | 16 | 18 | $22

Atlantic City | 164 St. James Pl. (bet. Boardwalk & Pacific Ave.) | 609-344-9063 | www.theirishpub.com

This 24/7 "slice of old Atlantic City" may have a monopoly on the "best-priced" food and beer in town, served in a "dark", "wood and memorabilia"-lined barroom; the "decent" grub has a decided Irish lilt and tastes even better "post-clubbing", but bring cash as it doesn't accept plastic.

Iron Hill Brewery ⓞ *American/Pub Food* 20 | 20 | 21 | $28

Maple Shade | 124 E. Kings Hwy. (Lenola Rd.) | 856-273-0300 | www.ironhillbrewery.com

Parked in Maple Shade, this lone outpost of the Delaware-based microbrewery chainlet offers "better-than-standard" pub fare ferried by an "aim-to-please" team; just be warned it's "popular", so "noise" and "long waits" are the norm.

Isabella's American Bistro ⓜ *American* 19 | 17 | 19 | $37

Westfield | 39 Elm St. (bet. Broad St. & North Ave.) | 908-233-8830 | www.isabellasbistro.com

Flanked by siblings Mojave Grille and Theresa's, this "casual" Westfield BYO vends "solid" American comfort food in "relaxed" digs; some find the "basic" menu "somewhat limiting" and the space "tight", but "enjoyable" alfresco tables offer excellent "people-watching" opportunities.

It's Greek To Me *Greek* 18 | 13 | 17 | $25

Clifton | Promenade Shops at Clifton | 852 Rte. 3 W. (Passaic Ave.) | 973-594-1777

Englewood | 36 E. Palisade Ave. (bet. Dean & Engle Sts.) | 201-568-0440

Fort Lee | 1611 Palisade Ave. (Angioletti St.) | 201-947-2050

Hoboken | 538 Washington St. (6th St.) | 201-216-1888

Jersey City | 194 Newark Ave. (Jersey Ave.) | 201-222-0844

Ridgewood | 21 E. Ridgewood Ave. (bet. Broad & Chestnut Sts.) | 201-612-2600

Westwood | 487 Broadway (bet. Irvington St. & Washington Ave.) | 201-722-3511

(continued)

It's Greek To Me

Holmdel | 2128 Rte. 35 (Laurel Ave.) | 732-275-0036
Long Branch | Pier Vill. | 44 Centennial Dr. (Chelsea Ave.) | 732-571-0222
www.itsgreektome.com

Folks needing a "souvlaki fix" tout these "serviceable" Greek BYOs offering all the "basics" in "modest", "diner"-esque environs; purists find them merely "average", but "fast" service and "moderate" prices make the overall experience more palatable.

Ivy Inn *American*   22 | 23 | 21 | $46

Hasbrouck Heights | 268 Terrace Ave. (bet. Kipp Ave. & Washington Pl.) | 201-393-7699 | www.ivyinn.com

The "sense of yesterday" pervades this "rustic" American housed in an erstwhile Hasbrouck Heights stagecoach inn, where the "interesting" menu includes "innovative" specials; the ultra-"romantic" setting – complete with a "cozy fireplace", "flickering candles" and an occasional "pianist on the ivories" – draws "lots of couples", while an "attractive" early-bird deal pleases penny-pinchers.

☑ Izakaya *Japanese*   23 | 25 | 21 | $59

Atlantic City | Borgata Hotel, Casino & Spa | 1 Borgata Way (Huron Ave.) | 609-317-1000 | www.theborgata.com

This "loungey" "new wave" Japanese pub in AC's Borgata Hotel may resemble a "swank" nightclub but turns out an "innovative" menu from star chef Michael Schulson that runs the gamut from sushi and sashimi to robatayaki to Kobe beef NY strip; the "striking" setting and "hip" crowd make the "minuscule" portions, "pricey" tabs and "loud" acoustics a bit more palatable.

Jack's Café ☒ *American/Eclectic*   20 | 10 | 18 | $26

Westwood | 325 Broadway (bet. Jefferson & Westwood Aves.) | 201-666-0400 | www.jackscafenj.com

A "worthy effort" in Westwood, this "small" cafe dishes out "homey" American-Eclectic eats that are "value" priced thanks to its BYO policy; though service can be "uneven" and the decor is on the "funky" side, fans see "much love" in evidence at this "upbeat" place.

J&K Steakhouse *Steak*   - | - | - | M

Dover | 34 W. Blackwell St. (Warren St.) | 862-244-4536 ☒ ☒
NEW Morristown | 56 South St. (Pine St.) | 973-998-8061
www.jandksteakhouse.com

A gentle Latin accent shows up in the sauces, sides and sangria mixers that complement the prime dry-aged beef at this pair of understated steakhouses in Dover and Morristown; BYO and three- and four-course prix fixe options help corral the tab.

Janice *American/Italian*   21 | 16 | 20 | $36

Ho-Ho-Kus | 23 Sheridan Ave. (bet. Orvil Ct. & Warren Ave.) | 201-445-2666 | www.janiceabistro.com

"Family-owned" Ho-Ho-Kus bistro offering a "surprisingly good", all-day Italian-American menu ferried by a "friendly" crew; some say the tabs are a tad "too expensive" given its "luncheonette"-like atmosphere, but the "gluten-free offerings" and "wonderful" desserts garner special praise.

Java Moon *American* 22 | 17 | 19 | $21

Newark | Newark Liberty Int'l Airport | Terminal A3 | no phone ◖

Newark | Newark Liberty Int'l Airport | Terminal B1 | no phone ◖

Jackson | 1022 Anderson Rd. (Rte. 537) | 732-928-3633

www.javamooncafe.com

Best for breakfast and lunch when visiting Jackson's nearby shopping outlets, this "small", diner-esque BYO purveys a wide-ranging American menu delivered by a crew that "moves fast"; the "relaxing" setting recalls a "log cabin", and there are also grab-and-go kiosks at Newark Airport.

NEW JBJ Soul Kitchen Ⓜ 🍽 *American* - | - | - | I

Red Bank | 207 Monmouth St. (bet. Bridge & Shrewsbury Aves.) | 732-842-0900 | www.jbjsoulkitchen.org

'Hope is delicious' is the motto behind this Red Bank project from Jon Bon Jovi's Soul Foundation, where diners pay a cash-only donation ($10 is suggested) for a professionally prepared three-course seasonal American meal (no alcohol), or volunteer at the eatery if they can't; with no reservations taken and limited hours, there's often a wait for the 30 seats in the cool modern digs.

JD's Steak Pit *Steak* 17 | 14 | 18 | $41

Fort Lee | 124 Main St. (Central Rd.) | 201-461-0444 | www.jdsteakpit.com

An "older crowd" says this "been-there-forever" Fort Lee steakhouse is a "real value in today's economy", even if it could "use some sprucing up"; but critics fret it's "become stale" and "suffered" after a change in ownership, even though it's still a "nice departure" from all the burger joints in these parts.

Jerry & Harvey's Noshery *Deli* 18 | 7 | 16 | $21

Marlboro | Marlboro Plaza | 96 Rte. 9 (Rte. 520) | 732-972-1122 | www.jerryandharveys.com

Set in a Marlboro strip mall, this "decent" kosher-style deli has "been around for quite some time" channeling NYC's "Lower East Side" with its "run-down" looks and "indifferent" staffers; while there's nothing wrong with the "good not great" food, many feel it's "long overdue" for a decor "makeover."

Je's Ⓜ *Southern* ∇ 25 | 11 | 20 | $21

Newark | 34 William St. (Halsey St.) | 973-623-8848

"Artery-clogging" soul food – and "plenty" of it – is yours at this "unassuming" Southerner in Downtown Newark slinging three squares a day since 1975; it's not much on looks, but the meals are "made and served with love" and it's a "good value" to boot.

Jimmy Buff's *Hot Dogs* 20 | 8 | 16 | $11

Kenilworth | 506 Blvd. (bet. 20th & 21st Sts.) | 908-276-2833 🍽

Scotch Plains | Rte. 22 W. (bet. Glenside & Mountain Aves.) | 908-233-2833 🍽

West Orange | 60 Washington St. (Columbus Ave.) | 973-325-9897 🍽

(continued)

Jimmy Buff's

East Hanover | Castle Ridge Plaza | 354 Rte. 10 W. (River Rd.) | 973-463-0099

NEW **Randolph** | 1594 Sussex Tpke. (Rt. 10 E.) | 973-584-3339
www.jimmybuff.com

"Killer" Italian hot dogs take "best in show" honors at these Jersey "institutions" where the weenies are fried in enough oil to keep "OPEC" in business, then stuffed into a 'pizza-bread' roll along with potatoes, peppers and onions; both service and decor "could use some work", and it's up to you to bring your own "Alka-Seltzer."

Jimmy's *Italian*   23 | 14 | 22 | $43

Asbury Park | 1405 Asbury Ave. (Prospect Ave.) | 732-774-5051 | www.jimmysitalianrestaurant.com

"Throwback" sums up the mood at this "time-machine" Italian in Asbury Park, where the traditional "red-sauce" cooking, "old-school" digs and "experienced" waiters are a match for the "Sinatra on the wall" (and "in the air"); given its "dicey" location, the "valet parking" is a plus.

Joe Pesce *Italian/Seafood*   24 | 15 | 23 | $43

Collingswood | 833 Haddon Ave. (bet. Collings Ave. & Cuthbert Blvd.) | 856-833-9888 | www.joepescerestaurant.com

"Simple", "expertly prepared" seafood comes with an Italian accent at this "small" Collingswood spot overseen by a willing-to-"please" host and serviced by an "outgoing" team; sure, it's "cramped" and "pricey for a BYO", but "worth every penny" since the food is so darn "delicious."

Joe's Peking Duck House Ⓜ⇗ *Chinese*   24 | 12 | 20 | $25

Marlton | Marlton Crossing Shopping Ctr. | 145 Rte. 73 S. (Rte. 70) | 856-985-1551

A "sprawling" Chinese menu awaits at this family-friendly, cash-only BYO in a Marlton shopping center that may be "not the fanciest place", but at least "everyone knows your name"; the namesake specialty is "as good as it gets", and adventurous eaters tout its "outside-the-box" options.

Jose's *Mexican*   ▽ 23 | 7 | 18 | $16

Spring Lake Heights | 101 Rte. 71 (Jersey Ave.) | 732-974-8080

Ok, this strip-mall Mexican BYO in Spring Lake Heights may be "tiny", but few mind given its "top-notch" cooking for "barely any money at all"; still, "schlocky" decor and staffers who "speak little English" lead insiders to opt for "takeout."

Jose's Mexican Cantina *Mexican*   19 | 15 | 18 | $26

New Providence | 24 South St. (Springfield Ave.) | 908-464-4360
Warren | Quail Run Ctr. | 125 Washington Valley Rd. (Morning Glory Rd.) | 732-563-0480
www.josescantina.com

"Voluminous" portions of "better-than-average" Mexicana turn up at these "dependable" BYOs in New Providence and Warren; some consider the cooking "inconsistent" and compare the decor to "Mayan ruins", but at least the tabs are "affordable" and the mood "kid-friendly."

Juanito's *Mexican*   23 | 17 | 20 | $26

Howell | 3930 Rte. 9 S. (Aldrich Rd.) | 732-370-1717 |
www.juanitos2howell.com
Red Bank | 159 Monmouth St. (West St.) | 732-747-9118 |
www.juanitosredbank.com

There's almost "always a crowd" at these Mexican BYOs in Howell and Red Bank thanks to "tasty", "authentic" cooking served for a "value" price; "cramped" seating and "no frills" in the decor department are overruled by the "bountiful" portions and "friendly" staffers.

NEW Just Restaurant *American*   - | - | - | VE

Old Bridge | 2280 Rte. 9 S. (bet. Arcade Ln. & Jake Brown Rd.) |
732-707-4800 | www.justrestaurantnj.com

Fine dining comes to an unexpected, underrepresented stretch of Route 9 in Old Bridge via this swank New American where veal cheeks, foie gras and the like are served in a dramatic setting bathed in pink and purple mood lighting; it's not just about the food, however, given specialty cocktails and a lounge scene with weekend DJs.

Kairo Kafe ⊠ *Mideastern*   - | - | - | M

New Brunswick | 49 Bayard St. (George St.) | 732-545-2476 |
www.kairokafe.com

"Decent" Mideastern platters, American burgers and crossover 'pitza' draw locals and Rutgers students to this underground New Brunswick lair also known for its hookahs, weekend belly dancers and "dorm-room" decor; Hopewell Valley wines are poured, but BYO is welcome.

Kanji *Japanese*   24 | 20 | 22 | $32

Tinton Falls | 980 Shrewsbury Ave. (Rte. 35) | 732-544-1600 |
www.kanjisteakhouse.com

"Fab" sushi and the "freshest" sashimi turn up at chef Roger Yang's Japanese BYO in Tinton Falls that's also praised for its "modern design", treat-you-like-"family" service and the "sizzle and show" at the hibachi grill; a convenient nearby liquor store offering "good sake selections" ices the cake.

Karma Kafe *Indian*   21 | 16 | 18 | $28

Hoboken | 505 Washington St. (bet. 5th & 6th Sts.) | 201-610-0900 |
www.karmakafe.com

"Addictive" Indian food that's "so good it should be illegal" is served at this "minimalist" Hoboken spot also known for its "bargain" $10 lunch buffet; though service "could be more attentive", the "large portions", validated parking and sidewalk seating are fine as is.

Kaya's Kitchen Ⓜ *Vegetarian*   ▽ 24 | 22 | 24 | $25

Belmar | 1000 Main St. (10th Ave.) | 732-280-1141 |
www.kayaskitchenbelmar.com

Since it relocated to more "upscale" quarters, this "healthy", "hippie" Belmar BYO is still offering an "extensive", "unusual" menu of vegan and vegetarian dishes so "delicious" that "even carnivores" are intrigued; "earnest" service and a "mellow vibe" keep its "tree-hugging" fan base satisfied.

KC Prime *Steak*

FOOD	DECOR	SERVICE	COST
22	20	21	$48

Lawrenceville | 4160 Quakerbridge Rd. (Clarksville Rd.) | 609-275-5418 | www.kcprimerestaurant.com

"One of the best nonchain steakhouses" in NJ, this "pleasant surprise" near Lawrenceville's Quaker Bridge Mall purveys "flavorful" chops in a "dark", "modern" room; "friendly", "well-paced" service and a "fabulous" $19 Sunday brunch buffet make the "expensive" tabs easier to swallow.

NEW Keg & Kitchen ● *American* (fka Cork)

FOOD	DECOR	SERVICE	COST
-	-	-	M

Westmont | 90 Haddon Ave. (Cuthbert Blvd.) | 856-833-9800 | kegnkitchen.com

The former Cork in Westmont has morphed into a casual, midpriced beer pub serving updated American comfort food; the renovated, eco-friendly digs have a rustic look, highlighted by a 16-ft. table built from a fallen Pennsylvania black walnut tree.

Kevin's Thyme ☒ *American*

FOOD	DECOR	SERVICE	COST
23	15	20	$35

Ho-Ho-Kus | 614 N. Maple Ave. (bet. Brookside Ave. & 1st St.) | 201-445-6400 | www.kevinsthyme.com

An "impressive" kitchen turns out "delicious" New American fare at this "tiny little" Ho-Ho-Kus BYO where the service is "warm" and the seating "limited", although a "cute" patio provides "excellent alfresco dining" in season.

NEW Khloe Bistrot ● *French*

FOOD	DECOR	SERVICE	COST
-	-	-	M

Fort Lee | 1643 Schosser St. (Main St.) | 201-461-9700 | www.khloebistrot.com

Within walking distance of the GW Bridge, this Fort Lee BYO French serves bistro fare at dinner (until midnight), as well as lunch and brunch in a funky, *très petit* space that charms with its mismatched vintage furnishings and crystal chandeliers.

Khun Thai *Thai*

FOOD	DECOR	SERVICE	COST
23	19	20	$30

Short Hills | 504 Millburn Ave. (Campbell Rd.) | 973-258-0586 | www.khunthairestaurant.com

"Flavorful" dishes – including "terrific" soups and "divine drunken noodles" – come with "just the right amount of spice" at this "casual" Thai duplex that's "close to Short Hills shopping"; BYO helps keep the cost down, while upstairs (and sidewalk) seating lets you "be away from it all."

NEW Khyber Grill *Indian*

FOOD	DECOR	SERVICE	COST
-	-	-	M

South Plainfield | 684 Oak Tree Ave. (Park Ave.) | 908-226-5544 | www.khybergrillusa.com

This midpriced BYO newcomer distinguishes itself from the other Indians lining South Plainfield's Oak Tree Avenue, serving fare from the Northwest frontier featuring top-quality ingredients and spices that are ground and mixed daily; co-owner/host Akshay Jhanjee, scion of the family behind NYC's Bukhara Grill, oversees service in the earth-toned room, which melds modern and traditional elements.

Kibitz Room *Deli*

FOOD	DECOR	SERVICE	COST
23	10	16	$19

Cherry Hill | Shoppes at Holly Ravine | 100 Springdale Rd. (Evesham Rd.) | 856-428-7878 | www.kibitzroom.com

Fans come for the "gargantuan" corned beef sandwiches "stacked a mile high" at this "New York City–style" joint that's the "closest thing" Cherry Hill has to a traditional Jewish deli; fressers don't mind overlooking the "who-cares?" decor, "elbow-to-elbow" seating and "snitty" countermen who treat customers "like chopped liver."

Kilkenny Alehouse *Pub Food* (aka Lynch's Kilkenny)

FOOD	DECOR	SERVICE	COST
∇ 18	17	18	$26

Newark | 27 Central Ave. (Halsey St.) | 973-824-8048 | www.kilkennyalehouse.net

"Decent" pub grub washed down with Guinness dispensed by "friendly" barkeeps makes this "average" Newark venue a natural for nearby students and professionals; firehouse regalia adds some distinction to its otherwise "typical" pub ambiance.

Kinara *Indian*

FOOD	DECOR	SERVICE	COST
22	14	19	$29

Edgewater | 800 River Rd. (Hilliard Ave.) | 201-313-0555 | www.kinararestaurant.com

Set in Edgewater (the name is Hindi for 'water's edge'), this "relaxing" BYO puts out a "wide-ranging" variety of "classic" Northern Indian fare, plus Chinese-influenced dishes at the dinner hour; regulars report the "interesting specials" and "affordable", all-you-can-eat buffet lunch are "worth checking out."

Kinchley's Tavern ⬤⊘ *Pizza*

FOOD	DECOR	SERVICE	COST
21	9	16	$21

Ramsey | 586 N. Franklin Tpke. (Orchard St.) | 201-934-7777

"Tissue paper–thin" pizza is the star of the show at this circa-1937 Ramsey tavern where "everything else on the menu is forgettable"; despite "cranky" service and "tacky", "beer-mirror" decor, it's always "bustling" with "happy, hungry" folks; P.S. it's "cheap", but bring "folding money" as it accepts no plastic.

Kitchen Consigliere *Italian*

FOOD	DECOR	SERVICE	COST
-	-	-	M

Collingswood | 8 Powell Ln. (Haddon Ave.) | 856-854-2156 | www.kitconcafe.com

Angelo Lutz – known for declaring 'I'm a cook, not a crook' during his 2001 racketeering trial – offers big-portioned Italian comfort food that won't break the bank at his cozy Collingswood BYO; the garrulous chef works the room, which is lined with articles about his colorful past and augmented by outdoor seating in season.

Klein's *Seafood*

FOOD	DECOR	SERVICE	COST
19	15	17	$35

Belmar | 708 River Rd. (bet. 7th & 8th Aves.) | 732-681-1177 | www.kleinsfish.com

Aficionados say the "simple", "nicely prepared" fish at this Belmar seafood "institution" tastes best when sitting "outside on the deck"

	FOOD	DECOR	SERVICE	COST

taking in the "salt air" and "watching the fishing boats go by"; a few feel the prices "jumped the shark" with the addition of a liquor license, but overall it stays "bustling" for a reason.

Komegashi *Japanese*

| | 22 | 18 | 21 | $33 |

Jersey City | 103 Montgomery St. (Warren St.) | 201-433-4567

Komegashi Too *Japanese*

Jersey City | 99 Town Square Pl. (Washington Blvd.) | 201-533-8888
www.komegashi.com

"Beautifully presented" sushi and sashimi at "reasonable" rates keep the trade brisk at these Jersey City Japanese siblings; though both share "pleasant" settings and "friendly" service, the Town Square Place branch near Newport Marina boasts "exquisite" views of Downtown Manhattan.

Konbu Ⓜ *Japanese*

| ▽ 26 | 13 | 20 | $32 |

Manalapan | Design Ctr. | 345 Rte. 9 S. (Center St.) | 732-462-6886

It's all about the "great" sushi at this "no-atmosphere" Manalapan BYO where the fish is "very fresh", albeit "a little more expensive" than the norm; still, the chefs are "constantly updating" the rolls, the cooked items are "excellent" and service is uniformly "friendly."

Krave Café Ⓑ *American*

| ▽ 24 | 22 | 24 | $41 |

Newton | 102 Sparta Ave. (bet. Merriman Ave. & Sussex St.) | 973-383-2600 | www.kravecaterers.com

Recently relocated to a "nicer" setting in Newton, this "sophisticated" New American BYO still serves the same "exquisite", "foodie"-friendly fare as before; "accommodating" owners and "excellent" staffers are other reasons why it's so "hard to get a reservation" here.

Kuzina by Sofia *Greek*

| 22 | 14 | 19 | $27 |

Cherry Hill | Sawmill Vill. | 404 Rte. 70 W. (Kings Hwy.) | 856-429-1061 | www.kuzinabysofia.com

A "little bit of Athens in Cherry Hill", this "cozy", "minimally decorated" Hellenic BYO offers "plentiful" portions of "authentic" chow for "reasonable" sums; expect "lots of regulars" in the crowd, especially on Saturday night, when a Greek band entertains; P.S. it has partnered with WineWorks, a nearby wine shop that will deliver your bottle.

NEW Kyma Greek Cuisine *Greek/Seafood*

| – | – | – | M |

Somerville | 24 E. Main St. (Bridge St.) | 908-864-4730 | www.kymacuisine.com

Classic Greek dishes get modern treatment at this sleek Somerville BYO, whose name means 'wave'; the biggest lure is charcoal-grilled whole fish that you select from the granite-counter display, but the midpriced menu offers plenty of choices for landlubbers too.

Labrador Lounge *Eclectic*

| 25 | 17 | 22 | $36 |

Normandy Beach | 3581 Rte. 35 N. (Peterson Ln.) | 732-830-5770 | www.kitschens.com

Brought to you by Shore restaurateuse Marilyn Schlossbach (Dauphin Grille, Langosta Lounge, etc.), this "laid-back" Normandy Beach eatery exudes a "cool vibe" and offers an Eclectic menu that's "diverse enough to satisfy all palates", served by a "surfer-dude" staff; BYO makes it "easy on the wallet", but bottles of wine can also be purchased on-site.

La Campagna *Italian*   23 | 19 | 22 | $44

Morristown | 5 Elm St. (South St.) | 973-644-4943 |
www.lacampagnaristorante.com

"Excellent" classic Italian cooking comes with some "creative" spins at this "special-night-out" Morristown BYO that maintains "high standards"; though "cramped" quarters make it a "challenge" to get a table, the quality of the food is "worth the squeeze."

La Campagne Ⓜ *Continental*   23 | 23 | 23 | $49

Cherry Hill | 312 Kresson Rd. (Brace Rd.) | 856-429-7647 |
www.lacampagne.com

Set in a "rustic" 1861 farmhouse (equipped with a fireplace and a "great" patio), this Cherry Hill Continental "respite" comprised of a series of "rambling", "intimate" rooms has the "feel of a country inn"; the food is "excellent", the service "first-rate", BYO keeps costs in check and the Thursday night "cooking classes" are a nice touch.

La Cipollina *Italian*   22 | 21 | 22 | $44

Freehold | 16 W. Main St. (South St.) | 732-308-3830 | www.lacipollina.com
Now at the quarter-century mark, this "dependable" (if "hard-to-find") Freehold Italian BYO maintains its old-world ways, with a "classic" menu of "quality" items served by an "excellent" tuxedoed team; "elegant" decor lends it "special-occasion" status, though "bargain" prix fixe specials keep costs under control.

La Esperanza *Mexican*   25 | 17 | 24 | $26

Lindenwold | 40 E. Gibbsboro Rd. (White Horse Pike) | 856-782-7114 |
www.mexicanhope.com

"Hearty, satisfying" Mexican food is yours at this "authentic" Lindenwold cantina that's the "exact opposite of chain places" since it's "family-run" with "lovingly prepared" grub and "super-friendly" service; a "huge selection of tequilas" keeps the crowd well lubricated.

La Focaccia *Italian*   23 | 18 | 22 | $46

Summit | 523 Morris Ave. (Aubrey St.) | 908-277-4006 |
www.lafocaccianj.com

"Tony Summit" is home to this "celebratory" Italian where the "consistently excellent" food is ferried by a "professional", "courteous" crew; BYO helps offset the "steep", "what-recession?" prices, and insiders sidestep the "long" weekend waits and "loud" noise level by going for lunch.

ᴺᴱᵂ La Fontana Coast *Italian*   - | - | - | E

Sea Isle City | 5000 Landis Ave. (50th St.) | 609-486-6088 |
www.lafontanacoast.com

Housemade mozzarella, gnocchi and desserts are just part of the extensive menu at this seasonal upscale Italian a block from the beach in Sea Isle City; BYO and enjoy water views, plus sunny decor and an outdoor patio that evoke a seaside Italian villa.

	FOOD	DECOR	SERVICE	COST

La Griglia ⌧ *Italian/Seafood*
`23` `20` `23` `$50`

Kenilworth | 740 Kenilworth Blvd. (Michigan Ave.) | 908-241-0031 | www.lagriglia.com

The fish is "cooked to perfection" at this "accessible" Kenilworth Italian seafooder right off the Garden State Parkway, a "dressy" kind of place where the "wonderful" food, "fantastic" wine list and "terrific" staffers jibe with its "upscale" aspirations; ok, it's on the "expensive" side, but penny-pinchers tout the $21 prix fixe lunch.

Laila's ⌧Ⓜ *Caribbean*
▽ `22` `15` `20` `$38`

Asbury Park | 808 Fifth Ave. (Main St.) | 732-988-8806 | www.lailaslatin.com

"Like eating at a relative's house", this "small" Asbury Park BYO is infused with "love", starting with its "full-of-flavor" Caribbean home cooking; some contend the prices are "not in line" with the "storefront" setting, though the "happy" atmosphere is fine as is.

La Isla *Cuban*
`25` `10` `17` `$24`

Hoboken | 104 Washington St. (bet. 1st & 2nd Sts.) | 201-659-8197 | www.laislarestaurant.com

Serving "incredible" Cuban food "morning, noon, and night", this "postage stamp"–size Hoboken BYO draws crowds with its "high-quality" Cuban cooking and "bang-for-your-buck" tabs; though service can be "variable" and the decor's strictly "hole-in-the-wall", there's usually a "line to get in" for good reason.

La Locanda *Italian*
▽ `28` `20` `23` `$45`

Voorhees | Echelon Village Plaza | 1120 White Horse Rd. (bet. Executive Dr. & Haddonfield Berlin Rd.) | 856-627-3700 | www.lalocandaonline.com

"Excellent" pastas are menu highlights at this "consistent" Italian yearling parked in a Voorhees shopping center; smooth service and a white-tablecloth setting signal its upscale aspirations, and though on the pricey side, the BYO policy helps keep tabs in check.

Lamberti's Cucina *Italian*
`20` `15` `19` `$26`

Turnersville | 3210 Rte. 42 (Black Horse Pike) | 856-728-4505 | www.lambertis.com

Bring on the "wonderful pizza bread" cry champions of this "unpretentious" Turnersville pasta chain link, reporting "generous portions" of "reliably good", "straightforward" "staples" in a "relaxing" setting; the Italian fare works equally well for a "fast" "before-the-movie meal" or a "large group" lunch.

Lambertville Station *American*
`17` `20` `20` `$38`

Lambertville | 11 Bridge St. (Delaware River) | 609-397-8300 | www.lambertvillestation.com

A "historic" Victorian-era train station overlooking Lambertville's canal is the site for this "touristy" American where "nice outdoor seating" distracts from the "routine" eats and "friendly" if "inexperienced" service; at least the prices are "lower" than most of the competition, and carnivores relish its wintertime wild game menu.

	FOOD	DECOR	SERVICE	COST

Langosta Lounge *Eclectic*
22 | 21 | 20 | $38

Asbury Park | Asbury Park Boardwalk | 1000 Ocean Ave. (2nd Ave.) |
732-455-3275 | www.kitschens.com

Another Asbury Park hit from "noted restaurateur" Marilyn
Schlossbach (Pop's Garage, Trinity & the Pope, etc.), this "busy"
boardwalk spot features her signature "vacation cuisine", an Eclectic
mix of "affordable" food items ferried by an "accommodating" crew;
the atmosphere is "alive", and it's hard to beat for "après-beach bev-
erages" on the patio.

La Pastaria *Italian*
19 | 16 | 18 | $32

Summit | 327 Springfield Ave. (Summit Ave.) | 908-522-9088
Red Bank | 30 Linden Pl. (Broad St.) | 732-224-8699
www.lapastaria.com

"Consistent" is the word on these Italian trattorias in Red Bank and
Summit where the food is "solid", the mood "cozy" and the costs
"reasonable"; sure, they can be "crowded" and "cacophonous", but
alfresco dining, "half portions" and "truly special specials" make
these BYOs "local favorites."

La Sorrentina *Italian*
∇ 24 | 13 | 22 | $28

North Bergen | 7831 Bergenline Ave. (79th St.) | 201-869-8100 |
www.sorrentinanb.com

"Superb" pizza and "great" pasta come "for a song" at this casual
North Bergen Italian trattoria that's steps away from North Hudson
Park; "gargantuan" portions and "friendly" service offset the lack of
decor and long waits to get in at prime times.

⏱ La Spiaggia *Italian*
24 | 20 | 25 | $49

Ship Bottom | 357 W. Eighth St. (Barnegat Ave.) | 609-494-4343 |
www.laspiaggialbi.com

"Excellent all-around", this "popular" Northern Italian BYO via the
brothers Stragapede draws seasonal visitors to Ship Bottom on Long
Beach Island; "well-prepared" food and "way-cute" staffers divert
attention from decor that's "in need of an update."

L'assiette *American*
∇ 20 | 15 | 19 | $45
(fka Plate)

Surf City | 1403 Long Beach Blvd. (14th St.) | 609-361-7800 |
www.lassiettelbi.com

An "ambitious" New American menu with a "nod toward local sup-
pliers" is the bait at this "locavore" BYO in Surf City on LBI; the food
is "good" – "sometimes very good" – but the digs are "not very attractive" and it would benefit from a "more professional staff."

La Strada Ⓜ *Italian*
23 | 19 | 22 | $40

Randolph | 1105 Rte. 10 E. (bet. Canfield & Eyland Aves.) |
973-584-4607 | www.lastradarestaurant.com

"Real Italian" cooking that "excites the palate" turns up at this "relaxing", "family-owned" spot in Randolph; despite "unimpressive"
decor and "pricey" specials, it's a "nice" option for an evening out,
and business types tout it as a "good lunch" destination.

Vote at zagat.com

	FOOD	DECOR	SERVICE	COST

🚩 Latour M *French* `26` `21` `24` `$56`

Ridgewood | 6 E. Ridgewood Ave. (Broad St.) | 201-445-5056 |
www.latourridgewood.com

Long an "outstanding" option in Ridgewood, this "romantic" BYO via
"hard-working" chef-owner Michael Latour offers a "sublime" slate
of "classic" French dishes delivered by a "genial" staff; some lament
"expensive" tabs, a "not-adventurous" menu and "too-close-for-
comfort" seating, but overall it's a natural choice for any "special occasion", and the $39.90 prix fixe (Sundays, Tuesdays–Thursdays) is an
"extraordinary value"; P.S. no relation to Hamburg's Restaurant Latour.

La Vecchia Napoli M *Italian* `21` `14` `19` `$44`

Edgewater | 2 Hilliard Ave. (River Rd.) | 201-941-6799 |
www.lavecchianapoli.com

"Down-home" cooking reminiscent of "grandmother's kitchen" is
featured at this "friendly" Edgewater Italian set in an "old-
fashioned" room that "needs a makeover"; penny-pinchers contend
it's "a bit pricey for what you get", but lunch and early-bird specials
are cost-cutting options.

Lazy Dog Saloon *American* `▽ 23` `21` `24` `$40`

Asbury Park | 716 Cookman Ave. (bet. Bond & Main Sts.) | 732-774-2200
"Down-to-earth" American fare comes as a "pleasant surprise" at
this "intimate" hangout on Asbury Park's "Restaurant Row"; since
it's all about the "service and the people" – "friendly" applies to both
the staff and the patrons – this "casual" spot is "right on the mark",
and there's a "great bar" scene to boot.

Le Fandy 🌿M *French* `25` `18` `23` `$54`

Fair Haven | 609 River Rd. (Haute St.) | 732-530-3338
"Charming" Fair Haven is the site of this "sweet" French BYO where
chef-owner Luke Peter Ong "knows his stuff", taking simple dishes and
"making them special"; service is "caring" and the tabs "expensive",
but what's "intimate" to some is just plain "cramped" to others.

🚩 Legal Sea Foods *Seafood* `21` `18` `19` `$42`

Paramus | Garden State Plaza | 1 Garden State Plaza (Roosevelt Ave.) |
201-843-8483
Short Hills | Short Hills Mall | 1200 Morris Tpke. (John F. Kennedy Pkwy.) |
973-467-0089
www.legalseafoods.com

"Chain shmain!" – fans of these seafood "institutions" in Paramus and
Short Hills tout their "consistent" delivery of "guaranteed-fresh, well-
prepared" fish washed down with a "surprisingly decent wine list"; the
"big, bustling" settings may be on the "plain-Jane" side and the tabs
"a little overpriced", but overall it's "worth it" given the "quality."

Le Jardin *Continental/French* `20` `23` `21` `$53`

Edgewater | 1257 River Rd. (North St.) | 201-224-9898 |
www.lejardinnj.com

Perched on a "cliff overlooking the Palisades", this Edgewater venue
is famed for its "spectacular" panorama of the Manhattan sky-

line (the GW Bridge is practically "in your lap"); many wish the French-Continental cooking "was as good as the view", yet the entire package is "lovely" enough to make it a "romantic" destination for "older" types.

Lemongrass *Thai/Vietnamese*   - | - | - | I

Morris Plains | 1729 Rte. 10 E. (Davis Ave.) | 973-998-6303 | www.lemongrassnj.com

Modern decor complements the fresh culinary compositions at this casual Viet-Thai BYO parked in a Morris Plains storefront; the inexpensive offerings include authentic phos and stir-fries that can be paired with bubble teas or an assortment of tropical fruit shakes.

⛝ Le Rendez-Vous Ⓜ *French*   27 | 18 | 24 | $55

Kenilworth | 520 Boulevard (21st St.) | 908-931-0888 | www.lerendez-vousnj.com

A bona fide "Parisian experience" awaits at this dinner-only French BYO in Kenilworth where the "memorable" meals "taste as good as they look"; though tabs are "pricey" and the "small" quarters strictly "cheek-by-jowl", admirers are too busy "swooning" over the "superb" bistro fare to notice.

NEW Levant Grille *Mediterranean*   - | - | - | M

Englewood | 34 E. Palisade Ave. (South Dean St.) | 201-503-1200 | www.levantgrille.com

Turkish and Persian accents dominate at this casual BYO Mediterranean on Englewood's main retail street, serving a mid-priced bill of fare featuring grilled seafood, stews and kebabs; long benches, exposed brick and floral accents highlight the contemporary space, and there's sidewalk seating in the warmer months.

Liberty House Ⓜ *American*   20 | 23 | 19 | $53

Jersey City | Liberty State Park | 76 Audrey Zapp Dr. (Freedom Way) | 201-395-0300 | www.libertyhouserestaurant.com

"Praiseworthy" American cooking and a "fabulous" Sunday jazz brunch play "second fiddle" to the "sweeping" views of lower Manhattan at this harborside venue in Jersey City's Liberty State Park, and "ferry" service to NYC makes it an option for city slickers too; a post-Survey chef change may not be reflected in the Food score.

Library IV ⌧Ⓜ *Steak*   - | - | - | E

Williamstown | 1030 N. Black Horse Pike (bet. Brookdale Blvd. & Lake Ave.) | 856-728-8064 | www.libraryiv.com

Carnivores can check out the hand-cut steaks ordered by the ounce at this upscale Williamstown meatery, which also offers seafood, veal and chicken selections, plus a 30-ft.-long salad bar; the dining room is lined with bookcases, as befits the name.

Light Horse Tavern *American*   22 | 23 | 21 | $41

Jersey City | 199 Washington St. (Morris St.) | 201-946-2028 | www.lighthorsetavern.com

Pub classics come with "contemporary twists" at this "hospitable" New American duplex situated in an "airy", "beautifully restored" old building in Jersey City's "up-and-coming" Paulus Hook area; though the tabs can be "pricey", its "young professional" following doesn't mind given the "excellent" beer list and bar menu.

Lilly's on the Canal Ⓜ *Eclectic*
21 | 21 | 20 | $37

Lambertville | 2 Canal St. (Bridge St.) | 609-397-6242 | www.lillysgourmet.com

The mood's "lively" at this "fun" Eclectic on the canal in Lambertville, known for its "fresh, tasty" main dishes and "amazing" desserts; the "very cool" setting in an old building encompasses an open kitchen, "magical" patio and a two-story waterfall wall, and though BYO is welcome, bottles from a local vineyard are available.

Limani Ⓜ *Greek*
24 | 17 | 22 | $42

Westfield | 235 North Ave. W. (Lenox Ave.) | 908-233-0052 | www.limaniwestfieldnj.com

"Sole with soul" is the specialty of this "scrumptious" Greek BYO seafooder parked in an "unpretentious" Downtown Westfield store-front, where the fish is "pristine", service "accommodating" and the tabs "pricey but not unreasonable"; though it can be "uncomfort-ably loud", regulars report it's "more civilized" on weeknights.

Lincroft Inn *Continental*
19 | 18 | 20 | $40

Lincroft | 700 Newman Springs Rd. (Middletown Lincroft Rd.) | 732-747-0890 | www.lincroftinn.com

"Dependable", "unpretentious" Continental classics arrive in a "his-toric" setting at this circa-1697 Lincroft inn that's long been a "lovely choice" for "special occasions", even though it's "a bit pricey"; while the main dining room is rather "sedate", the "fun" tav-ern lures more "lively" types.

Lithos *Greek*
- | - | - | E

Livingston | 405 Eisenhower Pkwy. (Nobhill Dr.) | 973-758-1111 | www.lithosnj.com

The fruits of the Mediterranean and Atlantic are on handsome dis-play, along with charcoal-grilled meats and a sea of greens, at this upscale Livingston Greek, whose name ('stone') references its floor-to-ceiling fireplace; an attractive bar and deck seating in good weather round out the Aegean adventure.

LITM ◑ *American*
▽ 14 | 18 | 16 | $29

Jersey City | 140 Newark Ave. (bet. Erie St. & Manila Ave.) | 201-536-5557 | www.litm.com

"Trendy" and "cool", this "unique" Jersey City eatery/art gallery hy-brid draws creative folks with a "nice bar scene" coupled with a usual-suspects American menu; though the name is short for 'Love Is The Message', service is just "so-so" here.

🔲 Little Café, A ⊠Ⓜ *Eclectic*
27 | 18 | 25 | $39

Voorhees | Plaza Shoppes | 118 White Horse Rd. E. (Burnt Mill Rd.) | 856-784-3344 | www.alittlecafenj.com

Like the name says, the space is "truly little", but the flavors and portions are "huge" at this "secret" Eclectic BYO in a Voorhees strip mall; though the decor's "too froufrou" for some, there's agreement on the "attentive" service and "pricey-but-worth-it" tabs; P.S. dinner served Wednesday–Saturday only.

Little Food Cafe *Sandwiches* ▽ 23 | 16 | 20 | $15

Bayonne | 330 Kennedy Blvd. (10th St.) | 201-436-6800
Pompton Plains | 585 Newark Pompton Tpke. (bet. Jackson & Poplar Aves.) | 973-616-8600
www.littlefood.fatcow.com

"Bright spots" in otherwise "mundane" culinary areas, these sandwich specialists in Bayonne and Pompton Plains earn praise for their "consistent" kitchens and "wonderful presentation"; there's "not much atmosphere", but service is "fast and friendly" and the price is right.

NEW Little Louie's Ⓜ *BBQ* - | - | - | I

Collingswood | 505 Haddon Ave. (Crestmont Terrace) | 856-854-0600 | www.littlelouiesbarbeque.com

Said Louie is a cartoon dachshund, and his sniffer points to all manner of barbecue from assorted regions at this Collingswood BYO, done up kitschy with old movie posters and a 70-in. flat-screen; chef Gerald Dougherty's longtime white-tablecloth past shows clearly in his out-there specialties, which include smoked duck and 'BBQ spaghetti.'

Little Saigon *Vietnamese* 25 | 10 | 20 | $26

Atlantic City | 2801 Arctic Ave. (Iowa Ave.) | 609-347-9119

"Authentic", "first-rate" Vietnamese cooking is the draw at this cash-only, off-the-boardwalk "find" in Atlantic City; granted, this small BYO has "no atmosphere" and is parked on an "uncharming street", but service is "friendly" and the price tags "relatively meager."

Little Tuna *Seafood* 23 | 20 | 22 | $35

Haddonfield | 141 Kings Hwy. E. (Haddon Ave.) | 856-795-0888 | www.thelittletuna.com

"Unencumbered" fish that's "as fresh as if you were in Hawaii" earns kudos at this "truly special" BYO seafooder set on the "quaint" main drag of "historic Haddonfield"; a "modern" setting, "attentive" service and "reasonable" prices add up to an overall "solid" dining experience.

LoBianco Ⓢ Ⓜ *American* - | - | - | M

Margate | 20 S. Douglas Ave. (bet. Atlantic & Ventnor Aves.) | 609-350-6493 | www.restaurantlobianco.com

From husband-and-wife team Nicholas and Stephanie LoBianco, this BYO New American bistro in Margate serves up moderately priced all-American faves such as short ribs, crab-cake sliders and fish 'n' chips in a bright, 'beach-casual' setting; hours vary by season, so call ahead or check the website.

Lobster House *Seafood* 20 | 17 | 18 | $40

Cape May | Fisherman's Wharf | 906 Schellengers Landing Rd. (Rte. 109) | 609-884-8296 | www.thelobsterhouse.com

This "quintessential" seafood experience-cum-"tourist trap" on Cape May's Fisherman's Wharf "never changes", providing "really good", "right-off-the-boat" fin fare in a "big", "not-fancy" setting since 1922; given the "long waits" and "too-fast" service, insiders opt for the raw bar or "take-out window" for speedier dining.

Locale *Italian* | 20 | 21 | 18 | $56

Closter | 208 Piermont Rd. (Ruckman Rd.) | 201-750-3233 | www.locale208closter.com

There's "nothing 'local'" about this ambitious, "special occasion"–worthy Closter spot serving "delicious" modern Italian food in "spacious", "beautiful" digs; it's "very pricey" and service is "competent", but fans feel it "has the potential to become an excellent restaurant."

Lola Latin Bistro Ⓜ *Pan-Latin* | - | - | - | M

Metuchen | 87 Central Ave. (bet. Durham & Middlesex Aves.) | 732-548-5652 | www.lolalatinbistro.com

The creative tapas and appetizers outnumber the entrees at this lively Pan-Latin BYO in Metuchen; it moved to its current Central Avenue location in September 2011.

Lola's *Spanish* | ▽ 18 | 18 | 18 | $40

Hoboken | 153 14th St. (Bloomfield St.) | 201-420-6062 | www.lolas-tapas-wine-bar-hoboken.com

Hot and cold tapas from both land and sea comprise the menu of this Hoboken Spanish wine bar, a decent "date-night" place thanks to an indoor courtyard with a "running fountain" and tables fashioned from wine barrels; sure, the small-plate tabs can really "add up", but it's "definitely worth the cost."

🄯 Lorena's Ⓜ *French* | 28 | 22 | 27 | $63

Maplewood | 168 Maplewood Ave. (Highland Pl.) | 973-763-4460 | www.restaurantlorena.com

Close to "perfect", this "spectacular" Maplewood BYO overseen by chef Humberto Campos Jr. offers "sublime" cuisine with such "superb attention to detail" that it's rated NJ's Top French restaurant; granted, it's "unaffordable on a regular basis" and the ultra-"compact" setting means "you'll need to reserve weeks in advance", but given the "flawless" service and "super-romantic" mood, many say it "doesn't get any better" than this.

Los Amigos *Mexican/Southwestern* | 23 | 18 | 22 | $31

Atlantic City | 1926 Atlantic Ave. (bet. Michigan & Ohio Aves.) | 609-344-2293
West Berlin | 461 Rte. 73 N. (Franklin Ave.) | 856-767-5216 Ⓜ www.losamigosrest.com

These "long-standing" cantinas in Atlantic City and West Berlin pair "mouthwatering" Mexican-Southwestern chow with "great" margaritas; fans ignore the "so-so" decor and focus instead on the "festive" mood and "consistently good" service.

Lotus Cafe *Chinese* | 23 | 13 | 19 | $24

Hackensack | Hackensack Plaza | 450 Hackensack Ave. (Rte. 4) | 201-488-7070 | www.lotuscafenj.com

An "unpretentious" Hackensack strip mall near the upscale Shops at Riverside houses this "deservedly popular", "white-tablecloth" BYO offering "high-quality" Chinese dishes for "reasonable" dough; those who find the "attentive" service too "hurried" opt for takeout.

LouCás *Italian*   23 | 18 | 21 | $40

Edison | Colonial Village Shopping Ctr. | 9 Lincoln Hwy. (Parsonage Rd.) | 732-549-8580 | www.loucasristorante.com

There's "value with a capital V" at this "upscale" Italian BYO in an Edison strip mall serving "large, luscious portions" of seafood and pasta abetted by an "array of creative specials"; maybe it's "noisy" and the decor's "not particularly memorable", but service is "attentive" and the atmosphere "family-friendly."

Luca's Ristorante *Italian*   24 | 20 | 21 | $34

Somerset | 2019 Rte. 27 (bet. Cozzens & Finnegans Lns.) | 732-297-7676 | www.lucasristorante.com

"Easily overlooked" in a "hidden" Somerset strip mall, this "step-up-from-the-ordinary" BYO serves a "unique" Italian menu that's "plated with serious attention"; though the decor splits surveyors – "cute" vs. "over-the-top" – there's agreement on the "midrange" pricing and "friendly" service.

Luce *Italian*   22 | 21 | 21 | $42

Caldwell | 115 Bloomfield Ave. (Elm Rd.) | 973-403-8500 | www.lucerestaurant.com

"Trendy" Caldwell types say this Italian BYO is *the* neighborhood place" thanks to its "tasty" vittles, "lovely presentation" and "feel-like-family" mood; maybe it's a tad "pricey", but in return you get a "diversified" menu, "terrific" service and a "lively" scene; the post-Survey arrival of chef Steven Saragnese (former sous-chef at Babbo) may not be reflected in the Food score.

Luciano's *Italian*   24 | 22 | 24 | $46

Rahway | 1579 Main St. (Monroe St.) | 732-815-1200 | www.lucianosristorante.com

Parked "in the center of Rahway", this Italian "delight" purveys an "outstanding" menu of "authentic" items in a "pretty", Tuscan-inspired setting, complete with a fireplace and a "busy" bar; the pricing suggests its "fine-dining" airs, but fans say it's worth it for a "special occasion."

Lucky Bones   20 | 16 | 18 | $32
Backwater Grille ☉ *American*

Cape May | 1200 Rte. 109 S. (3rd Ave.) | 609-884-2663 | www.luckybonesgrille.com

"Made-from-scratch comfort food" that's "fairly priced" draws a "family" crowd to this "downscale" Cape May American, an "oasis of normal" amid a stretch of fine-dining establishments; it's revered for its "yummy" thin-crust pizza, not the "high noise level."

Luigi's *Italian*   ▽ 26 | 18 | 25 | $38

East Hanover | Berkeley Plaza | 434 Ridgedale Ave. (McKinley Ave.) | 973-887-8408 | www.luigisrestaurant.info

"Cooked-to-perfection" Italian fare from a "creative" Puglia-born chef awaits at this "upscale" "hidden treasure" lodged in an East

Hanover strip mall; maybe the "tables are too close together", but overall it's "reliable" enough to have "special-night-out" appeal.

Luigi's Ⓜ️ *Italian* | - | - | - | M |

Ridgefield Park | 54 Mt. Vernon St. (Main St.) | 201-641-9869 | www.luigisinthepark.com

"Old-fashioned red sauce" right out of "nonna's" kitchen is yours at this Ridgefield Park "neighborhood" staple that's been a "longtime favorite" since 1948; devotees find everything at this "real thing" to be "totally delicious", save for the decor.

Luka's Ⓢ *Italian* | 23 | 12 | 20 | $34 |

Ridgefield Park | 238 Main St. (Park St.) | 201-440-2996 | www.lukasitaliancuisine.com

The "restaurant version of *Cheers*", this casual Ridgefield Park BYO draws locals with "wonderful" Italian chow at a "moderate" price, backed up by "friendly", "attentive" service; the "tables are close" in the "tiny" storefront setting and it's "a bit noisy", but that's why it feels "like dinner with the family."

Luke Palladino *Italian* | ▽ 26 | 18 | 23 | $49 |

NEW Atlantic City | Harrah's | 777 Harrah's Blvd. (Brigantine Blvd.) | 609-441-5576 | www.harrahsresort.com
Northfield | Plaza 9 Shopping Ctr. | 1333 New Rd. (Tilton Rd.) | 609-646-8189 | www.lukepalladino.com

Modern Italian "dining bliss" lands in Northfield via this storefront BYO from the eponymous chef, where the "beautifully prepared" seasonal menu emerges from an "open kitchen"; though it's so "tiny" that it's "hard to get a reservation", most are "ecstatic" to get one; P.S. the outpost in AC's Harrah's opened post-Survey.

Luna Rossa Ⓜ️ *Italian* | - | - | - | I |

Sicklerville | 3210 Rte. 42 (Woodlawn Ave.) | 856-728-4505 | www.lambertis.com

Locals are "fond" of Giuseppe Lamberti's contemporary Italian BYO in Sicklerville for generous portions "prepared to perfection" at "reasonable" prices; the attentive management "makes sure all is well."

Lu Nello Ⓢ *Italian* | 25 | 23 | 24 | $63 |

Cedar Grove | 182 Stevens Ave. (Lindsley Rd.) | 973-837-1660 | www.lunello.com

"Everyone knows everyone" at this "elegant" Cedar Grove Italian, famed for its cameo appearance in "*The Real Housewives of NJ*" and patronized for its "luscious" food served by a "sharp" team that rattles off an "impossible-to-remember" list of specials; the crowd's "half *Godfather*, half *Jersey Shore*", the tabs "best enjoyed on an expense account" and it really "helps to be a regular" here.

Madame Claude Cafe Ⓜ️⇄ *French* | 23 | 15 | 21 | $35 |

Jersey City | 364½ Fourth St. (Brunswick St.) | 201-876-8800 | www.madameclaudecafe.com

One of Jersey City's "best-kept secrets", this "cheerful", "cash-only" BYO offers "comforting", reasonably priced French bistro items in

| | FOOD | DECOR | SERVICE | COST |

"beat-up", "hipster-chic" environs; fans like the "down-to-earth" vibe and head for the outdoor tables when it gets too "cramped" inside.

Mad Batter *American*
23 | **19** | **21** | **$33**

Cape May | Carroll Villa Hotel | 19 Jackson St. (bet. Beach Ave. & Carpenter Ln.) | 609-884-5970 | www.madbatter.com

Renowned as a "great breakfast place", this "quaint" Cape May American also plies "prepared-to-perfection" lunches and dinners in a "homey" Victorian B&B (nothing beats "sitting on the veranda drinking something fun" here); still, fans say it's "worth a drive from anywhere" for its "classic eggs Benedict" alone.

Madeleine's Petit Paris Ⓜ *French*
25 | **21** | **25** | **$52**

Northvale | 416 Tappan Rd. (Paris Ave.) | 201-767-0063 | www.madeleinespetitparis.com

"*Très bien*" cooking and "gracious" service transport fans to "Paris" at this "charming" Northvale "neighborhood gem" where the "kitchen speaks fluent French"; some find the "Edith Piaf" mood a little too "old-world" (ditto the "grandmother's house" decor), but on the whole it's good for a "traditional" dining experience; P.S. Tuesday night welcomes BYO with no corkage fee.

Madison Bar & Grill *American*
19 | **19** | **19** | **$36**

Hoboken | 1316 Washington St. (14th St.) | 201-386-0300 | www.madisonbarandgrill.com

The food's "decent" enough, but the "scene" is better at this "neighborly" New American on a Hoboken corner that attracts "young, boisterous" things with its "simple" menu and "great-value" prix fixes; it's a "total meat market" on weekends, leading to service that's "adequate but not inspired."

Maggiano's Little Italy *Italian*
20 | **18** | **19** | **$34**

Hackensack | Riverside Sq. Mall | 390 Hackensack Ave. (Rte. 4) | 201-221-2030
Bridgewater | Village of the Bridgewater Commons | 600 Commons Way (bet. Prince Rodgers Ave. & Rte. 22) | 908-547-6045
Cherry Hill | Cherry Hill Mall | 2000 Rte. 38 (Haddonfield Rd.) | 856-792-4470
www.maggianos.com

"*Mangia, mangia!*" – you "get your money's worth and then some" at this "vintage", "family-style" chain known for "humongous" "feasts" of "commercial" "Italian standards done right", as well as "long waits" and "noise"; while some purists would leave the "fake" "corporate" experience to "tourists and suburbanites", the majority considers it "generally a crowd-pleaser."

Magic Pot Ⓜ *Fondue*
▽ **18** | **15** | **19** | **$41**

Edgewater | 934 River Rd. (bet. Dempsey & Hilliard Aves.) | 201-969-0400 | www.magicpotfondue.com

This "amiable" Edgewater BYO rolls out a "sumptuous choice" of Caribbean-, French- and Asian-accented fondues; though some find it "gimmicky" and "a little pricey", others say this "change of pace" is "fun" for a date or group outing.

		FOOD	DECOR	SERVICE	COST

Mahzu *Japanese*
20 | 16 | 18 | $31

East Windsor | 761 Rte. 33 W. (bet. Hickory Corner & Wyeth Rds.) | 609-371-2888
Aberdeen | Aberdeen Plaza | 1077 Rte. 34 (Lloyd Rd.) | 732-583-8985
Freehold | 430 Mounts Corner Dr. (Soloman Way) | 732-866-9668
www.mahzu.net

These centrally located triplets in Aberdeen, East Windsor and Freehold are "safe" bets for "good", "plain-Jane" sushi or "fun" hibachi shows that appeal to small fry; the decor's "minimal" and the service "variable" (sometimes "slow", sometimes "too rushed"), yet these BYOs are "decent" options given their "reasonable" costs.

Main Street *American/Continental*
19 | 18 | 19 | $35

Kingston | 4581 Rte. 27 (Laurel Ave.) | 609-921-2778
Princeton | Princeton Shopping Ctr. | 301 N. Harrison St. (Valley Rd.) | 609-921-2779
www.mainstreetprinceton.com

"What a 'local spot' is supposed to be", this Princeton "neighborhood bistro" and its Kingston sibling feature an "unfussy, moderately priced" menu of American-Continental standards that may be a little "mundane" but is perfect for "visiting parents"; the former's "cool patio bar" trumps the "dreary" dining room and "inconsistent" service, while the latter features a gourmet bakery.

Maize ● *American*
∇ 17 | 18 | 16 | $43

Newark | Best Western Robert Treat Hotel | 50 Park Pl. (bet. Center & Park Sts.) | 973-733-2202 | www.maizerestaurant.com

Portuguese accents add some zip to the "upscale" New Americana served at this Newark venue in the Best Western Robert Treat Hotel opposite NJPAC; though the setting's looking "tired" and the "decent" staffers "can't handle" the pre-theater crowds, at least it's "nice for drinks."

Makeda *Ethiopian*
24 | 23 | 21 | $38

New Brunswick | 338 George St. (bet. Bayard St. & Livingston Ave.) | 732-545-5115 | www.makedas.com

A "great excuse to eat with your hands", this "utensils-optional", "something-different" Ethiopian in Downtown New Brunswick lures "adventurous" eaters with "delicious" dishes served in "hip", "urban"-chic digs; it "adds to the cool factor of the city" and is a "pre-theater must" for showgoers headed for the nearby State Theater.

Manolo's *Mediterranean/Spanish*
∇ 25 | 20 | 24 | $45

Elizabeth | 91 Elizabeth Ave. (1st St.) | 908-353-7674 | www.manolosrestaurant.com

"Hidden" away in Elizabeth one block from Arthur Kill Park, this "classy" Spanish-Mediterranean has been on the scene since 1985 serving a "delicious" menu in an "intimate", white-tablecloth setting; fun fact: its courtly, old-world ambiance earned it the role of Vesuvio's in *The Sopranos*.

	FOOD	DECOR	SERVICE	COST

Manon ⓂⒷ French
25 | 21 | 22 | $48

Lambertville | 19 N. Union St. (Bridge St.) | 609-397-2596
For "authentic south-of-France cooking" in Lambertville, check out this "cute" French BYO that's been serving "sumptuous" Provençal fare since 1989; the "colorful" setting comes complete with a reproduction of Van Gogh's "'Starry Night' on the ceiling" that helps distract from its "tiny", "tight" dimensions; P.S. dinner only, Wednesday–Sunday.

Ⓩ Manor, The Ⓜ American
24 | 26 | 25 | $64

West Orange | 111 Prospect Ave. (Woodland Ave.) | 973-731-2360 | www.themanorrestaurant.com
Everything's pretty "perfect" at this "legendary" West Orange Traditional American, revered for its "high-class" food (especially that "overwhelming" lobster buffet) and "over-the-top", "fairy-tale" setting reminiscent of "dining at Versailles"; granted, it's "expensive" and a tad too "glitzy" for some, but overall this "first-class" experience can't be beat for "pomp-and-circumstance" dining.

Mantra Indian
22 | 22 | 21 | $41

NEW **Jersey City** | 253 Washington St. (bet. Montgomery & York Sts.) | 201-333-8699
Paramus | 275 Rte. 4 W. (bet. Bogert Rd. & Forest Ave.) | 201-342-8868 | www.mantranj.com
"Sleek, stylish" and "sophisticated", this "hip" contemporary Indian in a Paramus strip mall is known for its "unusual", "creative" cooking, "dark", "sexy" setting and "polite", "soft-spoken" staffers; maybe the pricing's rather "high" for the genre, but it compensates with a "great"-value all-you-can-eat lunch buffet; the Jersey City outpost opened post-Survey.

Marco & Pepe Ⓜ American
22 | 17 | 17 | $37

Jersey City | 289 Grove St. (Mercer St.) | 201-860-9688 | www.marcoandpepe.com
"Innovative" New American comfort food is offered in small plate- or entree-size portions at this "always crowded" Jersey City joint that seduces "local hipsters" with its "shabby-chic" looks and very "chilltown" vibe; though service can veer from "hurried" to "slow", most patrons are too "laid-back" to notice.

Margherita's Ⓜ Italian
22 | 13 | 18 | $26

Hoboken | 740 Washington St. (8th St.) | 201-222-2400
"Good for the classics", this Hoboken Italian BYO is touted for its "fantastic" pizzas, "big portions" of homemade pastas and "inexpensive" tabs; the "small, tight" setting and "no-reservations" policy detract, but outdoor seats help to ease the squeeze and sidestep the "hectic" goings-on inside during the warmer months.

Maritime Parc Ⓜ American/Seafood
- | - | - | E

Jersey City | Liberty State Park | 84 Audrey Zapp Dr. (bet. Freedom Way & Phillip St.) | 201-413-0050 | www.maritimeparc.com
Nestled by the marina in Liberty State Park, this high-end Jersey City eatery features a seasonally oriented New American seafood menu;

the yachtlike, blond-wood design is a match for the drop-dead views of the Hudson River and Lower Manhattan, best savored from its outdoor patio.

Market Roost Ⓜ Eclectic
▽ 22 | 12 | 15 | $23

Flemington | 65 Main St. (Bloomfield Ave.) | 908-788-4949 | www.marketroost.com

"Friendly" Flemington is home to this "interesting" Eclectic BYO that serves "terrific" chow and doubles as a gift gallery (the "junky trinkets" for sale help distract from the "blah" decor and so-so service); P.S. serves breakfast and lunch Tuesday–Sunday, and dinner on Thursday and Friday only.

NEW Marlene Mangia Bene Ⓢ Italian
- | - | - | M

Woodbury | 43 S. Broad St. (Curtis Ave.) | 856-848-8488 | www.marlenemangiabene.com

There's a friendly Sunday-dinner vibe at this low-key Italian BYO in the Gloucester County seat of Woodbury run by restaurant rookies armed with big dreams and Mamma Marlene's homey recipes; modest prices make it suitable for a weekday business lunch, and the white-tablecloth atmosphere has you covered for weekend date night.

Martini Bistro & Bar American
19 | 19 | 19 | $40

Millburn | 40 Main St. (Millburn Ave.) | 973-376-4444 | www.martinibistro.com

More about its "busy bar" than its dining room, this Millburn "meat-market" magnet for "cougars" and "mature men" serves a "well-prepared" New American menu that plays second fiddle to all the "frisky" goings-on; an "amazing" martini list blunts the somewhat "expensive" tabs.

Martini 494 Ⓢ American
- | - | - | E

Newark | 494 Broad St. (bet. Bridge & Orange Sts.) | 973-642-4900 | www.martini494bistro.com

A sibling to Millburn's Martini Bistro & Bar, this trendy Downtown Newark New American mixes high-end surf 'n' turf and specialty cocktails with more casual bar fare and tap brews; the upscale decor includes a communal table made from reclaimed pine wood.

Martino's Ⓜ Cuban
22 | 13 | 20 | $25

Somerville | 212 W. Main St. (Doughty Ave.) | 908-722-8602 | www.martinoscubanrestaurant.com

You get "a lot of flavor for little *dinero*" at this "family-run" Somerville Cuban dishing out "hearty", "hits-the-spot" chow in a distinctly "no-frills" setting; the $9 lunch buffet is the "best deal around", while BYO adds to the "good value."

Mastoris ◑ Diner
19 | 13 | 20 | $24

Bordentown | 144 Rte. 130 (Rte. 206) | 609-298-4650 | www.mastoris.com

NJ diners don't get more "typical" than this "ultimate" version parked on a "busy" Bordentown crossroads, which "seats hundreds" and slings an "immense" menu of usual-suspects eats (including its trademark complimentary cinnamon and cheese breads); it all comes "fast" and at "normal" prices, amid "seriously outdated" decor.

Matisse *American*

22	23	22	$49

Belmar | 1300 Ocean Ave. (13th Ave.) | 732-681-7680 | www.matissecatering.com

"Right on the beach", this "romantic" Belmar BYO boasts "stunning" ocean views that make the "exemplary", "well-prepared" American bill of fare taste even better; service is "knowledgeable" and the decor "bright and attractive", but some "wish it were more affordable."

☑ Mattar's Bistro ● *American*

24	23	25	$37

Allamuchy | 1115 Rte. 517 (Ridge Rd.) | 908-852-2300 | www.mattarsbistro.com

"Reinvention can be rewarding" at this "middle-of-nowhere" Allamuchy venue that's now "less formal" than before and plying a "delicious", more accessible New American menu backed up by a "happening happy hour"; old-timers say they "miss the old" place, but most say the "transformation has worked magic."

Matt's Red Rooster Grill Ⓜ *American*

26	22	25	$48

Flemington | 22 Bloomfield Ave. (Main St.) | 908-788-7050 | www.mattsredroostergrill.com

Chef-owner Matt McPherson turns out "ingenious" New American dishes ("perfectly cooked" on a wood-fired grill) at this "charming" Flemington BYO; "attentive" service and a "tastefully renovated" setting in a Victorian home make the "pricey" tabs more tolerable.

Max's Seafood Café 🅂Ⓜ *Seafood*

-	-	-	M

Gloucester | 34 N. Burlington St. (Hudson St.) | 856-456-9774 | www.maxsseafoodcafe.com

This Gloucester seafooder flexes its mussels and other fin fare in a building dating back to 1890 (and refurbished in 2000), notable for its handcrafted bar, stained-glass fixtures and Victorian-era tin ceiling; the moderately priced menu is backed by a solid lineup of beers from Belgium, Germany and elsewhere, plus selections from a 2,000-bottle wine cellar.

McCormick & Schmick's *Seafood*

20	19	19	$43

Hackensack | Shops at Riverside | 175 Riverside Sq. (Hackensack Ave.) | 201-968-9410

Bridgewater | Bridgewater Commons | 400 Commons Way (Rte. 206) | 908-707-9996

Atlantic City | Harrah's | 777 Harrah's Blvd. (Brigantine Blvd.) | 609-441-5579

Cherry Hill | Garden State Park | 941 Haddonfield Rd. (Rte. 70) | 856-317-1711

www.mccormickandschmicks.com

An "enjoyable" choice for "business and pleasure", this "upscale" seafood chain offers a "daily changing" menu of "freshly caught" fare in an "upbeat" atmosphere; though it feels too "stamped-out-of-a-mold" for some, its "professional" service is a plus and the "happy-hour bar menu" lures the after-work crowd.

	FOOD	DECOR	SERVICE	COST

McGovern's Tavern ● ⊘ 🅩 *Pub Food* ▽ 18 | 15 | 21 | $22

Newark | 58 New St. (bet. Halsey & Washington Sts.) | 973-643-3984 |
www.mcgovernstavern.com

Since 1936, this "dive bar extraordinaire" in Downtown Newark has
been drawing everyone from "business execs" to "dock workers" with
its "dependable" pub grub, washed down with a "fantastically poured"
Guinness; "friendly conversation" and "cheap" tabs are bonuses.

McLoone's *American* 17 | 22 | 19 | $42

NEW **West Orange** | South Mountain Recreation Complex |
9 Cherry Ln. (Northfield Ave.) | 862-252-7108 |
www.mcloonesboathouse.com
Fords | 3 Lafayette Rd. (Ford Ave.) | 732-512-5025 | www.mcloones.com
Asbury Park | 1200 Ocean Ave. (bet. 4th & 5th Aves.) | 732-774-1400 |
www.mcloones.com
Long Branch | 1 Ocean Ave. (Seaview Ave.) | 732-923-1006 |
www.mcloones.com
Sea Bright | 816 Ocean Ave. (Rumson Rd.) | 732-842-2894 |
www.mcloones.com

The casual vittles are "hit-or-miss" and "expensive for what you get"
at this American quintet from restaurateur Tim McLoone; the Shore
locations (Asbury Park, Sea Bright and Pier Village at Long Branch)
offer "spectacular" water views, as does the West Orange location
(which opened post-Survey) overlooking the Orange Reservoir,
while the Fords outlet, off an OTW parlor, allows you to "eat a
burger" while "watching a horse race" on the TV in your booth.

Mediterra *Mediterranean* 20 | 22 | 20 | $46

Princeton | 29 Hulfish St. (bet. Chambers & Witherspoon Sts.) |
609-252-9680 | www.mediterrarestaurant.com

Capturing the "essence of the Mediterranean", this "popular"
Princetonian via the Momo brothers (Eno Terra, Teresa Caffe) is "centrally located" on Palmer Square; admirers tout the "cosmopolitan" decor, "attentive" service and "quite nice" alfresco seats, but cynics
cite "Princeton prices" and think the "kitchen is treading water."

Meemah 🅜 *Chinese/Malaysian* 25 | 11 | 20 | $24

Edison | Colonial Village Shopping Ctr. | 9 Lincoln Hwy. (Parsonage Rd.) |
732-906-2223 | www.meemah.com

"Consistently good" food that "you can't easily find anyplace else"
turns up at this BYO "adventure" in an Edison strip mall, serving a
mix of "excellent", "old-school" Chinese with some "cut-above"
Malaysian dishes; but this "cramped" "hole-in-the-wall" has "no
ambiance", so aesthetes reserve it for "takeout."

Megu Sushi *Japanese* ▽ 23 | 17 | 20 | $30

Cherry Hill | Tuscany Mktpl. | 1990 Rte. 70 E. (Old Orchard Rd.) |
856-489-6228
Moorestown | 300 Young Ave. (bet. Centerton Rd. & County Rd. 537) |
856-780-6327
www.megusushi.com

"Creative sushi chefs" slice up "clean, fresh" fish at this Cherry Hill
BYO that also offers "pretty good" hibachi grilling (unlike the

Moorestown sibling); "friendly" staffers and "reasonable" tabs compensate for the "stark" surroundings.

Mehndi 🅼 Indian   24 | 24 | 22 | $44

Morristown | 88 Headquarters Plaza | 3 Speedwell Ave. (Park Pl.) | 973-871-2323 | www.mehtanirestaurantgroup.com

"Heavenly" Indian fare comes with "real heat if you want it" at this "exotic" spot set in a Morristown mall; "excellent" service and "modern" decor enhance the "sophisticated" experience, while a $13 lunch buffet is a low-cost alternative to the otherwise "high-end" tabs.

Meil's 🍴 American   24 | 16 | 20 | $29

Stockton | Bridge & Main Sts. | 609-397-8033 | www.meilsrestaurant.com

"Damn good", "seriously filling" American "home cooking" turns up at this "sincerely friendly", all-day affair set in a "nothing-fancy" "converted gas station" in Stockton; breakfast is the favorite 'meil', while BYO and cash-only policies keep prices down.

Mekong Grill 🅼 Vietnamese   - | - | - | I

Ridgewood | 24 Chestnut St. (bet. Franklin & Ridgewood Aves.) | 201-445-0011 | www.mekonggrillrestaurant.com

This casual little BYO storefront in Ridgewood focuses on traditional Southern Vietnamese specialties yet also includes some Northern dishes like pho; the contemporary space is outfitted in warm wood and decorated with oversize photos of menu favorites.

Mélange @ Haddonfield 🅼 Italian/Southern   25 | 22 | 23 | $40

Haddonfield | 18 Tanner St. (Kings Hwy.) | 856-354-1333 | www.melangerestaurants.com

"New Orleans meets Haddonfield" (with a dash of Italy in the mix) at this "interesting" Southern belle BYO helmed by the "delightful" Joe Brown, whose "unpretentious" Creole menu includes both "typical and unusual choices"; "warm" service and "festive" atmospherics make it a good alternative for those who "can't get to the Big Easy."

Melting Pot Fondue   19 | 20 | 20 | $46

Hoboken | 100 Sinatra Dr. (1st St.) | 201-222-1440
Westwood | 250 Center Ave. (Westwood Ave.) | 201-664-8877
Somerville | 190 W. Main St. (Doughty Ave.) | 908-575-8010
Whippany | Pine Plaza Shopping Ctr. | 831 Rte. 10 (Jefferson Rd.) | 973-428-5400
Red Bank | The Galleria | 2 Bridge Ave. (Front St.) | 732-219-0090
Atlantic City | 2112 Atlantic Ave. (Arkansas Ave.) | 609-441-1100
www.meltingpot.com

"It's all about sharing" and "cooking your own food" at this chain serving almost "every kind of fondue"; while it's a "romantic" "treat" for "younger couples" and "fun with a group", critics contend it's "overpriced"; P.S. go with a large party if you want "two burners."

Memphis Pig Out BBQ   19 | 13 | 17 | $29

Atlantic Highlands | 67 First Ave. (Center Ave.) | 732-291-5533 | www.memphispigout.com

The "name says it all" at this "kitschy" "neighborhood" fixture in Atlantic Highlands where "fall-off-the-bone-tasty" BBQ keeps customers "pigging out"; the "well-worn" digs done up with an "unending display of pig paraphernalia" could sure use a "makeover", but the "fun" mood and "cheap" tabs are fine as is.

Merion Inn *American*
24 | 22 | 24 | $44

Cape May | 106 Decatur St. (Columbia Ave.) | 609-884-8363 | www.merioninn.com

This "refined" Cape May "tradition" may be done up in "charming" Victorian style, but its "quite good" Traditional American cooking is decidedly "21st century" and draws a "polo-shirt" and "driving-mocs" crowd; "impeccable" service, nightly piano music and "hard-to-beat" early-bird deals make this a "throwback in a positive way."

Mesob Ⓜ *Ethiopian*
24 | 22 | 24 | $32

Montclair | 515 Bloomfield Ave. (bet. Fullerton Ave. & Park St.) | 973-655-9000 | www.mesobrestaurant.com

"Finger food never felt so refined" as at this Montclair Ethiopian BYO where the "exotic", "made-with-care" specialties can be scooped up with spongy injera bread; "informative" service and a "cool, calm", "high-ceilinged" setting enhance the "classy" mood at this "nice break from the standard."

Mesón Madrid *Spanish*
18 | 13 | 17 | $39

Palisades Park | 343 Bergen Blvd. (Palisades Blvd.) | 201-947-1038 | www.mesonmadridrestaurant.com

"Still reliable" after 30 years, this Palisades Park "standby" offers a "must-love-garlic" Spanish menu in "plentiful" portions for "bargain" sums; even though the decor's "dumpy" and the service "ho-hum", it sure "fills up fast on the weekend."

Metropolitan Cafe *Pacific Rim*
21 | 21 | 20 | $41

Freehold | 8 E. Main St. (South St.) | 732-780-9400 | www.greatrestaurantsnj.com

"Consistently good" Pacific Rim cuisine and a "lively" bar scene collide at this "trendy", "NYC-style" Freehold spot that's most beloved for its "large martini menu"; "energetic" service, "nice" patio seating and a "fun" vibe make the "pricey" tabs easier to swallow.

Mexican Food Factory *Mexican*
20 | 17 | 18 | $27

Marlton | 601 Rte. 70 W. (Cropwell Rd.) | 856-983-9222

Despite its name, this "low-key" Marlton Mexican is "not a chain", rather a "comfortable" family-owned indie around for more than three decades; though the "reasonably priced" food can be "hit-or-miss", the decor rises above the "stereotypical" with "Frida Kahlo art" on the walls.

Meyersville Inn Ⓜ *Eclectic*
19 | 19 | 19 | $38

Gillette | 632 Meyersville Rd. (New Vernon Rd.) | 908-647-6302 | www.meyersvilleinn.net

Patrons "never know what to expect" at this "remodeled" Gillette tavern – it "changes hands so frequently it's hard to keep up"; currently, the "tasty" Eclectic menu has a strong Cajun accent and seafood emphasis, while the "cozy" atmosphere and outdoor dining remain as "nice" as ever.

Mia 🛍Ⓜ *Italian* | 26 | 25 | 24 | $57 |

Atlantic City | Caesars on the Boardwalk | 2100 Pacific Ave. (Arkansas Ave.) | 609-441-2345 | www.miaac.com

An "amazing", "Roman temple–style" space just off the lobby of Caesars in Atlantic City is the site of this "classy" Italian "getaway" via Georges Perrier and Chris Scarduzio; patrons "feel like Zeus himself" as they dine on the "stellar" specialties, and though it's "quite expensive", the prix fixe dinner specials are an "outstanding value."

Mi Bandera *Cuban* | ∇ 24 | 14 | 21 | $34 |

Union City | 518 32nd St. (bet. Central & Summit Aves.) | 201-348-2828 | www.mibanderanj.com

Set above a same-named Latin American supermarket in Union City, this casual Cuban "mainstay" attracts expats with "traditional" "meaty" menus served in *"Flintstones"*-size portions; "cheap" lunchtime specials keep frugalistas coming back for more.

Midori *Japanese* | 21 | 15 | 20 | $29 |

Denville | Denville Commons Mall | 3130 Rte. 10 W. (bet. Franklin & Hill Rds.) | 973-537-8588 | www.midorirestaurant.com

"Excellent" sushi and an "extensive" menu of cooked items arrive "fast" at this "favorite" Japanese BYO located in a Denville strip mall; lunchbox specials, website coupons and an "endless", all-you-can-eat "bargain" buffet on Mondays please penny-pinchers.

Mie Thai *Thai* | 24 | 14 | 18 | $24 |

Woodbridge | 34 Main St. (Berry St.) | 732-596-9400 | www.miethai.com

"Amazing value" keeps regulars regular at this BYO Thai parked in a strip mall opposite Woodbridge Town Hall, where the "excellent", "authentic" specialties are on the "spicy" side; "generous" portions and "friendly" service make up for "very little ambiance."

Mignon Steakhouse *Steak* | 22 | 18 | 20 | $47 |

Rutherford | 72 Park Ave. (Franklin Pl.) | 201-896-0202 | www.villagerestaurantgroup.com

"Prime" meats weigh in at an "affordable price" at this Rutherford chop shop where BYO "helps keep the costs down"; though some beef about "inconsistent" cooking and only "fair" decor, others insist it's "as good as any NYC steakhouse."

Mikado *Japanese* | 23 | 20 | 21 | $32 |

Cherry Hill | 2320 Rte. 70 W. (Union Ave.) | 856-665-4411
Maple Shade | 468 S. Lenola Rd. (Kings Hwy.) | 856-638-1801
Marlton | Elmwood Shopping Ctr. | 793 Rte. 70 E. (Troth Rd.) | 856-797-8581
www.mikado-us.com

This "family-oriented" South Jersey Japanese trio earns kudos for its "well-done sushi" and "tasty" hibachi items, and the "comfortable" surroundings and "always good" service also earn praise; P.S. the Cherry Hill outpost is BYO.

	FOOD	DECOR	SERVICE	COST

☒ Milford Oyster House *Seafood* `27` `21` `26` `$45`

Milford | 92 Rte. 519 (York St.) | 908-995-9411 |
www.milfordoysterhouse.com

Set in a "cozy" stone structure, this Milford seafooder offers a "superb" menu that goes beyond oysters and "fancy fish" to include beef and pork (a tavern room features its own more casual menu); "genuine hospitality" and an "unpretentious" mood make the "pricey" tabs easier to digest.

Mill at Spring Lake Heights ☒ *American* `21` `24` `22` `$43`

Spring Lake Heights | 101 Old Mill Rd. (Ocean Rd.) | 732-449-1800 |
www.themillnj.com

A lakeside location – with "beautiful" views of Old Mill Pond – and a "modern" interior supply the "superb" atmosphere at this Spring Lake Heights "classic"; "better-than-average" American cuisine, "nice" service and "terrific" fixed-price meals appeal to "mature diners" and "special-occasion" celebrants.

Minado *Japanese* `20` `14` `16` `$34`

Little Ferry | 1 Valley Rd. (Waterside Dr.) | 201-931-1522
Morris Plains | 2888 Rte. 10 W. (bet. Powder Mill Rd. & Yacenda Dr.) |
973-734-4900
www.minado.com

These "popular" links of the Japanese buffet chain are "houses of gluttony", offering an "astonishing" array of "all-you-can-gorge" sushi and cooked items in "glorified cafeteria" settings; they're "fast-moving" (verging on "factorylike") and you get a lot for "little money" – hence their popularity with "families" and the "very hungry."

Ming ☒ *Asian* `24` `23` `22` `$40`

Edison | Oak Tree Shopping Ctr. | 1655-185 Oak Tree Rd. (bet. Grove & Wood Aves.) | 732-549-5051 | www.mingrestaurants.com

Ming II ☒ *Asian*

Morristown | 88 Headquarters Plaza | 3 Speedwell Ave. (Park Pl.) |
973-871-2323 | www.ming2morristown.com

"Out-of-the-ordinary" Pan-Asian fare with a pronounced Indian accent turns up at these ambitious eateries in Edison and Morristown; sure, they're a bit "pricey" for the genre, but partisans say it's worth it for a taste of something "totally different" from the norm.

Mister C's Beach Bistro *Seafood* `18` `18` `19` `$43`

Allenhurst | 1 Allen Ave. (Ocean Pl.) | 732-531-3665 |
www.mistercsbeachbistro.com

It's easy to "get lost" in the "fabulous" view of the ocean from the bar of this Allenhurst seafood "standby" (it's so close to the water that "you feel like you're on a cruise ship"); otherwise, the "ok" food and service are "inconsistent", and the interior "could be updated."

NEW MK Valencia *American/Italian* `-` `-` `-` `M`

Ridgefield Park | 228 Main St. (Park St.) | 201-494-4830 |
www.mkvalenciarestaurant.com

A stunning graphite-toned interior sets the stage for an elegant Italian–New American menu at this sexy Ridgefield Park newcomer;

singles mingle around the glitzy granite bar–cum–seafood display separating the lounge from the dining area, with its wall of personal wine lockers, while glass doors open onto a dramatically lit garden.

Moghul Ⓜ *Indian*
23 | 19 | 20 | $34

Edison | Oak Tree Shopping Ctr. | 1655-195 Oak Tree Rd. (bet. Grove & Wood Aves.) | 732-549-5050 | www.moghul.com
Despite "steep competition" in the Edison area, this "long-established" Indian BYO has a "dependable" reputation thanks to its "authentically spiced" subcontinental cuisine and "sophisticated" ambiance; though the à la carte prices are "on the upper side", the $11.50 lunchtime buffet is an "amazing value."

Mohawk House *American*
22 | 24 | 21 | $46

Sparta | 3 Sparta Jct. (Rte. 15) | 973-729-6464 | www.mohawkhouse.com
Quite the "hot spot" despite a "middle-of-nowhere" address in Sparta, this New American offers "creative takes on traditional" dishes, but is more renowned for its rustic setting that includes a "magnificent fireplace" and "beautiful" sunset views from the patio; even though it's on the "expensive" side, it's a "top choice" nonetheless.

Mojave Grille *Southwestern*
23 | 18 | 20 | $37

Westfield | 35 Elm St. (North Ave.) | 908-233-7772 | www.mojavegrille.com
"Robust flavors" fill out the menu of this casual Westfield Southwestern "staple" plying "excellent" fare "with flair" in "simple" digs; it's too bad they take "no reservations" and some "wish they served alcohol", but at least "BYO helps lower the cost."

☑ Molly Pitcher Inn *American*
22 | 25 | 23 | $48

Red Bank | Molly Pitcher Inn | 88 Riverside Ave. (Front St.) | 732-747-2500 | www.themollypitcher.com
Everything about this "old-world" Red Bank "grande dame" is "so civilized", from its "top-drawer" service and "going-back-in-time" ambiance to its jackets-required-at-dinner rule (Fridays and Saturdays); the "surprisingly good" Traditional American fare may be "on the expensive side", but few mind given the "gorgeous setting" overlooking the Navesink River.

Mompou *Spanish*
23 | 22 | 20 | $35

Newark | 77 Ferry St. (Congress St.) | 973-578-8114 | www.mompoutapas.com
An "improvement" on the "typical Newark" Ironbound options, this "mellow" Spanish wine bar plates "innovative" tapas in a "hip", brick-lined space or on the "nice" back patio; there's also an eclectic roster of musicians – it's named for a Catalan composer – and fans see lots of "potential", even if the tabs add up quickly.

Monster Sushi *Japanese*
20 | 14 | 18 | $34

Summit | 395 Springfield Ave. (Maple St.) | 908-598-1100 | www.monstersushi.com
The "giant-size" sushi is a match for the "inflated prices" at this "casual" Summit Japanese that's a spin-off of the Manhattan originals;

the mood can be "festive" and "fun", though critics complain this "just average" place "isn't what it used to be."

Montville Inn Ⓜ *American*   22 | 23 | 21 | $44

Montville | 167 Rte. 202 (River Rd.) | 973-541-1234 | www.montvilleinn.com

Dubbed "*the* place to be in Montville", this "charming" New American "hot spot" is set in a newly constructed building on the site of a pre-Revolutionary inn, with porch dining that "takes you back to another era"; though the "interesting" cooking and "weekend bar scene" draw an "older, sophisticated" crowd, a few find it too "noisy" and "pricey"; a post-Survey chef change may not be reflected in the Food score.

ᴺᴱᵂ MoonShine Modern   - | - | - | M
Supper Club *American*

Millburn | 57 Main St. (Millburn Ave.) | 973-509-1912 | www.moonshinesupperclub.com

For business by day or romance by night, this Millburn newcomer casts a sophisticated glow onto contemporary American comfort fare, serving a midpriced menu in a dramatic supper-club setting, highlighted by a 30-ft.-long oak bar and smoked mirror walls; happy-hour specials, seasonal specialty drinks and weekend live music further brighten the mood.

Ⓩ Moonstruck Ⓜ *American/Mediterranean*   25 | 25 | 25 | $51

Asbury Park | 517 Lake Ave. (bet. Main St. & Ocean Ave.) | 732-988-0123 | www.moonstrucknj.com

Folks are "awestruck" by the "magical atmosphere" at this three-story Victorian house overlooking Wesley Lake in Asbury Park, where a "top-flight" American-Mediterranean menu paired with "excellent" wines is served by an "exemplary" crew; it doesn't take reservations, but the "wait is worth it" – especially in the "cool" ground-floor piano bar.

Ⓩ Morton's The Steakhouse *Steak*   25 | 23 | 25 | $67

Hackensack | Shops at Riverside | 274 Riverside Sq. (Hackensack Ave.) | 201-487-1303
Atlantic City | Caesars on the Boardwalk | 2100 Pacific Ave. (Arkansas Ave.) | 609-449-1044
www.mortons.com

A steakhouse "standard-bearer", this "big-ticket" chain offers "excellently prepared" cuts of beef and "grand sides" "served professionally" amid an "ambiance of wealth and class"; some find it a bit "staid" and wish they'd "lose the raw-meat presentation" and "high" wine pricing, but overall it's considered "one of the best."

Mr. Chu *Chinese*   21 | 13 | 18 | $24

East Hanover | 44 Rte. 10 W. (Ridgedale Ave.) | 973-887-7555

"Authentic", "tastefully prepared" Chinese specialties at "can't-be-beat" prices keep things "hopping" at this East Hanover BYO parked in an erstwhile diner; given the "lacking" decor and "efficient if uninterested" service, regulars "stick with takeout."

	FOOD	DECOR	SERVICE	COST

Mud City Crab House *Seafood*
24 | 14 | 19 | $33

Manahawkin | 1185 E. Bay Ave. (bet. Heron St. & Marsha Dr.) | 609-978-3660 | www.mudcitycrabhouse.com

This seasonal Manahawkin crab "heaven" (on the mainland just minutes from LBI) is a "best-restaurant-in-a-swamp" contender thanks to some of the most "awesome" crab cakes "this side of Baltimore"; though the setting's strictly "hole-in-the-wall", the service is "good" and the tabs reasonable; P.S. it doesn't take rezzies, so brace yourself for "exhausting" waits.

NEW Mussel Bar by Robert Wiedmaier ● *Belgian*
- | - | - | M

Atlantic City | Revel | 500 Boardwalk (Metropolitan Ave.) | 609-225-9851 | www.revelresorts.com

DC chef Robert Wiedmaier brings Belgium to Atlantic City with this gastropub at Revel; it features mussels and other Flemish faves like tarte flambé, as well as steaks, salads and cured meats, not to mention 150 beers and live rock 'n' roll in a tavern atmosphere that includes beer-bottle light fixtures and mussel shells embedded in the bar top.

Mustache Bill's Diner ⊟ *Diner*
24 | 15 | 21 | $16

Barnegat Light | Broadway & Eighth St. (Central Ave.) | 609-494-0155

Featured on the Food Network, this "quintessential" BYO diner in Barnegat Light on Long Beach Island is a "real"-deal kind of place where everything's made from scratch; the "hours are a little crazy" (call ahead), but regulars tout the "out-of-this-world" breakfasts; P.S. it accepts neither plastic nor reservations.

Namaskaar Ⓜ *Indian*
20 | 15 | 20 | $30

Englewood | 120 Grand Ave. (bet. Dean & Franklin Sts.) | 201-567-0061 | www.namaskaar.com

"Surprises" (think chicken tikka Caesar salad) supplement the subcontinental standards on the menu of this "reinvented" Indian BYO transplanted from Paramus to a "smaller" setting in Englewood; its vegetarian specialties are "particularly good", while the $10 lunch buffet is a "total bargain."

Nana's Deli Ⓢ *Deli*
23 | 12 | 18 | $21

Livingston | 127 S. Livingston Ave. (Wilson Terrace) | 973-740-1940 | www.nanasdeli.com

Famed for its "outrageous tuna salad", this "gourmet" Livingston deli also vends "excellent" Jewish-style specialties; what with the limited seating and "lunch-only" hours in the dining room, most reserve it for "takeout"; the deli counter is open until 6:30 PM.

Napoli's Brick Oven Pizza *Pizza*
25 | 13 | 19 | $20

Hoboken | 1118 Washington St. (bet. 11th & 12th Sts.) | 201-216-0900

"Pizza-mad Hoboken" is home to this "bare-bones" BYO that "ranks high" for its "delicate" brick-oven pies sprinkled with "quality toppings"; the decor may be "generic", but service is "fast" and "friendly", and the costs on par for the genre.

	FOOD	DECOR	SERVICE	COST

National Hotel Restaurant Ⓜ *American/Eclectic*

-	-	-	M

Frenchtown | National Hotel | 31 Race St. (2nd St.) | 908-996-3200 | www.thenationalhotelnj.com

A former stagecoach stop along the Delaware River is home to this Eclectic–New American set in a Frenchtown boutique hotel; most surveyors have yet to discover it, but they're "trying hard" and there's early praise for its "endearing basement bar", the Rathskeller.

Nauvoo Grill Club *American*

18	25	19	$40

Fair Haven | 121 Fair Haven Rd. (River Rd.) | 732-747-8777 | www.nauvoogrillclub.com

Reminiscent of a "posh ski lodge", this "clubby" Fair Haven New American is set in a "lovely" "Arts and Crafts" space equipped with four fireplaces; since the menu is "average" and the service "inconsistent", regulars advise sticking with "simple preparations."

Navesink Fishery Ⓜ *Seafood*

25	10	19	$35

Navesink | A&P Shopping Ctr. | 1004 Rte. 36 S. (Valley Dr.) | 732-291-8017

"Easy to miss" in a Navesink shopping center, this "unpretentious" fish market–cum–BYO seafooder slings "simply prepared" fin fare that's "as fresh as it comes"; fans don't mind the "slow" service and "forget-about-it" decor – it's "all about the food" here.

Neelam *Indian*

20	13	18	$25

Berkeley Heights | 295 Springfield Ave. (Snyder Ave.) | 908-665-2212
South Orange | 115 S. Orange Ave. (Irvington Ave.) | 973-762-1100
Middletown | Village Mall | 1178 Rte. 35 S. (New Monmouth Rd.) | 732-671-8900 Ⓜ
www.neelamrestaurant.com

A "standard" sampling of "suburban" Indian chow that's "just plain good" turns up at these "unassuming", separately owned BYOs; the lunch buffets are such "good value" that it's easy to overlook the "slow" staffers and "tired" decor.

Negeen Persian Grill *Persian*

∇ 18	15	17	$29

Summit | 330 Springfield Ave. (Summit Ave.) | 908-277-2100 | www.negeengrill.com

The name is Farsi for 'gem', and this "small", "family-owned" Persian BYO shines with "authentic", "delicious" cooking for "reasonable" sums; converts ignore the "so-so" service, calling it a "nice addition to the Summit area."

Nero's Grille *Steak*

18	16	19	$47

Livingston | 618 S. Livingston Ave. (Hobart Gap Rd.) | 973-994-1410 | www.neros.com

There are "tons of regulars" at this "everyone-knows-everyone" Livingston chophouse where the "ordinary" steak-heavy menu features Italian accents as well as "lighter" cafe items; critics say this "1970s flashback" is "past its prime" and "pricey" to boot, but the bar scene stays "popular" for a reason; a post-Survey chef change may not be reflected in the Food score.

	FOOD	DECOR	SERVICE	COST

Next Door Ⓜ *American*

22 | 13 | 18 | $32

Montclair | 556 Bloomfield Ave. (bet. Midland Ave. & Park St.) | 973-744-3600

For a "down-market" alternative to next-door sibling Blu, try this "small" Montclair American BYO that's "just as good" although set in a "no-tablecloths" milieu; critics complain about "on-top-of-each-other" seating, but no one protests the "inexpensive" price point.

Nha Trang Place *Vietnamese*

23 | 6 | 14 | $19

Jersey City | 249 Newark Ave. (bet. Cole & 2nd Sts.) | 201-239-1988

"You eat for so little and leave so full" at this Jersey City BYO where "authentic Vietnamese" chow (including "restorative" pho noodle soups) comes at a "super-cheap" cost; too bad both decor and service are "nonexistent", but then again, there's usually "little wait" to get in.

☑ Nicholas Ⓜ *American*

29 | 27 | 28 | $84

Red Bank | 160 Rte. 35 S. (bet. Navesink River Rd. & Pine St.) | 732-345-9977 | www.restaurantnicholas.com

"Hot off its 10th-year anniversary", Nicholas and Melissa Harary's "fine-tuned" "crown jewel" in Red Bank is again voted New Jersey's Most Popular restaurant as well as No. 1 for Food and Service; look for "showstopping", prix fixe-only New American meals served by an "impeccable" team in an "understatedly elegant", jackets-suggested setting; it's a "flawless" experience that's "worth every hundred you spend", though insiders report you can dine for less (and à la carte) at the "hip", "more relaxed" bar.

Nicky's Firehouse *American*

18 | 15 | 15 | $22

Madison | 15 Central Ave. (Main St.) | 973-765-0565 | www.nickysfirehousenj.com

"Low-cost" and "family-friendly", this "reliable" American BYO in Madison is a decent "neighborhood" option with a "something-for-everyone" menu served in "firehouse-themed" digs; "noisy" acoustics, "poor" service and "crowded" conditions are part of the package.

🆕 Nico Kitchen & Bar Ⓢ *Eclectic*

- | - | - | M

Newark | New Jersey Performing Arts Ctr. | 1 Center St. (Park Pl.) | 973-642-1226 | nicokitchenbar.com

Under the direction of chef Ryan De Persio (Fascino, Bar Cara) globally inspired small plates take center stage at this midpriced Eclectic-Italian in Newark's NJPAC; the weekday lunch offerings attract local power brokers, while a market-driven, three-course prix fixe stars on performance nights and at matinees, all served in a sleek, high-ceilinged space.

Nifty Fifty's *Diner*

19 | 19 | 19 | $14

Clementon | 1310 Blackwood Clementon Rd. (Millbridge Rd.) | 856-346-1950

Turnersville | 4670 Black Horse Pike (Fries Mill Rd.) | 856-875-1950 www.niftyfiftys.com

For a dose of "'50s nostalgia", surveyors head to these "loud", "eye-blindingly" bright "throwback" diners where "you can feel your arteries clogging as you enjoy juicy burgers" and pick from a "mind-boggling" selection of "sodas" and "milkshakes" that "would even make the Fonz say aayyy"; a "wonderful" staff makes it easy to "bring the kids", and fans say the prices meet most "family budgets."

Nikko *Japanese*　24 | 16 | 20 | $38

Whippany | 881 Rte. 10 E. (Jefferson Rd.) | 973-428-0787 | www.nikkonj.com

The "flavors of the sea shine" at this Whippany Japanese known for its "tasty" sushi and sashimi specials; a post-Survey renovation (not reflected in the Decor score) may quell calls for a "face-lift" – regardless, "it's always packed for a reason."

☑ Ninety Acres at Natirar Ⓜ *American*　25 | 28 | 23 | $70

Peapack | Natirar Resort & Spa | 2 Main St. (bet. Old Dutch Rd. & Ramapo Way) | 908-901-9500 | www.ninetyacres.com

Set in a "stunning" restored carriage house on an "idyllic" estate once owned by the King of Morocco (and winner of Top Decor in New Jersey), this "sublime" Peapack New American showcases chef David Felton's "top-notch" "farm-to-table" menu, much of it prepared with ingredients grown on-site; it's true "destination dining" perfect for "special occasions", complete with "superb" service and a "see-and-be-seen" crowd, but don't forget your "trust fund" – you'll need it when the check arrives.

Nobi *Japanese*　▽ 26 | 17 | 22 | $30

Toms River | T.J. Maxx Plaza | 1338 Hooper Ave. (Bey Lea Rd.) | 732-244-7888

"Well-prepared" sushi made "true to form" from "always fresh" seafood is yours at this modest Japanese BYO, a "best-kept secret" in Toms River even though it's been around since 1997; "nice" sushi chefs and servers who "treat you like family" enhance the "cozy" mood.

Nomad Pizza ☒Ⓜ⇄ *Pizza*　26 | 17 | 23 | $23

Hopewell | 10 E. Broad St. (Greenwood Ave.) | 609-466-6623 | www.nomadpizzaco.com

Formerly prepared in a wood-fired brick oven mounted on a 1949 REO Speedwagon, the "inventive gourmet" pizza can now be accessed at this storefront BYO in Hopewell; ok, it's "small" and "crowded" – with no-reservations and cash-only policies – but the payoff is "out-of-this-world" pies.

Nori *Asian*　23 | 14 | 19 | $37

Caldwell | 406 Bloomfield Ave. (Academy Rd.) | 973-403-2400
Montclair | 561 Bloomfield Ave. (Maple Pl.) | 973-655-8805
www.nori-sushi.com

It's "all about the fish" at these neighborhood BYOs in Caldwell and Montclair best known for "innovative" sushi but also offering "tasty" Asian options; true, there's "no atmosphere" and service is "more functional than accomplished", but regulars call them "solid" choices.

	FOOD	DECOR	SERVICE	COST

Norma's *Mideastern*

22 | 14 | 20 | $23

Cherry Hill | Barclay Farms Shopping Ctr. | 132-145 Rte. 70 E. (Kings Hwy.) | 856-795-1373 | www.normasrestaurant.com

"Flavorful" Middle Eastern cooking is yours at this "solid" Cherry Hill BYO, where many "make a meal" of the "tasty" appetizers; weekend belly dancers distract from the so-so decor and service.

Nunzio *Italian*

24 | 22 | 22 | $41

Collingswood | 706 Haddon Ave. (Collings Ave.) | 856-858-9840 | www.nunzios.net

Channeling a "small Italian village", this "cozy" Collingswood trattoria matches its "beautiful" decor with "innovative", "mouthwatering" cooking for a "good price" (helped along by the BYO policy); the only sticking point is the "loud" sound level, so "don't expect to carry on a conversation."

NEW O Bistro & Wine Bar ◑ *American*

– | – | – | M

Atlantic City | Revel | 500 Boardwalk (Metropolitan Ave.) | 855-348-0500 | www.revelresorts.com

Take in ocean views, sip cocktails and wines and share stylish plates both small and large from top toque Michel Richard (Central Michel Richard in DC), who brings his signature New American fare with a French touch to this circular poolside bar at AC's Revel; the calypso vibe suits his playful takes on specialty burgers, fish tacos, skate meunière and the like.

Oceanos *Seafood*

23 | 21 | 22 | $51

Fair Lawn | 2-27 Saddle River Rd. (Meadow View Terrace) | 201-796-0546 | www.oceanosrestaurant.com

The "quality is undeniable" at this "first-class", family-run seafooder in Fair Lawn where the fin fare comes with a "Greek touch" and the ambiance is "dignified"; despite "splurge" prices, fans call it a "real catch" for its "wonderful" housemade bread and "welcoming" ambiance.

Octopus's Garden *Seafood*

22 | 23 | 23 | $37

West Creek | 771 S. Main St. (Mayetta Landing Rd.) | 609-597-8828 | www.theoctopussgardenfishhouse.com

"Classy" digs and "carefully prepared" seafood keep locals loyal to this "satisfying" option in West Creek, transplanted from Long Beach Island to the mainland a while back; the pricing is "reasonable", the specials "unbeatable" and a "pleasantly cheerful" staff pours NJ wines – or you can BYO.

Oddfellows *Cajun/Creole*

18 | 17 | 17 | $31

Hoboken | 80 River St. (bet. Hudson Pl. & Newark St.) | 201-656-9009 | www.oddfellowsrest.com

"Bayou cooking" comes to Hoboken at this "fun" Cajun-Creole pub near the PATH station that channels the "Big Easy" with its "Nola-inspired menu"; critics cite "indifferent" service and "noisy" acoustics, calling it "primarily a joint for a brew on the way to the train."

	FOOD	DECOR	SERVICE	COST

Oh! Calamares Ⓜ *Peruvian* — | - | - | - | M

Kearny | 102 Kearny Ave. (Dukes St.) | 201-998-4111

"Excellent" Peruvian fare turns up at this "surprising" find in Kearny serving "outstanding" ceviche, along with Lima-style seafood and braised meats; maybe the decor "leaves something to be desired" (a post-Survey redo may remedy that), but the "value" pricing is fine as is.

NEW Ohana Grill *Hawaiian/Seafood* — | - | - | - | M

Lavallette | 65 Grand Central Ave. (Bryn Mawr Ave.) | 732-830-4040 | www.theohanagrill.com

This cheerful Lavallette Eclectic (whose name is Hawaiian for 'extended family') offers an alternative to the usual seaside fare with creative Asian- and island-inspired surf 'n' turf; BYO means no boisterous bar crowds to disrupt the soothing setting, and there's a liquor store across the street; limited hours in the off-season.

Old Bay Ⓢ *Cajun/Creole* 19 | 17 | 18 | $33

New Brunswick | 61-63 Church St. (Neilson St.) | 732-246-3111 | www.oldbayrest.com

It's "always Mardi Gras" at this New Brunswick Cajun-Creole that's a hit with "Rutgers students" thanks to "pretty decent" grub and a nonstop "party atmosphere"; some say it's more "beer bar" than restaurant, but there's no debate about the "moderate prices" and "frat-house smell."

Ⓩ Old Homestead Ⓢ *Steak* 27 | 25 | 26 | $72

Atlantic City | Borgata Hotel, Casino & Spa | 1 Borgata Way (Huron Ave.) | 609-317-1000 | www.theoldhomesteadsteakhouse.com

"Killer" steaks are "cooked to perfection" at this "cavernous" spin-off of the NYC original occupying a double-decker setting in AC's Borgata Hotel; "typical leather" decor and "prompt, unobtrusive" service come with the territory, and don't forget to bring "deep pockets" to settle the "outrageous" bill.

Old Man Rafferty's *American* 18 | 17 | 18 | $29

Hillsborough | 284 Rte. 206 (Triangle Rd.) | 908-904-9731
New Brunswick | 106 Albany St. (George St.) | 732-846-6153
Asbury Park | Steinbach Bldg. | 541 Cookman Ave. (bet. Bangs & Mattison Aves.) | 732-774-1600
www.oldmanraffertys.com

"Dependable as a Swiss watch", this "casual" American chainlet slings "routine" "upscale diner food" and "ab-fab" desserts for "small" sums; "pleasant" settings and "large" menus with "lotsa choices" please the "pickiest" eaters, the "sophomoric" service not so much.

Oliver a Bistro Ⓜ *Eclectic* ∇ 27 | 21 | 24 | $41

Bordentown | 218 Farnsworth Ave. (Church St.) | 609-298-7177 | www.oliverabistro.com

'More, please' say "repeat" visitors to this "great little" storefront BYO on Bordentown's Restaurant Row, where "delicious" Eclectic dishes are prepared from "quality" "local" ingredients; "service with a smile" and a particularly "homey" setting complete the "exceptional" picture.

		SERVICE	
FOOD	DECOR		COST

One 53 *American*

| 23 | 19 | 22 | $50 |

Rocky Hill | 153 Washington St. (Princeton Ave.) | 609-924-1019 | www.one53nj.com

This New American bistro in Rocky Hill generates "buzz" with its "smart attention to detail", reflected in "delicious" cooking, "informed" service and a "sophisticated" mood; the "SoHo"-esque dining room draws mixed notices – "energizing" vs. "noisy" – but most agree on the "pricey" tabs and that "great" wine room downstairs.

Onieal's ● *American*

| 20 | 18 | 19 | $33 |

Hoboken | 343 Park Ave. (4th St.) | 201-653-1492 | www.onieals.com

"Great pub grub" is the order of the day at this "casual" Hoboken New American spun off from the SoHo original; even though the dining room's "a bit cramped", "friendly" service, reasonable tabs and "pleasant" outdoor seating keep business brisk.

Orange Squirrel ●Ⓩ *American*

| 22 | 14 | 18 | $48 |

Bloomfield | 412 Bloomfield Ave. (bet. Hill & Orange Sts.) | 973-337-6421 | www.theorangesquirrel.com

"Quirky" says it all about this "ambitious" New American set in a "hip storefront" in a "dicey" part of Bloomfield; voters split on the decor – "NY sophisticated" vs. "Laundromat"-esque – but agree on the "difficult parking", "close quarters" and "seriously good" cooking.

☑ Origin *French/Thai*

| 25 | 21 | 21 | $37 |

Basking Ridge | 25 Mountainview Blvd. (Liberty Corner Rd.) | 908-647-7781
Morristown | 10 South St. (Dehart St.) | 973-971-9933 Ⓜ
Somerville | 25 Division St. (Main St.) | 908-685-1344 Ⓜ
www.originthai.com

Thai-French "flavors dance on your tongue" at these "unbeatable" BYOs boasting "delicious, shareable" food and "hip", "modern" looks; maybe they're "a bit pricier than competitors", but no one seems to mind given the "crowded", "buzzing" settings that "hum with good energy."

☑ Osteria Giotto *Italian*

| 26 | 19 | 21 | $44 |

Montclair | 21 Midland Ave. (bet. Bloomfield Ave. & Portland Pl.) | 973-746-0111 | www.osteria-giotto.com

Given "absolutely delicious" Italian food with a "creative bent", it's "tough to get a reservation" at this "so popular" Montclair BYO where "everything is on the money"; "reasonable" tabs, "truly special specials" and overall "NY quality" make the "noise and crowds" more tolerable, and it's most pleasant "when they open the French doors in warm weather."

NEW Osteria La Fiamma Ⓜ *Italian*

| - | - | - | M |

Ridgewood | 119 E. Ridgewood Ave. (Oak Street) | 201-389-6400 | www.lafiammarestaurant.com

Overlooking Ridgewood's main shopping street, this warm, bustling Italian BYO (whose name means 'the flame') kindles appetites with crisp pizzas and rotisserie meats from a wood-fired oven, as well as housemade pastas and share-worthy desserts; large windows look out onto bucolic Van Neste Square, and there's outdoor seating as well.

NEW Osteria Morini *Italian*   - | - | - | E

Bernardsville | 107 Morristown Rd. (Finley Ave.) | 908-221-0040 | www.osteriamorini.com

Michael White replaced the former Due Terre in Bernardsville with this satellite of his popular high-end SoHo Italian, offering a pared-down menu of Emilia-Romagna regional cuisine; the dining space was reconfigured into a single level and imbued with a rustic feel to match the fare.

Ota-Ya M *Japanese*   21 | 13 | 19 | $35

Lambertville | 21 Ferry St. (Union St.) | 609-397-9228 | www.ota-ya.com

Nicknamed "Ota-Yum" by acolytes, this Lambertville BYO Japanese features "solid" sushi and "fun" hibachi items in a "rather average" setting that could "use a makeover"; some complain of "inconsistent quality", but others report "relaxing" meals and a "cheery" vibe.

Oyako Tso's *Japanese*   ▽ 23 | 18 | 21 | $28

Freehold | 6 W. Main St. (bet. South & Throckmorton Sts.) | 732-866-1988 | www.oyakotsos.com

A "nice place for a family meal" in Monmouth County, this Freehold Japanese slices "very good" sushi and also features hibachi dishes prepared by "talented", entertaining chefs in a pleasant setting; the "great prices" get a boost from the BYO policy.

NEW Pacific Grill *American*   - | - | - | E

Wildwood | 4801 Pacific Ave. (Taylor Ave.) | 609-523-2333 | www.pacificgrillwildwood.com

From the team behind Cape May's acclaimed Union Park, this up-scale seasonal BYO in Wildwood showcases executive chef John Schatz's global-inspired contemporary American lineup; warm colors, palms and bamboo give the casually elegant space a Pacific island flair.

Pad Thai *Thai*   24 | 14 | 19 | $25

Highland Park | 217 Raritan Ave. (bet. 2nd & 3rd Aves.) | 732-247-9636 | www.pad-thai.com

"Mild means moderately hot" at this "authentic" Thai in Highland Park, a "quite tasty" "neighborhood" joint on the scene since 1995; true, the "basic" setting "could use a little updating", but the staff is "accommodating" and the prices "cheap."

NEW Pairings M *American*   - | - | - | E

Cranford | 1 South Ave. E. (Walnut Ave.) | 908-276-4026 | www.pairingscranford.com

Chef/co-owner Carol Murphy Clyne strategically couples the comfort foods of her youth with global flavors at this elegant New American in Cranford, which serves a prix fixe dinner on Wednesdays and a bonus tapas menu on Thursdays; despite the name, it's BYO wine.

	FOOD	DECOR	SERVICE	COST

Palace of Asia *Indian*
- | - | - | M

Cherry Hill | 2389 Marlton Pike W. (bet. Hampton Rd. & Lexington Ave.) | 856-773-1200 | www.palace-of-asia.com

Tandoori dishes, biryanis and other Indian staples are served in a smart, white-tablecloth setting at this midpriced Cherry Hill eatery; in addition to a daily lunch buffet, it offers a Wednesday dinner spread.

Palm, The *Steak*
25 | 21 | 23 | $66

Atlantic City | Quarter at the Tropicana | 2801 Pacific Ave. (Iowa Ave.) | 609-344-7256 | www.thepalm.com

"Perfect" lobster, "superb" steaks and "hefty" cocktails are the signatures of this "bustling", "special-occasion" chophouse chain link in AC with a "dark men's-club" look; "old-school" service seals the deal, so while it's "not cheap", most conclude it's "worth it."

Pamir *Afghan*
22 | 20 | 22 | $32

Morristown | 11 South St. (Dehart St.) | 973-605-1095 | www.pamirrestaurant.com

Following a move to a "better Morristown location", this "special" Afghan BYO serves the "same great food", "full of exotic flavor", in an "upgraded" space with a "fine-dining atmosphere"; "eye-catching" preparations, "outstanding" service and "outdoor seating" all earn kudos at this "terrific change of pace."

Panico's *Italian*
21 | 19 | 22 | $51

New Brunswick | 103 Church St. (Neilson St.) | 732-545-6100 | www.panicosrestaurant.com

This "special-occasion" Italian in New Brunswick's theater district is known for its "excellent" cooking and "expense account"–worthy prices; some find it a bit "stuffy" and "trading on yesterday's reputation", but those seeking a more collegiate, "laid-back" atmosphere head for its pizzeria sibling across the street.

Papa Razzi *Italian*
18 | 18 | 19 | $32

Paramus | Garden State Plaza | 298 Garden State Plaza (Passaic St.) | 201-843-0990
Short Hills | Short Hills Mall | 1200 Morris Tpke. (John F. Kennedy Pkwy.) | 973-467-5544
www.paparazzitrattoria.com

Weary shoppers "fortify" themselves with wood-fired pizzas and "serviceable" Italian grub at these "upscale" mall chain links in Paramus and Short Hills; the tabs are fairly "reasonable", and "quick" service means you "won't lose your shopping momentum."

☑ Park & Orchard *Eclectic*
23 | 15 | 21 | $39

East Rutherford | 240 Hackensack St. (Union Ave.) | 201-939-9292 | www.parkandorchard.com

A vast, "health-minded" menu is paired with an "encyclopedic", "award-winning" wine list at this longtime East Rutherford Eclectic where the "creative" offerings can be "adapted to any dietary restrictions"; though there's "zero atmosphere" in the "industrial" setting, prices are "fair", the service "friendly" and it's "convenient to the Meadowlands."

		FOOD	DECOR	SERVICE	COST

Park Avenue
Bar & Grill *American/Pan-Latin* ▽ 18 | 16 | 16 | $38

Union City | 3417 Park Ave. (35th St.) | 201-617-7275 |
www.parkavenuebarandgrill.com

It's more scene than cuisine at this "fun" Union City venue that's
"ambitious for the area" given its bar/lounge/restaurant/rooftop
options; though both the American–Pan-Latin menu and service are
on the "so-so" side, a "lively atmosphere", "great NYC views" and
"NFL games" on the flat-screens provide distraction.

Park Steakhouse *Seafood/Steak*   23 | 19 | 21 | $61

Park Ridge | 151 Kinderkamack Rd. (bet. Grand & Park Aves.) |
201-930-1300 | www.theparksteakhouse.com

"Perfectly prepared meats" that are "on par with anything Manhattan
serves" turn up at this "classic" Park Ridge chophouse where the
"seafood is as good as the steaks"; "professional" service makes up
for "tired" decor and prices that are high "for what it is and where
you are"; Ridgewood sibling Park West Tavern opened in 2011.

NEW Park West Tavern *American*   - | - | - | E

Ridgewood | 30 Oak St. (Ridgewood Ave.) | 201-445-5400 |
www.parkwesttavern.com

Dry-aged steaks from the meat locker at Park Ridge sibling Park
Steakhouse beef up a lineup of surf 'n' turf and cleverly named comfort dishes at chef John Halligan's bustling New American pub in
Ridgewood; weekend brunch and extensive beer, wine and specialty
drink options make it fun for a crowd, while the sleek setting boasting a stone fireplace and sidewalk seating is casual date-cozy.

Pasquale's Ⓜ *Italian*   ▽ 24 | 21 | 22 | $33

Edison | Oak Tree Shopping Ctr. | 1655-200 Oak Tree Rd.
(bet. Grove & Wood Aves.) | 732-947-3010 |
www.pasqualesristoranteitaliano.com

Edison's Oak Tree Center is home to this "excellent" Italian yearling
where the extensive, "homemade" menu includes mix-and-match
sauces and pastas; the eponymous chef from Puglia has been replaced by his former assistant.

Patria Ⓜ *Pan-Latin*   - | - | - | E

Rahway | 169 W. Main St. (Elizabeth Ave.) | 732-943-7531 |
www.patrianj.com

Chef Andrew DiCataldo, who made his name at NYC's erstwhile
Patria, returns to his native NJ with this Rahway Pan-Latin, offering
serious Nuevo cooking and traditional plates; the dim, nightclubby
mood comes courtesy of an ambitious bar and two late-night
lounges with DJs and live music.

Patsy's *Italian*   23 | 15 | 20 | $37

Fairview | 332 Bergen Blvd. (bet. Cliff St. & Jersey Ave.) | 201-943-0627 |
www.patsysristorante.com

"Around for years", this "reliable" Fairview Italian is known for its
"consistent" cooking that "always tastes great"; the decor may be

"so-so", but the mood's reliably "comfortable" thanks to "treat-you-like-family" service and a strong "neighborhood" following.

Peacock Inn *American*
26 | 25 | 24 | $71

Princeton | Peacock Inn | 20 Bayard Ln. (bet. Boudinot & Stockton Sts.) | 609-924-1707 | www.peacockinn.com

"Looking great" following a 2010 renovation, this longtime Princetonian set in a modernized boutique hotel is "making a splash" with "simply divine" New American creations from a former Nicholas sous-chef; it's a "fine combination of old and new", with "want-to-please" service, a "serene" vibe and, of course, "big-ticket" tabs.

Penang *Malaysian/Thai*
22 | 17 | 18 | $26

Lodi | 334 N. Main St. (Garibaldi Ave.) | 973-779-1128 | www.penangnj.com

East Hanover | 200 Rte. 10 W. (bet. Ridgedale Ave. & River Rd.) | 973-887-6989 | www.penangnj.com

Edison | 505 Old Post Rd. (bet. Rte. 1 & Vineyard Rd.) | 732-287-3038 | www.penangnj.com

Princeton | Nassau Park Pavilion | 635 Nassau Park Blvd. (Rte. 1) | 609-897-9088 | www.penangnj.com

Maple Shade | 480 Rte. 38 E. (Cutler Ave.) | 856-755-0188 | www.penangmapleshade.com

"Lots of unique items" fill out the menu of this "interesting" Malaysian-Thai mini-chain that adventurous eaters call a "delicious departure from the usual"; menu "diversity" and "good-value" prices make up for the "aloof" service and "big-box" design; P.S. all but the Lodi outpost are BYO.

Perryville Inn Ⓜ *American*
26 | 23 | 23 | $56

Union Township | 167 Perryville Rd. (Rte. 78) | 908-730-9500 | www.theperryvilleinn.com

A "treat from beginning to end", this "romantic" Traditional American lies in a "beautiful", circa-1813 Union inn where chef-owner Paul Ingenito's "appetizing" preparations match the "lovely" setting and are served by a "professional" team; granted, the tabs are "high-end", but the "more relaxed" Brick Tavern offers comfort food at comfortable prices.

Pete & Elda's ● *Pizza*
22 | 10 | 18 | $23
(aka Carmen's Pizzeria)

Neptune City | 96 Woodland Ave. (Rte. 35) | 732-774-6010 | www.peteandeldas.com

Since 1957, this Neptune City "throwback" pizzeria has been slinging "amazing" "paper-thin-crust" pies; sure, it's "old", "loud" and a "world-class joint", but the mood's "friendly" and there's a fun "bar crowd."

⒵ Peter Shields Inn *American*
26 | 27 | 26 | $61

Cape May | 1301 Beach Ave. (Trenton Ave.) | 609-884-9090 | www.petershieldsinn.com

For "gracious dining" facing the ocean, it's hard to beat the "dreamlike" setting of this 1907 Georgian Revival mansion in Cape May, where

"A-plus" Americana is offered in a "quiet", "romantic" milieu with plenty of "space between tables"; "efficient" service and a "perfect-getaway" vibe distract from the fact that this BYO is "not cheap"; the 2011 arrival of chef Carl Messick (ex Ebbitt Room) and a dining room redo may not be reflected in the Food and Decor scores, respectively.

☑ P.F. Chang's China Bistro Chinese   20 | 21 | 19 | $34

Hackensack | Shops at Riverside | 390 Hackensack Ave. (Rte. 4) | 201-646-1565
West New York | 10 Port Imperial Blvd. (Riverbend Dr.) | 201-866-7790
Freehold | Freehold Raceway Mall | 3710 Rte. 9 S. (bet. Rtes. 33 & 537) | 732-308-1840
Atlantic City | Quarter at the Tropicana | 2801 Pacific Ave. (Iowa Ave.) | 609-348-4600
Princeton | Marketfair Mall | 3545 Rte. 1 (Meadow Rd.) | 609-799-5163
Marlton | Promenade at Sagemore | 500 Rte. 73 S. (bet. Brick Rd. & Marlton Pkwy.) | 856-396-0818
www.pfchangs.com
"Light, delicious", "Americanized" Chinese food (and "standout" lettuce wraps) keeps fans "coming back" to this "upscale" chain; though some call it "ordinary" and "loud", the "consistent" service is a plus, ditto the "smart" menu "catering to people with allergies" and other needs.

Pheasants Landing Ⓜ American/Continental   15 | 14 | 18 | $32

Hillsborough | 311 Amwell Rd. (Willow Rd.) | 908-281-1288 | www.pheasantslanding.com
Hillsborough locals like this "neighborhood-friendly" American-Continental for its "reasonable" tabs and "nice outdoor seating", but admit it's "too bad that the food isn't better"; the Underground Pub serves more casual grub in a Rathskeller-esque setting.

Phillips Seafood Seafood   20 | 20 | 20 | $41

Atlantic City | Pier Shops at Caesars | 1 Atlantic Ocean (Arkansas Ave.) | 609-348-2273 | www.phillipsseafood.com
Crab dishes are the menu "highlight" of this AC link in the crustacean-centric Maryland chain, which also features a view of the beach from its Pier Shops at Caesars setting; those who find "nothing exciting" going on say it "doesn't live up to the original", but admit it's still a "pleasant change" from the casino norm.

Pho Eden ⓈⓂ Vietnamese   - | - | - | M

Cherry Hill | 1900 Greentree Rd. (Springdale Rd.) | 856-424-0075
The eponymous soups are the phocus of this Vietnamese located in a Cherry Hill strip mall; it also serves a wide selection of moderately priced noodle and rice dishes, but no alcohol.

☑ Piccola Italia Ⓜ Italian   26 | 23 | 24 | $49

Ocean Township | 837 W. Park Ave. (Rte. 35) | 732-493-3090 | www.piccolaitalianj.com
"Sophisticated" Italian cooking via "superb" chef Brian Gualtieri "wows" locals at this "hidden gem" in a "hard-to-find" Ocean Township strip mall; an "extensive" wine list, "skilled" service and

an "attractive" setting make for "truly memorable" dining worthy of a "special occasion."

Pic-Nic *Portuguese/Spanish* ▽ 21 | 12 | 19 | $29

East Newark | Radburn Plaza Bldg. | 224 Grant Ave. (Central Ave.) | 973-481-3646 | www.picnicrestaurant.com

"Absolutely authentic" Iberian specialties arrive with "ubiquitous green sauce" at this East Newark joint that also boasts a "modestly priced" wine list and service "with a smile"; those who feel the "location leaves something to be desired" go the "take-out" route.

🅩 Picnic, the Restaurant 🅢🅜 *American* 27 | 24 | 26 | $52

Fair Lawn | Plaza Bldg. | 14-25 Plaza Rd. N. (Fair Lawn Ave.) | 201-796-2700 | www.picnictherestaurant.com

"Word is out" on this "destination-worthy" New American set in a "tiny" storefront in Fair Lawn's historic Radburn section, where the "excellent menu" is "adjusted daily according to market offerings"; BYO makes the "NYC prices" tolerable, and enthusiasts are "wowed" by the "charming" setting, "impeccable" service and "convivial" mood; P.S. wine lockers are available for regular customers.

Piero's 🅜 *Italian* ▽ 22 | 20 | 22 | $46

Union Beach | 1411 Rte. 36 W. (Patterson Ave.) | 732-264-5222 | www.pierosrestaurant.com

A "nice neighborhood place", this longtime Union Beach Italian offers "very good" cooking that "won't break the bank" in "homey" environs; while weekend "live music" ratchets up the "festive" atmosphere, some find it slightly "cheesy."

Pietro's Coal Oven Pizzeria *Pizza* ▽ 21 | 14 | 17 | $25

Marlton | 140 Rte. 70 W. (Rte. 73) | 856-596-5500 | www.pietrospizza.com

The crusts are "thin", "crisp" and "tasty" at this "simple" coal-fired-oven pizzeria in Marlton; service is "polite" and the mood "family-friendly", though ratings suggest the decor is best overlooked.

NEW Pilsener Haus & Biergarten ● *Austrian/Hungarian* - | - | - | M

Hoboken | 1422 Grand St. (15th St.) | 201-683-5465 | www.pilsenerhaus.com

Sausages and suds are savored at long wooden communal tables indoors and outdoors at this Hoboken Austrian-Hungarian beer garden, where Viennese chef Thomas Ferlesch (ex NYC's Café des Artistes) balances behemoth soft Bavarian pretzels and grilled Teutonic wursts with pub sandwiches and brunch fare, which are complemented by more than 60 local craft and imported brews; the kitchen is closed on Monday, but two grills are always fired up.

Pine Tavern *American* 20 | 14 | 18 | $34

Old Bridge | 151 Rte. 34 (Cottrell Rd.) | 732-727-5060 | www.pinetavern.net

There's "good value for the money" at this "publike" Old Bridge tavern where the "consistently good" American chow plays second fiddle to the "very busy bar scene"; the decor is "about what you'd expect from the name" and regulars say "stick to the basics" for best results.

Pino's La Forchetta *Italian*
21 | 22 | 22 | $55

Marlboro | 448 Rte. 9 N. (Union Hill Rd.) | 732-972-6933 | www.famouspinos.com

This "old-fashioned" Marlboro Italian is a "popular" choice thanks to its "excellent" cooking and "spacious" dining room done up in a "high-class", "old-world" style; ok, it's on the "expensive" side, but "pleasant" staffers and frequent live entertainment are pluses.

Pintxo y Tapas *Spanish*
▽ 21 | 18 | 19 | $39

Englewood | 47 N. Dean St. (bet. Palisade Ave. & Park Pl.) | 201-569-9999 | www.englewoodtapas.com

Bergen PAC-goers head for this Englewood Spaniard for its "outstanding" small plates and "excellent" paella washed down with "fantastic" sangria; though it's "loud" when crowded, service is "friendly" and the tabs fairly "reasonable."

Pithari Taverna *Greek*
23 | 18 | 20 | $31

Highland Park | 28 Woodbridge Ave. (Raritan Ave.) | 732-572-0616 | www.thepithari.com

Partisans of this "homey" Highland Park Hellenic BYO are "suckers" for the "reasonably priced" grilled seafood prepared in an open kitchen and served in "large portions"; though the dimensions are "cramped" and weekend waits can be "long", the host is "genial" and eating outdoors feels "like a mini-visit to Greece."

Pizzicato *Italian*
▽ 21 | 20 | 21 | $31

Marlton | Promenade at Sagemore | 500 Rte. 73 S. (bet. Brick Rd. & Marlton Pkwy.) | 856-396-0880 | www.pizzicatoristorante.com

Spun off from the mother trattoria in Philly, this Marlton Italian BYO vends brick-oven pizzette, panini and pastas in a "mall setting"; "efficient" service, "interesting variety" and "good-value" tabs complete the overall "pleasant" picture.

P.J. Whelihan's *Pub Food*
17 | 15 | 17 | $22

Cherry Hill | 1854 Rte. 70 E. (Greentree Rd.) | 856-424-8844 ◑
Haddonfield | 700 Haddon Ave. (Ardmore Ave.) | 856-427-7888 ◑
Maple Shade | 396 S. Lenola Rd. (Kings Hwy.) | 856-234-2345 ◑
Medford Lakes | 61 Stokes Rd. (Tabernacle Rd.) | 609-714-7900
Sewell | 425 Hurffville Crosskeys Rd. (Regulus Dr.) | 856-582-7774 ◑
www.pjspub.com

Most patrons of these "noisy" pubs-cum–"fraternity houses" in South Jersey and Pennsylvania show up for "sports, wings and beer", since the grub is "typical" and the service is "only good to look at" quip critics; still, "reasonable" prices and "plentiful" flat-screens save the day.

Plan B Ⓜ *American*
24 | 20 | 22 | $36

Asbury Park | 705 Cookman Ave. (Bond St.) | 732-807-4710 | www.restaurantplanbap.com

Asbury Park's "Restaurant Row" is home to this "small but mighty" eatery offering "original" New American fare in an "arty", brick-walled setting; "thoughtful" service and a "cool" vibe make it an "A-list" choice for "adult" locals, while the BYO policy helps keep costs in check; the post-Survey arrival of chef Evan Victor (ex Amanda's, Elements) may not be reflected in the Food score.

Plantation *American* | 18 | 20 | 18 | $41 |

Harvey Cedars | 7908 Long Beach Blvd. (80th St.) | 609-494-8191 | www.plantationrestaurant.com

There's always a "good bar crowd" at this "relaxing" spot on Long Beach Island's northern end, "one of the only places with a liquor license" in these parts; though the American chow can be "hit-or-miss" and the service "spotty", at least the decor is "pleasant" and it's "open year-round."

☑ Pluckemin Inn ⧄ *American* | 26 | 26 | 25 | $65 |

Bedminster | 359 Rte. 206 S. (Pluckemin Way) | 908-658-9292 | www.pluckemininn.com

"Classy but not pretentious", this Bedminster New American "never fails to impress" with "creative" cuisine paired with a "blow-you-away" list of wines stored in an "impressive" three-story tower; its "glitzy" crowd touts the "beautiful" re-created farmhouse setting that exudes "country elegance" and includes "stunning outdoor seating", and though you may need to "dip into the 401k" to settle the tab, the Plucky Tavern offers "more casual" dining in a "preppy" milieu.

Pointé, The Ⓜ *American* | ▽ 21 | 25 | 21 | $46 |

Jersey City | Port Liberté | 2 Chapel Ave. (Half Moon Isle) | 201-985-9854 | www.thepointerestaurant.com

It's "all about the view" of lower Manhattan and the Statue of Liberty at this "lovely" Jersey City American on the waterfront near Liberty State Park; the "enjoyable" interpretations of surf 'n' turf are "nicely prepared", though the cost is debatable: "overpriced" vs. "you get your money's worth."

Ponzio's *Diner* | 19 | 13 | 18 | $24 |

Cherry Hill | 7 Rte. 70 W. (Kings Hwy.) | 856-428-4808 | www.ponzios.com

A "prototypical", "South Jersey–style" diner, this "huge" Cherry Hill joint slings "satisfying" Americana plus treats from its "incredible bakery"; so even if the menu's "predictable", service is the "weak link" and the decor could "use a refresh", it still remains "wildly popular."

Pop's Garage *Mexican* | 22 | 16 | 20 | $21 |

Asbury Park | Asbury Park Boardwalk | 1000 Ocean Ave. (2nd Ave.) | 732-455-3275

Normandy Beach | 560 Rte. 35 N. (7th Ave.) | 732-830-5700

NEW **Shrewsbury** | The Grove | 520 Broad St. (bet. Meadow Dr. & Monroe Ave.) | 732-530-7677

www.popsgaragenj.com

These "fun", "come-as-you-are" taquerias via Marilyn Schlossbach (Labrador Lounge) dish out "fresh", "consistently good" Mexican chow in beachy, seasonal settings; "budget" pricing and "inexpe-

| | FOOD | DECOR | SERVICE | COST |

rienced" help come with the territory; the Shrewsbury branch opened post-Survey.

Pop Shop *American*   20 | 17 | 19 | $16

Collingswood | 729 Haddon Ave. (Collings Ave.) | 856-869-0111 | www.thepopshopusa.com

Even though it may be the "world's noisiest" restaurant, this "retro" soda fountain in Collingswood is a hit with kids of all ages thanks to its "back-to-the-'50s" menu famed for its "all-day", all-American breakfasts and "many varieties" of grilled cheese; just brace yourself for "slow service" and tons of "fattening" fare.

Portobello *Italian*   19 | 22 | 18 | $38

Oakland | 175 Ramapo Valley Rd. (Long Hill Rd.) | 201-337-8990 | www.portobellonj.com

"Large" is the word for this multiroom Oakland "behemoth" with an "over-the-top" "villa environment" that's "reminiscent of Tuscany" by way of "VFW hall"; the similarly expansive Italian menu may take "hours to read", but is worth the effort: its "standard favorites and inventive specials" are "really tasty" and "affordable."

Portofino 🅜 *Italian*   24 | 17 | 20 | $45

Tinton Falls | 720 Tinton Ave. (Sycamore Ave.) | 732-542-6068 | www.portofino-ristorante.com

Tinton Falls is the port of call for this "quite good" Italian known for staffers with an "outstanding memory" – the "list of specials is endless and provided verbally"; even though the tabs skew "expensive" and the service can be "slow", most leave here "stuffed and happy."

🅩 Porto Leggero 🅢 *Italian*   26 | 25 | 26 | $53

Jersey City | Harborside Financial Plaza 5 (Pearl St.) | 201-434-3200 | www.portoleggero.net

Bringing some "sophistication" to Jersey City's financial district, this Italian "oasis" co-owned by Michael Cetrulo (Scalini Fedeli) purveys a "unique", "sure-to-please" menu split into traditional and signature options; "top-notch" service and a "beautiful" setting – with "dramatic chandeliers", "giant windows" and "high ceilings" – distract from the "pricey" tabs.

Portuguese Manor *Portuguese/Spanish*   19 | 14 | 20 | $37

Perth Amboy | 310 Elm St. (bet. Fayette & Smith Sts.) | 732-826-2233 | www.portuguesemanorrestaurante.com

"Paella is king" and "sangria is queen" at this longtime Perth Amboy Iberian serving "enormous platters" of surf 'n' turf; although the "old-world" decor is looking "a little shopworn", service is "friendly" and "fantastic" weekend entertainment pulls in a "large, social crowd."

Primavera *Italian*   21 | 17 | 20 | $43

West Orange | 350 Pleasant Valley Way (bet. Marmon Terrace & Sullivan Dr.) | 973-731-4779 | www.primaverawestorange.com

"Many choices" fill out the menu of this "unpretentious" West Orange Italian known for its signature rock shrimp and "exceptional fish dishes"; too bad the "old-fashioned" interior looks like a "catering hall", but at least the "personable" staffers "try very hard to please."

Prime & Beyond
Meat House ☑ *Korean/Steak*

| - | - | - | E |

Fort Lee | 501 Main St. (bet. Edwin Ave. & Jones Rd.) | 201-461-0033
There's not much ambiance at this Fort Lee butcher shop–cum-eatery where the chops are priced by the pound and come with Korean-accented sides; maybe "your wallet will be empty by the time you leave", but lunch is cheaper.

Pub, The *Steak*

| 19 | 13 | 19 | $35 |

Pennsauken | 7600 Kaighns Ave. (Crescent Blvd.) | 856-665-6440 | www.thepubnj.com
Nostalgic types take a "walk down memory lane" at this Pennsauken "time machine" that's been serving "honest steaks" since 1951 in a faux medieval room the size of an "airplane hangar"; fans tout its "ginormous" salad bar and tolerate the "loud" decibels and "outdated" decor.

Quays, The *American*

| 18 | 20 | 17 | $43 |

Hoboken | 310 Sinatra Dr. (bet. 3rd & 4th Sts.) | 201-656-2521 | www.thequayshoboken.com
This "understated" Hoboken New American draws the "post-graduate set" with its "well-done" grub and "great outside dining"; set opposite the Hudson Riverfront promenade, it sports "nautical" decor that's a nice "nod to the sea", but sinkers say it's "pricey" and "known mostly as a bar."

Quiet Man, The ◑ *Pub Food*

| 22 | 17 | 21 | $33 |

Dover | 64 E. McFarlan St. (Hudson St.) | 973-366-6333 | www.quietmanpub.com
Fans of "great" pub grub laud this "authentic" Irish "staple" in Dover that's festooned with memorabilia from the John Wayne film of the same name; "warm" service and "live entertainment" enhance the overall "upbeat" experience.

Raagini *Indian*

| 23 | 18 | 20 | $36 |

Mountainside | 1085 Rte. 22 E. (Mill Ln.) | 908-789-9777 | www.raagini.com
For "upscale" Indian dining in Mountainside, check out this local "favorite" known for "lots of variety" on its "flavorful, tasty" menu; "attentive" service distracts from decor that "could use some sprucing up", but the "smashing" lunch buffet (a "steal for the quality") is fine as is.

Raimondo's *Italian*

| 24 | 18 | 22 | $45 |

Ship Bottom | 1101 Long Beach Blvd. (11th St.) | 609-494-5391 | www.raimondoslbi.com
"Busy all summer" (when reservations are at a premium), this Ship Bottom BYO on Long Beach Island draws crowds with "robust" Italian dishes that are "beautifully prepared with the freshest ingredients"; enthusiasts say it's "best off-season" when it's quieter, though its "fabulous" "bargain" early-bird deals are enjoyable year-round.

	FOOD	DECOR	SERVICE	COST

NEW Ralic's Steakhouse 🅂Ⓜ *Steak* | - | - | - | E |

Haddonfield | 26 S. Haddon Ave. (Ellis St.) | 856-616-1520 |
www.ralicssteakhouse.com

Chef Bryan Groff has replaced *Hell's Kitchen* alum Ed Battaglia at the
stove of this upscale BYO steakhouse in quaint Haddonfield; with
only 28 seats in its tasteful, contemporary space and dinner hours
only from Thursday–Sunday, reservations are a must here.

☒ Ram's Head Inn Ⓜ *American* | 24 | 26 | 25 | $57 |

Galloway | 9 W. White Horse Pike (bet. Ash & Taylor Aves.) |
609-652-1700 | www.ramsheadinn.com

A "short trek" but light years away from AC, this "elegant" Galloway
"class act" (and sibling of The Manor and Highlawn Pavilion) serves
"exquisitely presented" Traditional Americana with "wonderful for-
mality" in a jackets-suggested milieu; the "romantic", candlelit digs
appeal to "older" folks who think it's "outstanding in all areas" – save
for the "not-cheap" tabs – and particularly perfect at "Christmas."

Rare, The Steak House *Steak* | 24 | 21 | 24 | $55 |

Little Falls | 440 Main St. (bet. Pompton & Union Aves.) | 973-256-6699 |
www.rarestk.com

"Top" steaks and "excellent" presentation lure carnivores to this
"welcoming" Little Falls chophouse where the "creative" menu also
features Italian favorites from Il Tulipano (the owner's Cedar Grove
catering facility); many find it an "expensive" proposition, but lunch
is the "best deal" and the service is "superb."

☒ Rat's Ⓜ *French* | 24 | 28 | 24 | $60 |

Hamilton | Grounds for Sculpture | 16 Fairgrounds Rd. (Ward Ave.) |
609-584-7800 | www.ratsrestaurant.org

With its "dazzling" "fairy-tale" setting in a "whimsical" sculpture
park inspired by "Monet's garden at Giverny", this "unique" Hamilton
"destination" is beloved for its "not-to-be-missed" setting; now
managed by Stephen Starr Events, it offers a "creative" country
French menu that's less formal than before but still "delicious",
while the "attentive" service and "pricey" tabs remain in place.

☒ Raven and the Peach *American* | 24 | 25 | 23 | $61 |

Fair Haven | 740 River Rd. (Fair Haven Rd.) | 732-747-4666 |
www.ravenandthepeach.net

"Pretty", "softly lit" decor "reminiscent of *Casablanca*" is on par with
the "outstanding" New American food served at this "sophisticated" spot in Fair Haven; granted, it's "pricey", but "worth it" for a
"special evening" out, and the "splendid" staff makes a "genuine
effort to please."

Raymond's *American* | 21 | 17 | 19 | $27 |

Montclair | 28 Church St. (bet. Fullerton Ave. & Park St.) | 973-744-9263 |
www.raymondsnj.com

"Upscale diner" food and a "friendly" vibe make this "'50s-style"
American BYO in Montclair a "favorite three-meal option" and a perennial "hangout for the baby-carriage set"; though weekend waits

can be "long", "quick" service and "wonderful alfresco dining" leave most agreeing it's "what every town should have."

Ray's Little Silver Seafood *Seafood*   21 | 10 | 17 | $35

Little Silver | Markham Place Plaza | 125 Markham Pl. (Prospect Ave.) | 732-758-8166

Admirers "stick to the basics" and order the "simple, fresh" fish at this "low-key" strip-mall seafooder in Little Silver; the decor "hasn't moved into the 21st century" yet and it takes no reservations, but BYO keeps costs down and service is "nice" if "slow."

Rebecca's Ⓜ *Cuban*   23 | 20 | 23 | $43

Edgewater | 236 Old River Rd. (River Rd.) | 201-943-8808 | www.rebeccascubanrestaurant.com

"Splendid" Cuban cooking turns up at this "out-of-the-way" Edgewater BYO, an "intimate", "romantic" affair that's "perfect for a date"; sure, it's a bit "pricey" and the "tables can be close", but the "unique" outdoor courtyard, complete with gurgling fountain, is "very cool" indeed.

Red *American*   21 | 22 | 20 | $47

Red Bank | 3 Broad St. (Front St.) | 732-741-3232 | www.rednj.com

The "sexiest place to eat" in Red Bank, this "hip" resto/lounge slings "great" cocktails and "solid" New Americana (including "not-bad sushi") in a "modern", "nightclub-chic" setting; ok, it can be "pricey" and "loud", but its "trendy" followers are too busy "people-watching" to notice.

Red's Lobster Pot *Seafood*   24 | 16 | 19 | $37

Point Pleasant Beach | 57 Inlet Dr. (B'way) | 732-295-6622 | www.redslobsterpot.com

This "incredibly good" seasonal seafooder in Point Pleasant Beach is comprised of two parts: a basic, "self-serve" deck on the water where "you can watch the boats" come in, and a "cramped" indoor "shack" with a more ambitious, "fresh-caught" menu; either way, make sure to "get there early", since this BYO doesn't take reservations.

🅰 Red Square *Eclectic*   21 | 26 | 22 | $60

Atlantic City | Quarter at the Tropicana | 2801 Pacific Ave. (Iowa Ave.) | 609-344-9100 | www.chinagrillmgt.com

Renowned for its "sub-zero" vodka vault, this "upscale" restaurant/lounge in AC's Quarter at the Tropicana serves "creative", "expensive" Eclectic eats, but is probably most appreciated for its "amazing" cocktails; its perestroika-themed, "red velvet"-lined room includes "romantic" private booths that enhance the "enjoyable" experience.

Redstone American Grill *American*   21 | 23 | 21 | $36

Marlton | Promenade at Sagemore | 500 Rte. 73 S. (bet. Brick Rd. & Marlton Pkwy.) | 856-396-0332 | www.redstonegrill.com

An "inviting" outpost of a Midwestern mini-chain, this "lively" Marlton American offers "quite good" cooking for reasonable money; a "big bar" scene with a "pickup-city" vibe keeps things "lively" here, espe-

	FOOD	DECOR	SERVICE	COST

cially the "great people-watching" on its outdoor patio; P.S. there's another outpost in Plymouth Meeting, PA.

Redwood's *American* | 18 | 17 | 19 | $34

Chester | 459 Main St. (bet. Melville Pl. & Sentry Ln.) | 908-879-7909 | www.redwoodsgrillandbar.com

The aroma from the wood-burning grill "puts you in the mood to eat" at this "enjoyable" Chester American where the menu is "meat-centric" and the pricing "fair value"; though critics report "nothing spectacular" going on, it does host a "lively bar" scene and there's a "great loyalty program" via online coupons.

Remington's ☑ *American* | 21 | 22 | 22 | $47

Manasquan | 142 Main St. (bet. Parker & Taylor Aves.) | 732-292-1300 | www.remingtonsnj.com

Fans suggest that this Manasquan New American could be the "closest thing to a NYC restaurant on the Jersey Shore"; the "interesting" seasonal menu is "nicely presented", and service is "attentive" at this "classy" spot.

Renato's Pizza Master ◑ *Pizza* | ▽ 22 | 16 | 21 | $33

Jersey City | 278 Central Ave. (Hutton St.) | 201-659-2232

Ok, it "doesn't look like much from the front", but there's some "seriously good" Italian food offered in the discreet rear dining room of this Jersey City pizzeria; fans say it's "no garlic factory", while "terrific lunch specials" ensure that "you really get your money's worth."

Renault Winery Gourmet Restaurant ☑ *American* | 21 | 22 | 22 | $46

Egg Harbor | 72 N. Bremen Ave. (Moss Mill Rd.) | 609-965-2111 | www.renaultwinery.com

NJ's oldest winery (now a "secluded" Egg Harbor resort with its own inn) is the site of this "rustic" American offering an "escape from everything modern and urban"; while the six-course, set-price New American menu is "tasty" enough, the "so-so" wines are another story; P.S. dinner served Friday–Sunday only.

Reservoir Tavern ☒☑ *Italian* | 23 | 9 | 16 | $26

Boonton | 92 Parsippany Blvd. (Intervale Rd.) | 973-334-5708 | www.therestavern.com

"Legions of dedicated followers" applaud the "awesome" thin-crust pizza served at this "old-fashioned" Boonton Italian that's been family-owned since 1936; the rest of the "red-sauce" menu is "not so great", the waits can be "ridiculous" and the ambiance is strictly "church basement", but it stays "popular" by being so "easy on the wallet."

Restaurant L *American* | 18 | 18 | 19 | $47

Allendale | 9 Franklin Tpke. (bet. MacKay Ave. & Waibel Dr.) | 201-785-1112 | www.restaurantlnj.com

"Decent neighborhood dining" is the word on this Allendale American that may be better known for its "good bar scene" than its "just ok" food; although it's a bit "expensive", prix fixe deals and a Wednesday night DJ help keep it "packed"; P.S. regulars advise "try the patio."

	FOOD	DECOR	SERVICE	COST

❷ Restaurant Latour Ⓜ *American* `27` `26` `27` `$83`

Hamburg | Crystal Springs Resort | 1 Wild Turkey Way
(Crystal Springs Rd.) | 973-827-0548 | www.crystalgolfresort.com
Overlooking the Crystal Springs Resort golf course in Hamburg, this
"top table" showcases chef Michael Weisshaupt's "incredible"
French-accented New American cuisine, prepared from locally
sourced ingredients and complemented by an "amazing", 7,000-label
wine list; "white-glove" service and an "unhurried" pace enhance
the "extraordinary" mood, broken only when the super-"expensive"
check arrives; P.S. jackets suggested, open Thursday–Sunday only
and no relation to Latour of Ridgewood.

❷ Resto *French* `25` `18` `25` `$51`

Madison | 77 Main St. (bet. Central & Greenwood Aves.) | 973-377-0066 |
www.restonj.com
"Expertly crafted" contemporary French fare emerges from an open
kitchen at this "unpretentious" BYO storefront in Madison that
"crowds up rapidly"; true, it's "a bit pricey" and "Brooklyn-esque",
but "reservations are a necessity" here given its "tiny" dimensions.

Richard's ⌀ *Deli* `20` `12` `20` `$19`

Long Branch | 155 Brighton Ave. (Sairs Ave.) | 732-870-9133 |
www.richardsdeli.com
Now entering its fourth decade, this "old-school" Long Branch deli
presents a "large selection" of "consistent" noshes for "reasonable",
cash-only sums; "worn" decor comes with the territory, along with
"friendly", appropriately "intrusive" waitresses.

Rick's Ⓜ *Italian* `21` `13` `20` `$32`

Lambertville | 19 S. Main St. (Ferry St.) | 609-397-0051 |
www.ricksitalian.com
"Locals love" this "old-school" Lambertville BYO where surveyors
report the "excellent" Italian *cucina* is served in a "tiny", red-and-
white-checkered-tablecloth setting; regulars say it can be "claustro-
phobic" and say taking "reservations would be an improvement"
(currently accepted only for parties of four or more), but at least the
"prices are in line."

Rio Rodizio *Brazilian* `20` `19` `18` `$41`

Newark | 1034 McCarter Hwy. (Lombardy St.) | 973-622-6221
Union | 2185 Rte. 22 W. (Chestnut St.) | 908-206-0060
www.riorodizio.com
"Bring your appetite" to these Brazilian "meat feasts" in Newark and
Union, where the all-you-can-eat options can include sushi; although the chow is "good, not great" and the acoustics on the
"noisy" side, fans say you "can't beat the value" here.

Risotto House *Italian* `23` `15` `21` `$33`

Rutherford | 88 Park Ave. (bet. Passaic Ave. & Ridge Rd.) | 201-438-5344 |
www.therisottohouse.com
Like the name says, "they specialize in risotto" at this "excellent"
BYO in a Rutherford storefront, though the rest of the Italian offer-

ings are "well above average"; "helpful" service and "attractive" prices make the "not-much-to-look-at" decor more palatable.

⨂ Ristorante da Benito *Italian* 26 | 23 | 26 | $61

Union | 222 Galloping Hill Rd. (Walton Ave.) | 908-964-5850 | www.dabenito.com

Union "power brokers" – "politicians", "sports people" and other "high-visibility" folk – assemble at this "upscale" Italian where the food is "spectacular", the setting "beautiful" and the service "formal"; no surprise, it's "not inexpensive" and for best results, "go with a regular."

Ritz Seafood Ⓜ *Asian/Seafood* 26 | 15 | 22 | $39

Voorhees | Ritz Shopping Ctr. | 910 Haddonfield Berlin Rd. (bet. Laurel Oak Blvd. & White Horse Rd.) | 856-566-6650 | www.ritzseafood.com

"Small" dimensions are one reason this Pan-Asian seafood BYO in Voorhees' Ritz Shopping Center is usually "packed", but more credit goes to its "imaginative" cuisine; though there's "no atmosphere" and the "tables are too close" together, fans say "you can't go wrong" – "everything is cooked to perfection" here.

⨂ River Palm Terrace *Steak* 25 | 20 | 22 | $63

Edgewater | 1416 River Rd. (Palisade Terrace) | 201-224-2013
Fair Lawn | 41-11 Rte. 4 W. (Saddle River Rd.) | 201-703-3500
Mahwah | 209 Ramapo Valley Rd. (Rte. 17) | 201-529-1111
www.riverpalm.com

"Be prepared to spend" big time at this "upscale" chophouse trio where "succulent" steaks and "outstanding" seafood (including sushi at Edgewater and Mahwah) are paired with an "impressive" wine list; some beef that there's "always a wait" and "regulars get preference", but nearly everyone "wants to go back" – as soon as their "cash flow recovers."

RiverWinds Ⓢ Ⓜ *American* - | - | - | E

Deptford | 1075 Riverwinds Dr. | 856-579-7900 | www.theriverwindsrestaurant.com

Overlooking the Delaware River in Deptford, this spendy American steakhouse serves up surf 'n' turf in a slick contemporary setting; in addition to the lobby lounge, where a piano player tickles the ivories, there's a boat-shaped bar with views of the water.

Roberto's Dolce Vita *Italian* 21 | 17 | 19 | $40

Beach Haven | 12907 Long Beach Blvd. (130th St.) | 609-492-1001
For "good" "home-cooked" food at "fair" prices, check out this "informal" Beach Haven Italian on Long Beach Island that's open year-round; the atmosphere may be very "'70s", but service is "friendly" and "BYO adds to the value."

Roberto's II Ⓜ *Italian* 21 | 14 | 19 | $43

Edgewater | 936 River Rd. (bet. Dempsey & Hilliard Aves.) | 201-224-2524 | www.robertos2.com

"Old-school" sums up the mood at this longtime Edgewater venue with "Sinatra on the speakers" and "Italian standbys on the plates";

"pleasant", tuxedoed service and "value" pricing compensate for the "dated" decor and the "never-changes-never-improves" menu.

Robin's Nest *American*   ∇ 22 | 21 | 18 | $33
Mount Holly | 2 Washington St. (White St.) | 609-261-6149 | www.robinsnestmountholly.com

"Imagination guides the menu" at this "quaint" American set in a historic building along Rancocas Creek in Mount Holly; a "comfortable" setting with a "great patio", "friendly" service and "reasonable" tabs make for "pleasant" "small-town" dining; P.S. Sunday is brunch-only.

Robongi *Japanese*   24 | 15 | 20 | $33
Hoboken | 520 Washington St. (bet. 5th & 6th Sts.) | 201-222-8388
Weehawken | Port Imperial Ferry Terminal | 4800 Port Imperial Blvd. (Regency Pl.) | 201-558-1818
www.robongi.com

"Young, loud" crowds patronize this Hoboken Japanese BYO for its "creative" sushi, "reasonable" tabs and "hospitable" service; "cheesy" sea-shack decor and "long" weekend lines lead some to reserve it as a "solid take-out option"; P.S. the Weehawken branch has a full bar.

Rob's Bistro ⓂＭ *French*   - | - | - | M
Madison | 75 Main St. (bet. Central & Greenwood Aves.) | 973-377-0067 | www.robsbistro.com

Next to big brother Resto, this quaint Madison storefront BYO showcases chef-owner Robert Ubhaus' classic French bistro fare at midday and Sunday brunch, plus dinner; the $13 express lunch suits workers on the go, while moderate prices and a kids' menu tempt families.

Rocca Ⓜ *Italian*   24 | 18 | 21 | $41
Glen Rock | 203 Rock Rd. (bet. Glen Ave. & Main St.) | 201-670-4945 | www.roccaitalianrestaurant.com

"Sleepy Glen Rock" is the site of this "quality dining" experience, a "relaxing" BYO celebrated for its "upscale", "inventive" Italian cooking; though the atmosphere is just "ok" and service veers from "slow" to "eager", it's "affordable" and seems to be "getting better and better"; P.S. the adjacent Market at Rocca offers a roster of to-go items.

Rocky Hill Inn Ⓜ *American*   17 | 16 | 18 | $39
Rocky Hill | 137 Washington St. (Princeton Ave.) | 609-683-8930 | www.rockyhilltavern.com

"Early American" describes both the food and the atmosphere at this "quiet", "casual" venue in Rocky Hill that inhabits a "quaint" 18th-century inn; despite rather "average" food and "uneven" service, fans like its "good prices" and "ye olde neighborhood bar and grill" vibe.

Rod's Olde Irish Tavern *Pub Food*   18 | 15 | 19 | $30
Sea Girt | 507 Washington Blvd. (5th Ave.) | 732-449-2020 | www.rodstavern.com

Set on the "Irish Riviera" in Sea Girt, this "comfortable", "family-friendly" joint features a "decent", usual-suspects pub menu; maybe it's "loud at the bar" and the decor "needs a makeover", but no one complains about the "reasonable" tabs or "mammoth" portion sizes.

	FOOD	DECOR	SERVICE	COST

Rod's Steak & Seafood Grille *Seafood/Steak*

| 22 | 24 | 23 | $52 |

Morristown | Madison Hotel | 1 Convent Rd. (bet. Madison Ave. & Old Turnpike Rd.) | 973-539-6666 | www.rodssteak.com

"Charm and warmth" abound at this "longtime" Morristown surf 'n' turfer where patrons can dine in the "appealing" main room or in a pair of "romantic" antique Pullman cars recalling a "more elegant, cell-phone-free era"; though some lament the "expense-account" prices, it is a "good place to talk business" and the "outstanding" Sunday brunch is right on track.

Rolling Pin Cafe 🅱 *American/Sandwiches*

| 23 | 16 | 19 | $18 |

Westwood | 341 Broadway (bet. Jefferson & Westwood Aves.) | 201-666-4660 | www.therollingpincafe.com

"Off-the-charts-good" breakfast and lunch items turn up at this "low-key" American cafe in Westwood, where you can "gain 10 pounds just from the aroma emanating from the kitchen"; sure, it's "tiny" and "often crowded", but the "homemade scones" and "vintage" rolling-pin decor make it "worth the squeeze."

Rooney's Oceanfront *Seafood*

| 19 | 21 | 19 | $45 |

Long Branch | 100 Ocean Ave. N. (Cooper Ave.) | 732-870-1200 | www.rooneysocean.com

The "standard seafood" takes a backseat to the "breathtaking views" of "swaying palm trees" and the "roaring ocean" at this "happy" Long Branch "'in' place"; sure, service can be "spotty" and the chow's "pricey for the quality", but the "raw bar is a treat" and the "see-and-be-seen bar scene" is among the best in these parts.

Roots Steakhouse *Steak*

| 26 | 24 | 24 | $65 |

Summit | 401 Springfield Ave. (Maple St.) | 908-273-0027
NEW **Morristown** | 40 W. Park Pl. (Market St.) | 973-326-1800
www.rootssteakhouse.com

"Solid" steaks and "terrific" sides lure Summit's "movers and shakers" to this "swanky" chop shop set in a "handsome" former bank; a "hot" bar scene, "warm" environs and "crazy prices" are all part of the package; the Morristown satellite opened post-Survey.

Rosa Mexicano *Mexican*

| 22 | 21 | 20 | $40 |

Hackensack | Shops at Riverside | 390 Hackensack Ave. (Rte. 4) | 201-489-9100 | www.rosamexicano.com

A "NYC favorite without the tolls", this Hackensack spin-off supplies "contemporary" Mexican chow – notably "incredible" tableside guacamole and "fancy" pomegranate margaritas – in a "waterfall"-enhanced setting; the decibels can be "deafening" and the service "hit-or-miss", but overall it's a "fun" "change of pace."

🇿 Rosemary and Sage 🅱🅼 *American*

| 26 | 20 | 24 | $52 |

Riverdale | 26 Hamburg Tpke. (bet. Haycock & Morris Aves.) | 973-616-0606 | www.rosemaryandsage.com

"Hard-core foodies" tout the "well-crafted", "exquisitely prepared" New American menu at this "family-run" Riverdale "hideaway"; the staff "goes out of its way to make you feel welcome", and though prices skew "on the high side", the five-course prix fixe is an "excellent value"; P.S. dinner only, Wednesday–Saturday.

Rosie's Trattoria *Italian*

21	18	20	$36

Randolph | 1181 Sussex Tpke. (Brookside Rd.) | 973-895-3434 | www.rosiestrattoria.com

"What a neighborhood place should be", this "dependable" Randolph Italian serves "consistently good" "traditional" food paired with a "reasonably priced" wine list; though aesthetes think the decor "needs some freshening", the "outdoor dining" can't be beat on a nice night.

Royal Warsaw ◐Ⓜ *Polish*

23	18	20	$34

Elmwood Park | 871 River Dr. (bet. Garden Dr. & Roosevelt Ave.) | 201-794-9277 | www.royalwarsaw.com

"Pierogi mania" reigns at this Elmwood Parker serving "down-home", "stick-to-the-ribs" Polish fare (the "hefty" menu also includes French specialties like escargot and frogs' legs); "wonderful" service and "reasonable" tabs make this one "worth a try."

Rumba Cubana *Cuban*

▽ 23	18	22	$25

North Bergen | 7420 Broadway (75th St.) | 201-854-4000 | www.rumbacubanarestaurant.com

Rumba's Cafe *Cuban*

Jersey City | 513 Central Ave. (North St.) | 201-216-9655 | www.rumbascafe.com

"Huge portions" of "real-deal" *comida* accompanied by "fantastic" mojitos draw folks to this festive North Bergen Cuban and its JC sibling; fanciful island decor, "outdoor seating", "great prices" and a "so-much-fun" mood explain the perennial "lines out the door."

❷ Ruth's Chris Steak House *Steak*

25	22	24	$63

Weehawken | Lincoln Harbor | 1000 Harbor Blvd. (19th St.) | 201-863-5100
Parsippany | Hilton Parsippany | 1 Hilton Ct. (Campus Dr.) | 973-889-1400
Atlantic City | The Walk | 2020 Atlantic Ave. (bet. Arkansas & Michigan Aves.) | 609-344-5833
Princeton | Princeton Forrestal Vill. | 2 Village Blvd. (College Rd.) | 609-452-0041
www.ruthschris.com

Loyalists love the "sizzling platters" of "oh-so-good buttery steaks" at this "top-quality" chophouse chain that comes through with "winning" sides too; offering "old-style service" in a "traditional" setting, it's "expensive" but "utterly reliable", especially when you're "entertaining friends and clients."

Rutt's Hut ⑳ *Hot Dogs*

21	7	15	$13

Clifton | 417 River Rd. (bet. Delawanna Ave. & Peekay Dr.) | 973-779-8615

Deep-fried hot dogs (aka "rippers", aka "heaven on a bun") are the specialty of this circa-1928 cash-only Clifton "institution" where the service is "surly" and the weenies taste best at the "real-deal walk-up counter"; maybe the decor's "decrepit" (though a post-Survey

	FOOD	DECOR	SERVICE	COST

redo may change that), but "frankophiles" say it has the "best view of the highway around."

Sabor *Nuevo Latino*

22	21	19	$42

North Bergen | 8809 River Rd. (bet. Churchill & Old River Rds.) | 201-943-6366 | www.saborlatinbistro.com

The "sangria goes down easy" at this "upbeat" Nuevo Latino in North Bergen, where the "zesty" chow is just as "scrumptious" as the liquids; "low" lights, "loud music" and a "rockin' bar scene" make for a "salsa-party" mood for a crowd that's "clearly looking for an escape from the work week."

☑ Saddle River Inn ⑤Ⓜ *American/French*

28	25	26	$64

Saddle River | 2 Barnstable Ct. (Allendale Rd.) | 201-825-4016 | www.saddleriverinn.com

"Superb from beginning to end", this "gold-standard", "big-ticket" grande dame is set in a "casually elegant" 18th-century barn in Saddle River, where "impeccable" Franco-American preparations emerge from the "steady" kitchen; "serious" service and an "inviting" atmosphere burnish the "world-class" experience, and while it certainly "doesn't come cheap", BYO allows one to "indulge more than usual."

Saffron *Indian*

24	17	21	$33

East Hanover | 249 Rte. 10 (New Murray Rd.) | 973-599-0700 | www.saffronnj.com

"Creative use of seasoning" spices up the "high-quality" Indian fare at this "upscale" BYO in an East Hanover strip mall; "Zen" decor, a "Bollywood" soundtrack and "wonderful" service make for "pleasant" dining, while a "value"-priced lunch buffet ices the cake.

☑ Sagami Ⓜ *Japanese*

27	14	21	$38

Collingswood | 37 W. Crescent Blvd. (bet. Haddon Ave. & White Horse Pike) | 856-854-9773

"Still rocking" well into its third decade, this Collingswood BYO remains the "barometer to judge" Japanese fare in South Jersey; service is "quick", the decibel level "noisy" and the room "super-crowded", yet "reservations are a must" almost any night of the week at this "best-loved" spot.

Sage ⌀ *Mediterranean*

25	15	22	$39

Ventnor | 5206 Atlantic Ave. (Weymouth Ave.) | 609-823-2110 | www.sageventnor.com

"Outstanding" modern Mediterranean cuisine keeps this cash-only Ventnor BYO booked "even on weekends in the off-season"; a "diverse", "thoughtfully prepared" menu and "knowledgeable" service compensate for the "close" tables and "noisy" acoustics.

Sage Diner ❶ *Diner*

14	-	13	$19

Mount Laurel | 1170 Rte. 73 (Church Rd.) | 856-727-0770 | www.sagedinernj.com

Sage surveyors are split on this just-redecorated Mount Laurel stalwart – some cite its "reliable comfort food" as evidence that it's "just what a diner should be", but those who are "not impressed" find the eats "routine" and the "prices higher than warranted", saying "there are much better" examples of the genre.

Sakura Bana Ⓜ *Japanese* | 25 | 15 | 20 | $40 |

Ridgewood | 43 Franklin Ave. (Chestnut St.) | 201-447-6525 | www.sakurabana.com

"Exceptional" "raw delights", "fabulous" rolls and an "extensive" traditional menu keep this "longtime" Japanese BYO in Ridgewood "crowded"; there's "not much decor", but "attentive" service and "delicious" lunch boxes distract.

Sakura Spring *Chinese/Japanese* | ▽ 24 | 21 | 24 | $27 |

Cherry Hill | 1871 Rte. 70 E. (Greentree Rd.) | 856-489-8018 | www.sakuraspring.com

Surveyors says the "homey" surroundings are a bit more "attractive" than the norm at this "upscale" Cherry Hill BYO where the "beautifully prepared" Chinese and Japanese offerings are equally "excellent"; "great prices" and "lovely" service seal the deal.

Sallee Tee's Grille *American/Eclectic* | 18 | 16 | 18 | $34 |

Monmouth Beach | Channel Club Marina | 33 West St. (Channel Dr.) | 732-870-8999 | www.salleeteesgrille.com

"Hidden" in a "hard-to-find" location in Monmouth Beach's Channel Club Marina, this "congenial" spot serves NY-style deli items at lunchtime, then shifts to an Eclectic, "something-for-everyone" menu at the dinner hour; "inexpensive" tabs and a no-reservations policy translate into "long lines."

Salt Creek Grille *American* | 19 | 22 | 20 | $43 |

Rumson | 4 Bingham Ave. (River Rd.) | 732-933-9272
Princeton | Forrestal Village Shopping Ctr. | 1 Rockingham Row (Village Blvd.) | 609-419-4200
www.saltcreekgrille.com

"Aspen ski lodge meets NJ" at these "beautiful" "Arts and Crafts" Americans in Princeton and Rumson, where the "above-average", meat-centric menus are "tasty" if "not fancy"; fire pits and "noisy" bar scenes make for "jumping" "young scenes", and fans say they're "crowded for good reason."

Salute Brick Oven Bistro Ⓜ *Italian* | - | - | - | E |

Montclair | 173 Glen Ridge Ave. (Willow St.) | 973-746-2380 | www.salutebistro.com

Rustic Italian describes both the menu and the decor (think brick walls, bushel baskets of fresh produce) at this high-energy Montclair BYO; classic and modern takes on pizzette and assorted small bites emerge from the brick oven of its open kitchen, along with hearty pastas and entrees like braciole with gnocchi.

Samdan *Turkish* | 21 | 16 | 19 | $36 |

Cresskill | 178 Piermont Rd. (Union Ave.) | 201-816-7343 | www.samdanrestaurant.com

"Tender" kebabs "big enough to share" and "outstanding" mezes earn kudos at this "high-quality" Cresskill Turk that's particularly "good for groups"; "reasonable" tabs, "attentive" service and a "white-tablecloth" atmosphere complete the "solid" picture.

Sammy's Ye Old Cider Mill Steak   23 | 10 | 18 | $59

Mendham | 353 Mendham Rd. W. (Oak Knoll Rd.) | 973-543-7675 | www.sammyscidermill.com

"Not your typical dining experience", this "hard-to-find" Mendham steakhouse (appropriately a former speakeasy) serves "done-to-perfection" chops with a "gimmick": you "order on arrival" then "wait downstairs" in a "run-down" basement until the food's ready; what with the "expensive" tabs and "rough" service, some marvel at its "popularity."

Sanducci's Trattoria Italian   19 | 17 | 19 | $30

River Edge | 620 Kinderkamack Rd. (bet. Madison & Van Buren Aves.) | 201-599-0600 | www.sanduccis.com

"Generous portions" of "traditional" Italian fare and "excellent" pizzas make this "reliable" River Edge trattoria a "wonderful neighborhood" option; thanks to "moderate" prices and a "variety of deals", there's "usually a crowd."

San Remo Italian   22 | 15 | 22 | $40

Shrewsbury | 37 E. Newman Springs Rd. (Rte. 35) | 732-345-8200 | www.sanremoitaliana.com

Maybe it "doesn't look like much from the road", but this "small" Shrewsbury BYO supplies "reliable" chow from a menu that's all over the Italian map and served by a staff that's "on top of everything"; P.S. a move to Red Bank is in the works.

Santorini Taverna ❶ Greek   ▽ 21 | 17 | 19 | $43

Fort Lee | 2020 Central Rd. (Bruce Reynolds Blvd.) | 201-947-2055 | www.santorini-taverna.com

A "step above your average Greek", this "wonderfully authentic" Fort Lee Hellenic features grilled seafood at dinner and more casual dishes for lunch; there's also a "charming" outdoor deck, although the surrounding buildings "don't allow for much of a view."

Sanzari's New Bridge Inn Italian   22 | 21 | 22 | $51

New Milford | 105 Old New Bridge Rd. (New Bridge Rd.) | 201-692-7700 | www.sanzarisnewbridgeinn.com

"Old-fashioned" Italian meals turn up at this New Milford "treat" near the Shops at Riverside, where a steak- and seafood-centric menu makes it a "perfect businessman's hangout"; though it's "a bit pricey", "friendly" service enhances the "enjoyable" feel.

⧰ Sapori Italian   28 | 22 | 26 | $40

Collingswood | 601 Haddon Ave. (Harvard Ave.) | 856-858-2288 | www.sapori.info

A small but "fantastic" "taste of Italy" in Collingswood, this "exceptional" spot via chef Franco Lombardo serves "not-your-usual" fare (e.g. spaghetti with sea urchin) in "lovely" rustic quarters that he designed and constructed himself; a "relaxed" mood and "knowledgeable" servers make this one a "sure hit"; P.S. closed Tuesdays.

	FOOD	DECOR	SERVICE	COST

Satis ⓜ *European*

-	-	-	M

Jersey City | 212 Washington St. (Sussex St.) | 201-435-5151 | www.satisbistro.com

Taking its name from the Latin root for 'satisfy', this modern European BYO bistro/salumeria/cafe sates appetites in the Paulus Hook section of Jersey City with a roster of charcuterie and cheese plates, plus creative seasonal entrees, and some two dozen flavors of housemade gelato and sorbet; the bi-level space features exposed-brick walls, and there's a seasonal Euro-style outdoor cafe.

Sawa *Japanese*

23	20	20	$39

Eatontown | 42 Rte. 36 (Rte. 35) | 732-544-8885
Long Branch | Pier Vill. | 68 Ocean Ave. (Centennial Dr.) | 732-229-0600
www.sawasteakhouse.com

"Impressive" sushi and "entertaining" hibachi grills keep the trade brisk at this Japanese duo also touted for its "accommodating" service; Pier Village's "fun" outdoor seating offers "great people-watching" opportunities and a "lively" bar scene, while Eatontown's "giant" aquariums thrill small fry.

ⓩ Scalini Fedeli ⓢ *Italian*

27	25	26	$70

Chatham | 63 Main St. (bet. Parrott Mill Rd. & Tallmadge Ave.) | 973-701-9200 | www.scalinifedeli.com

"Fine dining" gets a "memorable" spin at Michael Cetrulo's "genuine article" in Chatham, where a "perfectly executed" Italian menu is "presented beautifully" by an "outstanding" team; the "romantic" 18th-century farmhouse setting "exudes class" and is "always packed", but for best results "bring your boss or your trust fund" to settle the "high-end" tabs; P.S. dinner is prix fixe only.

Scarborough Fair ⓜ *American*

23	25	21	$42

Sea Girt | 1414 Meetinghouse Rd. (Rte. 35) | 732-223-6658 | www.scarboroughfairrestaurant.com

Private alcoves on many levels enhance the "cozy", "wonderfully romantic" mood at this atmospheric Sea Girt spot set in a 19th-century farm building; "cooked-to-perfection" New Americana served by a "professional" team makes it perfect for "special occasions."

NEW Scarduzio's ⓜ *Japanese/Steak*

-	-	-	VE

Atlantic City | Showboat Casino | 801 Boardwalk (bet. Delaware & States Aves.) | 609-343-4330 | www.showboatac.com

This high-end steakhouse/sushi lounge in the Showboat is celeb chef Chris Scarduzio's second AC property (after Mia, at Caesars); Wagyu and other prime cuts of beef from NYC's DeBragga butchers fuel high rollers in a big, modern setting featuring an open kitchen, sushi bar and late-night lounge with live entertainment.

ⓩ SeaBlue *Seafood*

26	25	25	$69

Atlantic City | Borgata Hotel, Casino & Spa | 1 Borgata Way (Huron Ave.) | 609-317-8220 | www.theborgata.com

Celeb chef Michael Mina's "seafood experience" just off the Borgata casino floor in AC is famed for its "decadent" signature lobster pot pie, served in a "picture-worthy" Adam Tihany–designed space; "stellar" service and a swanky mood make the "mortgage-payment" price tags "worth the splurge."

Seabra's Marisqueira *Portuguese/Seafood* | 23 | 14 | 20 | $37 |

Newark | 87 Madison St. (Ferry St.) | 973-465-1250 | www.seabrasmarisqueira.com

This "old-time", "real-deal" Portuguese seafooder in Newark's Ironbound serves "bountiful" portions of "brilliant" fin fare in "brightly lit", rather "blah" digs; "bargain" tabs, "knowledgeable" service and "free parking" are reasons why it's "been around awhile."

NEW Sear House *Steak* | - | - | - | VE |

Closter | 411 Piermont Rd. (Irving Ave.) | 201-292-4612 | www.searhouse.com

A dramatically backlit honey onyx bar, glass-and-stone fire pit, expansive water wall and elegant striped booths leave a searing impression at this swanky bi-level Closter steakhouse from the brothers behind Dimora, where tender cuts of in-house dry-aged steaks spark the most interest on the pricey à la carte menu, but chops and seafood sizzle too; lunchers can bask in the glamor with slightly less of a burn to the wallet.

☒ Seasons 52 *American* | 22 | 25 | 23 | $38 |

Cherry Hill | Cherry Hill Mall | 2000 Rte. 38 (Haddonfield Rd.) | 856-665-1052 | www.seasons52.com

"Healthful" dining that "doesn't involve granola and sandals" is yours at this Cherry Hill link of the national chain, where every dish on the seasonally changing American menu is under 475 calories; admirers like the "guilt-free" eating, "well-trained" service and nice variety of by-the-glass wines.

Segovia *Portuguese/Spanish* | 23 | 14 | 21 | $39 |

Moonachie | 150 Moonachie Rd. (Garden St.) | 201-641-4266 | www.segoviarestaurant.com

Famed for its "huge portions" of "garlic-laden" grub, this "longtime" Moonachie "favorite" is a "popular" destination for Meadowlands fans seeking "excellent" Iberian cooking; given the "prompt" service and good "bang-for-the-buck" pricing, it's no wonder there are "long lines" on game days and weekend nights.

Segovia Steakhouse & | 23 | 18 | 23 | $39 |
Seafood *Spanish/Steak*

Little Ferry | 217 Main St. (Vogt Ln.) | 201-814-1100 | www.segoviasteakhouse.com

This Spanish chophouse in Little Ferry is an "updated" spin-off of nearby sister Segovia; although "pretty much undiscovered" to date, it's "just as delicious" as its sibling and a "good value" since it's "cheaper than your average steakhouse."

Senorita's Mexican Grill *Mexican* | 19 | 20 | 19 | $28 |

Bloomfield | 285 Glenwood Ave. (Conger St.) | 973-743-0099

(continued)

(continued)

Senorita's Mexican Grill

Clark | Hyatt Hills Golf Complex | 1300 Raritan Rd. (bet. Central & Walnut Aves.) | 732-669-9024 **M**
www.senoritasmexicangrill.com

"Always busy", this "family-friendly" Mexican duo in Bloomfield and Clark offers "better-than-average" chow at a "very inexpensive" price point; though service can be "spotty", "tasty" happy-hour margaritas supply a shot of "fun."

☑ Serenade *French*   27 | 26 | 26 | $74

Chatham | 6 Roosevelt Ave. (Main St.) | 973-701-0303 |
www.restaurantserenade.com

"Exquisite" cuisine in an "elegant" atmosphere inspires "super-latives all around" for this "upscale" Chatham French where chef James Laird's "creative" yet "approachable" cooking is paired with a "deep" wine list; granted, the price tags are super-"expensive", but "impeccable" service and the "romantic" mood make for "simply sublime" "celebration" dining.

Sergeantsville Inn **M** *American*   24 | 25 | 22 | $51

Sergeantsville | 601 Rosemont Ringoes Rd. (Rte. 604) | 609-397-3700 |
www.sergeantsvilleinn.com

"Dripping with atmosphere", this Colonial-era structure in Sergeantsville features enough "fireplaces" and "stone walls" to lend a "rustic" feel to the swooningly "romantic" mood; the "can't-go-wrong" American menu also includes "out-of-the-ordinary" game dishes, while the less expensive tavern has "neighborhood hangout" written all over it.

Settebello **⑤** *Italian*   20 | 18 | 19 | $38

Morristown | 2 Cattano Ave. (Speedwell Ave.) | 973-267-3355
A "reliable fallback", this "cozy" Morristown restaurant offers "tasty" Italian food in a "quiet" setting; the service is "friendly" and dining on the patio is a particular "treat", while BYO keeps the pricing manageable.

Sette Cucina Italiana **⑤** *Italian*   24 | 22 | 23 | $51

Bernardsville | 7 Mine Brook Rd. (Mt. Airy Rd.) | 908-502-5054 |
www.settecucina.com

"Unusually creative" Italian cooking comes via a "young", "person-able" chef at this Bernardsville BYO where it can be "hard to get a reservation" given its "tiny" dimensions; though prices skew "expensive", devotees say it's a "special" place with "lovely" service and an "enjoyable" atmosphere.

Settimo Cielo **⑤** *Italian*   ▽ 23 | 19 | 21 | $41

Trenton | 17 E. Front St. (bet. Broad & Warren Sts.) |
609-656-8877

For a "power lunch" - or a "first-rate" Italian dinner - this Downtown Trenton "oasis" is a natural choice given its "old-style charm"; "excellent" service, a white-tablecloth setting and "superb" drinks at the vintage bar complete the "outstanding" picture.

	FOOD	DECOR	SERVICE	COST

Shanghai Jazz ☑ Asian
22 | 20 | 23 | $44

Madison | 24 Main St. (Green Village Rd.) | 973-822-2899 | www.shanghaijazz.com

"Fabulous" jazz meets "delicious" riffs on Pan-Asian fare at this "sophisticated" Madison supper club where the "cool" tunes enhance the "metropolitan" mood; "warm service" compensates for the somewhat "high" tabs, and regulars say it's one of the "best date-night restaurants" around; P.S. there's "no cover charge", but per-person minimums vary, depending on the night.

Ship Inn Pub Food
17 | 18 | 18 | $30

Milford | 61 Bridge St. (Rte. 519) | 908-995-0188 | www.shipinn.com

Mateys yearning for "authentic" fish 'n' chips near the Delaware River drop anchor at this "friendly" Milford pub that's been on the scene since 1985; locals say the "hit-or-miss" grub plays second fiddle to the "spectacularly good" beer.

Shipwreck Grill American/Seafood
24 | 18 | 21 | $50

Brielle | 720 Ashley Ave. (Higgins Ave.) | 732-292-9380 | www.shipwreckgrill.com

"Always busy", this "unassuming" American seafooder in Brielle is a "consistent performer", with "top-notch" cooking and "exceptional" service; too bad the "way-too-loud" acoustics make for "sign-language" conversations, but overall it's a "nice local place."

Shipwreck Point Steak
- | - | - | E

Point Pleasant Beach | 20 Inlet Dr. (B'way) | 732-899-3800 | www.shipwreckpointsteakhouse.com

From the veterans behind Brielle's popular Shipwreck Grill comes this Point Pleasant Beach chophouse where NYC-style dining comes at NYC prices (i.e. most everything's à la carte); fortunately, the impressive wine list includes a good selection under $50.

Shogun Japanese/Steak
21 | 18 | 19 | $36

East Brunswick | Center 18 Mall | 1020 Rte. 18 N. (bet. Gunia St. & Hillsdale Rd.) | 732-390-1922 | www.shogun18.net
Green Brook | 166 Rte. 22 (Washington Ave.) | 732-968-3330 | www.shogun22.net
Kendall Park | 3376 Rte. 27 (Sand Hills Rd.) | 732-422-1117 | www.shogun27.com
Toms River | Bey Lea Golf Course | 1536 N. Bay Ave. (Oak Ave.) | 732-286-9888 | www.shogunbeylea.com

"Standard" hibachi shows keep the kiddies entertained at this "Benihana-type" Japanese mini-chain that also slices "pretty good" sushi; they're "fun" options and "great for celebrating birthdays", despite somewhat "sterile" decor and "rushed" service.

☑ Shumi ☑ Japanese
28 | 13 | 24 | $51

Somerville | 30 S. Doughty Ave. (Veterans Memorial Dr.) | 908-526-8596

"Experienced palates" tout the "fabulous" sushi at this Somerville BYO that's rated NJ's Top Japanese; true, it's "expensive", the location is "hidden" and there's a decided "lack of decor", but the chef is "dedicated", service is "excellent" and "you get what you pay for" here.

Siam ☑✍ *Thai*

| 23 | 13 | 18 | $27 |

Lambertville | 61 N. Main St (bet. Coryell & York Sts.) | 609-397-8128

"Real" Thai food for an "inexpensive" cost has kept this "basic" Lambertville venue in business since 1985; "slow" service, "no-frills" digs and a cash-only rule may detract, but at least "BYO makes it affordable."

Siam Garden *Thai*

| 24 | 22 | 22 | $33 |

Red Bank | The Galleria | 2 Bridge Ave. (Front St.) | 732-224-1233 | www.siamgardenrestaurant.com

"As good as it gets" in Red Bank for Thai cooking, this "popular" Siamese is also celebrated for its "beautiful" setting decorated with an exotic mix of silks, antiques and woodcarvings; "genuinely warm service" adds to the "pleasant experience", as does a location that's "perfect for a pre-theater dinner."

Silk Road ☑ *Afghan*

| 23 | 19 | 23 | $29 |

Warren | Village Square Mall | 41 Mountain Blvd. (Primrose Way) | 908-561-8288 | www.silkroadrestaurant.org

"Ample" portions of "authentic", "out-of-the-ordinary" fare – from "piping hot" bread, "right from the [clay] oven", to homemade desserts – turn up at this "attractive" Afghani BYO "hidden" in a Warren shopping center; "attentive", "accommodating" service completes the overall "wonderful" picture.

Simon Prime ☑ *Steak*

| - | - | - | E |

Atlantic City | Atlantic City Hilton | 3400 Pacific Ave. (Boston Ave.) | 609-347-7111 | www.hiltonac.com

'Rock 'n' roll chef' Kerry Simon lands inside AC's recently renovated Hilton with this "slick" steakhouse where the servers wear jeans and sneakers, and the tablecloth-free setting has a modern, sexy vibe; just be prepared to "wield a black Amex card" when the bill arrives.

Simply Vietnamese *Vietnamese*

| - | - | - | I |

Tenafly | 1 Highwood Ave. (bet. County Rd. & Jay St.) | 201-568-7770 | www.simplyvietnamese.com

Traditional Vietnamese cooking gets a market-driven, new-world spin at this BYO set in a Tenafly storefront; the casual room is on the cramped side, but bamboo partitions and photos of Vietnam provide some distraction.

Sirena *Italian*

| 23 | 25 | 18 | $52 |

Long Branch | Pier Vill. | 27 Ocean Ave. (Cooper Ave.) | 732-222-1119 | www.sirenaristorante.com

This "beauty at the beach" in Long Branch's Pier Village offers "delicious, beautifully presented" Italian food that tastes even better when gazing out the "floor-to-ceiling windows" at its "stand-out" ocean views; maybe the staff "needs an attitude adjustment", but otherwise this "sophisticated" joint more than "lives up to its prices."

Sirin *Thai* ▽ 21 | 20 | 21 | $36

Morristown | 3 Pine St. (South St.) | 973-993-9122 | www.sirinthairestaurant.com

"Top-notch" Thai food served by a "spot-on" team arrives in "quiet" "homey" digs at this Morristown BYO; adjacent to the Mayo Center for the Performing Arts, it's "convenient" for theatergoers and especially popular with "baby boomers."

Siri's Thai French Cuisine *French/Thai* 26 | 20 | 24 | $40

Cherry Hill | 2117 Rte. 70 W. (bet. Beideman & S. Washington Aves.) | 856-663-6781 | www.siris-nj.com

"Original" Thai-French cuisine is served at this "outstanding" Cherry Hill BYO, a "guaranteed winner" thanks to "delightful" dishes served by a "caring" crew in a "pleasant" milieu; don't let the "unassuming strip-mall location" fool you – this one's a "real treat."

Skylark *Diner/Eclectic* 22 | 20 | 20 | $29

Jersey City | 70 Townsquare Pl. (Washington Blvd.) | no phone | www.skylarkonthehudson.com 🌮Ⓜ
Edison | 17 Wooding Ave. (bet. Old Post Rd. & Rte. 1) | 732-777-7878 | www.skylarkdiner.com ◗

Aka the "anti-diner diner", this "upscale" Edison Eclectic offers a "creative" mix of "high- and lowbrow" dishes (including all-day breakfast offerings) paired with a "fine" wine list and served in a room done up in "retro", "Sputnik era"–style; after dark, the action shifts to the "hopping" lounge; P.S. the Jersey City location opened post-Survey.

Smashburger *Burgers* 19 | 13 | 16 | $13

Clifton | 700 Rte. 3 W. (Garden State Pkwy.) | 973-777-3600
Glen Ridge | 989 Bloomfield Ave. (bet. Highland & Maple Aves.) | 973-433-7343
Hackensack | Shops at Riverside | 390 Hackensack Ave. (Rte. 4) | 201-343-1488
Montclair | 15 Bloomfield Ave. (Maple Ave.) | 973-433-7343
New Providence | 1260 Springfield Ave. (Passaic St.) | 908-286-0100
NEW Paramus | 556 Rte. 17 N. (bet. A & S Dr. & Kalisa Way) | 201-670-1120
Ramsey | 984 Rte. 17 N. (bet. Brookside & Mountainview Rd.) | 201-825-3163
NEW East Hanover | Castle Ridge Plaza | 368 Rte. 10 W. (River Rd.) | 862-701-5411
Florham Park | 187 Columbia Tpke. (Park St.) | 973-520-8717
Morris Plains | 1755 Rte. 10 E. (Tabor Rd.) | no phone
www.smashburger.com
Additional locations throughout New Jersey

From the Denver-based burger chain comes these Jersey spin-offs where one can "build a perfect burger" with "many permutations and combinations" available; purists say it's a "small step up from typical fast food", though herb-seasoned fries and "somewhat healthy" veggie frites supply a change of pace.

	FOOD	DECOR	SERVICE	COST

Smithville Inn *American*

20 | 22 | 22 | $40

Smithville | 1 N. New York Rd. (Old New York Rd.) | 609-652-7777 | www.smithvilleinn.com

"Quaint and quiet" sums up the scene at this "charming" "throwback" set in a 1787 Smithville building that more than "lives up to its history"; "respectable" Traditional American cuisine, a "laid-back" atmosphere and "dependable" service all make for "nostalgic", "comfortable" dining.

Smoke Chophouse ⑤ *Seafood/Steak*

23 | 18 | 23 | $63

Englewood | 36 Engle St. (bet. Bergen St. & Spring Ln.) | 201-541-8530 | www.smokechophouse.com

"Awesome" steaks and seafood are plated at this "upscale" Englewood spot, touted as the "last bastion of old-world living" since cigar smoking is permitted (there is a nonsmoking section downstairs, however); an "excellent" wine list and "expense-account" tabs come with the territory; P.S. a post-Survey ownership change may not be reflected in the scores.

Sofia *Mediterranean*

23 | 25 | 22 | $42

Margate | 9314 Amherst Ave. (Adams Ave.) | 609-822-9111 | www.sofiaofmargate.com

"Homemade" Mediterranean dishes are served at this "delightful" Margate venue where the "beautiful" setting (complete with four working fireplaces and a "wonderful" patio) is on par with the "delicious" food; grilled whole fish is the specialty of the house, and although it's on the pricey side, the "early-bird deal is a steal."

Soho 33 *Eclectic*

18 | 13 | 18 | $33

Madison | 33 Main St. (bet. Green Village Rd. & Waverly Pl.) | 973-822-2600 | www.soho33.com

BYO keeps costs "reasonable" at this Madison Eclectic, a "great neighborhood place" with "better-than-you'd-expect" grub; cynics who find "nothing to write home about" feel it "needs an upgrade on decor and service."

Solaia *Italian*

17 | 19 | 17 | $55

Englewood | 22 N. Van Brunt St. (Palisade Ave.) | 201-871-7155 | www.solaiarestaurant.com

A "handy location" next to Bergen PAC keeps the trade brisk at this Englewood Italian serving "reliably good food" in a "pleasant" setting; but prices that "rival NYC" induce "sticker shock", and there are also complaints about "not consistent" service.

Solari's ⑤ *Italian*

19 | 17 | 19 | $43

Hackensack | 61 River St. (Bridge St.) | 201-487-1969 | www.solarisrestaurant.com

"Popular for lunch with the courthouse crowd", this "dependable", vintage-1938 Hackensack Italian turns more "family-oriented" after dark (with live music some nights); though the setting's rather "old-fashioned", it "stays relevant" with "satisfying" meals, "moderate" prices and "conversation-possible" noise levels.

	FOOD	DECOR	SERVICE	COST

Sol-Mar ● *Portuguese/Seafood*
▽ 26 | 20 | 24 | $37

(aka Vila Nova do Sol-Mar)

Newark | 267 Ferry St. (bet. Chambers & Niagara Sts.) | 973-344-3041 | www.solmar-restaurant.com

Located "off the main drag" in Newark's Ironbound, this "wonderful" Portuguese "find" is renowned for "top-notch seafood" served in a "nice", airy atmosphere; "helpful" service and "great prices" are reasons why it "passes the patronized-by-locals test."

Solo Bella *Italian*
22 | 18 | 21 | $28

Jackson | 426 Chandler Rd. (Jackson Mills Rd.) | 732-961-0951 | www.solobella.com

Locals and shoppers at the Jackson outlets hype the "outstanding" food at this "comfortable" BYO known for its "old-fashioned" Italian menu and "delicious" brick-oven pizza; "no reservations" is a drawback, but "modest prices" and "aim-to-please" service are pluses.

So Moon Nan Jip ● *Korean*
▽ 24 | 10 | 19 | $37

Palisades Park | 238 Broad Ave. (Brinkerhoff Ave.) | 201-944-3998

"Authentic" hibachi-grilled Korean BBQ is the draw at this "crowded, noisy" Palisades Parker that stays open till 3 AM; the "ordinary storefront" setting is strictly "no frills", but service is "efficient" enough and it's "very popular" with the locals.

Somsak *Thai*
▽ 22 | 15 | 22 | $24

Voorhees | Echo Shops | 200 White Horse Rd. (bet. Burnt Mill Rd. & Lucas Ln.) | 856-782-1771

Set in a modest Voorhees storefront, this "solid" Thai BYO is touted for its "pleasant" service and "good-value" tabs; fans praise its "authentic" fare, but aesthetes are less enthused about the so-so decor.

Son Cubano ● *Cuban*
- | - | - | M

West New York | 40-4 Riverwalk Pl. (Port Imperial Blvd.) | 201-399-2020 | www.soncubanonj.com

This glamorous West New York cousin of a Manhattan Cuban dishes up satisfying portions of authentic, artfully presented *comida* in a pair of crystal-chandeliered dining rooms, one with floor-to-ceiling views of the Hudson and NY skyline; drinks can jack up the tab, but compensations include nightly live Latin music and a riverfront patio scene.

Sono Sushi *Japanese*
25 | 15 | 21 | $32

Middletown | Village Mall | 1098 Rte. 35 S. (New Monmouth Rd.) | 732-706-3588 | www.sonosushi.net

"High-quality fresh fish" fills out the menu of this "family-run" Japanese BYO in Middletown, an "old favorite" esteemed for its "satisfying", "interesting" sushi; "faithful" followers like the "nice" service but feel that the decor "needs a serious revamp."

Sophie's Bistro Ⓜ *French*
24 | 20 | 24 | $41

Somerset | 700 Hamilton St. (Baier Ave.) | 732-545-7778 | www.sophiesbistro.net

Bringing the "Left Bank" to Somerset, this "delightful" French bistro serves an "authentic" menu in "charming" environs; "wonderful" servers ensure that patrons are "never rushed out", and if the menu skews "middle of the road", at least it "never disappoints."

Sorrento ⓜ Italian — ▽ 24 | 23 | 23 | $47

East Rutherford | 132 Park Ave. (Paterson Ave.) | 201-507-0093
This "elegant" East Rutherford BYO offers "outstanding" homemade pastas and "creative" Italian entrees, topped off with "fabulous" desserts; "old-school" service and "tasteful" decor make it a "must-go."

Soul Flavors ⓜ Soul Food — ▽ 21 | 12 | 17 | $29

Jersey City | 354 Grove St. (Bay St.) | 201-217-3004 | www.soulflavors.com
Downtown Jersey City is home to this "unassuming" soul food BYO plying "generous" portions of "affordable", "authentic" Southern cooking "with a kick"; the interior may resemble a "'70s diner", but there are outdoor seats and it's convenient to the Grove Street PATH.

Spain Portuguese/Spanish — 24 | 16 | 19 | $41

Newark | 419 Market St. (Raymond Blvd.) | 973-344-0994 | www.spainrestaurant.com
"Mouthwatering" classic dishes like paella and "great" steaks arrive in "huge portions" at this "reliable" Ironbound Iberian; though "cramped" quarters can make for "noisy" dining and there's "not much in the way of ambiance", at least the service is "pleasant" and free parking's a "big plus."

Spanish Tavern Spanish — 22 | 17 | 22 | $42

Mountainside | 1239 Rte. 22 E. (Locust Ave.) | 908-232-2171
Newark | 103 McWhorter St. (Green St.) | 973-589-4959
www.spanishtavern.com
"Feed-an-army" portion sizes and overall "dependable" cooking draw fans to this Spanish duo in Newark and Mountainside, where "dated" decor and "busy" atmospheres are trumped by "professional" service and "reasonable" prices; both have parking lots.

Spargo's Grille ⓜ American — 23 | 17 | 21 | $41

Manalapan | Andee Plaza | 130 Rte. 33 W. (Millhurst Rd.) | 732-294-9921 | www.spargosgrille.com
A chef who's "not averse to experimenting" concocts an "outstanding" New American menu at this "unexpectedly good" Manalapan BYO parked in a "nondescript" shopping plaza; the prix fixe and early-bird options are "great bargains", and "excellent" service seals the deal.

Spike's Seafood — 22 | 9 | 17 | $31

Point Pleasant Beach | 415 Broadway (Channel Dr.) | 732-295-9400
It's all about the "honest", "just-caught" fish at this Point Pleasant Beach fishmonger equipped with a "few tables" for dining; "dive" decor, "uncomfortable" bench seating and "eternal waits" (due to no reservations) come with the territory, but at least it's BYO.

Squan Tavern ⓜ Italian — 20 | 13 | 19 | $28

Manasquan | 15 Broad St. (Main St.) | 732-223-3324 | www.squantavern.com
"Everybody seems to know everybody" at this longtime Manasquan Southern Italian that's been serving an "old-fashioned red-sauce"

menu and "scrumptious" pizza since '64; the "homey" atmosphere distracts from the "average" decor, no-rezzie rule and weekend waits.

Sri Thai *Thai*   25 | 10 | 19 | $23

Hoboken | 234 Bloomfield St. (bet. 2nd & 3rd Sts.) | 201-798-4822
"Cheap, simple and delicious", this Hoboken BYO "institution" serves an "authentic" Thai menu in a "crowded" little setting; though there's "not much in the way of decor", "sweet" service compensates.

Stage House *American*   20 | 20 | 19 | $41

Scotch Plains | 366 Park Ave. (Front St.) | 908-322-4224 |
www.stagehousetavern.com
Housed in an 18th-century stagecoach stop, this "rustic" Scotch Plains New American serves "fancier entrees" in its "upscale" main dining room, but younger folk like the "lively" tavern that's "less expensive" and a magnet for "local drunks"; in the summer, pay-what-you-want BBQ keeps business brisk.

⊠ Stage Left *American*   27 | 24 | 26 | $66

New Brunswick | 5 Livingston Ave. (George St.) | 732-828-4444 |
www.stageleft.com
"Upscale in every sense of the word", this New Brunswick "jewel" convenient to the State Theater takes an "adventurous" approach with "novel" New American cuisine abetted by a "gem-studded", 1,000-label wine list; though it's "off the charts, pricewise", service is "extremely attentive" and the outdoor seating a refreshing "treat."

Stamna Greek Taverna *Greek*   23 | 15 | 20 | $33

Bloomfield | 1045 Broad St. (bet. Johnson & Watchung Aves.) |
973-338-5151 | www.stamnataverna.com
"Tiny" in size but "big in flavor", this Bloomfield Greek BYO boasts an "extensive" menu that's "well worth exploring" given its "reasonable" tabs (though the whole fish specials "can get expensive"); "tight" tables and "long waits" are trumped by the "happy buzz" in the air.

Steakhouse 85 *Steak*   26 | 24 | 25 | $58

New Brunswick | 85 Church St. (George St.) | 732-247-8585 |
www.steakhouse85.com
This "carnivore's dream" in New Brunswick stakes its reputation on "buttery" chops paired with an "impressive" wine list and served by an "exceptional" crew; a "terrific bar" and "handsome" setting involving "dark woods and clean lines" make the "costly" tabs easier to swallow.

Stella Marina *Italian*   23 | 23 | 20 | $46

Asbury Park | 800 Ocean Ave. (Asbury Ave.) | 732-775-7776 |
www.stellamarinarestaurant.com
Another "slick" Shore Italian from the Cetrulo restaurant group, this "trendy" Asbury Parker offers "really good" food and a "well-priced" wine list in a "stunning boardwalk" setting boasting "picture-perfect views of the Atlantic"; "irregular" service and a "deafening din" are the downsides, yet many call it "outstanding all around."

	FOOD	DECOR	SERVICE	COST

Steve & Cookie's by the Bay *American* `25` `22` `23` `$52`

Margate | 9700 Amherst Ave. (Monroe Ave.) | 609-823-1163 |
www.steveandcookies.com

Known as a year-round Margate "mainstay", this "locavore heaven"
near the AC casinos is also renowned for its "crazy good" seasonal
New Americana as well as its "friendly" owner, Cookie Till; it's *the*
place to be seen" and "mobbed in summer", though retiring types
"ask to be seated in the piano room where you're entertained."

NEW St. Eve's Ⓜ *American* `-` `-` `-` `M`

Ho-Ho-Kus | 611 North Maple Ave. (Brookside Ave.) | 201-857-4717 |
www.stevesnj.com

Locally sourced, seasonal flavors highlight the artful American fare at
this Ho-Ho-Kus BYO bearing a playful contraction of chef-owner Steve
Christianson's first name; seafood and meat dishes grilled over a
wood fire and housemade desserts are served in a rustically elegant
space with high ceilings, natural wood and black-walnut tables.

Steve's Sizzling Steaks ⑤Ⓜ *Steak* `-` `-` `-` `M`

Carlstadt | 620 Rte. 17 S. (bet. Berry & Passaic Aves.) | 201-438-9677 |
www.stevessizzlingsteaks.com

Not far from the Meadowlands, this veteran (circa 1936) Carlstadt
steakhouse serves moderately priced steaks and burgers in a wood-
paneled lodge setting festooned with taxidermy, vintage photos and
Giants and Devils memorabilia.

Ⓩ Stone House at `22` `28` `23` `$56`
Stirling Ridge Ⓜ *American*

Warren | 50 Stirling Rd. (Stiles Rd.) | 908-754-1222 |
www.stonehouseatstirlingridge.com

"Fine dining" doesn't get much more "sophisticated" than at this
Warren New American that's part of a Watchung Mountain catering
facility, where the "inventive" menu is just as "lovely" as the
"unique" setting in a "spectacular" Craftsman-style lodge;
"Manhattan prices" are part of the package, but the midweek prix
fixe is a "fantastic value."

Stony Hill Inn *Continental/Italian* `22` `25` `23` `$59`

Hackensack | 231 Polifly Rd. (Mary St.) | 201-342-4085 |
www.stonyhillinn.com

"Truly special", this "formal" Hackensack "favorite" oozes "class"
with its "lovely" 1818 farmhouse setting and "excellent" Continental-
Italian cuisine; "high prices", "attentive" service and an "older,
dressier crowd" come with the territory, while live music and dancing on weekends embellish its "beautiful ambiance."

Strip House *Steak* `25` `23` `23` `$63`

Livingston | Westminster Hotel | 550 W. Mt. Pleasant Ave.
(bet. Daven Ave. & Microlab Rd.) | 973-548-0050 | www.striphouse.com

A "bit of NYC chic" lands in Livingston's Westminster Hotel via this
"not-stuffy" steakhouse spin-off best known for its "sexy" "bor-
dello" decor featuring "red-flocked wallpaper" and naughty bur-

lesque photos; granted, the "to-die-for" chops and "killer martinis" may "set you back a paycheck or two", but it's "worth the money" since the "scene is cool."

Sublime Ⓜ Eclectic
▽ 20 | 21 | 21 | $67

Gladstone | 12 Lackawanna St. (bet. Main St. & Park Ave.) | 908-781-1888 | www.sublimenj.com

"Refreshingly different" cuisine with an international spin is the hall-mark of this "high-end" Gladstone Eclectic whose menu and hours change with the seasons; though naysayers find the cooking "erratic" and the bar area "more interesting" than the restaurant, there's nothing wrong with the "modern" decor and "accommodating" service.

Sumo Japanese
▽ 25 | 21 | 25 | $30

Wall | Allaire Plaza | 1933 Rte. 35 (Allaire Rd.) | 732-282-1388 | www.sumowalltwp.com

Sushi and hibachi fans rave about this under-the-radar Japanese set in a Wall shopping center, where "fresh" sushi and "really good" hibachi items are dispensed by a "smiling" crew; there are "lots of choices" on the menu, and thanks to the BYO policy, the price is right.

Surf Taco Mexican
21 | 14 | 17 | $14

Belmar | 1003 Main St. (10th Ave.) | 732-681-3001
Forked River | 44 Manchester Ave. (Lacey Rd.) | 609-971-9996
Jackson | 21 Hope Chapel Rd. (Veterans Hwy.) | 732-364-8226 ◗
Long Branch | 94 Brighton Ave. (2nd Ave.) | 732-229-7873
Manasquan | 121 Parker Ave. (Stockton Lake Blvd.) | 732-223-7757
Point Pleasant Beach | 1300 Richmond Ave. (Marcia Ave.) | 732-701-9000
NEW **Red Bank** | 35 Broad St. (bet. Mechanic & White Sts.) | 732-936-1800
Seaside Park | 212 SE Central Ave. (Brighton Ave.) | 732-830-2111
Toms River | 1887 Hooper Ave. (bet. Church & Moore Rds.) | 732-255-3333
www.surftaco.com

Folks in the mood for a "quickie" tout this "popular" counter-service chainlet for "cheap", "tasty" Mexican chow served in "no-ambiance", surfer-themed settings; the Jackson outpost has a bar, the rest are BYO.

Sushi Lounge Japanese
22 | 20 | 18 | $41

Hoboken | 200 Hudson St. (2nd St.) | 201-386-1117
Totowa | 235 Rte. 46 W. (bet. Riverview Dr. & Union Blvd.) | 973-890-0007
Morristown | 12 Schuyler Pl. (Washington St.) | 973-539-1135
www.sushilounge.com

"High-quality" sushi arrives in "loud, dark" dens at these "trendy" Japanese triplets in Hoboken, Morristown and Totowa; even though you'll pay "top dollar" for the food, its "young, hip" followers don't mind since these "singles bar scenes" feature DJs and "techno music."

Sushi X Japanese
▽ 21 | 18 | 20 | $35

Ridgewood | 23 Chestnut St. (bet. Franklin & Ridgewood Aves.) | 201-689-7878

"All-you-can-eat" sushi and cooked items at a fixed price is the "novelty" at this "new-breed", not-a-buffet Ridgewood Japanese; fans say the chow is "well prepared" and tout the BYO policy, but critics scoff "you get what you pay for"; your call.

Sweet Basil's Cafe *American* `21 | - | 19 | $26`

Livingston | 498 S. Livingston Ave. (Concord Dr.) | 973-325-3340 | www.sweetbasilscafe.com

For "unassuming" but "flavorful" fare at "reasonable" tabs, check out this "intimate" New American BYO in Livingston offering three squares a day; though service can be "slow", it's a favorite with "ladies who lunch" and those in the mood for a "sumptuous" weekend brunch; P.S. it relocated post-Survey.

Tabor Road Tavern *American* `21 | 24 | 21 | $49`

Morris Plains | 510 Tabor Rd. (Rte. 10) | 973-267-7004 | www.taborroadtavern.com

"Creative" comfort food comes in an appropriately "comfy" setting at this "fresh-faced" Morris Plains New American, with "high-end mountain-cabin" decor that makes "you feel far away from the 'burbs"; "grown-ups" say it works for "business" or "fun" occasions thanks to an "excellent" happy hour, "attentive" service and "rustic charm."

Tacconelli's Pizzeria Ⓜ⊉ *Pizza* `23 | 12 | 17 | $18`

Maple Shade | 450 S. Lenola Rd. (Rte. 38) | 856-638-0338 | www.tacconellispizzerianj.com

"Superlative" thin-crust pizza emerges from the brick oven at this "cash-only" BYO across from the Moorestown Mall in Maple Shade; though the room is "barren", service so-so and the hours "crazy" (call ahead), many say it's still "good for a quick fix."

Taj Mahal Ⓜ *Indian* `- | - | - | I`

Jersey City | 663 Newark Ave. (Summit Ave.) | 201-963-9100 | www.tajmahalromanceindining.com

The traditional flavors and decor of India's Mughal Court are re-created a short walk from the Hudson County Courthouse at this exotic Jersey City BYO, spun off from the Washington, DC, original; an expansive, inexpensive lunch buffet attracts Five Corners–area office workers, while those who can't get away from their desks go the take-out route.

Taka Ⓜ *Japanese* `25 | 25 | 24 | $41`

Asbury Park | 632 Mattison Ave. (Main St.) | 732-775-1020 | www.takaapnj.com

Chef Taka Hirai's "Nuevo Japanese" in Asbury Park draws huzzahs for his "exceptional" sushi and "delicious" cooked fare; the "sophis-ticated" "Zen" setting is abetted by "great service" from an "easy-on-the-eyes" staff and, best of all, "BYO keeps tabs low."

Takara *Japanese* `▽ 20 | 19 | 15 | $32`

Oakhurst | Orchard Plaza | 1610 Rte. 35 S. (bet. Deal Rd. & Park Ave.) | 732-663-1899 | www.takarasteakhousenj.com

An "interesting mix of all things Asian" – think sushi, hibachi and tatami rooms – distinguishes this family-run Japanese in the Oakhurst section of Ocean Township; pricing is reasonable and the decor "unusually pleasant and peaceful", despite a full bar equipped with high-def TVs.

Tapas de Espana *Spanish* ∇ 22 | 16 | 21 | $41

North Bergen | 7909 Bergenline Ave. (79th St.) | 201-453-1690 | www.tapasnj.com

A "little bit of everything goes a long way" at this North Bergen Spaniard where the "lively" crowd digs the small plates, "superb" entrees and "low" prices; Friday night flamenco helps "bring you back to Spain", but those who "want to avoid the crowds" may prefer to go during the week.

Taqueria Downtown Ⓜ *Mexican* 24 | 13 | 14 | $15

Jersey City | 236 Grove St. (Grand St.) | 201-333-3220

"Brilliant" Mexican is slung at this "hip" Jersey City cantina where the *comida* is "so authentic" you can almost "smell the ocean off the Baja"; counter service with a "serious attitude problem" is a drag, but "cheap" tabs, patio seats and "posters of hair metal bands" on the walls compensate.

Taste of Asia Ⓜ *Malaysian* 22 | 17 | 21 | $29

Chatham | 245 Main St. (Passaic Ave.) | 973-701-8821 | www.atasteofasianj.com

"Charming Chatham" is the site of this "oh-so-good" Malaysian offering "abundant" portions of "beautifully presented" chow in a "small", "kind of boring" setting; prices are "fair", the service "friendly" and Sunday's dim sum brunch is "not to be missed."

Taste of Portugal *Portuguese* ∇ 22 | 16 | 19 | $37

Newark | 148 Delancey St. (Van Buren St.) | 973-274-0600 | www.tasteofportugalnj.com

"Enormous" portions mean you "won't leave hungry" from this "tasty" Portuguese in Newark's Ironbound; though parking can be a "challenge", the decor is "comfy", the service "very accommodating" and you'll exit "pleased" after sampling the "tasty" chow.

Taverna Mykonos Ⓜ *Greek* 25 | 22 | 22 | $39

Elmwood Park | 238 Broadway (bet. 53rd St. & Lyncrest Ave.) | 201-703-9200 | www.tavernamykonos.com

A "budget" version of Fair Lawn sibling Oceanos, this "traditional" Elmwood Park Greek features "wonderful" Hellenic specialties served in a "casual" but "beautiful" room; "accommodating" staffers and an "authentic" mood make this one an overall "nice surprise."

Tbones Tuscan Steakhouse *Steak* ∇ 22 | 20 | 22 | $50

Bridgewater | Bridgewater Marriott | 700 Commons Way (bet. Crossing Blvd. & Prince Rodgers Ave.) | 908-482-0007 | www.tbonessteak.com

Although it bills itself as a steakhouse and is done up with the usual leather and dark wood, this "exceptional" spot in the Bridgewater Marriott goes beyond chops to include "delightful specials" made with "local ingredients"; since the "quiet" dining room is "never crowded", service is uniformly "great."

	FOOD	DECOR	SERVICE	COST

Teak *Asian* — 21 | 21 | 18 | $44

Red Bank | 64 Monmouth St. (Drummond Pl.) | 732-747-5775 | www.teakrestaurant.com

"Trendy" sums up the setting, crowd and staffers at this "hip" Asian near Red Bank's Theater District, where the "quality" menu takes a backseat to the happening vibe; regulars say it's "all about the bar scene", citing an "overpowering din" and "crazy-busy" weekends, while bargain-hunters sidestep the "high" tabs on "half-price Monday nights"; a post-Survey renovation may not be reflected in the Decor score.

Teplitzky's *Diner* — ▽ 18 | 18 | 19 | $26

Atlantic City | Chelsea Hotel | 111 S. Chelsea Ave. (Pacific Ave.) | 609-428-4550 | www.thechelsea-ac.com

AC's "über-trendy" Chelsea Hotel houses this "kitschy" diner that's a "good getaway" from the casino bustle; service is "pleasant", the "retro" '50s setting "fun" and breakfasts may be "the best" choice on the "small, focused" menu.

Teresa Caffe *Italian* — 21 | 17 | 19 | $32

Princeton | Palmer Sq. | 23 Palmer Sq. E. (Nassau St.) | 609-921-1974 | www.terramomo.com

Now in its 20th year on Palmer Square, this "dependable" Princeton trattoria is ever a "best bet" for "gourmet" pizza and "fresh" pasta; sure, the "cheerful" quarters can be "tight" and "noisy", and many wish they'd "take reservations", but the staff is "hardworking" and it could be the "best value-to-price ratio" in town.

Terra Nova *American* — - | - | - | E

Sewell | 590 Delsea Dr. (bet. Bethel Mill Rd. & Parke Place Blvd.) | 856-589-8883 | www.terranovawineanddine.com

With a gurgling fountain out front and sophisticated Napa Valley-inspired decor, this midpriced New American on Delsea Drive is turning heads in the chain country of Gloucester County.

Tewksbury Inn *American* — 23 | 20 | 21 | $50

Oldwick | 55 Main St. (King St.) | 908-439-2641 | www.thetewksburyinn.com

A former stagecoach stop in Oldwick is the site of this "charming" New American where patrons can choose from a "quiet", "formal" dining room, more casual "rustic" tavern or "lovely outdoor terrace"; no matter where you end up, the food's "high-level", the crowd "landed gentry" and the cost "fairly expensive."

Thai Chef *French/Thai* — 21 | 17 | 18 | $33

Montclair | 664 Bloomfield Ave. (bet. Orange & Valley Rds.) | 973-783-4994 | www.thaichefusa.com

"Cut-above" French-Thai food is served at this Montclair BYO, the last remaining outpost of a former mini-chain; value-conscious diners don't mind the "inexperienced" service given the "reasonable prices", "comfortable" setting and that "out-of-this-world" chocolate soufflé.

	FOOD	DECOR	SERVICE	COST

Thai Kitchen *Thai*
23 | 16 | 21 | $25

Bridgewater | 1351 Prince Rodgers Ave. (Commons Way) | 908-231-8822
Bridgewater | Somerset Shopping Ctr. | 327 Hwy. 202 (Rte. 206) | 908-722-8983
Chester | Streets of Chester | 320 Rte. 206 S. (bet. Colby Farm Rd. & Maple Ave.) | 908-879-9800
Hillsborough | Hillsborough Shopping Ctr. | 649 Rte. 206 (Amwell Rd.) | 908-904-8038
www.thaikitchennj.com

"Not Bangkok" but "pretty great for NJ", this "outstanding" Thai quartet plies "authentic", "not-afraid-to-be-spicy" dishes for "economical" tabs that "won't break the budget" (they're all BYO); "bland" decor is the trade-off, but at least the service is "friendly" and "quick."

Thai Thai *Thai*
23 | 15 | 21 | $27

Stirling | 1168 Valley Rd. (Poplar Dr.) | 908-903-0790 | www.thaithaifinecuisine.com

"Deliciously seasoned" Thai specialties come at "reasonable" rates at this Stirling BYO that "gets all the basics right" – save for "hole-in-the-wall" looks that could stand a "remodel"; "reasonable" prices and "super-friendly" staffers complete the overall "satisfying" picture.

Theresa's *Italian*
22 | 17 | 19 | $38

Westfield | 47 Elm St. (bet. Broad St. & North Ave.) | 908-233-9133 | www.theresasrestaurant.com

"Amazing flavors" shine through the "uncomplicated" dishes at this "inviting" Italian (a sibling of Isabella's and Mojave Grille) set on Westfield's Restaurant Row; BYO helps keep the costs "reasonable", while sidewalk seating is an alternative to the "noisy, tight" interior.

3 Forty Grill *American*
20 | 22 | 19 | $41

Hoboken | 340 Sinatra Dr. (bet. 3rd & 4th Sts.) | 201-217-3406 | www.3fortygrill.com

The "cuisine is almost as delicious as the view" at this "hip" Hoboken New American celebrated for its "drop-dead gorgeous" vistas of the NYC skyline and best enjoyed from the patio; though a "great place to take a date or meet a future one" (it morphs into a "messy night-life scene" late-night), it's a tad "overpriced" for some.

3 West *American*
23 | 24 | 22 | $49

Basking Ridge | Riverwalk Village Ctr. | 665 Martinsville Rd. (Independence Blvd.) | 908-647-3000 | www.3westrest.com

"Artfully presented" New Americana is matched with a "fantastic" wine list and "super-friendly" service at this Basking Ridge "class act" known for its "energetic" bar scene and "upscale après-ski" mood; its "fortysomething" crowd can get "noisy" and it's "easy to run up a big bill", but the "roaring fireplace" makes it a "must" visit.

Tick Tock Diner ● *Diner*
18 | 13 | 18 | $20

Clifton | 281 Allwood Rd. (bet. Bloomfield & Passaic Aves.) | 973-777-0511 | www.theticktockdiner.com

Jersey diners don't get much more "quintessential" than this circa-1948 Clifton joint doling out "excessive" portions of the usual suspects from a "menu the size of the *Oxford English Dictionary*"; "fast" service, "affordable" tabs and a 24/7 open-door policy keep it "packed."

Tiger Noodles *Noodle Shop* 19 | 9 | 18 | $19

Princeton | 260 Nassau St. (Pine St.) | 609-252-0663
Princeton | Shops at Windsor Green | 3495 Rte. 1 S. (Emmons Dr.) | 609-799-1469 **M**

These "nothing-fancy" BYO Princeton noodle shops are "reliable" enough for "fast, cheap" meals, ladled out by a "friendly" crew; the Nassau Street patio seating is a "delight" compared to the "cramped" interior, while the shopping-center satellite is a tad more "comfy."

Tim McLoone's Supper Club *American* 20 | 23 | 20 | $50

Asbury Park | 1200 Ocean Ave. (bet. 4th & 5th Aves.) | 732-774-1155 | www.timmcloonessupperclub.com

An homage to the "old-style" "NY supper club", this Asbury Park eatery set on the boardwalk above McLoone's Asbury Grille offers "oceanfront" views; a "great" show with "talented musicians" makes the "decent but overpriced" New American fare taste even better.

Tim Schafer's *American* 23 | 18 | 23 | $47

Morristown | 82 Speedwell Ave. (bet. Cattano Ave. & Clinton Pl.) | 973-538-3330 | www.timschafersrestaurant.com

An "experience like no other", this Morristown New American features "cutting-edge" cooking with "lots of game options" and many "interesting" dishes infused with beer; though it's "on the expensive side", prix fixe menus and a BYO policy help "keep the price down."

Tina Louise *Asian* 23 | 16 | 22 | $32

Carlstadt | 403 Hackensack St. (bet. Broad St. & Division Ave.) | 201-933-7133 | www.villagerestaurantgroup.com

"Not-your-normal" Asian fare is served at this "hole-in-the-wall" Carlstadt BYO near the Meadowlands, run by the eponymous sisters Tina and Louise Wong; "reasonable" tabs and "enthusiastic" service compensate for the "small" setting and "cramped" quarters.

Tisha's Fine Dining *American* 25 | 20 | 24 | $48

Cape May | Washington Street Mall | 322 Washington St. (Jackson St.) | 609-884-9119 | www.tishasfinedining.com

Now "open year-round" for breakfast, lunch and dinner, this Cape May New American BYO moved to larger digs in the Washington Street Mall in 2010 but still offers "excellent" grub and "attentive" service; though it "lacks the ocean view" of old and feels a bit more "sterile" than before, most report it's just as "fantastic" as ever.

Tito's Burritos *Mexican* 20 | 11 | 15 | $13

Ridgewood | 166 E. Ridgewood Ave. (bet. Cottage Pl. & Walnut St.) | 201-857-4619
Summit | 356 Springfield Ave. (Summit Ave.) | 908-277-3710
Morristown | 26 Washington Ave. (bet. John Glenn Rd. & Valley View Dr.) | 973-267-8486
www.titosburritos.com

Either "totally tubular" or "totally juvenile", this Mexican chainlet does supply "good, quick", "inexpensive" eats; fans say the "huge", "made-to-order" burritos are a "step up" from fast food, although the "counter service" and "beach-shack" decor "get old fast."

Toast *American*   22 | 15 | 18 | $21

Montclair | 700 Bloomfield Ave. (bet. Orange Rd. & St. Luke's Pl.) | 973-509-8099 | www.toastmontclair.com

Asbury Park | 516 Cookman Ave. (bet. Bangs & Grand Aves.) | 732-776-5900 | www.toastasbury.com

This Montclair breakfast-and-lunch specialist offers "tasty" American meals, a "homey" duplex setting and "efficient" service; the ground floor is "lively" and the top floor "more quiet", but wherever you wind up, come "early" as this BYO doesn't take reservations; the Asbury Park outpost opened post-Survey.

Tomatoes *Californian/Eclectic*   25 | 23 | 23 | $51

Margate | 9300 Amherst Ave. (Washington Ave.) | 609-822-7535 | www.tomatoesmargate.com

There's "major bar activity" at this Cal-Eclectic in Margate, a "Shore favorite" where the "excellent" chow is a match for the "beautiful-people scene"; granted, it's "pricey" and can get "loud" during prime times, but it's a "no-brainer" for those in the mood for "lively" dining.

Tony Da Caneca *Portuguese*   23 | 16 | 22 | $39

Newark | 72 Elm Rd. (Houston St.) | 973-589-6882 | www.tonydacanecarestaurant.com

"Consistently delicious", this 1969 Portuguese "throwback" in an "off-the-beaten-path" section of Newark's Ironbound serves "high-quality" "traditional" dishes; although "nothing fancy" to look at, it's "quiet", "friendly" and there's a "free guarded parking" lot across the street.

Tony Luke's ❶ *Cheesesteaks*   20 | 11 | 16 | $16

Atlantic City | Borgata Hotel, Casino & Spa | 1 Borgata Way (Huron Ave.) | 609-317-1000 | www.theborgata.com

NEW **Wildwood** | 6200 New Jersey Ave. (bet. Sweetbriar & Wisteria Rds.) | 609-770-7033 | www.tonylukes.com

"Not the same as eating on a Philly street corner" – but "just as messy" – this cheesesteak specialist in the food court of AC's Borgata draws mixed responses: "can't beat it" vs. "close but no cigar"; all agree there's "no atmosphere", but it's not true "you can gain weight just looking at them"; the Wildwood sibling opened post-Survey.

Tony's Baltimore Grill ❶ *Pizza*   18 | 8 | 16 | $20

Atlantic City | 2800 Atlantic Ave. (Iowa Ave.) | 609-345-5766 | www.tonysbaltimoregrill.com

"Like stepping into an Edward Hopper painting", this AC pizzeria is a "cross between a dive bar and a cafeteria", with "stark lighting", "faded linoleum" and table-mounted jukeboxes; the "bar is open 24/7", and the "old-fashioned", "gum-chewing" waitresses add to the "blast-from-the-past" atmosphere.

Tortilla Press *Mexican*   24 | 19 | 22 | $28

Collingswood | 703 Haddon Ave. (Collings Ave.) | 856-869-3345 | www.thetortillapress.com

(continued)

	FOOD	DECOR	SERVICE	COST

(continued)

Tortilla Press Cantina *Mexican*

Merchantville | 7716 Maple Ave. (Haddonfield Rd.) | 856-356-2050 |
www.tortillapresscantina.com

"Varied, inventive" menus, "fun" settings and "quick" staffers
make these South Jersey Mexicans popular "powerhouses"; the
Collingswood original is BYO, while the newer Merchantville outpost
has a "liquor license", but both are "good value for your money."

Tortuga's Mexican Village ⊅ *Mexican* | 22 | 11 | 18 | $24 |

Princeton | 44 Leigh Ave. (bet. John & Witherspoon Sts.) |
609-924-5143 | www.tortugasmv.com

"Hidden away" in Princeton, this "unassuming", cash-only BYO
serves "tasty", "cheese-gooey" Mexicana that "fills your belly without emptying your wallet"; "slow" service and "shabby" decor are
downsides, and since they don't take reservations on weekends,
"expect a wait."

Toscano *Italian*   ▽ | 22 | 19 | 21 | $43 |

Bordentown | 136 Farnsworth Ave. (Park St.) | 609-291-0291 |
www.toscano-ristorante.com

"Traditional" Italian food fills out the menu of this "old-school"
Bordentown trattoria where "everything's well prepared"; "generous
portions" mean you'll "be taking something home" while "friendly"
service makes for a lot of regulars.

Trap Rock *American* | 21 | 22 | 20 | $45 |

Berkeley Heights | 279 Springfield Ave. (bet. Snyder & Union Aves.) |
908-665-1755 | www.traprockrestaurant.net

"Surprisingly good for a place that makes its own beer", this "upscale"
Berkeley Heights pub-cum-microbrewery puts a Southern-Cajun spin
on the "solid" New American menu; admirers like the "chic", lodge-
like setting and "ask-and-ye-shall-receive" service, though the
somewhat "steep" prices and "loud" acoustics are another story.

Trattoria Bel Paese *Italian* | - | - | - | M |

Cranford | 104 N. Union Ave. (Alden St.) | 908-276-3336 |
www.trattoriabelpaese.com

A luncheonette by day, this unassuming family-run Cranford
BYO morphs into a sit-down restaurant at night, and while it may
look like a typical neighborhood red-sauce joint, the authentic
Sicilian and Southern Italian dishes conjure Little Italy in its pre-
tourist trap heyday with offerings such as stuffed artichokes and
pasta with sardines; locals take advantage of the bargain take-out
dinners for $10.

Trattoria Mediterranea Ⓜ *Italian*   ▽ | 24 | 17 | 23 | $44 |

Bedminster | 2472 Lamington Rd. (Somerville Rd.) | 908-781-7131 |
www.trattoriamediterranea.com

There's lots of "family pride" evident at this "small" "Calabrian-
style" Italian in Bedminster, renowned for its "wonderful" "homemade" pasta; "attentive" service, "moderate" prices and a BYO policy keep it a "perennial favorite."

	FOOD	DECOR	SERVICE	COST

NEW **Trattoria Primavera** Ⓜ *Italian* — | — | — | M

West Orange | 500 Pleasant Valley Way (bet. Eagle Rock &
Greenwood Aves.) | 973-669-0966

An in-town sibling of West Orange's Primavera, this casual strip-
maller kicks it old-school with a midpriced menu of Italian staples,
including a family Sunday special featuring all-you-can-eat homemade pasta and a complimentary glass of red wine; reasonably
priced soups and panini make it an affordable weekday lunch option.

Treno *Italian* — | — | — | M

Westmont | 233 Haddon Ave. (Crystal Lake Rd.) | 856-833-9233 |
www.trenopizzabar.com

Wood-fired pizza, wine by the glass and a local beer list bring
Westmonters to this lively, affordable Italian, which does a tidy
happy-hour trade too; a modern enclosed patio (with fireplace) is a
draw as are seats at the pizza counter with views of the 800-degree
oven; P.S. families will like the 'Sunday gravy' deal.

Tre Piani Ⓩ *Italian/Mediterranean* 20 | 21 | 19 | $47

Princeton | Forrestal Village Shopping Ctr. | 120 Rockingham Row
(Village Blvd.) | 609-452-1515 | www.trepiani.com

Set in Princeton's Forrestal Village off Route 1, this "upscale" Italian-
Mediterranean "tries hard" and is "sometimes very good", sometimes just "decent" foodwise; the "roomy" setting (three floors plus
a patio) is certainly "comfortable" and the service "attentive",
though "trendy" types tout Tre Bar, its "fun" small-plates adjunct.

Très Yan & Wu *Asian* ∇ 23 | 19 | 23 | $27
(fka Très Elena Wu)

Mount Laurel | Bank of America Shopping Ctr. | 3131 Rte. 38
(Larchmont Blvd.) | 856-608-8888 | www.tresyanandwu.com

South Jersey dining fixture Elena Wu has ceded her "classy", French-
accented Asian in Mount Laurel to her two chefs, Paul Yan and Jian
Min Wu (who also happen to be her brother and cousin, respectively); the "delicious", "not-typical" vittles range from "authentic"
Cantonese to sushi and chocolate mousse, served by the "same old
reliable group" for the same BYO-friendly tabs.

Trinity Ⓜ *American* 25 | 24 | 22 | $40

Keyport | 84 Broad St. (bet. Front & 3rd Sts.) | 732-888-1998 |
www.trinitykeyport.com

"Heavenly" cooking issues from the "ambitious" kitchen of this
Keyport New American set in a "converted church" and praised for its
"sinful", seasonal menu; the "magnificent" setting with "soaring ceilings" and frosted-glass windows is a match for the "outstanding"
service, and there's "live entertainment" on weekends to boot.

Trinity ☽ *Irish* 18 | 19 | 19 | $36

Hoboken | 306 Sinatra Dr. (3rd St.) | 201-533-4446 |
www.hobokentrinity.com

"Upscale" pub food lies ahead at this "big" Irish joint on the Hoboken
waterfront that "covers all the bases" and comes with a "beautiful"

NYC skyline view to boot; "breezy" service and "good-value" lunchtime tabs are pluses, though many just "go for the Guinness on tap."

Trinity & the Pope ☑ *Cajun/Creole* | 21 | 23 | 22 | $35 |

Asbury Park | 649 Mattison Ave. (Bond St.) | 732-807-3435 |
www.trinityandthepope.com

This "good-time" outpost of the Marilyn Schlossbach "empire" set in a "beautiful" old Asbury Park bank puts a "sexy" spin on New Orleans–style Cajun-Creole cooking in a "noisy" setting fueled by "great" music and "very strong" drinks; a post-Survey renovation may not be reflected in the Decor score.

Triumph Brewing Co. *American/Eclectic* | 16 | 19 | 17 | $32 |

Princeton | 138 Nassau St. (Washington Rd.) | 609-924-7855 |
www.triumphbrewing.com

The mood's "hoppy" at this multilevel Princeton microbrewery where the "crazy-good" housemade brews trump the just "passable" Eclectic-American eats; though service is "extremely casual", the pricing's "reasonable" and a "great location" on Nassau Street keeps it "popular" – and "noisy."

Trovato's *Italian* | 19 | 16 | 19 | $36 |

Elmwood Park | 206 Rte. 46 (Mill St.) | 201-797-5552 |
www.trovatosnj.com

Trovato's Due *Italian*

Oakland | 4 Barbara Ln. (Oakland Ave.) | 201-337-0813 |
www.trovatosduenj.com

"Generous portions" of "tried-and-true" favorites draw pasta, veal and seafood lovers to these Southern Italian twins in Elmwood Park and Oakland; "old-school", "white-tablecloth" settings and "gracious" service complete the "delicious" picture.

Tsuki ☒ *Japanese* | 22 | 13 | 18 | $34 |

Bernardsville | 23 Mine Brook Rd. (Mt. Airy Rd.) | 908-953-0450 |
www.tsukirestaurant.com

"Convenient to the Bernardsville cinema", this "neighborhood" Japanese BYO offers "reasonably priced" sushi and cooked items; "spotty" service, not much decor and a "nothing-special" vibe lead some to yawn "uninspired."

Tula ☒ *Eclectic*   ∇ | 19 | 20 | 19 | $43 |

New Brunswick | 47 Easton Ave. (bet. Hamilton & Somerset Sts.) | 732-246-0014 | www.tulalounge.com

Given the emphasis on small plates, you can sample lots of "different" options at this "lively" New Brunswick Eclectic, a "trendy college town spot" that's "not too expensive"; "NYC decor" and occasional DJs keep its "young" crowd happy.

Tun Tavern ❶ *American* | 18 | 17 | 17 | $32 |

Atlantic City | Sheraton Atlantic City | 2 Convention Blvd. (Baltic Ave.) | 609-347-7800 | www.tuntavern.com

"Beer is the star" of the show at this "casual" American microbrewery set in the AC Sheraton "near the convention center"; though service is "slow" and the chow's merely "acceptable", there are "lots of TVs" for sports fans, the decor is "cool" and the mood is "fun."

Tuptim *Thai*   21 | 17 | 19 | $29

Montclair | 600 Bloomfield Ave. (bet. Park St. & Valley Rd.) | 973-783-3800 | www.tuptimthaicuisine.com

"Pleasantly authentic" Thai dishes are abetted by a "great veggie menu" at this Montclair BYO "stalwart"; some find the cooking "run-of-the-mill" and the "casual" setting a bit "tired", but at least service is "friendly" and the tabs won't "break the budget."

Tutto a Modo Mio *Italian*   ▽ 21 | 15 | 20 | $37

Ridgefield | 482 Bergen Blvd. (Edgewater Ave.) | 201-313-9690

This "unexpected little BYO" in Ridgefield serves a "classic" menu that's "as Italian as it gets" in a room where "everyone seems to know each other"; "pleasant", "nothing-fancy" decor, "reasonable" costs and "nice" service make it a "solid local spot."

Tuzzio's *Italian*   20 | 11 | 20 | $30

Long Branch | 224 Westwood Ave. (Morris Ave.) | 732-222-9614 | www.tuzzios.com

"No fuss", "no pretense" and no reservations sum up the scene at this "old-time" "neighborhood" Italian in Long Branch; though "decor isn't its strong point", locals like its "welcoming" service and "family-oriented" approach, adding that the "reliable" cooking is also a "good value."

27 Mix ⓩ *Eclectic*   21 | 19 | 17 | $30

Newark | 27 Halsey St. (bet. Bleeker St. & Central Ave.) | 973-648-0643 | www.27mix.com

"Consistently good" Latin, Asian and American fare (plus a convenient location near NJPAC and the Newark Museum) makes this "fun" Eclectic a "great option", particularly for lunch; it also features an "arty SoHo" vibe – i.e. an "exposed-brick wall" – along with a popular summer patio where its "lively" crowd can escape the "noise" but not the "erratic" service.

TwoFiftyTwo ⓩ *American*   - | - | - | E

Bedminster | 252 Somerville Rd. (Main St.) | 908-234-9093 | www.twofiftytworestaurant.com

Artfully prepared New American cuisine, tagged with all the right buzzwords – like fresh, local, sustainable, seasonal – is yours at this tiny Bedminster BYO set in a beautiful 1922 Arts and Crafts bungalow; regulars store their wines under lock and key in vintage mailboxes.

Ugly Mug ● *Pub Food*   15 | 14 | 16 | $25

Cape May | 426 Washington St. (Decatur St.) | 609-884-3459

"Simple is better" could be the motto of this way-"casual" American pub in Cape May's Washington Street Mall, where the "average" grub plays second fiddle to the "fun bar" scene; while it attracts a "younger crowd" bent on "getting its drink on", some "old salts drift in" too.

	FOOD	DECOR	SERVICE	COST

Umeya ⓜ *Japanese* ▽ 23 | 14 | 17 | $46

Cresskill | 156 Piermont Rd. (Union Ave.) | 201-816-0511 |
www.umeyasushi.com

"Quality" Japanese food lures Cresskill locals to this "quiet" spot
that's pretty darn "close to authentic"; sure, it "needs some ambiance" and a few feel that the tabs are "too expensive", but there is a
bargain, $31 six-course prix fixe available.

Umpasri Ⓢ *Thai* - | - | - | M

Cherry Hill | Plaza 38 | 2442 Rte. 38 (Church Rd.) | 856-482-0377 |
www.umpasrithaicuisine.com

The family behind this Cherry Hill establishment named it after a
beloved grandmother, who would be proud of its authentic Thai
cooking with spice levels that can be adjusted to patrons' heat
tolerance; the ambiance is bright and welcoming, while BYO
keeps tabs affordable.

Undici *Italian* 22 | 24 | 20 | $57

Rumson | 11 W. River Rd. (Bingham Ave.) | 732-842-3880 |
www.undicirestaurant.com

"Gorgeous" "Tuscan villa" design "transports you to Italy" at this
"sophisticated" Italian, a Rumson favorite famed for its "profoundly
authentic" cooking and "extensive" wine list; the "lively" bar can be
"loud" and it's an "expensive endeavor", so "get someone else to
pick up the check" – or else stick with the "great" appetizers and
wood-fired pizza.

Union Park Dining Room *American* 25 | 24 | 24 | $55

Cape May | Hotel Macomber | 727 Beach Ave. (Howard St.) |
609-884-8811 | www.unionparkdiningroom.com

This "elegant" venue in Cape May's Hotel Macomber serves "innovative", "expertly prepared" New Americana in a "spacious" setting
complete with a veranda sporting ocean views; it's the epitome of
"classy", "memorable" dining – with "formal" service and appropriately "upscale" tabs – and although a BYO, it also serves local wines.

Uproot *American* 22 | 24 | 21 | $65

Warren | 9 Mt. Bethel Rd. (Mountain Blvd.) | 908-834-8194 |
www.uprootrestaurant.com

A "middle-of-nowhere" Warren strip mall is the unlikely setting for
this "stylish" New American praised for its "spectacular" regional
fare paired with an "extensive" wine list; "chic, modern" digs and
"pleasing" service attract a "trendy" crowd that doesn't mind the
"above-average prices"; a post-Survey chef change and a shift to a
more casual menu format may not be reflected in the Food score.

NEW Upstairs ⓜ *American/Continental* - | - | - | E

Upper Montclair | 608 Valley Rd., 2nd fl. (Bellevue Ave.) | 973-744-4144 |
www.upstairsmontclair.com

Seasonal ingredients shine in chef Dave Van Morrelgem's New
American small and large plates, which are showcased in a sleek
modern setting atop sibling Dai-Kichi in Montclair; custom cocktails

| | FOOD | DECOR | SERVICE | COST |

dazzle as well at the sexy bar, making the trek up the stairs the only downer; P.S. the kitchen is closed on Monday, although sushi is served.

NEW Urban Table Eclectic — | — | — | M

Morristown | 40 W. Park Pl. (Market St.) | 973-326-9200 | www.urbantablerestaurant.com

Breakfast, brunch, lunch and dinner come to the table quickly and at modest cost at the Harvest Restaurant Group's latest offspring, a casual Eclectic in Downtown Morristown; there's booth and banquette seating in the casual, subway-themed space plus sidewalk tables in season.

NEW Ursino ⑤ American — | — | — | E

Union | STEM Bldg., Kean University | 1075 Morris Ave. (bet. Green Ln. & North Ave.) | 908-249-4099 | www.ursinorestaurant.com

Kean University's state-of-the-art STEM Building in Union is the unlikely home of this eye-popping, upscale Modern American; the glittering two-story space by designer Glen Coben (NYC's Del Posto) is the setting for farm-to-table cuisine from chef Peter Turso, a veteran of the erstwhile Restaurant David Drake, with many ingredients coming from the restaurant's own four-acre farm.

Valdebenito's Bistro ⑤Ⓜ Argentinean — | — | — | M

Somerville | 18 W. Main St. (bet. Bridge & Maple Sts.) | 908-231-9244 | www.valbistro.com

Argentinean cuisine comes to Downtown Somerville via this BYO specializing in churrasco and empanadas – although some Italian standards are also on the menu; the setting is casual, the pricing reasonable and in the summer there's live music on Friday nights.

Varka Greek/Seafood 26 | 22 | 22 | $59

Ramsey | 30 N. Spruce St. (Main St.) | 201-995-9333 | www.varkarestaurant.com

The "finest catch of the day" gets a Mediterranean spin at this "classy" Greek seafooder in Ramsey that specializes in "you-pick-it-they-cook-it" whole fish, as well as steaks; while the setting's "seductive", the "vibrant" bar scene is so "very noisy" that it almost manages to drown out the "expensive" pricing.

Vasili's Taverna ⑤ Greek 21 | 13 | 20 | $35

Teaneck | 365 Queen Anne Rd. (Degraw St.) | 201-287-1007 | www.vasilistaverna.com

"Traditional" Greek dishes and "divine" seafood for those with a "hankering for whole fish" are "lovingly prepared" at this "welcoming" Teaneck BYO; the dimensions may be "small", but staffers are "friendly" and the pricing "gentle."

Ventura's Greenhouse ◑ Italian 18 | 16 | 17 | $34

Margate | 106 S. Benson Ave. (Atlantic Ave.) | 609-822-0140 | www.venturasgreenhouse.com

More "social experience" than fine-dining experience, this "enjoyable" Margate double-decker features a "basic" Italian menu upstairs and more "pub"-like chow on the ground floor, but is probably most memorable for its views of the ocean and seaside attraction Lucy the Elephant; you can always count on "lots of action" at the bar, however.

Verjus ⓂFrench
25 | 19 | 22 | $50

Maplewood | 1790 Springfield Ave. (Rutgers St.) | 973-378-8990 | www.verjusrestaurant.com

Run by a "caring" husband-and-wife team, this "well-oiled" Maplewood French features "scrumptious" cuisine abetted by a "smart" wine list; maybe the mood's too "sedate" for some, but there's "lots of elbow room" and "attention to detail", as well as "superb value for the money."

Verve Ⓢ American/French
23 | 20 | 23 | $46

Somerville | 18 E. Main St. (bet. Bridge & Grove Sts.) | 908-707-8655 | www.vervestyle.com

There's a "distinctly urban" vibe to this Somerville Franco-American where "top-notch" surf 'n' turf is served by a "spot-on" crew; though it's "kind of pricey", the prix fixe is a "real steal" and there are bonuses like a "fun" bar scene and occasional DJs.

Vespa's Italian
17 | 16 | 19 | $38

Edgewater | 860 River Rd. (Hilliard Ave.) | 201-943-9393 | www.vespasrestaurant.com

"Steady" is the word on this Edgewater "neighborhood standby" where the "above-average" Italian food is "not breaking records for innovation" but comes in "bountiful" portions for "reasonable" dough; motor scooter-themed decor separates it from the pack.

Vic's Ⓜ Italian/Pizza
21 | 12 | 19 | $24

Bradley Beach | 60 Main St. (Evergreen Ave.) | 732-774-8225 | www.vicspizza.com

Experience "bygone days at the Jersey Shore" at this fourth-generation family pizzeria in Bradley Beach, where regulars stick to the "addictive" thin-crust pies and "avoid the rest of the menu"; service can be "indifferent" and there's "no ambiance" in the "loud", "knotty pine"-lined room, but the tabs are really "cheap."

Victor's Pub, The ● Pub Food
- | - | - | M

Camden | Victor Luxury Lofts | 1 Market St. (Delaware Ave.) | 856-635-0600 | www.victorspub.com

Camden's waterfront, already home to an aquarium, ballpark and concert hall, also boasts this American pub, located in the Victor Luxury Lofts, offering a midpriced bar menu that draws residents and local workers; P.S. despite the requisite 20 plasma-screen TVs, the best view is of the Philly skyline across the Delaware.

Villa Amalfi Ⓜ Italian
23 | 21 | 21 | $49

Cliffside Park | 793 Palisade Ave. (Marion Ave.) | 201-886-8626 | www.villaamalfi.com

"Old-world in every way", this circa-1982 Cliffside Park Italian is an "upscale" affair with "beautiful" decor, a "friendly" ambiance and "gracious" service; sure, it's "pretty expensive" and some note it's

	FOOD	DECOR	SERVICE	COST

"never crowded" due to "changing tastes", but diehards still reserve it for "special occasions."

Village Gourmet *Eclectic*
21 | **16** | **18** | **$30**

Rutherford | 75 Park Ave. (Ridge Rd.) | 201-438-9404 | www.villagerestaurantgroup.com

An "expansive" Eclectic menu circles the globe from Asia to Mexico at this "informal" Rutherford BYO that includes an on-site wine store; the "no-ambiance" quarters are "tight", but staffers are "friendly", the food "hearty" and it's certainly "affordable."

Village Green *American*
24 | **19** | **23** | **$57**

Ridgewood | 36 Prospect St. (Hudson St.) | 201-445-2914 | www.villagegreenrestaurant.com

"Spectacular" multicourse tasting menus and other "interesting" prix fixe options are the lure at this "charming little" Ridgewood American BYO; though some say it's "mastered the art of teeny, pricey portions", there are à la carte options available; CIA grad Kevin Portscher (ex Latour) took over as chef-owner in 2011, a change that may not be reflected in the scores.

Villa Vittoria *Italian*
23 | **19** | **22** | **$41**

Brick | 2700 Hooper Ave. (Cedar Bridge Ave.) | 732-920-1550 | www.villavittoria.com

Look for a "big menu" of "old-fashioned" "red-sauce" standards at this "white-tablecloth" Italian in Brick that draws locals with its "uncompromising quality"; ok, maybe the decor is "a bit dated" and the crowd is from the "Sinatra" era, but genuinely "friendly" service makes for a "pleasant evening out."

Vincentown Diner ◑ *Diner*
▽ **20** | **13** | **20** | **$21**

Vincentown | 2357 Rte. 206 (Rte. 38) | 609-267-3033 | www.vincentowndiner.com

Fans say the word 'diner' is a "misnomer" at this "locavore delight" in Vincentown, where the "not-typical" menu includes "seasonal" produce, organic eggs and NJ wines; otherwise, it's known for "generous" portions, "friendly" service and breakfast offered "anytime."

Vine ☒ *American/Mediterranean*
23 | **23** | **23** | **$56**

Basking Ridge | 95 Morristown Rd. (bet. Finley & Maple Aves.) | 908-221-0017 | www.vinerestaurant.net

"De-vine" sums up the scene at this "cosmopolitan" Med–New American that's always on the "short list" of Basking Ridge's "horse-country crowd" thanks to its "superb" cooking and "spacious", "contemporary" digs; "excellent" service and a "vibrant bar scene" make the "special-occasion" tabs easier to digest.

Vu ◑ *American*
▽ **16** | **25** | **16** | **$54**

Jersey City | Hyatt Regency Jersey City | 2 Exchange Pl. (Christopher Columbus Dr.) | 201-469-4650 | www.jerseycity.hyatt.com

Floor-to-ceiling windows supply "unequaled" vistas of the NYC skyline at this "stylish" New American in Jersey City's Hyatt Regency; too bad about the "pricey" tabs, "pretty good" food and the "poor" though "well-meaning" service, but most say you're "paying for the vu" here.

Walpack Inn ☒ *American* | 20 | 22 | 20 | $43 |

Wallpack Center | Rte. 615 (Rte. 206) | 973-948-3890 | www.walpackinn.com

"Grazing deer" come with the territory at this "out-of-the-way" spot in Wallpack Center that's celebrated for its "major-league wilderness" setting and "hunting-lodge" looks; the "old-style" Traditional American menu is famed for its "fabulous" housemade bread, though some complain the "prices are rising faster" than the dough.

Wasabi Asian Plates *Japanese* | 24 | 17 | 21 | $34 |

Somerville | 12 W. Main St. (Bridge St.) | 908-203-8881

Wasabi House *Japanese*

East Brunswick | Colchester Plaza | 77 Tices Ln. (Rte. 18) | 732-254-9988 | www.wasabieb.com

Wasabi 34 *Japanese*

Matawan | 392 State Rte. 34 (Clover Hill Rd.) | 732-566-1888 | www.wasabi34.com

Though the menu differs slightly at each branch of this Japanese threesome, all feature "wonderful" sushi and service "with a smile"; East Brunswick and Matawan are BYO, while the Somerville outpost offers sake, a larger menu and "fancier", "modern" digs.

☒ Washington Inn *American* | 28 | 26 | 27 | $57 |

Cape May | 801 Washington St. (Jefferson St.) | 609-884-5697 | www.washingtoninn.com

Still the "gold standard" for "benchmark" fine dining in Cape May, this "classy" destination is all about "flawless attention to detail", from its "sensational", "artistically presented" Traditional American menu and "nice wine list" to the "gets-everything-right" service and "romantic" setting in a former plantation home; the "pricey" tabs notwithstanding, this one's a natural for "special occasions."

☒ Waterside *Mediterranean* | 21 | 25 | 21 | $59 |

North Bergen | 7800B River Rd. (Ferry Rd.) | 201-861-7767 | www.watersiderestaurantandcatering.com

"Jaw-dropping" views of the Manhattan skyline can be savored along with "excellent" Mediterranean seafood at this North Bergen venue; the "big prices" are counterbalanced by "modern Miami" decor, "happy" atmospherics and a hopping "singles scene" at the bar, which was renovated and enlarged post-Survey.

🆕 Wayne Steakhouse ☒ *Steak* | - | - | - | E |

Wayne | 2230 Hamburg Turnpike. (Westview Rd.) | 973-616-0047 | www.waynesteakhouse.com

BYO helps corral the high-end tabs at this Wayne steakhouse run by Peter Luger alumni, where dry-aged steaks and seafood dominate the menu, but complimentary onion rings and salad boost the value, and housemade schlag makes for a sweet finish; the casual space has a traditional German look, and there's patio seating in good weather.

	FOOD	DECOR	SERVICE	COST

West Lake Seafood *Chinese*
25 | 12 | 19 | $29

Matawan | Pine Crest Plaza | 1016 Rte. 34 (Broad St.) | 732-290-2988 | www.westlakeseafood.com

Like "Chinatown in Matawan", this shopping-plaza BYO is known for its "fresh", right-"from-the-tank" seafood as well as "authentic" specialties "rarely served outside the big city"; too bad the decor and service "don't match the food", but it is "moderately priced" and there's "nice" dim sum on weekends.

What's Your Beef? *Steak*
22 | 14 | 18 | $40

Rumson | 21 W. River Rd. (Lafayette St.) | 732-842-6205 | www.whatsyourbeefrumsonnj.com

You "pick your own cut" then decide "how you want it cooked" at this longtime steakhouse "standard" in Rumson where "high-quality" chops and a "marvelous" salad bar keep regulars regular; "tired", "Elks Lodge"–esque decor, "long" weekend waits and a no-rezzie policy are the main beefs here.

Z Whispers *American*
27 | 24 | 26 | $58

Spring Lake | Hewitt Wellington Hotel | 200 Monmouth Ave. (2nd Ave.) | 732-974-9755 | www.whispersrestaurant.com

A bit of "heaven" in Spring Lake's Hewitt Wellington Hotel, this "romantic" BYO is "outstanding in every respect", starting with its "stellar" New American cooking and extending to its "spot-on" service and "elegant" Victorian inn setting; fans murmur it's "as good as it gets" for an "intimate candlelit dinner" with that special someone.

White House *Sandwiches*
26 | 8 | 16 | $14

Atlantic City | 2301 Arctic Ave. (Mississippi Ave.) | 609-345-1564 ⇗

Atlantic City | Trump Taj Mahal | 1000 Boardwalk (Virginia Ave.) | 609-345-7827 | www.trumptaj.com

"Ridiculously large" submarine sandwiches arrive on "paper plates" at this cash-only AC "institution" that's "always crowded" but certainly "worth the wait in line", despite "tacky" decor and "major attitude" from the staff; P.S. the spin-off in the Trump Taj Mahal opened post-Survey.

White Mana ◑⇗ *Burgers*
17 | 8 | 13 | $10

Jersey City | 470 Tonnele Ave. (Manhattan Ave.) | 201-963-1441

"Dripping with history", this 24/7 "greasy pit stop" in "one of the least scenic parts of Jersey City" was built for the 1939 NY World's Fair and has been a slider-slinging "landmark" ever since; though "bad service and decor" are "part of the experience", some just "don't get the draw"; P.S. once part of a chain that included White Manna in Hackensack, this venue lost an 'n' because of a misspelled sign.

White Manna ◑ *Burgers*
23 | 9 | 15 | $10

Hackensack | 358 River St. (Passaic Ave.) | 201-342-0914

"Wicked good" sliders draw crowds to this "dumpy" Hackensack burger joint that's been around since 1946; though some "don't know what all the fuss is about", fans insist this "guilty pleasure" stays "busy" for a reason; P.S. it's not affiliated with White Mana in Jersey City.

Wicked Wolf Tavern *Pub Food*   ▽ 19 | 22 | 18 | $30

Hoboken | 120 Sinatra Dr. (bet. 1st & 2nd Sts.) | 201-659-7500 | www.wickedwolfhoboken.com

This "casual" Hoboken sports bar serves "simple" pub grub for "reasonable" sums; no surprise, it can be "extremely loud", but it's a "fun" enough option for those in the mood to shout at "tons of flatscreens" - and the outdoor seats offer a "great river view."

William Douglas Steakhouse 🅂🅼 *Steak*   ▽ 25 | 25 | 25 | $55

Cherry Hill | Garden State Park | 941 Haddonfield Rd. (Rte. 70) | 856-665-6100 | www.williamdouglassteakhouse.com

Owned by McCormick & Schmick's (and sharing its kitchen in Cherry Hill's former Garden State Park racetrack), this "quiet, clubby" steakhouse is "never crowded", so diners can "take their time" and "actually converse"; "tender", "juicy" chops, "excellent" service and live jazz Thursdays-Saturdays explain its appeal; P.S. closed Monday-Wednesdays.

Windansea *Seafood*   17 | 19 | 19 | $38

Highlands | 56 Shrewsbury Ave. (Bay Ave.) | 732-872-2266 | www.windanseanj.com

"Great" views of the Shrewsbury River and Sandy Hook Bay trump the "solid if unspectacular" seafood slung at this "laid-back" Highlands "summer hangout"; "friendly" staffers, "surfer-chic" decor and a "popular bar scene" ratchet up the "cheery" vibe.

WindMill, The *Hot Dogs*   19 | 8 | 14 | $12

Westfield | 256 E. Broad St. (Central Ave.) | 908-233-2001
Belmar | 1201 River Rd. (Rte. 71) | 732-681-9628 ◑
Brick | 856 Rte. 70 (Rte. 88) | 732-458-7774
Freehold | 3338 Rte. 9 S. (Adelphia Rd.) | 732-303-9855
Long Branch | 200 Ocean Blvd. (Morris Ave.) | 732-870-6098
Long Branch | 586 Ocean Blvd. (Brighton Ave.) | 732-229-9863 ◑
Ocean Grove | 18 S. Main St. (Lake Ave.) | 732-988-5277
Red Bank | 22 N. Bridge Ave. (Front St.) | 732-747-5958
www.windmillhotdogs.com

Nothing less than "Jersey Shore icons", these "decent" hot dog stands are known for their "crispy-skinned" red hots, not their "unattractive" looks and "counter-style service"; still, dog people say these "guilty pleasures" are just right when you're in the mood for cheap "seaside sustenance."

Wine Bar 🅂🅼 *Eclectic/Mediterranean*   ▽ 22 | 25 | 23 | $46

Atlantic Highlands | 40 First Ave. (Ocean Blvd.) | 732-291-1377 | www.ahwinebar.com

Oenophiles tout this "classy" second-story loft in Atlantic Highlands for its "wonderful" vino selection that makes the "delicious" Mediterranean-Eclectic food taste even better; the "romantic",

	FOOD	DECOR	SERVICE	COST

"beautifully decorated" space includes French doors, "soft" chairs and a baby grand for cabaret shows.

Witherspoon Grill *Seafood/Steak*   21 | 22 | 20 | $46

Princeton | 57 Witherspoon St. (bet. Hulfish & Wiggins Sts.) | 609-924-6011 | www.jmgroupprinceton.com

"Princeton's best-known secret", this "popular" surf 'n' turfer proffers "ample" portions of "outstanding" grub for an "ample" price; when the "hopping" bar and "masculine" dining room get "as noisy as a Jadwin gym basketball game", insiders slip outside to the "perfect" patio.

Wolfgang Puck
American Grille *American*   23 | 23 | 23 | $56

Atlantic City | Borgata Hotel, Casino & Spa | 1 Borgata Way (Huron Ave.) | 609-317-1000 | www.theborgata.com

Marquee chef Wolfgang Puck lands in Atlantic City's Borgata Hotel with this "pleasurable dining experience" that "never disappoints" thanks to "creative" New Americana served by a "highly professional" crew in a room that's "relaxing" even though open to the casino; frugal folks who find the prices "way out of line" opt for the "tavern menu."

Wondee's *Thai*   22 | 7 | 15 | $23

Hackensack | 296 Main St. (Camden St.) | 201-883-1700 | www.wondeenj.com

"Wonderful" Thai cooking is dispensed from the "fast" kitchen of this "far from fancy" Hackensack storefront where "what they lack in decor they make up in flavor"; "bargain" tabs and a BYO policy compensate for the so-so service.

Wonder Seafood *Chinese*   26 | 10 | 16 | $23

Edison | 1984 Rte. 27 (Langstaff Ave.) | 732-287-6328

"Outstanding" seafood may be the specialty of this Edison Cantonese BYO, but its real claim to fame is "exceptional" dim sum, available all the time; sure, the service is "gruff", the acoustics "noisy" and the decor strictly "low rent", but it's "cheap", "authentic" and definitely "worth trying."

Yankee Doodle Tap Room *Pub Food*   13 | 19 | 16 | $33

Princeton | Nassau Inn | 10 Palmer Sq. (Nassau St.) | 609-921-7500 | www.nassauinn.com

"Uniquely Princeton", this "been-there-forever" pub in the Nassau Inn offers "nothing-to-write-home-about" American grub in a "dark" rathskeller setting famed for its Norman Rockwell mural behind the bar; a recent patio addition "takes advantage of the village green setting", but "strains" the just "fair" service.

Ya Ya Noodles *Noodle Shop*   21 | 13 | 18 | $25

Skillman | Montgomery Shopping Ctr. | 1325 Rte. 206 N. (Rte. 518) | 609-921-8551 | www.yayanoodles.com

Noodle soups are the "specialty" but all the Chinese dishes are "well done" at this Skillman BYO set in the Montgomery Shopping Center;

while the "fraying" decor and service "need work", the "wide selection" and "reasonable prices" are fine as is.

☑ Yellow Fin *American* | 27 | 18 | 21 | $59 |

Surf City | 104 24th St. (Long Beach Blvd.) | 609-494-7001

The tuna's "perfect" and all else is "consistently great" at this "artful" Surf City New American BYO that offers some of the "best dining" – for a "big-city" price – on LBI; despite "small" dimensions, "cramped" seating and "noisy" sound levels, it books up fast in season and is "worth it" for the "pulsing" vibe alone.

☑ Yumi *Asian* | 26 | 19 | 22 | $43 |

Sea Bright | 1120 Ocean Ave. (bet. Church & New Sts.) | 732-212-0881 | www.yumirestaurant.com

Downtown Sea Bright is home to this "delightful" Asian BYO known for its "amazing", "artistic" sushi and "large" menu of "beautifully prepared" cooked dishes; "courteous" staffers and a "well-appointed" setting help make it a "summer hot spot."

Za *American* | 23 | 17 | 20 | $44 |

Pennington | 147 W. Delaware Ave. (bet. Green Ave. & Rte. 31) | 609-737-4400 | www.zarestaurants.com

This "creative" New American BYO in a Pennington strip mall delights fans with its "imaginative" menu served by a team that "makes you feel like part of the family"; although "small" inside, it also features "romantic" outdoor seats that are "magical" when the wisteria garden is in bloom.

Zafra *Pan-Latin* | 23 | 15 | 19 | $30 |

Hoboken | 301 Willow Ave. (3rd St.) | 201-610-9801 | www.zafrakitchens.com

A "fantastic variety" of small plates "encourages sharing" at this "flavorful" Pan-Latin BYO in Hoboken that's a "cheaper", more "laid-back" alternative to sibling Cucharamama; sure, the setting is pretty "tiny", but it slings three meals a day and the "warm" atmosphere makes regulars "feel like *familia*."

Zen Zen ❶ *Japanese/Korean* ∇ | 21 | 16 | 17 | $41 |

Fairview | 356 Bergen Blvd. (Jersey Ave.) | 201-840-1820

"Delicious" tabletop-grilled Korean *galbi* (short ribs) and Japanese shabu-shabu are among the specialties on the menu at this casual Fairview venue; valet parking is a plus, while late-night hours please night owls.

NEW Zeppoli *Italian* | - | - | - | M |

Collingswood | 618 Collings Ave. (Richey Ave.) | 856-854-2670 | www.zeppolirestaurant.com

Unsung chef Joey Baldino, who ran the kitchen for years at Philly's Vetri, is turning out homespun, moderately priced fresh pastas and other hearty Sicilian tastes (including handmade desserts) at his cozy BYO trattoria in Collingswood; many dishes are available in full and half sizes to encourage sharing, and reservations are a must (closed Tuesdays).

	FOOD	DECOR	SERVICE	COST
	-	-	-	M

Zinburger *Burgers*

Clifton | Promenade Shops at Clifton | 853 Rte. 3 W. (Passaic Ave.) | 973-272-1492 | www.zinburgernj.com

Burgers topped with red zinfandel-braised onions are paired with offerings from a full bar at this trendy Clifton outpost of an Arizona-based chain; the spacious, bovine-themed setting features a mural of grazing cows and milk-bottle droplights, along with patio seating.

	FOOD	DECOR	SERVICE	COST
	21	25	19	$53

Zylo *Steak*

Hoboken | W Hotel | 225 River St. (bet. 2nd & 3rd Sts.) | 201-253-2500 | www.zylorestaurant.com

An "incredible" Manhattan skyline view and "creative" cuisine attract a "swanky young crowd" to this "classy" Tuscan steakhouse in Hoboken's W Hotel; the setting is "beautiful" and the mood "trendy", so the "splurge" price tags and "dress-to-impress" scene shouldn't be a surprise.

INDEXES

Cuisines

Includes names, locations and Food ratings.

AFGHAN

Ariana	**Voorhees**	18
Pamir	**Morristown**	22
Silk Road	**Warren**	23

AMERICAN

Acacia	**Lawrenceville**	23
NEW Adara	**Montclair**	-
Alchemist/Barrister	**Princeton**	16
Alice's	**Lake Hopatcong**	21
Z Amanda's	**Hoboken**	26
Amelia's	**Jersey City**	19
Z Andre's	**Newton**	27
Anton's/Swan	**Lambertville**	22
NEW Aqua Blu	**Toms River**	-
Atlantic B&G	**S Seaside Pk**	26
Z A Toute Heure	**Cranford**	26
Ave. Bistro	**Verona**	19
Avon Pavilion	**Avon-by-Sea**	19
Backyards	**Hoboken**	18
Barnacle Bill's	**Rumson**	22
Barnsboro Inn	**Sewell**	22
Basil T's	**Red Bank**	20
Z Baumgart's	**multi.**	19
Z Bay Ave.	**Highlands**	28
Z Belford Bistro	**Belford**	26
Bell's Mansion	**Stanhope**	15
Bell's Tavern	**Lambertville**	20
Z Bernards Inn	**Bernardsville**	27
Biagio's	**Paramus**	17
Bibi'z	**Westwood**	-
Bicycle Club	**Englewood Cliffs**	14
NEW Biddy O'Malley's	**Northvale**	-
Bistro 55	**Rochelle Pk**	19
Black-Eyed Susans	**Harvey Cedars**	-
Black Horse	**Mendham**	18
Black Trumpet	**Spring Lake**	24
Blu	**Montclair**	25
Blue Bottle	**Hopewell**	26
NEW Blue Morel	**Morristown**	-
Blue Pig	**Cape May**	21
Blueplate	**Mullica Hill**	-
Bonefish Grill	**multi.**	21
Blvd. Five 72	**Kenilworth**	25

Braddock's	**Medford**	19
Brandl	**Belmar**	24
Brass Rail	**Hoboken**	19
NEW Breakfast Room	**A.C.**	-
Brick City B&G	**Newark**	18
Brickwall Tavern	**Asbury Pk**	18
Brothers Moon	**Hopewell**	23
Cabin	**Howell**	18
Cafe Loren	**Avalon**	25
Z Cafe Madison	**Riverside**	22
Z Chakra	**Paramus**	20
Chambers Walk	**Lawrenceville**	21
Charley's	**Long Branch**	18
Z Cheesecake Factory	**multi.**	19
Chickie's/Pete's	**Egg Harbor Twp**	17
Clydz	**New Bruns.**	22
Copper Fish	**W Cape May**	20
Country Pancake	**Ridgewood**	19
Cranbury Inn	**Cranbury**	14
Z CulinAriane	**Montclair**	27
Daddy O	**Long Beach**	19
NEW Daryl	**New Bruns.**	-
Dauphin	**Asbury Pk**	22
Z David Burke	**Rumson**	25
Delicious Hts.	**Berkeley Hts**	18
Dish	**Red Bank**	25
Z Drew's Bayshore	**Keyport**	27
Z Ebbitt Room	**Cape May**	26
Z Elements	**Princeton**	26
Elements	**Haddon Hts**	23
Elevation Burg.	**Moorestown**	19
Esposito's Pk. Cafe	**Cliffside Pk**	-
Esty St.	**Park Ridge**	25
Ferry House	**Princeton**	-
Fiddleheads	**Jamesburg**	23
55 Main	**Flemington**	22
Fire/Oak	**multi.**	19
NEW Firecreek	**Voorhees**	-
NEW 5 Seasons	**Ridgewood**	-
Z Frog/Peach	**New Bruns.**	26
Gazelle Café	**Ridgewood**	23
GG's	**Mt Laurel**	25
Gladstone	**Gladstone**	21
Grain House	**Basking Ridge**	19

Gusto Grill	**E Brunswick**	19
Harvest Bistro	**Closter**	21
Harvest Moon	**Ringoes**	25
Hat Tavern	**Summit**	-
☑ Highlawn Pavilion	**W Orange**	25
High St. Grill	**Mt Holly**	20
Hoboken B&G	**Hoboken**	19
Ho-Ho-Kus Inn	**Ho-Ho-Kus**	21
Holsten's	**Bloomfield**	16
Huntley Taverne	**Summit**	22
Inn at Millrace Pond Restaurant	**Hope**	23
Inn/Sugar Hill	**Mays Landing**	18
Inn of the Hawke Restaurant	**Lambertville**	20
Iron Hill Brewery	**Maple Shade**	20
Isabella's	**Westfield**	19
Ivy Inn	**Hasbrouck Hts**	22
Jack's	**Westwood**	20
Janice	**Ho-Ho-Kus**	21
Java Moon	**multi.**	22
NEW JBJ Soul Kitchen	**Red Bank**	-
NEW Just	**Old Bridge**	-
NEW Keg/Kitchen	**Westmont**	-
Kevin's Thyme	**Ho-Ho-Kus**	23
Krave Café	**Newton**	24
Lambertville Station	**Lambertville**	17
L'assiette	**Surf City**	20
Lazy Dog Saloon	**Asbury Pk**	23
Liberty House	**Jersey City**	20
Library IV	**Williamstown**	-
Light Horse	**Jersey City**	22
LITM	**Jersey City**	14
LoBianco	**Margate**	-
Lucky Bones	**Cape May**	20
Mad Batter	**Cape May**	23
Madison B&G	**Hoboken**	19
Main St.	**multi.**	19
Maize	**Newark**	17
☑ Manor	**W Orange**	24
Marco/Pepe	**Jersey City**	22
Maritime Parc	**Jersey City**	-
Martini Bistro	**Millburn**	19
Martini 494	**Newark**	-
Mastoris	**Bordentown**	19
Matisse	**Belmar**	22
☑ Mattar's Bistro	**Allamuchy**	24
Matt's/Rooster	**Flemington**	26
McLoone's	**multi.**	17
Meil's	**Stockton**	24
Merion Inn	**Cape May**	24
Mill/Spring Lake Hts.	**Spring Lake Hts**	21
NEW MK Valencia	**Ridgefield Pk**	-
Mohawk House	**Sparta**	22
☑ Molly Pitcher Inn Restaurant	**Red Bank**	22
Montville Inn	**Montville**	22
NEW MoonShine	**Millburn**	-
☑ Moonstruck	**Asbury Pk**	25
National Hotel Rest.	**Frenchtown**	-
Nauvoo Grill	**Fair Haven**	18
Next Door	**Montclair**	22
☑ Nicholas	**Red Bank**	29
Nicky's	**Madison**	18
☑ Ninety Acres	**Peapack**	25
NEW O Bistro	**A.C.**	-
Old Man Rafferty's	**multi.**	18
One 53	**Rocky Hill**	23
Onieal's	**Hoboken**	20
Orange Squirrel	**Bloomfield**	22
NEW Pacific Grill	**Wildwood**	-
NEW Pairings	**Cranford**	-
Park Ave. B&G	**Union City**	18
NEW Park West	**Ridgewood**	-
Peacock Inn Restaurant	**Princeton**	26
Perryville Inn	**Union Twp**	26
☑ Peter Shields	**Cape May**	26
Pheasants Landing	**Hillsborough**	15
☑ Picnic	**Fair Lawn**	27
Pine Tavern	**Old Bridge**	20
P.J. Whelihan's	**multi.**	17
Plan B	**Asbury Pk**	24
Plantation	**Harvey Cedars**	18
☑ Pluckemin Inn	**Bedminster**	26
Pointé	**Jersey City**	21
Ponzio's	**Cherry Hill**	19
Pop Shop	**Collingswood**	20
Quays	**Hoboken**	18
☑ Ram's Head Inn	**Galloway**	24
☑ Raven/Peach	**Fair Haven**	24
Raymond's	**Montclair**	21
Red	**Red Bank**	21

Redstone | **Marlton**	21
Redwood's | **Chester**	18
Remington's | **Manasquan**	21
Renault Winery | **Egg Harbor**	21
Rest. L | **Allendale**	18
Z Rest. Latour | **Hamburg**	27
RiverWinds | **Deptford**	–
Robin's Nest | **Mt Holly**	22
Rocky Hill Inn | **Rocky Hill**	17
Rod's Olde Irish | **Sea Girt**	18
Rolling Pin | **Westwood**	23
Z Rosemary/Sage | **Riverdale**	26
Z Saddle River Inn | **Saddle River**	28
Sallee Tee's | **Monmouth Bch**	18
Salt Creek | **multi.**	19
Scarborough Fair | **Sea Girt**	23
Z Seasons 52 | **Cherry Hill**	22
Sergeantsville Inn | **Sergeantsville**	24
Shipwreck Grill | **Brielle**	24
Smithville Inn | **Smithville**	20
Spargo's | **Manalapan**	23
Stage House | **Scotch Plains**	20
Z Stage Left | **New Bruns.**	27
Steve/Cookie's | **Margate**	25
NEW St. Eve's | **Ho-Ho-Kus**	–
Z Stone House | **Warren**	22
Sweet Basil's | **Livingston**	21
Tabor Rd. | **Morris Plains**	21
Terra Nova | **Sewell**	–
Tewksbury Inn | **Oldwick**	23
Grenville | **Bay Hd.**	17
3 Forty Grill | **Hoboken**	20
3 West | **Basking Ridge**	23
Tim McLoone's | **Asbury Pk**	20
Tim Schafer's | **Morristown**	23
Tisha's | **Cape May**	25
Toast | **multi.**	22
Trap Rock | **Berkeley Hts**	21
Trinity | **Keyport**	25
Triumph Brew. | **Princeton**	16
Tun Tavern | **A.C.**	18
TwoFiftyTwo | **Bedminster**	–
Ugly Mug | **Cape May**	15
Union Park | **Cape May**	25
Uproot | **Warren**	22
NEW Upstairs | **Upper Montclair**	–
NEW Ursino | **Union**	–
Verve | **Somerville**	23

Village Green | **Ridgewood**	24
Vine | **Basking Ridge**	23
Vu | **Jersey City**	16
Walpack Inn | **Wallpack**	20
Z Washington Inn | **Cape May**	28
Z Whispers | **Spring Lake**	27
White Mana | **Jersey City**	17
White Manna | **Hackensack**	23
Wolfgang Puck | **A.C.**	23
Yankee Doodle | **Princeton**	13
Z Yellow Fin | **Surf City**	27
Za | **Pennington**	23
Zinburger | **Clifton**	–

ARGENTINEAN

Valdebenito's | **Somerville**	–

ASIAN

Z Baumgart's | **multi.**	19
Z Buddakan | **A.C.**	26
NEW Chinese Mirch | **N Brunswick**	–
Coconut Bay | **Voorhees**	22
Z Hotoke | **New Bruns.**	20
Ming | **multi.**	24
Ritz Seafood | **Voorhees**	26
Teak | **Red Bank**	21
Tina Louise | **Carlstadt**	23
Très Yan & Wu | **Mt Laurel**	23

AUSTRIAN

NEW Pilsener Haus | **Hoboken**	–

BAKERIES

NEW Bucu | **Paramus**	–
Mastoris | **Bordentown**	19
Ponzio's | **Cherry Hill**	19

BARBECUE

Big Ed's BBQ | **Matawan**	18
NEW Blind Boar | **Norwood**	–
Cubby's BBQ | **Hackensack**	19
D&L BBQ | **Bradley Bch**	24
Grub Hut | **Manville**	21
Memphis Pig Out | **Atlantic Highlands**	19

BELGIAN

NEW Mussel Bar | **A.C.**	–

BRAZILIAN

Brasilia | **Newark**	22
Rio Rodizio | **multi.**	20

BRITISH

Ship Inn | Milford   17

BURGERS

Barnacle Bill's | Rumson   22
Bobby's | multi.   21
NEW Bucu | Paramus   -
Elevation Burg. | multi.   19
Z Five Guys | multi.   21
Hiram's | Fort Lee   21
Nifty Fifty's | multi.   19
Pop Shop | Collingswood   20
Smashburger | multi.   19
WindMill | multi.   19
White Mana | Jersey City   17
White Manna | Hackensack   23
Zinburger | Clifton   -

CAJUN

Oddfellows | Hoboken   18
Old Bay | New Bruns.   19
Trinity/Pope | Asbury Pk   21

CALIFORNIAN

Surf Taco | multi.   21
Tomatoes | Margate   25

CARIBBEAN

Bahama Breeze | multi.   17
410 Bank St. | Cape May   26
Laila's | Asbury Pk   22

CHEESESTEAKS

Tony Luke's | multi.   20

CHINESE

(* dim sum specialist)
Cathay 22 | Springfield   22
Chef Jon's | Whippany   24
Chengdu 46 | Clifton   24
Chez Elena Wu | Voorhees   22
Crown Palace* | multi.   20
Dim Sum Dynasty* | Ridgewood   20
NEW Duck King | Edgewater   -
Edo Sushi | Pennington   20
Far East Taste | Eatontown   23
Fortune Cookie | Bridgewater   21
Hanami | multi.   20
Hunan Chinese | Morris Plains   20
Hunan Spring | Springfield   18
Hunan Taste | Denville   24
Joe's Peking* | Marlton   24

Lotus Cafe | Hackensack   23
Meemah | Edison   25
Mr. Chu | E Hanover   21
Z P.F. Chang's | multi.   20
Sakura Spring | Cherry Hill   24
Shanghai Jazz | Madison   22
Tiger Noodles | Princeton   19
West Lake Seafood | Matawan   25
Wonder Seafood* | Edison   26

COFFEEHOUSES

Rolling Pin | Westwood   23

COFFEE SHOPS/ DINERS

Mastoris | Bordentown   19
Mustache Bill's | Barnegat Light   24
Nifty Fifty's | multi.   19
Ponzio's | Cherry Hill   19
Sage Diner | Mt Laurel   14
Skylark | Edison   22
Teplitzky's | A.C.   18
Tick Tock | Clifton   18
Vincentown Diner | Vincentown   20
White Mana | Jersey City   17
White Manna | Hackensack   23

COLOMBIAN

El Familiar | Toms River   -

CONTINENTAL

Black Forest Inn | Stanhope   23
Café Gallery | Burlington   20
Court St. | Hoboken   22
Daniel's Bistro | Pt. Pleas. Bch   -
Farnsworth House | Bordentown   22
Inn at Millrace Pond Restaurant | 23
  Hope
La Campagne | Cherry Hill   23
Le Jardin | Edgewater   20
Lincroft Inn | Lincroft   19
Main St. | Princeton   19
Pheasants Landing | Hillsborough   15
Stony Hill Inn | Hackensack   22
NEW Upstairs | Upper Montclair   -

CREOLE

Clementine's | Avon-by-Sea   23
410 Bank St. | Cape May   26
Oddfellows | Hoboken   18
Old Bay | New Bruns.   19
Trinity/Pope | Asbury Pk   21

CUBAN

A Little Bit of Cuba | **Freehold** 19
Azúcar | **Jersey City** 20
Casona | **Collingswood** 22
NEW Cubacan | **Asbury Pk** -
Cuba Libre | **A.C.** 21
Cuban Pete's | **Montclair** 19
Cubanu | **Rahway** 21
El Caney | **Bergenfield** -
La Isla | **Hoboken** 25
Martino's | **Somerville** 22
Mi Bandera | **Union City** 24
Rebecca's | **Edgewater** 23
Rumba Cubana/Cafe | **multi.** 23
Son Cubano | **W New York** -

DELIS/ SANDWICH SHOPS

Eppes Essen | **Livingston** 20
Hobby's | **Newark** 24
Jerry/Harvey's | **Marlboro** 18
Kibitz Room | **Cherry Hill** 23
Nana's Deli | **Livingston** 23
Richard's | **Long Branch** 20

DESSERT

Z Cheesecake Factory | **multi.** 19
Old Man Rafferty's | **multi.** 18

EASTERN EUROPEAN

Blue Danube | **Trenton** 22

ECLECTIC

Z Little Café | **Voorhees** 27
NEW Aqua Blu | **Toms River** -
Ariel's | **Englewood** 20
NEW Baia | **Somers Point** -
Bistro/Red Bank | **Red Bank** 21
Black Duck | **W Cape May** 26
Z Cafe Matisse | **Rutherford** 27
Cafe Metro | **Denville** 22
Z Cafe Panache | **Ramsey** 27
Caffe Galleria | **Lambertville** 21
Christopher | **Cherry Hill** -
Continental | **A.C.** 23
DelMonico | **Cedar Grove** 27
Eurasian | **Red Bank** 23
Fedora Café | **Lawrenceville** 20
Frenchtown Inn | **Frenchtown** 23
Full Moon | **Lambertville** 19
Z Gables | **Beach Haven** 24

Garlic Rose | **multi.** 20
Jack's | **Westwood** 20
Kilkenny Ale | **Newark** 18
Labrador | **Normandy Bch** 25
Langosta | **Asbury Pk** 22
Lilly's/Canal | **Lambertville** 21
Main St. | **Kingston** 19
Market Roost | **Flemington** 22
Meyersville Inn | **Gillette** 19
National Hotel Rest. | **Frenchtown** -
NEW Nico | **Newark** -
Oliver a Bistro | **Bordentown** 27
Z Park/Orchard | **E Rutherford** 23
Z Red Square | **A.C.** 21
Sallee Tee's | **Monmouth Bch** 18
Skylark | **Edison** 22
Soho 33 | **Madison** 18
Sublime | **Gladstone** 20
Tomatoes | **Margate** 25
Triumph Brew. | **Princeton** 16
Tula | **New Bruns.** 19
27 Mix | **Newark** 21
NEW Urban Table | **Morristown** -
Village Gourmet | **Rutherford** 21
Wine Bar | **Atlantic Highlands** 22

ETHIOPIAN

Makeda | **New Bruns.** 24
Mesob | **Montclair** 24

EURASIAN

Coconut Bay | **Voorhees** 22

EUROPEAN

Satis | **Jersey City** -

FONDUE

Magic Pot | **Edgewater** 18
Melting Pot | **multi.** 19

FRENCH

Aozora | **Montclair** 24
Blackbird | **Collingswood** 24
Z Chez Catherine | **Westfield** 26
Claude's | **N Wildwood** 27
Dream Cuisine | **Cherry Hill** 27
Ferry House | **Princeton** -
Frenchtown Inn | **Frenchtown** 23
Z Grand Cafe | **Morristown** 25
NEW Khloe Bistrot | **Fort Lee** -
Z Latour | **Ridgewood** 26

Le Jardin | **Edgewater**	20
☑ Lorena's | **Maplewood**	28
Madeleine's | **Northvale**	25
Manon | **Lambertville**	25
☑ Origin | **multi.**	25
☑ Rat's | **Hamilton**	24
☑ Resto | **Madison**	25
Robin's Nest | **Mt Holly**	22
☑ Saddle River Inn | **Saddle River**	28
☑ Serenade | **Chatham**	27
Siri's | **Cherry Hill**	26
Thai Chef | **Montclair**	21
Très Yan & Wu | **Mt Laurel**	23
Verjus | **Maplewood**	25
Verve | **Somerville**	23

FRENCH (BISTRO)

Bienvenue | **Red Bank**	22
☑ Chef's Table | **Franklin Lakes**	28
Circa | **High Bridge**	17
Elysian Café | **Hoboken**	21
Epernay | **Montclair**	21
Harvest Bistro | **Closter**	21
Le Fandy | **Fair Haven**	25
☑ Le Rendez-Vous | **Kenilworth**	27
Madame Claude | **Jersey City**	23
Rob's Bistro | **Madison**	–
Sophie's | **Somerset**	24

FRENCH (BRASSERIE)

☑ Avenue | **Long Branch**	22

GASTROPUB

NEW Biddy O'Malley's | New American | **Northvale**	–

GERMAN

Alps Bistro | **Allentown**	–
Black Forest Inn | **Stanhope**	23
Helmers' | **Hoboken**	19

GREEK

Athenian Gdn. | **Galloway Twp**	23
Axia Taverna | **Tenafly**	23
Greek Taverna | **multi.**	20
It's Greek To Me | **multi.**	18
Kuzina/Sofia | **Cherry Hill**	22
NEW Kyma | **Somerville**	–
Limani | **Westfield**	24
Lithos | **Livingston**	–
Pithari | **Highland Pk**	23

Santorini | **Fort Lee**	21
Stamna | **Bloomfield**	23
Taverna Mykonos | **Elmwood Pk**	25
Varka | **Ramsey**	26
Vasili's | **Teaneck**	21

HAWAIIAN

NEW Ohana Grill | **Lavallette**	–

HOT DOGS

Hiram's | **Fort Lee**	21
Hot Dog Johnny's | **Buttzville**	21
Jimmy Buff's | **multi.**	20
Rutt's Hut | **Clifton**	21
WindMill | **multi.**	19

HUNGARIAN

NEW Pilsener Haus | **Hoboken**	–

ICE CREAM PARLORS

☑ Baumgart's | **multi.**	19
Holsten's | **Bloomfield**	16

INDIAN

Aamantran | **Toms River**	21
Aangan | **Freehold Twp**	23
Akbar | **Edison**	20
Amiya | **Jersey City**	19
NEW Bombay Bistro | **Summit**	–
NEW Brick Lane Curry | **multi.**	–
Chand Palace | **multi.**	23
Cinnamon | **Morris Plains**	23
Cross Culture | **Haddonfield**	–
IndeBlue | **Collingswood**	25
India/Hudson | **Hoboken**	21
Karma Kafe | **Hoboken**	21
NEW Khyber Grill | **South Plainfield**	–
Kinara | **Edgewater**	22
Mantra | **multi.**	22
Mehndi | **Morristown**	24
Moghul | **Edison**	23
Namaskaar | **Englewood**	20
Neelam | **multi.**	20
Palace of Asia | **Cherry Hill**	–
Raagini | **Mountainside**	23
Saffron | **E Hanover**	24
Taj Mahal | **Jersey City**	–

IRISH

Egan/Sons | **multi.**	19
Irish Pub | **A.C.**	18

Quiet Man | **Dover**	22
Trinity | **Hoboken**	18

ITALIAN

(N=Northern; S=Southern)

Acquaviva/Fonti | N | **Westfield**	22
Aldo/Gianni | **Montvale**	21
A Mano | **Ridgewood**	22
Amarone | N | **Teaneck**	21
Amici Milano | N | **Trenton**	22
Andreotti's | **Cherry Hill**	-
Angelo's | **A.C.**	21
Anjelica's | S | **Sea Bright**	24
Anna's Kitchen | **Middletown**	23
NEW Anna's Rist. | **Summit**	-
Anthony David's | N | **Hoboken**	25
Anthony's | **Haddon Hts**	24
Antonia's | **N Bergen**	20
Armando's | **Fort Lee**	19
Armando's Tuscan | **River Vale**	20
Arturo's | S | **Midland Pk**	23
Arturo's | **Maplewood**	24
Arugula | **Sewell**	-
Assaggini/Roma | **Newark**	24
A Tavola | **Old Bridge**	20
Augustino's | S | **Hoboken**	26
NEW Baia | **Somers Point**	-
Bar Cara | **Bloomfield**	20
Bareli's | **Secaucus**	23
Barone's/Villa Barone/Tuscan | N | **multi.**	22
Barrels | **multi.**	21
☑ Basilico | N | **Millburn**	23
Basil T's | **Red Bank**	20
☑ Bay Ave. | **Highlands**	28
Bazzarelli | **Moonachie**	19
Bella Sogno | **Bradley Bch**	21
Bell's Tavern | **Lambertville**	20
Belmont Tavern | **Belleville**	23
Benito's | N | **Chester**	23
Berta's | N | **Wanaque**	22
Biagio's | **Paramus**	17
Bin 14 | **Hoboken**	22
Bistro/Marino | **Collingswood**	22
Blackbird | **Collingswood**	24
Bottagra | **Hawthorne**	20
Brioso | **Marlboro**	24
Brio | **multi.**	19
Bruschetta | N | **Fairfield**	21
BV Tuscany | N | **Teaneck**	23

Cafe Arugula | **S Orange**	21
Café Azzurro | N | **Peapack**	24
Cafe Bello | **Bayonne**	22
Cafe Coloré | **Freehold Twp**	19
Cafe Emilia | **Bridgewater**	22
Cafe Graziella | **Hillsborough**	20
Cafe Italiano | **Englewood Cliffs**	19
Caffe Aldo | **Cherry Hill**	24
☑ Capriccio | **A.C.**	25
Cara Mia | **Millburn**	-
Carmine's | **A.C.**	21
Casa Dante | **Jersey City**	24
Casa Giuseppe | N | **Iselin**	22
Cassie's | **Englewood**	18
☑ Catherine Lombardi | **New Bruns.**	24
Cenzino | **Oakland**	24
☑ Chef Vola's | **A.C.**	26
Christie's | **Howell**	26
Ciao | **Basking Ridge**	21
Columbia Inn | **Montville**	21
Corso 98 | **Montclair**	22
Cucina Calandra | S | **Fairfield**	21
Cucina Rosa | **Cape May**	21
Da Filippo's | **Somerville**	24
Dante's | **Mendham**	20
NEW Da Soli | **Haddonfield**	-
Davia | **Fair Lawn**	20
DeAnna's | **Lambertville**	24
Dimora | N | **Norwood**	24
Dinallo's | **River Edge**	22
Dino's | **Harrington Pk**	22
DiPalma Brothers | **N Bergen**	21
Due Mari | **New Bruns.**	26
E & V | **Paterson**	23
Eccola | **Parsippany**	23
☑ Eno Terra | **Kingston**	24
Espo's | S | **Raritan**	23
Esposito's Pk. Cafe | **Cliffside Pk**	-
☑ Fascino | **Montclair**	26
Federici's | **Freehold**	21
15 Fox Pl. | **Jersey City**	23
Filomena Italiana | S | **Clementon**	25
Filomena Lake. | S | **Deptford**	23
Filomena Rustica | S | **W Berlin**	18
Fiorino | N | **Summit**	24
Fontana/Trevi | **Leonia**	23
Fornelletto | **A.C.**	24

Franco's Metro | **Fort Lee** 19

Frankie Fed's | **Freehold Twp** 21

Fredo's | **Freehold Twp** 22

Frescos | **Cape May** 22

Gaetano's | **Red Bank** 20

Gianna's | **Carlstadt** 20

Girasole | S | **A.C.** 26

Girasole | **Bound Brook** 26

Giumarello | N | **Westmont** 25

GoodFellas | N | **Garfield** 21

Z Grato | **Morris Plains** 22

Grissini | **Englewood Cliffs** 22

Homestead Inn | **Trenton** 22

I Gemelli | **S Hackensack** 24

Z Il Capriccio | **Whippany** 25

NEW Il Cinghiale | **Little Ferry** –

Il Fiore | **Collingswood** 26

Il Michelangelo | **Boonton** 20

Z Il Mondo | N | **Madison** 26

Z Il Mulino | **A.C.** 27

Il Vecchio Cafe | **Caldwell** 20

Il Villaggio | **Carlstadt** 24

In Napoli | S | **Fort Lee** 17

Janice | **Ho-Ho-Kus** 21

Jimmy's | S | **Asbury Pk** 23

Joe Pesce | **Collingswood** 24

Kinchley's | **Ramsey** 21

Kitchen Consigliere | **Collingswood** –

La Campagna | **Morristown** 23

La Cipollina | **Freehold** 22

La Focaccia | N | **Summit** 23

NEW La Fontana Coast | **Sea Isle City** –

La Griglia | **Kenilworth** 23

La Locanda | **Voorhees** 28

Lamberti's Cucina | **Turnersville** 20

La Pastaria | **multi.** 19

NEW Tratt. Primavera | **W Orange** –

La Sorrentina | N | **N Bergen** 24

Z La Spiaggia | **Ship Bottom** 24

La Strada | **Randolph** 23

La Vecchia | **Edgewater** 21

Locale | **Closter** 20

LouCás | **Edison** 23

Luca's Rist. | **Somerset** 24

Luce | **Caldwell** 22

Luciano's | **Rahway** 24

Luigi's | **E Hanover** 26

Luigi's | **Ridgefield Pk** –

Luka's | **Ridgefield Pk** 23

Luke Palladino | **multi.** 26

Luna Rossa | **Sicklerville** –

Lu Nello | **Cedar Grove** 25

Maggiano's | **multi.** 20

Margherita's | **Hoboken** 22

NEW Marlene Mangia Bene | **Woodbury** –

Mélange | **Haddonfield** 25

Mia | **A.C.** 26

NEW MK Valencia | **Ridgefield Pk** –

NEW Nico | **Newark** –

Nunzio | **Collingswood** 24

Z Osteria Giotto | **Montclair** 26

NEW Osteria/Fiamma | **Ridgewood** –

NEW Osteria Morini | **Bernardsville** –

Panico's | **New Bruns.** 21

Papa Razzi | **multi.** 18

Pasquale's | **Edison** 24

Patsy's | **Fairview** 23

Pete/Elda's | **Neptune City** 22

Z Piccola | **Ocean Twp** 26

Piero's | **Union Beach** 22

Pietro's Pizza | **Marlton** 21

Pino's | **Marlboro** 21

Pizzicato | **Marlton** 21

Portobello | N | **Oakland** 19

Portofino | **Tinton Falls** 24

Z Porto Leggero | **Jersey City** 26

Primavera | **W Orange** 21

Raimondo's | **Ship Bottom** 24

Renato's | **Jersey City** 22

Reservoir | **Boonton** 23

Rick's | **Lambertville** 21

Risotto House | **Rutherford** 23

Z Rist./Benito | **Union** 26

Roberto's | N | **Beach Haven** 21

Roberto's II | **Edgewater** 21

Rocca | **Glen Rock** 24

Rosie's | **Randolph** 21

Saluté | **Montclair** –

Sanducci's | **River Edge** 19

San Remo | **Shrewsbury** 22

Sanzari's | **New Milford** 22

Z Sapori | **Collingswood** 28

🇿 Scalini Fedeli | N | **Chatham**	27
Settebello | **Morristown**	20
Sette | **Bernardsville**	24
Settimo Cielo | **Trenton**	23
Sirena | **Long Branch**	23
Solaia | **Englewood**	17
Solari's | **Hackensack**	19
Solo Bella | **Jackson**	22
Sorrento | **E Rutherford**	24
Squan Tavern | S | **Manasquan**	20
Stella Marina | **Asbury Pk**	23
Stony Hill Inn | **Hackensack**	22
Tbones Tuscan Steakhouse | N | **Bridgewater**	22
Teresa Caffe | **Princeton**	21
Theresa's | **Westfield**	22
Toscano | **Bordentown**	22
Trattoria Bel Paese | **Cranford**	-
Trattoria Med. | **Bedminster**	24
Treno | **Westmont**	-
Tre Piani | **Princeton**	20
Trovato's | S | **multi.**	19
Tutto/Modo Mio | **Ridgefield**	21
Tuzzio's | **Long Branch**	20
Undici | **Rumson**	22
Ventura's | **Margate**	18
Vespa's | **Edgewater**	17
Vic's | **Bradley Bch**	21
Villa Amalfi | **Cliffside Pk**	23
Villa Vittoria | **Brick**	23
🆕 Zeppoli | S | **Collingswood**	-
Zylo | N | **Hoboken**	21

JAPANESE

(* sushi specialist)

Ajihei* | **Princeton**	25
Akai* | **Englewood**	24
Aligado* | **Hazlet**	24
Aozora | **Montclair**	24
Benihana | **multi.**	18
🆕 Bushido | **Cliffside Pk**	-
Chez Elena Wu* | **Voorhees**	22
Dai-Kichi* | **Upper Montclair**	23
East* | **Teaneck**	19
Edo Sushi* | **Pennington**	20
Elements Asia* | **Lawrenceville**	23
Flirt Sushi* | **Allendale**	23
Fuji | **Haddonfield**	25
Hanami | **multi.**	20

🇿 Ikko* | **Brick**	25
🇿 Izakaya | **A.C.**	23
Kanji* | **Tinton Falls**	24
Komegashi* | **Jersey City**	22
Konbu* | **Manalapan**	26
Mahzu* | **multi.**	20
Megu* | **multi.**	23
Midori* | **Denville**	21
Mikado* | **multi.**	23
Minado* | **multi.**	20
Monster Sushi* | **Summit**	20
Nikko* | **Whippany**	24
Nobi* | **Toms River**	26
Nori* | **multi.**	23
Ota-Ya* | **Lambertville**	21
Oyako Tso's* | **Freehold**	23
Rio Rodizio* | **multi.**	20
Robongi | **multi.**	24
🇿 Sagami* | **Collingswood**	27
Sakura-Bana* | **Ridgewood**	25
Sakura Spring | **Cherry Hill**	24
Sawa* | **multi.**	23
🆕 Scarduzio's* | **A.C.**	-
Shogun* | **multi.**	21
🇿 Shumi* | **Somerville**	28
Sono* | **Middletown**	25
Sumo* | **Wall**	25
Sushi Lounge* | **multi.**	22
Sushi X | **Ridgewood**	21
Taka* | **Asbury Pk**	25
Takara | **Oakhurst**	20
Tsuki* | **Bernardsville**	22
Umeya | **Cresskill**	23
Wasabi* | **multi.**	24
🇿 Yumi* | **Sea Bright**	26
Zen Zen | **Fairview**	21

JEWISH

Eppes Essen | **Livingston**	20
Hobby's | **Newark**	24
Kibitz Room | **Cherry Hill**	23
Nana's Deli | **Livingston**	23

KOREAN

(* barbecue specialist)

Dong Bang Grill* | **Fort Lee**	22
Gam Mee Ok | **Fort Lee**	21
Prime/Beyond | **Fort Lee**	-
So Moon Nan Jip* | **Palisades Pk**	24
Zen Zen* | **Fairview**	21

KOSHER/ KOSHER-STYLE

Ariel's | **Englewood**	20
Etc. Steak | **Teaneck**	25
Hummus Elite | **Englewood**	21
Jerry/Harvey's | **Marlboro**	18

MALAYSIAN

Meemah | **Edison**	25
Penang | **multi.**	22
Taste of Asia | **Chatham**	22

MEDITERRANEAN

Babylon | **River Edge**	21
Calandra's/Grill | **Fairfield**	21
Frescos | **Cape May**	22
Hamilton's | **Lambertville**	26
Hummus Elite | **Englewood**	21
NEW Levant Grille | **Englewood**	-
Manolo's | **Elizabeth**	25
Mediterra | **Princeton**	20
☑ Moonstruck | **Asbury Pk**	25
Sage | **Ventnor**	25
Satis | **Jersey City**	-
Sofia | **Margate**	23
Tre Piani | **Princeton**	20
Vine | **Basking Ridge**	23
☑ Waterside | **N Bergen**	21
Wine Bar | **Atlantic Highlands**	22

MEXICAN

Aby's | **Matawan**	20
Animo Juice | **Haddonfield**	-
Baja | **multi.**	18
Baja Fresh | **multi.**	17
Casa Maya | **multi.**	24
Charrito's/El Charro | **multi.**	22
Chilangos | **Highlands**	21
NEW Dos Caminos | **A.C.**	-
El Azteca | **Mt Laurel**	21
El Familiar | **Toms River**	-
El Mesón Café | **Freehold**	24
NEW El Tule | **Lambertville**	-
Grub Hut | **Manville**	21
Jose's | **Spring Lake Hts**	23
Jose's Cantina | **multi.**	19
Juanito's | **multi.**	23
La Esperanza | **Lindenwold**	25
Los Amigos | **multi.**	23
Mexican Food | **Marlton**	20

Pop's Garage | **multi.**	22
Rosa Mexicano | **Hackensack**	22
Senorita's | **multi.**	19
Surf Taco | **multi.**	21
Taqueria Downtown | **Jersey City**	24
Tito's | **multi.**	20
Tortilla Press | **multi.**	24
Tortuga's | **Princeton**	22

MIDDLE EASTERN

Ali Baba | **Hoboken**	19
Ibby's | **multi.**	22
Kairo | **New Bruns.**	-
Norma's | **Cherry Hill**	22

NOODLE SHOPS

Tiger Noodles | **Princeton**	19
Ya Ya | **Skillman**	21

NUEVO LATINO

NEW Cubacan | **Asbury Pk**	-
Sabor | **N Bergen**	22

PACIFIC RIM

Metropolitan Cafe | **Freehold**	21

PAKISTANI

NEW Bombay Bistro | **Summit**	-

PAN-LATIN

Casa Solar | **Belmar**	23
Lola/Bistro | **Metuchen**	-
Park Ave. B&G | **Union City**	18
Patria | **Rahway**	-
Zafra | **Hoboken**	23

PERSIAN

Negeen | **Summit**	18

PERUVIAN

Costanera | **Montclair**	24
NEW El Tule | **Lambertville**	-
Oh! Calamares | **Kearny**	-

PIZZA

Ah'Pizz | **Montclair**	22
A Mano | **Ridgewood**	22
Arturo's | **Maplewood**	24
Bar Cara | **Bloomfield**	20
Benny Tudino's | **Hoboken**	22
Brooklyn's Pizza | **multi.**	22
Cassie's | **Englewood**	18
Columbia Inn | **Montville**	21

Conte's | **Princeton**	25
DeLorenzo's Pizza | **multi.**	24
🇿 DeLorenzo's/Pies | **Robbinsville**	27
Esposito's Pk. Cafe | **Cliffside Pk**	-
Federici's | **Freehold**	21
Frankie Fed's | **Freehold Twp**	21
Grimaldi's | **multi.**	25
Kinchley's | **Ramsey**	21
La Sorrentina | **N Bergen**	24
Margherita's | **Hoboken**	22
Napoli's Pizza | **Hoboken**	25
Nicky's | **Madison**	18
Nomad Pizza | **Hopewell**	26
Pete/Elda's | **Neptune City**	22
Pietro's Pizza | **Marlton**	21
Pino's | **Marlboro**	21
Pizzicato | **Marlton**	21
Renato's | **Jersey City**	22
Reservoir | **Boonton**	23
Solo Bella | **Jackson**	22
Tacconelli's | **Maple Shade**	23
Tony's Baltimore Grill | **A.C.**	18
Vic's | **Bradley Bch**	21

POLISH

Royal Warsaw | **Elmwood Pk**	23

PORTUGUESE

Adega Grill | **Newark**	22
Bistro Olé | **Asbury Pk**	23
Campino Mercado | **Newark**	22
Don Pepe | **multi.**	22
Europa South | **Pt. Pleas. Bch**	21
Fernandes | **Newark**	24
Gabriela's | **Somerville**	18
Iberia | **Newark**	20
Maize | **Newark**	17
Pic-Nic | **E Newark**	21
Portuguese Manor | **Perth Amboy**	19
Seabra's | **Newark**	23
Segovia | **Moonachie**	23
Sol-Mar | **Newark**	26
Spain | **Newark**	24
Taste/Portugal | **Newark**	22
Tony/Caneca | **Newark**	23

PUB FOOD

Alchemist/Barrister | **Princeton**	16
Barnacle Bill's | **Rumson**	22
🆕 Biddy O'Malley's | **Northvale**	-
Black Horse | **Mendham**	18
Brick City B&G | **Newark**	18
Brickwall Tavern | **Asbury Pk**	18
Cabin | **Howell**	18
Chickie's/Pete's | **multi.**	17
🆕 GK's Red Dog | **Morristown**	-
Inn of the Hawke Restaurant | **Lambertville**	20
Irish Pub | **A.C.**	18
Iron Hill Brewery | **Maple Shade**	20
Kilkenny Ale | **Newark**	18
Light Horse | **Jersey City**	22
McGovern's | **Newark**	18
🆕 Park West | **Ridgewood**	-
P.J. Whelihan's | **multi.**	17
Quiet Man | **Dover**	22
Rod's Olde Irish | **Sea Girt**	18
Ship Inn | **Milford**	17
Ugly Mug | **Cape May**	15
Victor's Pub | **Camden**	-
Wicked Wolf | **Hoboken**	19
Yankee Doodle | **Princeton**	13

SANDWICHES

(See also Delis)

Little Food Cafe | **multi.**	23
Rolling Pin | **Westwood**	23
Sallee Tee's | **Monmouth Bch**	18
White House | **A.C.**	26

SEAFOOD

Allen's | **New Gretna**	22
Atlantic B&G | **S Seaside Pk**	26
Axelsson's | **Cape May**	23
Bahrs Landing | **Highlands**	17
Berkeley | **S Seaside Pk**	20
Blue Fish | **Flemington**	21
🇿 Blue Point | **Princeton**	26
Bobby Chez | **multi.**	24
Bonefish Grill | **multi.**	21
Capt'n Ed's | **Pt. Pleas.**	20
🇿 Chart House | **multi.**	21
Chophouse | **Gibbsboro**	23
Copper Fish | **W Cape May**	20
Crab House | **Edgewater**	16
Crab's Claw Inn | **Lavallette**	18
Crab Trap | **Somers Point**	21
Da Filippo's | **Somerville**	24

Diving Horse | **Avalon**	24
Dock's | **A.C.**	26
Don Quijote | **Fairview**	18
Due Mari | **New Bruns.**	26
Fin | **A.C.**	25
Fin Raw Bar | **Montclair**	-
Fishery | **S Amboy**	20
Fredo's | **Freehold Twp**	22
Fresco Steak | **Milltown**	25
NEW GK's Red Dog | **Morristown**	-
Grabbe's | **Westville**	-
Hamilton's | **Lambertville**	26
Harvey Cedars | **multi.**	23
Il Villaggio | **Carlstadt**	24
Inlet Café | **Highlands**	20
Joe Pesce | **Collingswood**	24
Klein's | **Belmar**	19
NEW Kyma | **Somerville**	-
La Griglia | **Kenilworth**	23
Z Legal Sea Foods | **multi.**	21
Limani | **Westfield**	24
Little Tuna | **Haddonfield**	23
Lobster House | **Cape May**	20
Maritime Parc | **Jersey City**	-
Max's Seafood | **Gloucester**	-
McCormick/Schmick | **multi.**	20
Z Milford Oyster | **Milford**	27
Mill/Spring Lake Hts. | **Spring Lake Hts**	21
Mister C's/Bistro | **Allenhurst**	18
Mud City | **Manahawkin**	24
Navesink Fishery | **Navesink**	25
Oceanos | **Fair Lawn**	23
Octopus's Gdn. | **West Creek**	22
NEW Ohana Grill | **Lavallette**	-
Park Steak | **Park Ridge**	23
Phillips Seafood | **A.C.**	20
Ray's | **Little Silver**	21
Red's Lobster | **Pt. Pleas. Bch**	24
Ritz Seafood | **Voorhees**	26
Rod's Steak | **Morristown**	22
Rooney's | **Long Branch**	19
Santorini | **Fort Lee**	21
Z SeaBlue | **A.C.**	26
Seabra's | **Newark**	23
Shipwreck Grill | **Brielle**	24
Smoke Chophouse | **Englewood**	23
Sol-Mar | **Newark**	26
Spike's | **Pt. Pleas. Bch**	22

Varka | **Ramsey**	26
West Lake Seafood | **Matawan**	25
Windansea | **Highlands**	17
Witherspoon | **Princeton**	21
Wonder Seafood | **Edison**	26

SMALL PLATES

(See also Spanish tapas specialist)

Z A Toute Heure | Amer. | **Cranford**	26
Bin 14 | Italian | **Hoboken**	22
NEW Bushido | Japanese | **Cliffside Pk**	-
Elements | Amer. | **Haddon Hts**	23
Marco/Pepe | Amer. | **Jersey City**	22
Trinity/Pope | Cajun/Creole | **Asbury Pk**	21
Tula | Eclectic | **New Bruns.**	19
NEW Upstairs | Amer./Continental | **Upper Montclair**	-
Wine Bar | Eclectic/Med. | **Atlantic Highlands**	22

SOUL FOOD

Aunt Berta's | **Oaklyn**	-
Delta's | **New Bruns.**	22
Je's | **Newark**	25
Soul Flavors | **Jersey City**	21

SOUTH AMERICAN

Cucharamama | **Hoboken**	26

SOUTHERN

Aunt Berta's | **Oaklyn**	-
NEW Bell & Whistle | **Hopewell**	-
Delta's | **New Bruns.**	22
Freshwaters | **Plainfield**	21
Je's | **Newark**	25
Mélange | **Haddonfield**	25
Soul Flavors | **Jersey City**	21

SOUTHWESTERN

Copper Canyon | **Atlantic Highlands**	23
Los Amigos | **multi.**	23
Mojave | **Westfield**	23

SPANISH

(* tapas specialist)

Adega Grill | **Newark**	22
Bistro Olé | **Asbury Pk**	23
Casa Vasca* | **Newark**	24

Chateau/Spain | **Newark**	23
Don Pepe | **multi.**	22
Don Quijote | **Fairview**	18
El Cid | **Paramus**	22
Europa South | **Pt. Pleas. Bch**	21
Fernandes | **Newark**	24
☑ Fornos/Spain | **Newark**	24
Iberia | **Newark**	20
Lola's* | **Hoboken**	18
Manolo's | **Elizabeth**	25
Mesón Madrid | **Palisades Pk**	18
Mompou* | **Newark**	23
Patria | **Rahway**	-
Pic-Nic | **E Newark**	21
Pintxo y Tapas* | **Englewood**	21
Portuguese Manor | **Perth Amboy**	19
Segovia | **Moonachie**	23
Segovia Steak | **Little Ferry**	23
Spain | **Newark**	24
Spanish Tavern | **multi.**	22
Tapas/Espana* | **N Bergen**	22

STEAKHOUSES

Arthur's Steak | **N Brunswick**	19
Arthur's Tavern | **multi.**	20
Assembly | **Englewood Cliffs**	16
Bobby Flay | **A.C.**	25
Bonefish Grill | **Deptford**	21
Brennen's | **Neptune City**	23
☑ Capital Grille | **multi.**	26
Capt'n Ed's | **Pt. Pleas.**	20
Char | **Raritan**	22
Chelsea Prime | **A.C.**	24
Chophouse | **Gibbsboro**	23
Danny's | **Red Bank**	20
DelMonico | **Cedar Grove**	27
☑ Dino/Harry's | **Hoboken**	27
Don Pepe's Steak | **Pine Brook**	22
Edward's Steak | **Jersey City**	23
Etc. Steak | **Teaneck**	25
Fernandes | **Newark**	24
Fleming's | **multi.**	23
Fresco Steak | **Milltown**	25
Gallagher's | **multi.**	22
NEW GK's Red Dog | **Morristown**	-
Hamilton/Ward | **Paterson**	23
J&K Steak | **multi.**	-
JD's Steak Pit | **Fort Lee**	17
KC Prime | **Lawrenceville**	22

Mignon Steak | **Rutherford**	22
Mill/Spring Lake Hts. | **Spring Lake Hts**	21
☑ Morton's | **multi.**	25
Nero's Grille | **Livingston**	18
☑ Old Homestead | **A.C.**	27
Park Steak | **Park Ridge**	23
Prime/Beyond | **Fort Lee**	-
Pub | **Pennsauken**	19
NEW Ralic's Steak | **Haddonfield**	-
Rare | **Little Falls**	24
☑ River Palm | **multi.**	25
Rod's Steak | **Morristown**	22
Roots Steak | **multi.**	26
☑ Ruth's Chris | **multi.**	25
Sammy's | **Mendham**	23
NEW Scarduzio's | **A.C.**	-
NEW Sear House | **Closter**	-
Segovia Steak | **Little Ferry**	23
Shipwreck Point | **Pt. Pleas. Bch**	-
Shogun | **multi.**	21
Simon Prime | **A.C.**	-
Smoke Chophouse | **Englewood**	23
Steakhouse 85 | **New Bruns.**	26
Steve's Sizzling | **Carlstadt**	-
Strip House | **Livingston**	25
Tbones Tuscan Steakhouse | **Bridgewater**	22
Palm | **A.C.**	25
NEW Wayne Steak | **Wayne**	-
What's Your Beef? | **Rumson**	22
William Douglas | **Cherry Hill**	25
Witherspoon | **Princeton**	21
Zylo | **Hoboken**	21

SYRIAN

Aleppo | **Paterson**	-

THAI

Aligado | **Hazlet**	24
Aroma | **Franklin Pk**	22
Bamboo Leaf | **multi.**	22
Bangkok Gdn. | **Hackensack**	23
Chao Phaya | **multi.**	22
NEW Da's Kitchen | **Hopewell**	-
Far East Taste | **Eatontown**	23
Khun Thai | **Short Hills**	23
Lemongrass | **Morris Plains**	-
Mie Thai | **Woodbridge**	24
☑ Origin | **multi.**	25
Pad Thai | **Highland Pk**	24

Penang	multi.	22
Siam	Lambertville	23
Siam Gdn.	Red Bank	24
Sirin	Morristown	21
Siri's	Cherry Hill	26
Somsak	Voorhees	22
Sri Thai	Hoboken	25
Thai Chef	Montclair	21
Thai Kitchen	multi.	23
Thai Thai	Stirling	23
Tuptim	Montclair	21
Umpasri	Cherry Hill	-
Wondee's	Hackensack	22

TURKISH

Beyti Kebab	Union City	21
Bosphorus	Lake Hiawatha	22
Samdan	Cresskill	21

VEGETARIAN

(* vegan)

Chand Palace	multi.	23
Hummus Elite	Englewood	21
Kaya's*	Belmar	24
Tuptim	Montclair	21

VIETNAMESE

Bamboo Leaf	multi.	22
Lemongrass	Morris Plains	-
Little Saigon	A.C.	25
Mekong Grill	Ridgewood	-
Nha Trang Pl.	Jersey City	23
Pho Eden	Cherry Hill	-
Simply Viet.	Tenafly	-

CUISINES

Locations

Includes names, cuisines and Food ratings.

Metro New York Area

ALLENDALE

Flirt Sushi | *Japanese*   23
Rest. L | *Amer.*   18

BAYONNE

Cafe Bello | *Italian*   22
Little Food Cafe | *Sandwiches*   23

BELLEVILLE

Belmont Tavern | *Italian*   23

BERGENFIELD

El Caney | *Cuban*   -

BERKELEY HEIGHTS

Delicious Hts. | *Amer.*   18
Neelam | *Indian*   20
Trap Rock | *Amer.*   21

BLOOMFIELD

Bar Cara | *Italian*   20
Holsten's | *Amer.*   16
Orange Squirrel | *Amer.*   22
Senorita's | *Mex.*   19
Stamna | *Greek*   23

CALDWELL

Il Vecchio Cafe | *italian*   20
Luce | *Italian*   22
Nori | *Asian*   23

CARLSTADT

Gianna's | *Italian*   20
Il Villaggio | *Italian/Seafood*   24
Steve's Sizzling | *Steak*   -
Tina Louise | *Asian*   23

CEDAR GROVE

DelMonico | *Eclectic/Steak*   27
Lu Nello | *Italian*   25

CLARK

Senorita's | *Mex.*   19

CLIFFSIDE PARK

NEW Bushido | *Japanese*   -
Esposito's Pk. Cafe | *Amer./Italian*   -
Villa Amalfi | *Italian*   23

CLIFTON

Chengdu 46 | *Chinese*   24
It's Greek To Me | *Greek*   18
Rutt's Hut | *Hot Dogs*   21
Smashburger | *Burgers*   19
Tick Tock | *Diner*   18
Zinburger | *Burgers*   -

CLOSTER

Harvest Bistro | *Amer./French*   21
Locale | *Italian*   20
NEW Sear House | *Steak*   -

CRANFORD

Z A Toute Heure | *Amer.*   26
Garlic Rose | *Eclectic*   20
NEW Pairings | *Amer.*   -
Trattoria Bel Paese | *Italian*   -

CRESSKILL

Hanami | *Chinese/Japanese*   20
Samdan | *Turkish*   21
Umeya | *Japanese*   23

EAST NEWARK

Pic-Nic | *Portug./Spanish*   21

EAST RUTHERFORD

Baja Fresh | *Mex.*   17
Z Park/Orchard | *Eclectic*   23
Sorrento | *Italian*   24

EDGEWATER

Z Baumgart's | *Amer./Asian*   19
Brooklyn's Pizza | *Pizza*   22
Crab House | *Seafood*   16
NEW Duck King | *Chinese*   -
Fleming's | *Steak*   23
Greek Taverna | *Greek*   20
Kinara | *Indian*   22
La Vecchia | *Italian*   21
Le Jardin | *Continental/French*   20
Magic Pot | *Fondue*   18
Rebecca's | *Cuban*   23
Z River Palm | *Steak*   25
Roberto's II | *Italian*   21
Vespa's | *Italian*   17

ELIZABETH

Manolo's | Med./Spanish — 25

ELMWOOD PARK

Royal Warsaw | Polish — 23
Taverna Mykonos | Greek — 25
Trovato's | Italian — 19

ENGLEWOOD

Akai | Japanese — 24
Ariel's | Eclectic — 20
Z Baumgart's | Amer./Asian — 19
Cassie's | Italian — 18
Hummus Elite | Med. — 21
It's Greek To Me | Greek — 18
NEW Levant Grille | Med. — –
Namaskaar | Indian — 20
Pintxo y Tapas | Spanish — 21
Smoke Chophouse | Seafood/Steak — 23
Solaia | Italian — 17

ENGLEWOOD CLIFFS

Assembly | Steak — 16
Bicycle Club | Amer. — 14
Cafe Italiano | Italian — 19
Grissini | Italian — 22

FAIRFIELD

Bruschetta | Italian — 21
Calandra's/Grill | Med. — 21
Cucina Calandra | Italian — 21

FAIR LAWN

Davia | Italian — 20
Oceanos | Seafood — 23
Z Picnic | Amer. — 27
Z River Palm | Steak — 25

FAIRVIEW

Don Quijote | Spanish — 18
Patsy's | Italian — 23
Zen Zen | Japanese/Korean — 21

FORT LEE

Armando's | Italian — 19
Dong Bang Grill | Korean — 22
Franco's Metro | Italian — 19
Gam Mee Ok | Korean — 21
Hiram's | Hot Dogs — 21
In Napoli | Italian — 17
It's Greek To Me | Greek — 18

JD's Steak Pit | Steak — 17
NEW Khloe Bistrot | French — –
Prime/Beyond | Korean/Steak — –
Santorini | Greek — 21

FRANKLIN LAKES

Z Chef's Table | French — 28

GARFIELD

GoodFellas | Italian — 21

GLEN RIDGE

Smashburger | Burgers — 19

GLEN ROCK

Greek Taverna | Greek — 20
Rocca | Italian — 24

HACKENSACK

Bangkok Gdn. | Thai — 23
Brooklyn's Pizza | Pizza — 22
Z Cheesecake Factory | Amer. — 19
Cubby's BBQ | BBQ — 19
Z Five Guys | Burgers — 21
Lotus Cafe | Chinese — 23
Maggiano's | Italian — 20
McCormick/Schmick | Seafood — 20
Z Morton's | Steak — 25
Z P.F. Chang's | Chinese — 20
Rosa Mexicano | Mex. — 22
Smashburger | Burgers — 19
Solari's | Italian — 19
Stony Hill Inn | Continental/Italian — 22
White Manna | Burgers — 23
Wondee's | Thai — 22

HARRINGTON PARK

Dino's | Italian — 22

HASBROUCK HEIGHTS

Ivy Inn | Amer. — 22

HAWTHORNE

Bottagra | Italian — 20

HOBOKEN

Ali Baba | Mideast. — 19
Z Amanda's | Amer. — 26
Anthony David's | Italian — 25
Arthur's Tavern | Steak — 20
Augustino's | Italian — 26
Backyards | Amer. — 18

Baja | *Mex.*	18
Benny Tudino's | *Pizza*	22
Bin 14 | *Italian*	22
Brass Rail | *Amer.*	19
Charrito's/El Charro | *Mex.*	22
Court St. | *Continental*	22
Cucharamama | *S Amer.*	26
🔣 Dino/Harry's | *Steak*	27
Elysian Café | *French*	21
Grimaldi's | *Pizza*	25
Helmers' | *German*	19
Hoboken B&G | *Amer.*	19
Ibby's | *Mideast.*	22
India/Hudson | *Indian*	21
It's Greek To Me | *Greek*	18
Karma Kafe | *Indian*	21
La Isla | *Cuban*	25
Lola's | *Spanish*	18
Madison B&G | *Amer.*	19
Margherita's | *Italian*	22
Melting Pot | *Fondue*	19
Napoli's Pizza | *Pizza*	25
Oddfellows | *Cajun/Creole*	18
Onieal's | *Amer.*	20
NEW Pilsener Haus | *Austrian/Hungarian*	-
Quays | *Amer.*	18
Robongi | *Japanese*	24
Sri Thai | *Thai*	25
Sushi Lounge | *Japanese*	22
3 Forty Grill | *Amer.*	20
Trinity | *Irish*	18
Wicked Wolf | *Pub*	19
Zafra | *Pan-Latin*	23
Zylo | *Steak*	21

HO-HO-KUS

Ho-Ho-Kus Inn | *Amer.*	21
Janice | *Amer./Italian*	21
Kevin's Thyme | *Amer.*	23
NEW St. Eve's | *Amer.*	-

JERSEY CITY

Amelia's | *Amer.*	19
Amiya | *Indian*	19
Azúcar | *Cuban*	20
Baja | *Mex.*	18
Casa Dante | *Italian*	24
Edward's Steak | *Steak*	23
15 Fox Pl. | *Italian*	23

Fire/Oak | *Amer.*	19
Ibby's | *Mideast.*	22
It's Greek To Me | *Greek*	18
Komegashi | *Japanese*	22
Liberty House | *Amer.*	20
Light Horse | *Amer.*	22
LITM | *Amer.*	14
Madame Claude | *French*	23
Mantra | *Indian*	22
Marco/Pepe | *Amer.*	22
Maritime Parc | *Amer./Seafood*	-
Nha Trang Pl. | *Viet.*	23
Pointé | *Amer.*	21
🔣 Porto Leggero | *Italian*	26
Renato's | *Pizza*	22
Rumba Cubana/Cafe | *Cuban*	23
Satis | *Med.*	-
Skylark | *Diner/Eclectic*	22
Soul Flavors | *Soul Food*	21
Taj Mahal | *Indian*	-
Taqueria Downtown | *Mex.*	24
Vu | *Amer.*	16
White Mana | *Burgers*	17

KEARNY

Oh! Calamares | *Peruvian*	-

KENILWORTH

Blvd. Five 72 | *Amer.*	25
Jimmy Buff's | *Hot Dogs*	20
La Griglia | *Italian/Seafood*	23
🔣 Le Rendez-Vous | *French*	27

LEONIA

Fontana/Trevi | *Italian*	23

LITTLE FALLS

Rare | *Steak*	24

LITTLE FERRY

NEW Il Cinghiale | *Italian*	-
Minado | *Japanese*	20
Segovia Steak | *Spanish/Steak*	23

LIVINGSTON

🔣 Baumgart's | *Amer./Asian*	19
Eppes Essen | *Deli*	20
Lithos | *Greek*	-
Nana's Deli | *Deli*	23
Nero's Grille | *Steak*	18
Strip House | *Steak*	25
Sweet Basil's | *Amer.*	21

LODI

Penang | *Malaysian/Thai*	22

MAHWAH

☑ River Palm | *Steak*	25

MAPLEWOOD

Arturo's | *Pizza*	24
☑ Lorena's | *French*	28
Verjus | *French*	25

MIDLAND PARK

Arturo's | *Italian*	23

MILLBURN

☑ Basilico | *Italian*	23
Cara Mia | *Italian*	-
☑ Five Guys | *Burgers*	21
Martini Bistro | *Amer.*	19
NEW MoonShine | *Amer.*	-

MONTCLAIR

NEW Adara | *Amer.*	-
Ah'Pizz | *Pizza*	22
Aozora | *French/Japanese*	24
Blu | *Amer.*	25
Corso 98 | *Italian*	22
Costanera | *Peruvian*	24
Cuban Pete's | *Cuban*	19
☑ CulinAriane | *Amer.*	27
Egan/Sons | *Irish*	19
Elevation Burg. | *Burgers*	19
Epernay | *French*	21
☑ Fascino | *Italian*	26
Fin Raw Bar | *Seafood*	-
Greek Taverna | *Greek*	20
Mesob | *Ethiopian*	24
Next Door | *Amer.*	22
Nori | *Asian*	23
☑ Osteria Giotto | *Italian*	26
Raymond's | *Amer.*	21
Saluté | *Italian*	-
Smashburger | *Burgers*	19
Thai Chef | *French/Thai*	21
Toast | *Amer.*	22
Tuptim | *Thai*	21

MONTVALE

Aldo/Gianni | *Italian*	21
Fire/Oak | *Amer.*	19

MOONACHIE

Bazzarelli | *Italian*	19
Segovia | *Portug./Spanish*	23

MOUNTAINSIDE

Raagini | *Indian*	23
Spanish Tavern | *Spanish*	22

NEWARK

Adega Grill | *Portug./Spanish*	22
Assaggini/Roma | *Italian*	24
Brasilia | *Brazilian*	22
Brick City B&G | *Pub*	18
Campino Mercado | *Portug.*	22
Casa Vasca | *Spanish*	24
Chateau/Spain | *Spanish*	23
Don Pepe | *Portug./Spanish*	22
Fernandes | *Portug./Spanish*	24
☑ Fornos/Spain | *Spanish*	24
Gallagher's | *Steak*	22
Hobby's | *Deli*	24
Iberia | *Portug./Spanish*	20
Java Moon | *Amer.*	22
Je's | *Southern*	25
Kilkenny Ale | *Pub*	18
Maize | *Amer.*	17
Martini 494 | *Amer.*	-
McGovern's | *Pub*	18
Mompou | *Spanish*	23
NEW Nico | *Eclectic*	-
Rio Rodizio | *Brazilian*	20
Seabra's | *Portug./Seafood*	23
Sol-Mar | *Portug./Seafood*	26
Spain | *Portug./Spanish*	24
Spanish Tavern | *Spanish*	22
Taste/Portugal | *Portug.*	22
Tony/Caneca | *Portug.*	23
27 Mix | *Eclectic*	21

NEW MILFORD

Sanzari's | *Italian*	22

NEW PROVIDENCE

Jose's Cantina | *Mex.*	19
Smashburger | *Burgers*	19

NORTH BERGEN

Antonia's | *Italian*	20
DiPalma Brothers | *Italian*	21
La Sorrentina | *Italian*	24
Rumba Cubana/Cafe | *Cuban*	23
Sabor | *Nuevo Latino*	22
Tapas/Espana | *Spanish*	22
☑ Waterside | *Med.*	21

LOCATIONS

METRO NY AREA

NORTHVALE

NEW Biddy O'Malley's | _Amer./Pub_ | -

Madeleine's | _French_ | 25

NORWOOD

NEW Blind Boar | _BBQ_ | -

Dimora | _Italian_ | 24

OAKLAND

Cenzino | _Italian_ | 24

Portobello | _Italian_ | 19

Trovato's | _Italian_ | 19

PALISADES PARK

Mesón Madrid | _Spanish_ | 18

So Moon Nan Jip | _Korean_ | 24

PARAMUS

Biagio's | _Italian_ | 17

Bobby's | _Burgers_ | 21

Bonefish Grill | _Seafood_ | 21

NEW Bucu | _Bakery/Burgers_ | -

Z Capital Grille | _Steak_ | 26

Z Chakra | _Amer._ | 20

El Cid | _Spanish_ | 22

Z Legal Sea Foods | _Seafood_ | 21

Mantra | _Indian_ | 22

Papa Razzi | _Italian_ | 18

Smashburger | _Burgers_ | 19

PARK RIDGE

Esty St. | _Amer._ | 25

Park Steak | _Seafood/Steak_ | 23

PATERSON

Aleppo | _Syrian_ | -

E & V | _Italian_ | 23

Hamilton/Ward | _Steak_ | 23

PLAINFIELD

Freshwaters | _Southern_ | 21

RAHWAY

Cubanu | _Cuban_ | 21

Luciano's | _Italian_ | 24

Patria | _Pan-Latin_ | -

RAMSEY

Z Cafe Panache | _Eclectic_ | 27

Kinchley's | _Pizza_ | 21

Smashburger | _Burgers_ | 19

Varka | _Greek/Seafood_ | 26

RIDGEFIELD

Tutto/Modo Mio | _Italian_ | 21

RIDGEFIELD PARK

Luigi's | _Italian_ | -

Luka's | _Italian_ | 23

NEW MK Valencia | _Amer./Italian_ | -

RIDGEWOOD

A Mano | _Pizza_ | 22

Z Baumgart's | _Amer./Asian_ | 19

NEW Brick Lane Curry | _Indian_ | -

Brooklyn's Pizza | _Pizza_ | 22

Country Pancake | _Amer._ | 19

Dim Sum Dynasty | _Chinese_ | 20

NEW 5 Seasons | _Amer._ | -

Gazelle Café | _Amer._ | 23

It's Greek To Me | _Greek_ | 18

Z Latour | _French_ | 26

Mekong Grill | _Viet._ | -

NEW Osteria/Fiamma | _Italian_ | -

NEW Park West | _Amer._ | -

Sakura-Bana | _Japanese_ | 25

Sushi X | _Japanese_ | 21

Tito's | _Mex._ | 20

Village Green | _Amer._ | 24

RIVER EDGE

Babylon | _Med._ | 21

Dinallo's | _Italian_ | 22

Sanducci's | _Italian_ | 19

RIVER VALE

Armando's Tuscan | _Italian_ | 20

ROCHELLE PARK

Bistro 55 | _Amer._ | 19

RUTHERFORD

Z Cafe Matisse | _Eclectic_ | 27

Mignon Steak | _Steak_ | 22

Risotto House | _Italian_ | 23

Village Gourmet | _Eclectic_ | 21

SADDLE RIVER

Z Saddle River Inn | _Amer./ French_ | 28

SCOTCH PLAINS

Jimmy Buff's | _Hot Dogs_ | 20

Stage House | _Amer._ | 20

SECAUCUS

Bareli's | *Italian* — 23

SHORT HILLS

Benihana | *Japanese* — 18
Z Cheesecake Factory | *Amer.* — 19
Khun Thai | *Thai* — 23
Z Legal Sea Foods | *Seafood* — 21
Papa Razzi | *Italian* — 18

SOUTH HACKENSACK

I Gemelli | *Italian* — 24

SOUTH ORANGE

Cafe Arugula | *Italian* — 21
Neelam | *Indian* — 20

SPRINGFIELD

Cathay 22 | *Chinese* — 22
Hunan Spring | *Chinese* — 18

SUMMIT

NEW Anna's Rist. | *Italian* — -
NEW Bombay Bistro | *Indian* — -
Fiorino | *Italian* — 24
Hat Tavern | *Amer.* — -
Huntley Taverne | *Amer.* — 22
La Focaccia | *Italian* — 23
La Pastaria | *Italian* — 19
Monster Sushi | *Japanese* — 20
Negeen | *Persian* — 18
Roots Steak | *Steak* — 26
Tito's | *Mex.* — 20

TEANECK

Amarone | *Italian* — 21
BV Tuscany | *Italian* — 23
East | *Japanese* — 19
Etc. Steak | *Kosher/Steak* — 25
Vasili's | *Greek* — 21

TENAFLY

Axia Taverna | *Greek* — 23
Simply Viet. | *Viet.* — -

TOTOWA

Sushi Lounge | *Japanese* — 22

UNION

Rio Rodizio | *Brazilian* — 20
Z Rist./Benito | *Italian* — 26
NEW Ursino | *Amer.* — -

UNION CITY

Beyti Kebab | *Turkish* — 21
Mi Bandera | *Cuban* — 24
Park Ave. B&G | — 18
  Amer./Pan-Latin

UPPER MONTCLAIR

NEW Brick Lane Curry | *Indian* — -
Dai-Kichi | *Japanese* — 23
NEW Upstairs | — -
  Amer./Continental

VERONA

Ave. Bistro | *Amer.* — 19

WANAQUE

Berta's | *Italian* — 22

WAYNE

Bahama Breeze | *Carib.* — 17
Baja Fresh | *Mex.* — 17
Z Cheesecake Factory | *Amer.* — 19
NEW Wayne Steak | *Steak* — -

WEEHAWKEN

Z Chart House | *Seafood* — 21
Charrito's/El Charro | *Mex.* — 22
Robongi | *Japanese* — 24
Z Ruth's Chris | *Steak* — 25

WESTFIELD

Acquaviva/Fonti | *Italian* — 22
Z Chez Catherine | *French* — 26
Isabella's | *Amer.* — 19
Limani | *Greek* — 24
Mojave | *SW* — 23
Theresa's | *Italian* — 22
WindMill | *Hot Dogs* — 19

WEST NEW YORK

Z P.F. Chang's | *Chinese* — 20
Son Cubano | *Cuban* — -

WEST ORANGE

Egan/Sons | *Irish* — 19
Z Highlawn Pavilion | *Amer.* — 25
Jimmy Buff's | *Hot Dogs* — 20
NEW Tratt. Primavera | *Italian* — -
Z Manor | *Amer.* — 24
McLoone's | *Amer.* — 17
Primavera | *Italian* — 21

LOCATIONS

METRO NY AREA

WESTWOOD

Restaurant	Rating
Bibi'z | *Amer.*	-
Hanami | *Chinese/Japanese*	20
It's Greek To Me | *Greek*	18
Jack's | *Amer./Eclectic*	20
Melting Pot | *Fondue*	19
Rolling Pin | *Amer./Sandwiches*	23

Central

BASKING RIDGE

Restaurant	Rating
Ciao | *Italian*	21
Grain House | *Amer.*	19
☑ Origin | *French/Thai*	25
3 West | *Amer.*	23
Vine | *Amer./Med.*	23

BEDMINSTER

Restaurant	Rating
☑ Pluckemin Inn | *Amer.*	26
Trattoria Med. | *Italian*	24
TwoFiftyTwo | *Amer.*	-

BERNARDSVILLE

Restaurant	Rating
☑ Bernards Inn | *Amer.*	27
NEW Osteria Morini | *Italian*	-
Sette | *Italian*	24
Tsuki | *Japanese*	22

BOONTON

Restaurant	Rating
Il Michelangelo | *Italian*	20
Reservoir | *Italian*	23

BOUND BROOK

Restaurant	Rating
Girasole | *Italian*	26

BRIDGEWATER

Restaurant	Rating
Cafe Emilia | *Italian*	22
☑ Cheesecake Factory | *Amer.*	19
Fortune Cookie | *Chinese*	21
Maggiano's | *Italian*	20
McCormick/Schmick | *Seafood*	20
Tbones Tuscan Steakhouse | *Steak*	22
Thai Kitchen | *Thai*	23

CHATHAM

Restaurant	Rating
☑ Scalini Fedeli | *Italian*	27
☑ Serenade | *French*	27
Taste of Asia | *Malaysian*	22

CHESTER

Restaurant	Rating
Benito's | *Italian*	23
Redwood's | *Amer.*	18
Thai Kitchen | *Thai*	23

CRANBURY

Restaurant	Rating
Cranbury Inn | *Amer.*	14

DENVILLE

Restaurant	Rating
Cafe Metro | *Eclectic*	22
Hunan Taste | *Chinese*	24
Midori | *Japanese*	21

DOVER

Restaurant	Rating
J&K Steak | *Steak*	-
Quiet Man | *Pub*	22

EAST BRUNSWICK

Restaurant	Rating
Baja Fresh | *Mex.*	17
Bonefish Grill | *Seafood*	21
Gusto Grill | *Amer.*	19
Shogun | *Japanese/Steak*	21
Wasabi | *Japanese*	24

EAST HANOVER

Restaurant	Rating
Baja Fresh | *Mex.*	17
Jimmy Buff's | *Hot Dogs*	20
Luigi's | *Italian*	26
Mr. Chu | *Chinese*	21
Penang | *Malaysian/Thai*	22
Saffron | *Indian*	24
Smashburger | *Burgers*	19

EAST WINDSOR

Restaurant	Rating
Mahzu | *Japanese*	20

EDISON

Restaurant	Rating
Akbar | *Indian*	20
Benihana | *Japanese*	18
☑ Cheesecake Factory | *Amer.*	19
☑ Five Guys | *Burgers*	21
LouCás | *Italian*	23
Meemah | *Chinese/Malaysian*	25
Ming | *Asian*	24
Moghul | *Indian*	23
Pasquale's | *Italian*	24
Penang | *Malaysian/Thai*	22
Skylark | *Diner/Eclectic*	22
Wonder Seafood | *Chinese*	26

FLORHAM PARK

Restaurant	Rating
Smashburger | *Burgers*	19

FORDS

Restaurant	Rating
McLoone's | *Amer.*	17

FRANKLIN PARK

Restaurant	Rating
Aroma | *Thai*	22

GILLETTE

Casa Maya | Mex. — 24
Meyersville Inn | Eclectic — 19

GLADSTONE

Gladstone | Amer. — 21
Sublime | Eclectic — 20

GREEN BROOK

Bonefish Grill | Seafood — 21
Shogun | Japanese/Steak — 21

HIGHLAND PARK

Pad Thai | Thai — 24
Pithari | Greek — 23

HILLSBOROUGH

Cafe Graziella | Italian — 20
Old Man Rafferty's | Amer. — 18
Pheasants Landing |
  Amer./Continental — 15
Thai Kitchen | Thai — 23

ISELIN

Bonefish Grill | Seafood — 21
Casa Giuseppe | Italian — 22

JAMESBURG

Fiddleheads | Amer. — 23

KENDALL PARK

Shogun | Japanese/Steak — 21

KINGSTON

🅉 Eno Terra | Italian — 24
Main St. | Amer./Continental — 19

LAKE HIAWATHA

Bosphorus | Turkish — 22

LAKE HOPATCONG

Alice's | Amer. — 21

MADISON

Garlic Rose | Eclectic — 20
🅉 Il Mondo | Italian — 26
Nicky's | Amer. — 18
🅉 Resto | French — 25
Rob's Bistro | French — -
Shanghai Jazz | Asian — 22
Soho 33 | Eclectic — 18

MANVILLE

Grub Hut | BBQ/Mexican — 21

MENDHAM

Black Horse | Amer. — 18
Dante's | Italian — 20
Sammy's | Steak — 23

METUCHEN

Lola/Bistro | Pan-Latin — -

MILLTOWN

Fresco Steak | Seafood/Steak — 25

MONTVILLE

Columbia Inn | Italian — 21
Montville Inn | Amer. — 22

MORRIS PLAINS

Arthur's Tavern | Steak — 20
Cinnamon | Indian — 23
🅉 Grato | Italian — 22
Hunan Chinese | Chinese — 20
Lemongrass | Thai/Viet. — -
Minado | Japanese — 20
Smashburger | Burgers — 19
Tabor Rd. | Amer. — 21

MORRISTOWN

NEW Blue Morel | Amer. — -
NEW GK's Red Dog | Pub — -
🅉 Grand Cafe | French — 25
J&K Steak | Steak — -
La Campagna | Italian — 23
Mehndi | Indian — 24
Ming | Asian — 24
🅉 Origin | French/Thai — 25
Pamir | Afghan — 22
Rod's Steak | Seafood/Steak — 22
Roots Steak | Steak — 26
Settebello | Italian — 20
Sirin | Thai — 21
Sushi Lounge | Japanese — 22
Tim Schafer's | Amer. — 23
Tito's | Mex. — 20
NEW Urban Table | Eclectic — -

NEW BRUNSWICK

🅉 Catherine Lombardi | Italian — 24
Clydz | Amer. — 22
NEW Daryl | Amer. — -
Delta's | Southern — 22
Due Mari | Italian — 26
🅉 Frog/Peach | Amer. — 26
🅉 Hotoke | Asian — 20

Kairo | *Mideast.* — ‾

Makeda | *Ethiopian* 24

Old Bay | *Cajun/Creole* 19

Old Man Rafferty's | *Amer.* 18

Panico's | *Italian* 21

Z Stage Left | *Amer.* 27

Steakhouse 85 | *Steak* 26

Tula | *Eclectic* 19

NORTH BRUNSWICK

Arthur's Steak | *Steak* 19

NEW Chinese Mirch | *Asian* ‾

OLD BRIDGE

A Tavola | *Italian* 20

NEW Just | *Amer.* ‾

Pine Tavern | *Amer.* 20

PARSIPPANY

Chand Palace | *Indian* 23

Eccola | *Italian* 23

Z Five Guys | *Burgers* 21

Z Ruth's Chris | *Steak* 25

PEAPACK

Café Azzurro | *Italian* 24

Z Ninety Acres | *Amer.* 25

PERTH AMBOY

Portuguese Manor | 19
  Portug./Spanish

PINE BROOK

Bonefish Grill | *Seafood* 21

Don Pepe | *Portug./Spanish* 22

Don Pepe's Steak | *Steak* 22

PISCATAWAY

Chand Palace | *Indian* 23

POMPTON PLAINS

Little Food Cafe | *Sandwiches* 23

RANDOLPH

Jimmy Buff's | *Hot Dogs* 20

La Strada | *Italian* 23

Rosie's | *Italian* 21

RARITAN

Char | *Steak* 22

Espo's | *Italian* 23

RIVERDALE

Z Rosemary/Sage | *Amer.* 26

ROCKY HILL

One 53 | *Amer.* 23

Rocky Hill Inn | *Amer.* 17

SKILLMAN

Ya Ya | *Noodle Shop* 21

SOMERSET

Chao Phaya | *Thai* 22

Luca's Rist. | *Italian* 24

Sophie's | *French* 24

SOMERVILLE

Chao Phaya | *Thai* 22

Da Filippo's | *Italian/Seafood* 24

Gabriela's | *Portug.* 18

NEW Kyma | *Greek/Seafood* ‾

Martino's | *Cuban* 22

Melting Pot | *Fondue* 19

Z Origin | *French/Thai* 25

Z Shumi | *Japanese* 28

Valdebenito's | *Argent.* ‾

Verve | *Amer./French* 23

Wasabi | *Japanese* 24

SOUTH AMBOY

Fishery | *Seafood* 20

SOUTH PLAINFIELD

Baja Fresh | *Mex.* 17

NEW Khyber Grill | *Indian* ‾

STIRLING

Thai Thai | *Thai* 23

WARREN

Jose's Cantina | *Mex.* 19

Silk Road | *Afghan* 23

Z Stone House | *Amer.* 22

Uproot | *Amer.* 22

WATCHUNG

Baja Fresh | *Mex.* 17

Z Five Guys | *Burgers* 21

WHIPPANY

Chef Jon's | *Chinese* 24

Z Il Capriccio | *Italian* 25

Melting Pot | *Fondue* 19

Nikko | *Japanese* 24

WOODBRIDGE

Bahama Breeze | *Carib.* 17

Z Five Guys | *Burgers* 21

Mie Thai | *Thai* 24

North Shore

ABERDEEN

Mahzu | *Japanese* — 20

ALLENHURST

Mister C's/Bistro | *Seafood* — 18

ALLENTOWN

Alps Bistro | *German* — -

ASBURY PARK

Bistro Olé | *Portug./Spanish* — 23
Brickwall Tavern | *Pub* — 18
NEW Cubacan | *Cuban* — -
Dauphin | *Amer.* — 22
Jimmy's | *Italian* — 23
Laila's | *Carib.* — 22
Langosta | *Eclectic* — 22
Lazy Dog Saloon | *Amer.* — 23
McLoone's | *Amer.* — 17
Z Moonstruck | *Amer./Med.* — 25
Old Man Rafferty's | *Amer.* — 18
Plan B | *Amer.* — 24
Pop's Garage | *Mex.* — 22
Stella Marina | *Italian* — 23
Taka | *Japanese* — 25
Tim McLoone's | *Amer.* — 20
Toast | *Amer.* — 22
Trinity/Pope | *Cajun/Creole* — 21

ATLANTIC HIGHLANDS

Copper Canyon | *SW* — 23
Memphis Pig Out | *BBQ* — 19
Wine Bar | *Eclectic/Med.* — 22

AVON-BY-THE-SEA

Avon Pavilion | *Amer.* — 19
Clementine's | *Creole* — 23

BARNEGAT LIGHT

Mustache Bill's | *Diner* — 24

BAY HEAD

Grenville | *Amer.* — 17

BEACH HAVEN

Z Gables | *Eclectic* — 24
Harvey Cedars | *Seafood* — 23
Roberto's | *Italian* — 21

BELFORD

Z Belford Bistro | *Amer.* — 26

BELMAR

Brandl | *Amer.* — 24
Casa Solar | *Pan-Latin* — 23
Kaya's | *Veg.* — 24
Klein's | *Seafood* — 19
Matisse | *Amer.* — 22
Surf Taco | *Mex.* — 21
WindMill | *Hot Dogs* — 19

BRADLEY BEACH

Bamboo Leaf | *Thai/Viet.* — 22
Bella Sogno | *Italian* — 21
D&L BBQ | *BBQ* — 24
Vic's | *Italian/Pizza* — 21

BRICK

Bonefish Grill | *Seafood* — 21
Z Five Guys | *Burgers* — 21
Z Ikko | *Japanese* — 25
WindMill | *Hot Dogs* — 19
Villa Vittoria | *Italian* — 23

BRIELLE

Shipwreck Grill | *Amer./Seafood* — 24

EATONTOWN

Bobby's | *Burgers* — 21
Far East Taste | *Chinese/Thai* — 23
Sawa | *Japanese* — 23

FAIR HAVEN

Le Fandy | *French* — 25
Nauvoo Grill | *Amer.* — 18
Z Raven/Peach | *Amer.* — 24

FORKED RIVER

Surf Taco | *Mex.* — 21

FREEHOLD

A Little Bit of Cuba | *Cuban* — 19
Z Cheesecake Factory | *Amer.* — 19
El Mesón Café | *Mex.* — 24
Federici's | *Pizza* — 21
Ibby's | *Mideast.* — 22
La Cipollina | *Italian* — 22
Mahzu | *Japanese* — 20
Metropolitan Cafe | *Pac. Rim* — 21
Oyako Tso's | *Japanese* — 23

P.F. Chang's | *Chinese* — 20
WindMill | *Hot Dogs* — 19

FREEHOLD TOWNSHIP

Aangan | *Indian* — 23
Cafe Coloré | *Italian* — 19
Frankie Fed's | *Italian* — 21
Fredo's | *Italian* — 22

HARVEY CEDARS

Black-Eyed Susans | *Amer.* — -
Harvey Cedars | *Seafood* — 23
Plantation | *Amer.* — 18

HAZLET

Aligado | *Thai* — 24

HIGHLANDS

Bahrs Landing | *Seafood* — 17
Bay Ave. | *Amer./Italian* — 28
Chilangos | *Mex.* — 21
Grimaldi's | *Pizza* — 25
Inlet Café | *Seafood* — 20
Windansea | *Seafood* — 17

HOLMDEL

It's Greek To Me | *Greek* — 18

HOWELL

Bamboo Leaf | *Thai/Viet.* — 22
Cabin | *Amer.* — 18
Christie's | *Italian* — 26
Juanito's | *Mex.* — 23

JACKSON

Java Moon | *Amer.* — 22
Solo Bella | *Italian* — 22
Surf Taco | *Mex.* — 21

KEYPORT

Drew's Bayshore | *Amer.* — 27
Trinity | *Amer.* — 25

LAVALLETTE

Crab's Claw Inn | *Seafood* — 18
NEW Ohana Grill | *Hawaiian/Seafood* — -

LINCROFT

Lincroft Inn | *Continental* — 19

LITTLE SILVER

Ray's | *Seafood* — 21

LONG BEACH TOWNSHIP

Daddy O | *Amer.* — 19

LONG BRANCH

Avenue | *French* — 22
Charley's | *Amer.* — 18
It's Greek To Me | *Greek* — 18
McLoone's | *Amer.* — 17
Richard's | *Deli* — 20
Rooney's | *Seafood* — 19
Sawa | *Japanese* — 23
Sirena | *Italian* — 23
Surf Taco | *Mex.* — 21
WindMill | *Hot Dogs* — 19
Tuzzio's | *Italian* — 20

MANAHAWKIN

Mud City | *Seafood* — 24

MANALAPAN

Konbu | *Japanese* — 26
Spargo's | *Amer.* — 23

MANASQUAN

Remington's | *Amer.* — 21
Squan Tavern | *Italian* — 20
Surf Taco | *Mex.* — 21

MARLBORO

Brioso | *Italian* — 24
Crown Palace | *Chinese* — 20
Jerry/Harvey's | *Deli* — 18
Pino's | *Italian* — 21

MATAWAN

Aby's | *Mex.* — 20
Big Ed's BBQ | *BBQ* — 18
Wasabi | *Japanese* — 24
West Lake Seafood | *Chinese* — 25

MIDDLETOWN

Anna's Kitchen | *Italian* — 23
Crown Palace | *Chinese* — 20
Neelam | *Indian* — 20
Sono | *Japanese* — 25

MONMOUTH BEACH

Sallee Tee's | *Amer./Eclectic* — 18

NAVESINK

Navesink Fishery | *Seafood* — 25

NEPTUNE CITY

Brennen's | *Steak* — 23
Pete/Elda's | *Pizza* — 22

NORMANDY BEACH

Labrador | *Eclectic* — 25
Pop's Garage | *Mex.* — 22

OAKHURST/ OCEAN TOWNSHIP

🅉 Piccola | *Italian* — 26
Takara | *Japanese* — 20

OCEAN GROVE

WindMill | *Hot Dogs* — 19

POINT PLEASANT

Capt'n Ed's | *Seafood/Steak* — 20

POINT PLEASANT BEACH

Daniel's Bistro | *Continental* — -
Europa South | *Portug./Spanish* — 21
Red's Lobster | *Seafood* — 24
Shipwreck Point | *Steak* — -
Spike's | *Seafood* — 22
Surf Taco | *Mex.* — 21

RED BANK

Basil T's | *Amer./Italian* — 20
Bienvenue | *French* — 22
Bistro/Red Bank | *Eclectic* — 21
Bonefish Grill | *Seafood* — 21
Danny's | *Steak* — 20
Dish | *Amer.* — 25
Eurasian | *Eclectic* — 23
Gaetano's | *Italian* — 20
NEW JBJ Soul Kitchen | *Amer.* — -
Juanito's | *Mex.* — 23
La Pastaria | *Italian* — 19
Melting Pot | *Fondue* — 19
🅉 Molly Pitcher Inn Restaurant | *Amer.* — 22
🅉 Nicholas | *Amer.* — 29
Red | *Amer.* — 21
Siam Gdn. | *Thai* — 24
Surf Taco | *Mex.* — 21
Teak | *Asian* — 21
WindMill | *Hot Dogs* — 19

RUMSON

Barnacle Bill's | *Burgers* — 22
🅉 David Burke | *Amer.* — 25

Salt Creek | *Amer.* — 19
Undici | *Italian* — 22
What's Your Beef? | *Steak* — 22

SEA BRIGHT

Anjelica's | *Italian* — 24
McLoone's | *Amer.* — 17
🅉 Yumi | *Asian* — 26

SEA GIRT

Rod's Olde Irish | *Pub* — 18
Scarborough Fair | *Amer.* — 23

SHIP BOTTOM

🅉 La Spiaggia | *Italian* — 24
Raimondo's | *Italian* — 24

SHREWSBURY

Pop's Garage | *Mex.* — 22
San Remo | *Italian* — 22

SOUTH SEASIDE PARK

Atlantic B&G | *Amer./Seafood* — 26
Berkeley | *Seafood* — 20
Surf Taco | *Mex.* — 21

SPRING LAKE

Black Trumpet | *Amer.* — 24
🅉 Whispers | *Amer.* — 27

SPRING LAKE HEIGHTS

Jose's | *Mex.* — 23
Mill/Spring Lake Hts. | *Amer.* — 21

SURF CITY

L'assiette | *Amer.* — 20
🅉 Yellow Fin | *Amer.* — 27

TINTON FALLS

Kanji | *Japanese* — 24
Portofino | *Italian* — 24

TOMS RIVER

Aamantran | *Indian* — 21
NEW Aqua Blu | *Amer.* — -
Benihana | *Japanese* — 18
El Familiar | *Colombian/Mex.* — -
🅉 Five Guys | *Burgers* — 21
Nobi | *Japanese* — 26
Shogun | *Japanese/Steak* — 21
Surf Taco | *Mex.* — 21

LOCATIONS

NORTH SHORE

UNION BEACH

Piero's | *Italian* — 22

WALL

Sumo | *Japanese* — 25

WEST CREEK

Octopus's Gdn. | *Seafood* — 22

Delaware Valley

ALLAMUCHY

🅩 Mattar's Bistro | *Amer.* — 24

BUTTZVILLE

Hot Dog Johnny's | *Hot Dogs* — 21

FLEMINGTON

Blue Fish | *Seafood* — 21
55 Main | *Amer.* — 22
Market Roost | *Eclectic* — 22
Matt's/Rooster | *Amer.* — 26

FRENCHTOWN

Frenchtown Inn | *Eclectic/French* — 23
National Hotel Rest. | *Amer./Eclectic* — -

HAMBURG

🅩 Rest. Latour | *Amer.* — 27

HAMILTON

DeLorenzo's Pizza | *Pizza* — 24
🅩 Rat's | *French* — 24

HIGH BRIDGE

Casa Maya | *Mex.* — 24
Circa | *French* — 17

HOPE

Inn at Millrace Pond Restaurant | *Amer./Continental* — 23

HOPEWELL

NEW Bell & Whistle | *American/Southern* — -
Blue Bottle | *Amer.* — 26
Brothers Moon | *Amer.* — 23
NEW Da's Kitchen | *Thai* — -
Nomad Pizza | *Pizza* — 26

LAMBERTVILLE

Anton's/Swan | *Amer.* — 22
Bell's Tavern | *Amer./Italian* — 20
Caffe Galleria | *Eclectic* — 21

DeAnna's | *Italian* — 24
NEW El Tule | *Mex./Peruvian* — -
Full Moon | *Eclectic* — 19
Hamilton's | *Med.* — 26
Inn of the Hawke Restaurant | *Amer.* — 20
Lambertville Station | *Amer.* — 17
Lilly's/Canal | *Eclectic* — 21
Manon | *French* — 25
Ota-Ya | *Japanese* — 21
Rick's | *Italian* — 21
Siam | *Thai* — 23

LAWRENCEVILLE

Acacia | *Amer.* — 23
Chambers Walk | *Amer.* — 21
Elements Asia | *Asian* — 23
Fedora Café | *Eclectic* — 20
KC Prime | *Steak* — 22

MILFORD

🅩 Milford Oyster | *Seafood* — 27
Ship Inn | *Pub* — 17

NEWTON

🅩 Andre's | *Amer.* — 27
Krave Café | *Amer.* — 24

OLDWICK

Tewksbury Inn | *Amer.* — 23

PENNINGTON

Edo Sushi | *Chinese/Japanese* — 20
Za | *Amer.* — 23

PRINCETON

Ajihei | *Japanese* — 25
Alchemist/Barrister | *Amer.* — 16
🅩 Blue Point | *Seafood* — 26
Conte's | *Pizza* — 25
🅩 Elements | *Amer.* — 26
Ferry House | *Amer./French* — -
Main St. | *Amer./Continental* — 19
Mediterra | *Med.* — 20
Peacock Inn Restaurant | *Amer.* — 26
Penang | *Malaysian/Thai* — 22
🅩 P.F. Chang's | *Chinese* — 20
🅩 Ruth's Chris | *Steak* — 25
Salt Creek | *Amer.* — 19
Teresa Caffe | *Italian* — 21
Tiger Noodles | *Noodle Shop* — 19
Tortuga's | *Mex.* — 22

Tre Piani | *Italian/Med.* 20
Triumph Brew. | *Amer./Eclectic* 16
Witherspoon | *Seafood/Steak* 21
Yankee Doodle | *Pub* 13

RINGOES

Harvest Moon | *Amer.* 25

ROBBINSVILLE

☑ DeLorenzo's/Pies | *Pizza* 27

SERGEANTSVILLE

Sergeantsville Inn | *Amer.* 24

SPARTA

Mohawk House | *Amer.* 22

STANHOPE

Bell's Mansion | *Amer.* 15
Black Forest Inn | 23
 Continental/German

STOCKTON

Meil's | *Amer.* 24

TRENTON

Amici Milano | *Italian* 22
Blue Danube | *E Euro.* 22
DeLorenzo's Pizza | *Pizza* 24
Homestead Inn | *Italian* 22
Settimo Cielo | *Italian* 23

UNION TOWNSHIP

Baja Fresh | *Mex.* 17
Perryville Inn | *Amer.* 26

WALLPACK CENTER

Walpack Inn | *Amer.* 20

South Shore

ATLANTIC CITY

Angelo's | *Italian* 21
Bobby Flay | *Steak* 25
NEW Breakfast Room | *Amer.* –
☑ Buddakan | *Asian* 26
☑ Capriccio | *Italian* 25
Carmine's | *Italian* 21
☑ Chart House | *Seafood* 21
☑ Chef Vola's | *Italian* 26
Chelsea Prime | *Steak* 24
Continental | *Eclectic* 23
Cuba Libre | *Cuban* 21
Dock's | *Seafood* 26

NEW Dos Caminos | *Mex.* –
Fin | *Seafood* 25
Fornelletto | *Italian* 24
Gallagher's | *Steak* 22
Girasole | *Italian* 26
☑ Il Mulino | *Italian* 27
Irish Pub | *Pub* 18
☑ Izakaya | *Japanese* 23
Little Saigon | *Viet.* 25
Los Amigos | *Mex./SW* 23
Luke Palladino | *Italian* 26
McCormick/Schmick | *Seafood* 20
Melting Pot | *Fondue* 19
Mia | *Italian* 26
☑ Morton's | *Steak* 25
NEW Mussel Bar | *Belgian* –
NEW O Bistro | *Amer.* –
☑ Old Homestead | *Steak* 27
☑ P.F. Chang's | *Chinese* 20
Phillips Seafood | *Seafood* 20
☑ Red Square | *Eclectic* 21
☑ Ruth's Chris | *Steak* 25
NEW Scarduzio's | –
 Japanese/Steak
☑ SeaBlue | *Seafood* 26
Simon Prime | *Steak* –
Teplitzky's | *Diner* 18
Palm | *Steak* 25
Tony Luke's | *Cheesestks.* 20
Tony's Baltimore Grill | *Pizza* 18
Tun Tavern | *Amer.* 18
White House | *Sandwiches* 26
Wolfgang Puck | *Amer.* 23

AVALON

Cafe Loren | *Amer.* 25
Diving Horse | *Seafood* 24

CAPE MAY

Axelsson's | *Seafood* 23
Blue Pig | *Amer.* 21
Cucina Rosa | *Italian* 21
☑ Ebbitt Room | *Amer.* 26
410 Bank St. | *Carib./Creole* 26
Frescos | *Italian/Med.* 22
Lobster House | *Seafood* 20
Lucky Bones | *Amer.* 20
Mad Batter | *Amer.* 23
Merion Inn | *Amer.* 24
☑ Peter Shields | *Amer.* 26

Tisha's | Amer. 25
Ugly Mug | Pub 15
Union Park | Amer. 25
Z Washington Inn | Amer. 28

EGG HARBOR

Bonefish Grill | Seafood 21
Chickie's/Pete's | Pub 17
Renault Winery | Amer. 21

GALLOWAY

Z Ram's Head Inn | Amer. 24

GALLOWAY TOWNSHIP

Athenian Gdn. | Greek 23

LINWOOD

Barrels | Italian 21

MARGATE

Barrels | Italian 21
Bobby Chez | Seafood 24
LoBianco | Amer. -
Sofia | Med. 23
Steve/Cookie's | Amer. 25
Tomatoes | Cal./Eclectic 25
Ventura's | Italian 18

MAYS LANDING

Bobby Chez | Seafood 24
Inn/Sugar Hill | Amer. 18

NEW GRETNA

Allen's | Seafood 22

NORTHFIELD

Luke Palladino | Italian 26

NORTH WILDWOOD

Claude's | French 27

OCEAN CITY

Chickie's/Pete's | Pub 17

SEA ISLE CITY

NEW La Fontana Coast | Italian -

SICKLERVILLE

Luna Rossa | Italian -

SMITHVILLE

Smithville Inn | Amer. 20

SOMERS POINT

NEW Baia | Italian -
Crab Trap | Seafood 21

VENTNOR

Sage | Med. 25

WEST CAPE MAY

Black Duck | Eclectic 26
Copper Fish | Amer./Seafood 20

WILDWOOD

Chickie's/Pete's | Pub 17
NEW Pacific Grill | Amer. -
Tony Luke's | Cheesestks. 20

Suburban Philly Area

BORDENTOWN

Chickie's/Pete's | Pub 17
Farnsworth House | Continental 22
Mastoris | Diner 19
Oliver a Bistro | Eclectic 27
Toscano | Italian 22

BURLINGTON

Café Gallery | Continental 20

CAMDEN

Victor's Pub | Pub -

CHERRY HILL

Andreotti's | Italian -
Bahama Breeze | Carib. 17
Baja Fresh | Mex. 17
Bobby Chez | Seafood 24
Bobby's | Burgers 21
Brio | Italian 19
Caffe Aldo | Italian 24
Z Capital Grille | Steak 26
Z Cheesecake Factory | Amer. 19
Christopher | Eclectic -
Dream Cuisine | French 27
Kibitz Room | Deli 23
Kuzina/Sofia | Greek 22
La Campagne | Continental 23
Maggiano's | Italian 20
McCormick/Schmick | Seafood 20
Megu | Japanese 23
Mikado | Japanese 23
Norma's | Mideast. 22
Palace of Asia | Indian -
Pho Eden | Viet. -
P.J. Whelihan's | Pub 17
Ponzio's | Diner 19

Sakura Spring | *Chinese/Japanese*	24
Z Seasons 52 | *Amer.*	22
Siri's | *French/Thai*	26
Umpasri | *Thai*	-
William Douglas | *Steak*	25

CLEMENTON

Filomena Italiana | *Italian*	25
Nifty Fifty's | *Diner*	19

COLLINGSWOOD

Barone's/Villa Barone/Tuscan | *Italian*	22
Bistro/Marino | *Italian*	22
Blackbird | *French/Italian*	24
Bobby Chez | *Seafood*	24
Casona | *Cuban*	22
Il Fiore | *Italian*	26
IndeBlue | *Indian*	25
Joe Pesce | *Italian/Seafood*	24
Kitchen Consigliere | *Italian*	-
Nunzio | *Italian*	24
Pop Shop | *Amer.*	20
Z Sagami | *Japanese*	27
Z Sapori | *Italian*	28
Tortilla Press | *Mex.*	24
NEW Zeppoli | *Italian*	-

DEPTFORD

Bonefish Grill | *Seafood*	21
Filomena Lake. | *Italian*	23
RiverWinds | *Amer.*	-

GIBBSBORO

Chophouse | *Seafood/Steak*	23

GLOUCESTER

Max's Seafood | *Seafood*	-

HADDONFIELD

Animo Juice | *Mex.*	-
Cross Culture | *Indian*	-
NEW Da Soli | *Italian*	-
Fuji | *Japanese*	25
Little Tuna | *Seafood*	23
Mélange | *Italian/Southern*	25
P.J. Whelihan's | *Pub*	17
NEW Ralic's Steak | *Steak*	-

HADDON HEIGHTS

Anthony's | *Italian*	24
Elements | *Amer.*	23

LINDENWOLD

La Esperanza | *Mex.*	25

MAPLE SHADE

Iron Hill Brewery | *Amer./Pub*	20
Mikado | *Japanese*	23
Penang | *Malaysian/Thai*	22
P.J. Whelihan's | *Pub*	17
Tacconelli's | *Pizza*	23
Barone's/Villa Barone/Tuscan | *Italian*	22

MARLTON

Bonefish Grill | *Seafood*	21
Brio | *Italian*	19
Fleming's | *Steak*	23
Joe's Peking | *Chinese*	24
Mexican Food | *Mex.*	20
Mikado | *Japanese*	23
Z P.F. Chang's | *Chinese*	20
Pietro's Pizza | *Pizza*	21
Pizzicato | *Italian*	21
Redstone | *Amer.*	21

MEDFORD

Braddock's | *Amer.*	19

MEDFORD LAKES

P.J. Whelihan's | *Pub*	17

MERCHANTVILLE

Tortilla Press | *Mex.*	24

MOORESTOWN

Barone's/Villa Barone/Tuscan | *Italian*	22
Elevation Burg. | *Burgers*	19
Megu | *Japanese*	23

MOUNT EPHRAIM

Z Five Guys | *Burgers*	21

MOUNT HOLLY

High St. Grill | *Amer.*	20
Robin's Nest | *Amer.*	22

MOUNT LAUREL

Baja Fresh | *Mex.*	17
Bobby Chez | *Seafood*	24
El Azteca | *Mex.*	21
GG's | *Amer.*	25
Sage Diner | *Diner*	14
Très Yan & Wu | *Asian*	23

LOCATIONS

SUB. PHILLY AREA

MULLICA HILL

Blueplate | *Amer.* | - |

OAKLYN

Aunt Berta's | *Soul/Southern* | - |

PENNSAUKEN

Benihana | *Japanese* | 18 |
Pub | *Steak* | 19 |

RIVERSIDE

2 Cafe Madison | *Amer.* | 22 |

SEWELL

Arugula | *Italian* | - |
Barnsboro Inn | *Amer.* | 22 |
Bobby Chez | *Seafood* | 24 |
P.J. Whelihan's | *Pub* | 17 |
Terra Nova | *Amer.* | - |

TURNERSVILLE

Lamberti's Cucina | *Italian* | 20 |
Nifty Fifty's | *Diner* | 19 |

VINCENTOWN

Vincentown Diner | *Diner* | 20 |

VOORHEES

2 Little Café | *Eclectic* | 27 |
Ariana | *Afghan* | 18 |

Baja Fresh | *Mex.* | 17 |
Chez Elena Wu | *Chinese/Japanese* | 22 |
Coconut Bay | *Asian* | 22 |
NEW Firecreek | *Amer.* | - |
2 Five Guys | *Burgers* | 21 |
La Locanda | *Italian* | 28 |
Ritz Seafood | *Asian/Seafood* | 26 |
Somsak | *Thai* | 22 |

WEST BERLIN

Filomena Rustica | *Italian* | 18 |
Los Amigos | *Mex./SW* | 23 |

WESTMONT

Giumarello | *Italian* | 25 |
NEW Keg/Kitchen | *Amer.* | - |
Treno | *Italian* | - |

WESTVILLE

Grabbe's | *Seafood* | - |

WILLIAMSTOWN

Library IV | *Steak* | - |

WOODBURY

NEW Marlene Mangia Bene | *Italian* | - |

Special Features

Listings cover the best in each category and include names, locations and Food ratings. Multi-location restaurants' features may vary by branch.

ADDITIONS

(Properties added since the last edition of the book)

Adara | **Montclair** ⌐
Alps Bistro | **Allentown** ⌐
Andreotti's | **Cherry Hill** ⌐
Animo Juice | **Haddonfield** ⌐
Anna's Rist. | **Summit** ⌐
Aqua Blu | **Toms River** ⌐
Arugula | **Sewell** ⌐
Aunt Berta's | **Oaklyn** ⌐
Baia | **Somers Point** ⌐
Bell & Whistle | **Hopewell** ⌐
Biddy O'Malley's | **Northvale** ⌐
Black-Eyed Susans | **Harvey Cedars** ⌐
Blind Boar | **Norwood** ⌐
Blue Morel | **Morristown** ⌐
Bombay Bistro | **Summit** ⌐
Breakfast Room | **A.C.** ⌐
Brick Lane Curry | **multi.** ⌐
Bucu | **Paramus** ⌐
Bushido | **Cliffside Pk** ⌐
Chinese Mirch | **N Brunswick** ⌐
Christopher | **Cherry Hill** ⌐
Cross Culture | **Haddonfield** ⌐
Cubacan | **Asbury Pk** ⌐
Daryl | **New Bruns.** ⌐
Da's Kitchen | **Hopewell** ⌐
Da Soli | **Haddonfield** ⌐
Dos Caminos | **A.C.** ⌐
Duck King | **Edgewater** ⌐
El Caney | **Bergenfield** ⌐
El Tule | **Lambertville** ⌐
Fin Raw Bar | **Montclair** ⌐
Firecreek | **Voorhees** ⌐
5 Seasons | **Ridgewood** ⌐
GK's Red Dog | **Morristown** ⌐
Grabbe's | **Westville** ⌐
Il Cinghiale | **Little Ferry** ⌐
J&K Steak | **multi.** ⌐
JBJ Soul Kitchen | **Red Bank** ⌐
Just | **Old Bridge** ⌐
Keg/Kitchen | **Westmont** ⌐
Khloe Bistrot | **Fort Lee** ⌐

Khyber Grill | **South Plainfield** ⌐
Kitchen Consigliere | **Collingswood** ⌐
Kyma | **Somerville** ⌐
La Fontana Coast | **Sea Isle City** ⌐
Tratt. Primavera | **W Orange** ⌐
Levant Grille | **Englewood** ⌐
Library IV | **Williamstown** ⌐
Lithos | **Livingston** ⌐
LoBianco | **Margate** ⌐
Marlene Mangia Bene | **Woodbury** ⌐
Max's Seafood | **Gloucester** ⌐
MK Valencia | **Ridgefield Pk** ⌐
MoonShine | **Millburn** ⌐
Mussel Bar | **A.C.** ⌐
Nico | **Newark** ⌐
O Bistro | **A.C.** ⌐
Ohana Grill | **Lavallette** ⌐
Osteria/Fiamma | **Ridgewood** ⌐
Osteria Morini | **Bernardsville** ⌐
Pacific Grill | **Wildwood** ⌐
Pairings | **Cranford** ⌐
Palace of Asia | **Cherry Hill** ⌐
Park West | **Ridgewood** ⌐
Patria | **Rahway** ⌐
Pho Eden | **Cherry Hill** ⌐
Pilsener Haus | **Hoboken** ⌐
Ralic's Steak | **Haddonfield** ⌐
RiverWinds | **Deptford** ⌐
Rob's Bistro | **Madison** ⌐
Saluté | **Montclair** ⌐
Satis | **Jersey City** ⌐
Scarduzio's | **A.C.** ⌐
Sear House | **Closter** ⌐
Son Cubano | **W New York** ⌐
St. Eve's | **Ho-Ho-Kus** ⌐
Steve's Sizzling | **Carlstadt** ⌐
Trattoria Bel Paese | **Cranford** ⌐
Treno | **Westmont** ⌐
Upstairs | **Upper Montclair** ⌐
Urban Table | **Morristown** ⌐
Ursino | **Union** ⌐
Wayne Steak | **Wayne** ⌐
Zeppoli | **Collingswood** ⌐

BREAKFAST

(See also Hotel Dining)

Alice's | **Lake Hopatcong**	21
Avon Pavilion | **Avon-by-Sea**	19
Backyards | **Hoboken**	18
Blueplate | **Mullica Hill**	-
Country Pancake | **Ridgewood**	19
Eppes Essen | **Livingston**	20
Full Moon | **Lambertville**	19
Hobby's | **Newark**	24
Jack's | **Westwood**	20
Janice | **Ho-Ho-Kus**	21
Java Moon | **Jackson**	22
Je's | **Newark**	25
La Isla | **Hoboken**	25
Little Food Cafe | **multi.**	23
Market Roost | **Flemington**	22
Mastoris | **Bordentown**	19
Meil's | **Stockton**	24
Mustache Bill's | **Barnegat Light**	24
Ponzio's | **Cherry Hill**	19
Pop Shop | **Collingswood**	20
Raymond's | **Montclair**	21
Rolling Pin | **Westwood**	23
Skylark | **Edison**	22
Tick Tock | **Clifton**	18
Tisha's | **Cape May**	25
Toast | **Montclair**	22
NEW Urban Table | **Morristown**	-
Vincentown Diner | **Vincentown**	20
Zafra | **Hoboken**	23

BRUNCH

☑ Amanda's | **Hoboken**	26
Amelia's | **Jersey City**	19
Anthony David's | **Hoboken**	25
Assembly | **Englewood Cliffs**	16
Aunt Berta's | **Oaklyn**	-
NEW Blue Morel | **Morristown**	-
Brass Rail | **Hoboken**	19
Brothers Moon | **Hopewell**	23
Café Gallery | **Burlington**	20
☑ Chart House | **Weehawken**	21
Court St. | **Hoboken**	22
Crown Palace | **Middletown**	20
☑ David Burke | **Rumson**	25
Dim Sum Dynasty | **Ridgewood**	20
☑ Elements | **Princeton**	26
Elysian Café | **Hoboken**	21
Esty St. | **Park Ridge**	25

Fiddleheads | **Jamesburg**	23
NEW 5 Seasons | **Ridgewood**	-
☑ Gables | **Beach Haven**	24
Harvest Bistro | **Closter**	21
Ho-Ho-Kus Inn | **Ho-Ho-Kus**	21
KC Prime | **Lawrenceville**	22
NEW Khloe Bistrot | **Fort Lee**	-
La Campagne | **Cherry Hill**	23
Lambertville Station | **Lambertville**	17
NEW Levant Grille | **Englewood**	-
Liberty House | **Jersey City**	20
Light Horse | **Jersey City**	22
Little Food Cafe | **Bayonne**	23
Madame Claude | **Jersey City**	23
Madeleine's | **Northvale**	25
☑ Manor | **W Orange**	24
Marco/Pepe | **Jersey City**	22
Maritime Parc | **Jersey City**	-
Matisse | **Belmar**	22
Moghul | **Edison**	23
☑ Molly Pitcher Inn Restaurant | **Red Bank**	22
Montville Inn | **Montville**	22
NEW MoonShine | **Millburn**	-
☑ Ninety Acres | **Peapack**	25
NEW Park West | **Ridgewood**	-
Peacock Inn Restaurant | **Princeton**	26
NEW Pilsener Haus | **Hoboken**	-
Pointé | **Jersey City**	21
☑ Rat's | **Hamilton**	24
Raymond's | **Montclair**	21
Robin's Nest | **Mt Holly**	22
Rob's Bistro | **Madison**	-
Rod's Steak | **Morristown**	22
Satis | **Jersey City**	-
☑ Stone House | **Warren**	22
Sweet Basil's | **Livingston**	21
Taqueria Downtown | **Jersey City**	24
Taste of Asia | **Chatham**	22
3 Forty Grill | **Hoboken**	20
3 West | **Basking Ridge**	23
Toast | **Montclair**	22
Tortilla Press | **Collingswood**	24
NEW Urban Table | **Morristown**	-
Verjus | **Maplewood**	25
Villa Amalfi | **Cliffside Pk**	23

West Lake Seafood	**Matawan**	25
Za	**Pennington**	23
Zafra	**Hoboken**	23

BUFFET

(Check availability)

Aamantran	**Toms River**	21
Aangan	**Freehold Twp**	23
Akbar	**Edison**	20
Amiya	**Jersey City**	19
Antonia's	**N Bergen**	20
Assembly	**Englewood Cliffs**	16
☑ Bernards Inn	**Bernardsville**	27
Bicycle Club	**Englewood Cliffs**	14
Bistro 55	**Rochelle Pk**	19
Bistro/Marino	**Collingswood**	22
Black Forest Inn	**Stanhope**	23
NEW Brick Lane Curry	**multi.**	-
Café Gallery	**Burlington**	20
☑ Capriccio	**A.C.**	25
Chand Palace	**multi.**	23
Cinnamon	**Morris Plains**	23
Cranbury Inn	**Cranbury**	14
☑ David Burke	**Rumson**	25
Grain House	**Basking Ridge**	19
Hat Tavern	**Summit**	-
India/Hudson	**Hoboken**	21
Karma Kafe	**Hoboken**	21
Kaya's	**Belmar**	24
KC Prime	**Lawrenceville**	22
Kinara	**Edgewater**	22
Madison B&G	**Hoboken**	19
☑ Manor	**W Orange**	24
Mantra	**Paramus**	22
Martino's	**Somerville**	22
McLoone's	**multi.**	17
Mehndi	**Morristown**	24
Mill/Spring Lake Hts.	**Spring Lake Hts**	21
Minado	**multi.**	20
Moghul	**Edison**	23
☑ Molly Pitcher Inn Restaurant	**Red Bank**	22
Namaskaar	**Englewood**	20
Neelam	**multi.**	20
Old Man Rafferty's	**New Bruns.**	18
Raagini	**Mountainside**	23
Saffron	**E Hanover**	24
Salt Creek	**Rumson**	19
Spargo's	**Manalapan**	23

Taj Mahal	**Jersey City**	-
Tbones Tuscan Steakhouse	**Bridgewater**	22
Villa Amalfi	**Cliffside Pk**	23

BUSINESS DINING

Acquaviva/Fonti	**Westfield**	22
Aldo/Gianni	**Montvale**	21
Assembly	**Englewood Cliffs**	16
Benihana	**multi.**	18
☑ Bernards Inn	**Bernardsville**	27
Biagio's	**Paramus**	17
Bicycle Club	**Englewood Cliffs**	14
NEW Biddy O'Malley's	**Northvale**	-
Blackbird	**Collingswood**	24
NEW Blue Morel	**Morristown**	-
Bonefish Grill	**Deptford**	21
Blvd. Five 72	**Kenilworth**	25
NEW Breakfast Room	**A.C.**	-
Café Azzurro	**Peapack**	24
Cafe Emilia	**Bridgewater**	22
Cara Mia	**Millburn**	-
Casa Dante	**Jersey City**	24
Cenzino	**Oakland**	24
Char	**Raritan**	22
☑ Chez Catherine	**Westfield**	26
NEW Daryl	**New Bruns.**	-
☑ David Burke	**Rumson**	25
☑ Dino/Harry's	**Hoboken**	27
Due Mari	**New Bruns.**	26
Eccola	**Parsippany**	23
Edward's Steak	**Jersey City**	23
Egan/Sons	**W Orange**	19
☑ Eno Terra	**Kingston**	24
☑ Fascino	**Montclair**	26
55 Main	**Flemington**	22
Fiorino	**Summit**	24
Fire/Oak	**Jersey City**	19
NEW Firecreek	**Voorhees**	-
NEW 5 Seasons	**Ridgewood**	-
Franco's Metro	**Fort Lee**	19
Fuji	**Haddonfield**	25
Gallagher's	**A.C.**	22
Gianna's	**Carlstadt**	20
Gladstone	**Gladstone**	21
Grissini	**Englewood Cliffs**	22
Harvest Bistro	**Closter**	21
Hat Tavern	**Summit**	-

SPECIAL FEATURES

🇿 Highlawn Pavilion | **W Orange**		25
Ho-Ho-Kus Inn | **Ho-Ho-Kus**		21
Huntley Taverne | **Summit**		22
Iberia | **Newark**		20
🇿 Il Capriccio | **Whippany**		25
Il Fiore | **Collingswood**		26
Il Villaggio | **Carlstadt**		24
J&K Steak | **multi.**		-
NEW Kyma | **Somerville**		-
La Strada | **Randolph**		23
Light Horse | **Jersey City**		22
Lithos | **Livingston**		-
Locale | **Closter**		20
Luke Palladino | **A.C.**		26
Lu Nello | **Cedar Grove**		25
Maritime Parc | **Jersey City**		-
NEW Marlene Mangia Bene | **Woodbury**		-
Martini Bistro | **Millburn**		19
Martini 494 | **Newark**		-
McCormick/Schmick | **Cherry Hill**		20
Mekong Grill | **Ridgewood**		-
Mill/Spring Lake Hts. | **Spring Lake Hts**		21
NEW MK Valencia | **Ridgefield Pk**		-
Montville Inn | **Montville**		22
NEW MoonShine | **Millburn**		-
🇿 Morton's | **Hackensack**		25
NEW Nico | **Newark**		-
🇿 Ninety Acres | **Peapack**		25
NEW O Bistro | **A.C.**		-
Oceanos | **Fair Lawn**		23
🇿 Old Homestead | **A.C.**		27
NEW Osteria/Fiamma | **Ridgewood**		-
NEW Osteria Morini | **Bernardsville**		-
Panico's | **New Bruns.**		21
Papa Razzi | **multi.**		18
Park Steak | **Park Ridge**		23
Peacock Inn Restaurant | **Princeton**		26
Phillips Seafood | **A.C.**		20
🇿 Picnic | **Fair Lawn**		27
🇿 Pluckemin Inn | **Bedminster**		26
Pointé | **Jersey City**		21
Portofino | **Tinton Falls**		24

🇿 Porto Leggero | **Jersey City**		26
Quays | **Hoboken**		18
NEW Ralic's Steak | **Haddonfield**		-
Rare | **Little Falls**		24
🇿 Raven/Peach | **Fair Haven**		24
🇿 River Palm | **multi.**		25
Rod's Steak | **Morristown**		22
Roots Steak | **Summit**		26
🇿 Ruth's Chris | **Princeton**		25
Sanzari's | **New Milford**		22
🇿 Scalini Fedeli | **Chatham**		27
NEW Sear House | **Closter**		-
Segovia Steak | **Little Ferry**		23
🇿 Serenade | **Chatham**		27
Settimo Cielo | **Trenton**		23
Sirena | **Long Branch**		23
Smoke Chophouse | **Englewood**		23
Solari's | **Hackensack**		19
Son Cubano | **W New York**		-
Spain | **Newark**		24
Spanish Tavern | **multi.**		22
Steakhouse 85 | **New Bruns.**		26
🇿 Stone House | **Warren**		22
Stony Hill Inn | **Hackensack**		22
Tabor Rd. | **Morris Plains**		21
Taj Mahal | **Jersey City**		-
Terra Nova | **Sewell**		-
3 West | **Basking Ridge**		23
Tim Schafer's | **Morristown**		23
Treno | **Westmont**		-
Très Yan & Wu | **Mt Laurel**		23
NEW Ursino | **Union**		-
Victor's Pub | **Camden**		-
Villa Amalfi | **Cliffside Pk**		23
Vine | **Basking Ridge**		23
Vu | **Jersey City**		16
Wasabi | **Somerville**		24
🇿 Waterside | **N Bergen**		21
NEW Wayne Steak | **Wayne**		-
William Douglas | **Cherry Hill**		25
NEW Zeppoli | **Collingswood**		-

BYO

Aamantran | **Toms River**		21
Aangan | **Freehold Twp**		23
Aby's | **Matawan**		20
Acacia | **Lawrenceville**		23
NEW Adara | **Montclair**		-
Ah'Pizz | **Montclair**		22

Ajihei | **Princeton**	25
Ali Baba | **Hoboken**	19
Aligado | **Hazlet**	24
A Little Bit of Cuba | **Freehold**	19
Z **Little Café** | **Voorhees**	27
Allen's | **New Gretna**	22
Alps Bistro | **Allentown**	﹣
Animo Juice | **Haddonfield**	﹣
Anjelica's | **Sea Bright**	24
Anna's Kitchen | **Middletown**	23
NEW Anna's Rist. | **Summit**	﹣
Anthony David's | **Hoboken**	25
Anthony's | **Haddon Hts**	24
Aozora | **Montclair**	24
Ariana | **Voorhees**	18
Ariel's | **Englewood**	20
Armando's Tuscan | **River Vale**	20
Aroma | **Franklin Pk**	22
Arturo's | **Maplewood**	24
Arugula | **Sewell**	﹣
A Tavola | **Old Bridge**	20
Athenian Gdn. | **Galloway Twp**	23
Z A Toute Heure | **Cranford**	26
Aunt Berta's | **Oaklyn**	﹣
Avon Pavilion | **Avon-by-Sea**	19
Babylon | **River Edge**	21
Backyards | **Hoboken**	18
Bamboo Leaf | **multi.**	22
Barone's/Villa Barone/Tuscan | **multi.**	22
Barrels | **multi.**	21
Z Basilico | **Millburn**	23
Z Baumgart's | **multi.**	19
Z Bay Ave. | **Highlands**	28
Z Belford Bistro | **Belford**	26
NEW Bell & Whistle | **Hopewell**	﹣
Bella Sogno | **Bradley Bch**	21
Benito's | **Chester**	23
Beyti Kebab | **Union City**	21
Bienvenue | **Red Bank**	22
Bistro/Marino | **Collingswood**	22
Bistro Olé | **Asbury Pk**	23
Blackbird | **Collingswood**	24
Black Duck | **W Cape May**	26
Black-Eyed Susans | **Harvey Cedars**	﹣
Black Trumpet | **Spring Lake**	24
Blu | **Montclair**	25
Blue Bottle | **Hopewell**	26
Blue Fish | **Flemington**	21
Blueplate | **Mullica Hill**	﹣
Z Blue Point | **Princeton**	26
Bobby Chez | **multi.**	24
NEW Bombay Bistro | **Summit**	﹣
Bosphorus | **Lake Hiawatha**	22
Brandl | **Belmar**	24
Brasilia | **Newark**	22
NEW Brick Lane Curry | **multi.**	﹣
Brioso | **Marlboro**	24
Brooklyn's Pizza | **multi.**	22
Brothers Moon | **Hopewell**	23
Cafe Arugula | **S Orange**	21
Café Azzurro | **Peapack**	24
Cafe Coloré | **Freehold Twp**	19
Cafe Graziella | **Hillsborough**	20
Z Cafe Matisse | **Rutherford**	27
Z Cafe Panache | **Ramsey**	27
Caffe Galleria | **Lambertville**	21
Capt'n Ed's | **Pt. Pleas.**	20
Cara Mia | **Millburn**	﹣
Casa Maya | **multi.**	24
Casa Solar | **Belmar**	23
Casona | **Collingswood**	22
Chambers Walk | **Lawrenceville**	21
Chand Palace | **multi.**	23
Chao Phaya | **multi.**	22
Charrito's/El Charro | **Hoboken**	22
Chef Jon's | **Whippany**	24
Z Chef's Table | **Franklin Lakes**	28
Z Chef Vola's | **A.C.**	26
Chez Elena Wu | **Voorhees**	22
NEW Chinese Mirch | **N Brunswick**	﹣
Christie's | **Howell**	26
Christopher | **Cherry Hill**	﹣
Cinnamon | **Morris Plains**	23
Clementine's | **Avon-by-Sea**	23
Coconut Bay | **Voorhees**	22
Costanera | **Montclair**	24
Country Pancake | **Ridgewood**	19
Cross Culture | **Haddonfield**	﹣
Cuban Pete's | **Montclair**	19
Z CulinAriane | **Montclair**	27
Da Filippo's | **Somerville**	24
D&L BBQ | **Bradley Bch**	24
Daniel's Bistro | **Pt. Pleas. Bch**	﹣
NEW Da's Kitchen | **Hopewell**	﹣
NEW Da Soli | **Haddonfield**	﹣

DeLorenzo's Pizza | **Trenton**	24
Z DeLorenzo's/Pies | **Robbinsville**	27
Dim Sum Dynasty | **Ridgewood**	20
DiPalma Brothers | **N Bergen**	21
Dish | **Red Bank**	25
Diving Horse | **Avalon**	24
Dream Cuisine | **Cherry Hill**	27
Z Drew's Bayshore | **Keyport**	27
NEW Duck King | **Edgewater**	-
Edo Sushi | **Pennington**	20
El Azteca | **Mt Laurel**	21
El Caney | **Bergenfield**	-
Elements Asia | **Lawrenceville**	23
Elements | **Haddon Hts**	23
El Familiar | **Toms River**	-
El Mesón Café | **Freehold**	24
NEW El Tule | **Lambertville**	-
Epernay | **Montclair**	21
Eppes Essen | **Livingston**	20
Etc. Steak | **Teaneck**	25
Eurasian | **Red Bank**	23
Far East Taste | **Eatontown**	23
Z Fascino | **Montclair**	26
Fedora Café | **Lawrenceville**	20
Ferry House | **Princeton**	-
Fiddleheads | **Jamesburg**	23
15 Fox Pl. | **Jersey City**	23
55 Main | **Flemington**	22
Fin Raw Bar | **Montclair**	-
Fishery | **S Amboy**	20
NEW 5 Seasons | **Ridgewood**	-
Flirt Sushi | **Allendale**	23
Fontana/Trevi | **Leonia**	23
Fortune Cookie | **Bridgewater**	21
Frankie Fed's | **Freehold Twp**	21
Fredo's | **Freehold Twp**	22
Fresco Steak | **Milltown**	25
Freshwaters | **Plainfield**	21
Fuji | **Haddonfield**	25
Full Moon | **Lambertville**	19
Gabriela's | **Somerville**	18
Garlic Rose | **Madison**	20
Gazelle Café | **Ridgewood**	23
Girasole | **Bound Brook**	26
Greek Taverna | **multi.**	20
Grub Hut | **Manville**	21
Hamilton's | **Lambertville**	26
Hanami | **multi.**	20

Harvey Cedars | **multi.**	23
Hummus Elite | **Englewood**	21
Hunan Spring | **Springfield**	18
I Gemelli | **S Hackensack**	24
Z Ikko | **Brick**	25
NEW Il Cinghiale | **Little Ferry**	-
Il Fiore | **Collingswood**	26
Z Il Mondo | **Madison**	26
IndeBlue | **Collingswood**	25
Isabella's | **Westfield**	19
It's Greek To Me | **multi.**	18
Jack's | **Westwood**	20
J&K Steak | **multi.**	-
Janice | **Ho-Ho-Kus**	21
Java Moon | **Jackson**	22
Jerry/Harvey's | **Marlboro**	18
Joe Pesce | **Collingswood**	24
Joe's Peking | **Marlton**	24
Jose's | **Spring Lake Hts**	23
Jose's Cantina | **Warren**	19
Juanito's | **Howell**	23
Kanji | **Tinton Falls**	24
Kaya's | **Belmar**	24
Kevin's Thyme | **Ho-Ho-Kus**	23
NEW Khloe Bistrot | **Fort Lee**	-
Khun Thai | **Short Hills**	23
NEW Khyber Grill | **South Plainfield**	-
Kibitz Room | **Cherry Hill**	23
Kinara | **Edgewater**	22
Kitchen Consigliere | **Collingswood**	-
Konbu | **Manalapan**	26
Krave Café | **Newton**	24
Kuzina/Sofia | **Cherry Hill**	22
NEW Kyma | **Somerville**	-
Labrador | **Normandy Bch**	25
La Campagna | **Morristown**	23
La Campagne | **Cherry Hill**	23
La Cipollina | **Freehold**	22
La Focaccia | **Summit**	23
NEW La Fontana Coast | **Sea Isle City**	-
Laila's | **Asbury Pk**	22
La Isla | **Hoboken**	25
La Locanda | **Voorhees**	28
La Pastaria | **multi.**	19
Z La Spiaggia | **Ship Bottom**	24
L'assiette | **Surf City**	20

Z Latour | **Ridgewood**	26
Le Fandy | **Fair Haven**	25
Lemongrass | **Morris Plains**	-
Z Le Rendez-Vous | **Kenilworth**	27
NEW Levant Grille | **Englewood**	-
Limani | **Westfield**	24
Little Food Cafe | **Pompton Plains**	23
Little Saigon | **A.C.**	25
Little Tuna | **Haddonfield**	23
LoBianco | **Margate**	-
Lola/Bistro | **Metuchen**	-
Z Lorena's | **Maplewood**	28
Lotus Cafe | **Hackensack**	23
LouCás | **Edison**	23
Luca's Rist. | **Somerset**	24
Luce | **Caldwell**	22
Luka's | **Ridgefield Pk**	23
Luke Palladino | **Northfield**	26
Luna Rossa | **Sicklerville**	-
Madame Claude | **Jersey City**	23
Magic Pot | **Edgewater**	18
Mahzu | **multi.**	20
Manon | **Lambertville**	25
Margherita's | **Hoboken**	22
Market Roost | **Flemington**	22
NEW Marlene Mangia Bene | **Woodbury**	-
Martino's | **Somerville**	22
Matisse | **Belmar**	22
Matt's/Rooster | **Flemington**	26
Meemah | **Edison**	25
Megu | **multi.**	23
Meil's | **Stockton**	24
Mekong Grill | **Ridgewood**	-
Mélange | **Haddonfield**	25
Mesob | **Montclair**	24
Midori | **Denville**	21
Mie Thai | **Woodbridge**	24
Mignon Steak | **Rutherford**	22
Mikado | **Cherry Hill**	23
Ming | **Edison**	24
Mojave | **Westfield**	23
Monster Sushi | **Summit**	20
Mr. Chu | **E Hanover**	21
Mud City | **Manahawkin**	24
Mustache Bill's | **Barnegat Light**	24
Namaskaar | **Englewood**	20
Napoli's Pizza | **Hoboken**	25
Navesink Fishery | **Navesink**	25
Neelam | **multi.**	20
Negeen | **Summit**	18
Next Door | **Montclair**	22
Nha Trang Pl. | **Jersey City**	23
Nicky's | **Madison**	18
Nobi | **Toms River**	26
Nomad Pizza | **Hopewell**	26
Nori | **multi.**	23
Norma's | **Cherry Hill**	22
Nunzio | **Collingswood**	24
NEW Ohana Grill | **Lavallette**	-
Oliver a Bistro | **Bordentown**	27
Z Origin | **multi.**	25
Z Osteria Giotto | **Montclair**	26
NEW Osteria/Fiamma | **Ridgewood**	-
Ota-Ya | **Lambertville**	21
Oyako Tso's | **Freehold**	23
NEW Pacific Grill | **Wildwood**	-
NEW Pairings | **Cranford**	-
Pamir | **Morristown**	22
Penang | **multi.**	22
Z Peter Shields | **Cape May**	26
Z Picnic | **Fair Lawn**	27
Pithari | **Highland Pk**	23
Plan B | **Asbury Pk**	24
Pop's Garage | **multi.**	22
Prime/Beyond | **Fort Lee**	-
Raimondo's | **Ship Bottom**	24
NEW Ralic's Steak | **Haddonfield**	-
Raymond's | **Montclair**	21
Ray's | **Little Silver**	21
Rebecca's | **Edgewater**	23
Red's Lobster | **Pt. Pleas. Bch**	24
Z Resto | **Madison**	25
Richard's | **Long Branch**	20
Rick's | **Lambertville**	21
Risotto House | **Rutherford**	23
Ritz Seafood | **Voorhees**	26
Roberto's | **Beach Haven**	21
Robongi | **Hoboken**	24
Rob's Bistro | **Madison**	-
Rocca | **Glen Rock**	24
Rolling Pin | **Westwood**	23
Z Saddle River Inn | **Saddle River**	28
Saffron | **E Hanover**	24
Z Sagami | **Collingswood**	27
Sage | **Ventnor**	25

Sakura-Bana | **Ridgewood**	25
Sakura Spring | **Cherry Hill**	24
Saluté | **Montclair**	-
San Remo | **Shrewsbury**	22
⚡ Sapori | **Collingswood**	28
Satis | **Jersey City**	-
Settebello | **Morristown**	20
Sette | **Bernardsville**	24
⚡ Shumi | **Somerville**	28
Siam | **Lambertville**	23
Siam Gdn. | **Red Bank**	24
Silk Road | **Warren**	23
Sirin | **Morristown**	21
Siri's | **Cherry Hill**	26
Soho 33 | **Madison**	18
Solo Bella | **Jackson**	22
Somsak | **Voorhees**	22
Sono | **Middletown**	25
Soul Flavors | **Jersey City**	21
Spargo's | **Manalapan**	23
Spike's | **Pt. Pleas. Bch**	22
Sri Thai | **Hoboken**	25
Stamna | **Bloomfield**	23
NEW St. Eve's | **Ho-Ho-Kus**	-
Sumo | **Wall**	25
Surf Taco | **multi.**	21
Sushi X | **Ridgewood**	21
Sweet Basil's | **Livingston**	21
Tacconelli's | **Maple Shade**	23
Taj Mahal | **Jersey City**	-
Taka | **Asbury Pk**	25
Taste of Asia | **Chatham**	22
Thai Chef | **Montclair**	21
Thai Kitchen | **multi.**	23
Thai Thai | **Stirling**	23
Theresa's | **Westfield**	22
Tiger Noodles | **Princeton**	19
Tim Schafer's | **Morristown**	23
Tina Louise | **Carlstadt**	23
Tisha's | **Cape May**	25
Toast | **Montclair**	22
Tortilla Press | **Collingswood**	24
Tortuga's | **Princeton**	22
Trattoria Bel Paese | **Cranford**	-
Trattoria Med. | **Bedminster**	24
Très Yan & Wu | **Mt Laurel**	23
Tsuki | **Bernardsville**	22
Tuptim | **Montclair**	21
Tutto/Modo Mio | **Ridgefield**	21

TwoFiftyTwo | **Bedminster**	-
Umpasri | **Cherry Hill**	-
Valdebenito's | **Somerville**	-
Vasili's | **Teaneck**	21
Village Gourmet | **Rutherford**	21
Village Green | **Ridgewood**	24
Wasabi | **E Brunswick**	24
NEW Wayne Steak | **Wayne**	-
West Lake Seafood | **Matawan**	25
⚡ Whispers | **Spring Lake**	27
Wondee's | **Hackensack**	22
Wonder Seafood | **Edison**	26
Ya Ya | **Skillman**	21
⚡ Yellow Fin | **Surf City**	27
Za | **Pennington**	23
Zafra | **Hoboken**	23
NEW Zeppoli | **Collingswood**	-

CATERING

Aamantran | **Toms River**	21
Aangan | **Freehold Twp**	23
⚡ Amanda's | **Hoboken**	26
⚡ Andre's | **Newton**	27
Anjelica's | **Sea Bright**	24
Anthony David's | **Hoboken**	25
Athenian Gdn. | **Galloway Twp**	23
Augustino's | **Hoboken**	26
Backyards | **Hoboken**	18
⚡ Basilico | **Millburn**	23
⚡ Bernards Inn | **Bernardsville**	27
Brioso | **Marlboro**	24
Brothers Moon | **Hopewell**	23
Cafe Loren | **Avalon**	25
⚡ Cafe Matisse | **Rutherford**	27
⚡ Cafe Panache | **Ramsey**	27
Casa Dante | **Jersey City**	24
Cucharamama | **Hoboken**	26
⚡ CulinAriane | **Montclair**	27
Da Filippo's | **Somerville**	24
DiPalma Brothers | **N Bergen**	21
Eppes Essen | **Livingston**	20
Far East Taste | **Eatontown**	23
⚡ Fascino | **Montclair**	26
15 Fox Pl. | **Jersey City**	23
Filomena Rustica | **W Berlin**	18
Franco's Metro | **Fort Lee**	19
Freshwaters | **Plainfield**	21
⚡ Gables | **Beach Haven**	24
Girasole | **Bound Brook**	26

☑ Grand Cafe | **Morristown**		25
Harvest Moon | **Ringoes**		25
Hobby's | **Newark**		24
Hunan Taste | **Denville**		24
☑ Il Capriccio | **Whippany**		25
Jack's | **Westwood**		20
Kevin's Thyme | **Ho-Ho-Kus**		23
Little Tuna | **Haddonfield**		23
Makeda | **New Bruns.**		24
Market Roost | **Flemington**		22
☑ Mattar's Bistro | **Allamuchy**		24
Ming | **Edison**		24
Moghul | **Edison**		23
Mud City | **Manahawkin**		24
☑ Nicholas | **Red Bank**		29
☑ Origin | **multi.**		25
☑ Picnic | **Fair Lawn**		27
☑ Ram's Head Inn | **Galloway**		24
Rebecca's | **Edgewater**		23
☑ Resto | **Madison**		25
Robongi | **Hoboken**		24
☑ Rosemary/Sage | **Riverdale**		26
Soul Flavors | **Jersey City**		21
Squan Tavern | **Manasquan**		20
Stage House | **Scotch Plains**		20
☑ Stage Left | **New Bruns.**		27
☑ Stone House | **Warren**		22
Tim Schafer's | **Morristown**		23
Tina Louise | **Carlstadt**		23
Villa Amalfi | **Cliffside Pk**		23
☑ Washington Inn | **Cape May**		28
☑ Waterside | **N Bergen**		21
☑ Whispers | **Spring Lake**		27
Zafra | **Hoboken**		23

CELEBRITY CHEFS

Scott Anderson
☑ Elements | **Princeton**		26

Zod Arifai
Blu | **Montclair**		25
NEW Daryl | **New Bruns.**		–
Next Door | **Montclair**		22

Claude Baills
☑ Chef's Table | **Franklin Lakes**		28

Ed Battaglia
NEW Ralic's Steak | **Haddonfield**		–

David Burke
☑ David Burke | **Rumson**		25

Humberto Campos
☑ Lorena's | **Maplewood**		28

Andrea Carbine
☑ A Toute Heure | **Cranford**		26

Michael Cetrulo
☑ Il Mondo | **Madison**		26
☑ Scalini Fedeli | **Chatham**		27
Sirena | **Long Branch**		23
Stella Marina | **Asbury Pk**		23

Michael Cetrulo, Angelo Stella
☑ Porto Leggero | **Jersey City**		26

Thomas Ciszak
☑ Chakra | **Paramus**		20

Thomas Ciszak, Kevin Takafuji
NEW Blue Morel | **Morristown**		–

Juan Jose Cuevas
☑ Pluckemin Inn | **Bedminster**		26

Ryan DePersio
Bar Cara | **Bloomfield**		20
☑ Fascino | **Montclair**		26
NEW Nico | **Newark**		–

David Drake
Alice's | **Lake Hopatcong**		21

Ariane Duarte
☑ CulinAriane | **Montclair**		27

David Felton
☑ Ninety Acres | **Peapack**		25

Bobby Flay
Bobby Flay | **A.C.**		25
Bobby's | **multi.**		21

Nicholas Harary
☑ Nicholas | **Red Bank**		29

Corey Heyer
☑ Bernards Inn | **Bernardsville**		27

Paul Ingenito
Perryville Inn | **Union Twp**		26

Matt Ito
Fuji | **Haddonfield**		25

Kevin Kohler
☑ Cafe Panache | **Ramsey**		27

James Laird
☑ Serenade | **Chatham**		27

Michael Latour
☑ Latour | **Ridgewood**		26

Bruce Lefebvre
☑ Frog/Peach | **New Bruns.**		26

Peter Loria
 🔁 Cafe Matisse | **Rutherford** 27

Angelo Lutz
 Kitchen Consigliere | —
 Collingswood

Nelson Martinez
 Bibi'z | **Westwood** —

Michael Mina
 🔁 SeaBlue | **A.C.** 26

Luke Palladino
 Luke Palladino | **multi.** 26

Nunzio Patruno
 Nunzio | **Collingswood** 24

Georges Perrier, Chris Scarduzio
 Mia | **A.C.** 26

Anthony Pino
 Anthony David's | **Hoboken** 25
 Bin 14 | **Hoboken** 22

Maricel Presilla
 Cucharamama | **Hoboken** 26
 Zafra | **Hoboken** 23

Wolfgang Puck
 Wolfgang Puck | **A.C.** 23

Michel Richard
 🆕 Breakfast Room | **A.C.** —
 🆕 O Bistro | **A.C.** —

Daniel Richer
 Arturo's | **Maplewood** 24

Joe Romanowski
 🔁 Bay Ave. | **Highlands** 28

Chris Scarduzio
 🆕 Scarduzio's | **A.C.** —

John Schatz
 🆕 Pacific Grill | **Wildwood** —
 Union Park | **Cape May** 25

Kerry Simon
 Simon Prime | **A.C.** —

Tony Sindaco
 Hat Tavern | **Summit** —

Scott Snyder
 Blvd. Five 72 | **Kenilworth** 25

Kenneth Trickilo
 Liberty House | **Jersey City** 20

Michael Weisshaupt
 🔁 Rest. Latour | **Hamburg** 27

Michael White
 🆕 Osteria Morini | —
 Bernardsville

CHEF'S TABLE

Bella Sogno | **Bradley Bch**	21
🔁 Cafe Madison | **Riverside**	22
Chophouse | **Gibbsboro**	23
🔁 CulinAriane | **Montclair**	27
🔁 Elements | **Princeton**	26
🔁 Nicholas | **Red Bank**	29
Nunzio | **Collingswood**	24
🔁 Old Homestead | **A.C.**	27
🔁 Rat's | **Hamilton**	24
🔁 Seasons 52 | **Cherry Hill**	22
Tbones Tuscan Steakhouse |	22
Bridgewater	
Wolfgang Puck | **A.C.**	23

CHILD-FRIENDLY

(Alternatives to the usual fast-food places; * children's menu available)

Aby's* | **Matawan**	20
A Mano* | **Ridgewood**	22
Anjelica's | **Sea Bright**	24
Axelsson's* | **Cape May**	23
Bahama Breeze* | **Cherry Hill**	17
Baja Fresh* | **multi.**	17
Bamboo Leaf | **Bradley Bch**	22
Bareli's | **Secaucus**	23
Barone's/Villa Barone/Tuscan* |	22
multi.	
🔁 Baumgart's* | **multi.**	19
Bell's Tavern | **Lambertville**	20
Benihana* | **multi.**	18
Beyti Kebab | **Union City**	21
Big Ed's BBQ* | **Matawan**	18
Black Duck | **W Cape May**	26
Black Forest Inn | **Stanhope**	23
🆕 Blind Boar* | **Norwood**	—
🔁 Blue Point* | **Princeton**	26
Bobby Chez | **multi.**	24
Braddock's* | **Medford**	19
Brioso | **Marlboro**	24
Cabin* | **Howell**	18
Cafe Loren | **Avalon**	25
Calandra's/Grill | **Fairfield**	21
🔁 Capriccio | **A.C.**	25
Casa Giuseppe | **Iselin**	22
Casa Vasca | **Newark**	24
Cassie's | **Englewood**	18
Chao Phaya | **Somerville**	22
🔁 Cheesecake Factory* | **multi.**	19
Chengdu 46 | **Clifton**	24

Christie's* | **Howell**	26
Cucina Calandra* | **Fairfield**	21
Dai-Kichi | **Upper Montclair**	23
Delicious Hts.* | **Berkeley Hts**	18
Dock's* | **A.C.**	26
E & V | **Paterson**	23
East | **Teaneck**	19
El Azteca* | **Mt Laurel**	21
El Cid | **Paramus**	22
El Mesón Café | **Freehold**	24
Espo's | **Raritan**	23
Far East Taste | **Eatontown**	23
Filomena Italiana* | **Clementon**	25
Filomena Lake.* | **Deptford**	23
Filomena Rustica* | **W Berlin**	18
Fire/Oak* | **multi.**	19
☑ Five Guys* | **multi.**	21
☑ Fornos/Spain | **Newark**	24
Frankie Fed's* | **Freehold Twp**	21
Frenchtown Inn | **Frenchtown**	23
NEW GK's Red Dog* | **Morristown**	-
Gusto Grill* | **E Brunswick**	19
Harvest Moon* | **Ringoes**	25
Hiram's | **Fort Lee**	21
Hobby's | **Newark**	24
Ho-Ho-Kus Inn* | **Ho-Ho-Kus**	21
Holsten's* | **Bloomfield**	16
Hot Dog Johnny's | **Buttzville**	21
☑ Ikko* | **Brick**	25
Il Vecchio Cafe | **Caldwell**	20
Inn of the Hawke Restaurant* | **Lambertville**	20
It's Greek To Me* | **multi.**	18
Jack's | **Westwood**	20
Java Moon* | **Jackson**	22
Jose's Cantina | **multi.**	19
Kibitz Room* | **Cherry Hill**	23
La Campagne | **Cherry Hill**	23
La Esperanza* | **Lindenwold**	25
☑ Legal Sea Foods* | **multi.**	21
Little Tuna* | **Haddonfield**	23
LouCás* | **Edison**	23
Lu Nello | **Cedar Grove**	25
Margherita's | **Hoboken**	22
Meil's* | **Stockton**	24
Mexican Food* | **Marlton**	20
Mikado | **Cherry Hill**	23
Monster Sushi* | **Summit**	20
Mud City* | **Manahawkin**	24
Nana's Deli | **Livingston**	23
Navesink Fishery | **Navesink**	25
Nicky's* | **Madison**	18
Nifty Fifty's* | **multi.**	19
Nomad Pizza | **Hopewell**	26
Norma's* | **Cherry Hill**	22
Ota-Ya | **Lambertville**	21
☑ Park/Orchard* | **E Rutherford**	23
☑ P.F. Chang's | **Marlton**	20
Pietro's Pizza* | **Marlton**	21
Pizzicato* | **Marlton**	21
Ponzio's* | **Cherry Hill**	19
Pop Shop* | **Collingswood**	20
Pub* | **Pennsauken**	19
Raimondo's* | **Ship Bottom**	24
☑ Ram's Head Inn* | **Galloway**	24
☑ Rat's | **Hamilton**	24
Raymond's* | **Montclair**	21
Reservoir | **Boonton**	23
Robongi | **Hoboken**	24
Rob's Bistro* | **Madison**	-
Saffron | **E Hanover**	24
☑ Sagami | **Collingswood**	27
Sage Diner* | **Mt Laurel**	14
Sawa* | **Eatontown**	23
Senorita's* | **multi.**	19
Shipwreck Grill | **Brielle**	24
Shogun* | **multi.**	21
Siri's* | **Cherry Hill**	26
Skylark* | **Edison**	22
Solari's | **Hackensack**	19
Somsak | **Voorhees**	22
Sono* | **Middletown**	25
Steve/Cookie's* | **Margate**	25
Surf Taco* | **multi.**	21
Sushi X | **Ridgewood**	21
Thai Kitchen | **multi.**	23
Thai Thai | **Stirling**	23
Theresa's* | **Westfield**	22
WindMill* | **multi.**	19
Tick Tock* | **Clifton**	18
Tina Louise | **Carlstadt**	23
Toast* | **Montclair**	22
Tortilla Press* | **Collingswood**	24
NEW Urban Table | **Morristown**	-
Verjus | **Maplewood**	25
Wasabi | **multi.**	24
West Lake Seafood | **Matawan**	25

White House	**A.C.**	26
White Mana	**Jersey City**	17
White Manna	**Hackensack**	23
Zafra	**Hoboken**	23

DANCING

Andreotti's	**Cherry Hill**	-
Azúcar	**Jersey City**	20
Cabin	**Howell**	18
Casa Dante	**Jersey City**	24
Cuba Libre	**A.C.**	21
Cubanu	**Rahway**	21
Delta's	**New Bruns.**	22
Dinallo's	**River Edge**	22
Filomena Italiana	**Clementon**	25
Filomena Rustica	**W Berlin**	18
ⓩ Manor	**W Orange**	24
Mohawk House	**Sparta**	22
Park Ave. B&G	**Union City**	18
Portobello	**Oakland**	19
Portuguese Manor	**Perth Amboy**	19
ⓩ Rat's	**Hamilton**	24
Sabor	**N Bergen**	22
Skylark	**Edison**	22
Solari's	**Hackensack**	19
Stony Hill Inn	**Hackensack**	22
Villa Amalfi	**Cliffside Pk**	23
Windansea	**Highlands**	17

DELIVERY/TAKEOUT

(D=delivery, T=takeout)

Aamantran	D, T	**Toms River**	21
Aby's	D, T	**Matawan**	20
A Mano	T	**Ridgewood**	22
Ariel's	D, T	**Englewood**	20
Athenian Gdn.	T	**Galloway Twp**	23
Bahama Breeze	T	**Cherry Hill**	17
ⓩ Baumgart's	T	**multi.**	19
Bell's Tavern	T	**Lambertville**	20
Belmont Tavern	T	**Belleville**	23
Beyti Kebab	T	**Union City**	21
NEW Biddy O'Malley's	T	**Northvale**	-
Big Ed's BBQ	T	**Matawan**	18
NEW Blind Boar	T	**Norwood**	-
Blue Danube	T	**Trenton**	22
Bobby Chez	T	**multi.**	24
NEW Brick Lane Curry	T	**multi.**	-

Brooklyn's Pizza	T	**multi.**	22
Casa Maya	T	**Gillette**	24
Chao Phaya	T	**Somerville**	22
Chilangos	T	**Highlands**	21
Crown Palace	T	**multi.**	20
ⓩ DeLorenzo's/Pies	T	**Robbinsville**	27
DiPalma Brothers	T	**N Bergen**	21
NEW Duck King	D, T	**Edgewater**	-
El Familiar	T	**Toms River**	-
El Mesón Café	T	**Freehold**	24
Eppes Essen	T	**Livingston**	20
Far East Taste	T	**Eatontown**	23
Federici's	T	**Freehold**	21
Filomena Italiana	T	**Clementon**	25
Filomena Lake.	T	**Deptford**	23
Filomena Rustica	T	**W Berlin**	18
Franco's Metro	T	**Fort Lee**	19
Frankie Fed's	T	**Freehold Twp**	21
Full Moon	T	**Lambertville**	19
Grimaldi's	D	**Hoboken**	25
Harvey Cedars	T	**Beach Haven**	23
Hiram's	T	**Fort Lee**	21
Hobby's	D, T	**Newark**	24
Hot Dog Johnny's	T	**Buttzville**	21
Hunan Chinese	T	**Morris Plains**	20
Ibby's	D, T	**multi.**	22
India/Hudson	D	**Hoboken**	21
It's Greek To Me	T	**multi.**	18
Java Moon	T	**Jackson**	22
Je's	D, T	**Newark**	25
Joe's Peking	T	**Marlton**	24
Juanito's	T	**multi.**	23
Karma Kafe	D	**Hoboken**	21
Komegashi	D, T	**Jersey City**	22
NEW Tratt. Primavera	T	**W Orange**	-
La Sorrentina	T	**N Bergen**	24
NEW Levant Grille	D, T	**Englewood**	-
Los Amigos	T	**multi.**	23
Lotus Cafe	D	**Hackensack**	23
Madeleine's	T	**Northvale**	25
Madison B&G	T	**Hoboken**	19
Mahzu	T	**Aberdeen**	20
Margherita's	D	**Hoboken**	22
Market Roost	T	**Flemington**	22

Mastoris | T | **Bordentown**	19
Meemah | T | **Edison**	25
Meil's | T | **Stockton**	24
Memphis Pig Out | T | **Atlantic Highlands**	19
Mie Thai | T | **Woodbridge**	24
Mikado | T | **Cherry Hill**	23
Moghul | T | **Edison**	23
Monster Sushi | D, T | **Summit**	20
Mustache Bill's | T | **Barnegat Light**	24
Napoli's Pizza | D, T | **Hoboken**	25
Nobi | T | **Toms River**	26
Norma's | T | **Cherry Hill**	22
Old Man Rafferty's | T | **multi.**	18
Ota-Ya | T | **Lambertville**	21
Pad Thai | T | **Highland Pk**	24
Penang | D, T | **multi.**	22
Z P.F. Chang's | T | **multi.**	20
Raagini | T | **Mountainside**	23
Renato's | T | **Jersey City**	22
Reservoir | T | **Boonton**	23
Richard's | T | **Long Branch**	20
Robongi | D, T | **Hoboken**	24
Rob's Bistro | T | **Madison**	-
Rosa Mexicano | D, T | **Hackensack**	22
Rutt's Hut | T | **Clifton**	21
Saffron | D | **E Hanover**	24
Sakura-Bana | T | **Ridgewood**	25
Satis | T | **Jersey City**	-
Shogun | T | **multi.**	21
Z Shumi | T | **Somerville**	28
Siam | T | **Lambertville**	23
Sono | T | **Middletown**	25
Spike's | T | **Pt. Pleas. Bch**	22
Sri Thai | D | **Hoboken**	25
Sushi Lounge | D, T | **multi.**	22
Taste of Asia | T | **Chatham**	22
Thai Chef | T | **Montclair**	21
Thai Kitchen | T | **multi.**	23
Tina Louise | T | **Carlstadt**	23
Tortuga's | T | **Princeton**	22
Très Yan & Wu | T | **Mt Laurel**	23
Tuzzio's | T | **Long Branch**	20
NEW Urban Table | T | **Morristown**	-
Vic's | T | **Bradley Bch**	21
Wasabi | D, T | **multi.**	24

West Lake Seafood | T | **Matawan**	25
White House | T | **A.C.**	26
White Mana | T | **Jersey City**	17
White Manna | T | **Hackensack**	23
Wonder Seafood | T | **Edison**	26

DESSERT SPECIALISTS

Bar Cara | **Bloomfield**	20
Z Baumgart's | **multi.**	19
Z Chakra | **Paramus**	20
Z Cheesecake Factory | **multi.**	19
Z CulinAriane | **Montclair**	27
Z Fascino | **Montclair**	26
Fedora Café | **Lawrenceville**	20
NEW 5 Seasons | **Ridgewood**	-
Z Frog/Peach | **New Bruns.**	26
Holsten's | **Bloomfield**	16
Janice | **Ho-Ho-Kus**	21
Madeleine's | **Northvale**	25
Old Man Rafferty's | **multi.**	18
Z Picnic | **Fair Lawn**	27
Z Pluckemin Inn | **Bedminster**	26
Raymond's | **Montclair**	21
Robin's Nest | **Mt Holly**	22
Rolling Pin | **Westwood**	23
Satis | **Jersey City**	-
NEW St. Eve's | **Ho-Ho-Kus**	-

ENTERTAINMENT

(Call for days and times of performances)

NEW Aqua Blu | live music | **Toms River**	-
Atlantic B&G | live music | **S Seaside Pk**	26
Bahama Breeze | steel drum band: Thu-Sun | **Cherry Hill**	17
NEW Baia | live music | **Somers Point**	-
Z Bernards Inn | piano | **Bernardsville**	27
Z Blue Point | jazz | **Princeton**	26
Casa Dante | varies | **Jersey City**	24
Z Chakra | DJs/jazz | **Paramus**	20
NEW Cubacan | Latin music | **Asbury Pk**	-
Da Filippo's | piano | **Somerville**	24
Dock's | piano | **A.C.**	26
Z Ebbitt Room | jazz | **Cape May**	26

Filomena Italiana | live music | **Clementon** — 25

Filomena Lake. | live music | **Deptford** — 23

Filomena Rustica | live music | **W Berlin** — 18

Z Grand Cafe | piano | **Morristown** — 25

Harvest Moon | piano | **Ringoes** — 25

Z Il Capriccio | piano | **Whippany** — 25

Le Jardin | live music | **Edgewater** — 20

Makeda | varies | **New Bruns.** — 24

Z Manor | live music | **W Orange** — 24

Z Mattar's Bistro | varies | **Allamuchy** — 24

McLoone's | jazz/rock | **Sea Bright** — 17

Mohawk House | varies | **Sparta** — 22

Z Molly Pitcher Inn Restaurant | piano | **Red Bank** — 22

Mompou | bossa nova/flamenco/jazz | **Newark** — 23

NEW MoonShine | live music | **Millburn** — -

Z Moonstruck | jazz | **Asbury Pk** — 25

Norma's | belly dancing | **Cherry Hill** — 22

Park Ave. B&G | DJs/jazz | **Union City** — 18

Z Peter Shields | piano | **Cape May** — 26

Portuguese Manor | DJs/live music | **Perth Amboy** — 19

Z Ram's Head Inn | piano | **Galloway** — 24

Z Rat's | varies | **Hamilton** — 24

Z Raven/Peach | guitar/piano | **Fair Haven** — 24

Rumba Cubana/Cafe | Cuban music | **N Bergen** — 23

Sabor | DJs/flamenco | **N Bergen** — 22

NEW Scarduzio's | DJs/live music | **A.C.** — -

Shanghai Jazz | jazz | **Madison** — 22

Shipwreck Grill | jazz | **Brielle** — 24

Stage House | live music | **Scotch Plains** — 20

Steve/Cookie's | live music | **Margate** — 25

Stony Hill Inn | live music | **Hackensack** — 22

Sushi Lounge | DJs/jazz | **Morristown** — 22

Tapas/Espana | flamenco | **N Bergen** — 22

Tim McLoone's | live music | **Asbury Pk** — 20

Trinity/Pope | live music | **Asbury Pk** — 21

Triumph Brew. | live music | **Princeton** — 16

Tula | DJs | **New Bruns.** — 19

Valdebenito's | varies | **Somerville** — -

Verve | varies | **Somerville** — 23

Villa Amalfi | live music | **Cliffside Pk** — 23

Windansea | DJs/live music | **Highlands** — 17

FAMILY-STYLE

Adega Grill	**Newark**	22
Brio	**Cherry Hill**	19
Carmine's	**A.C.**	21
Cassie's	**Englewood**	18
Z Chef Vola's	**A.C.**	26
E & V	**Paterson**	23
Gaetano's	**Red Bank**	20
Gianna's	**Carlstadt**	20
GoodFellas	**Garfield**	21
Maggiano's	**multi.**	20
Melting Pot	**multi.**	19
Mesob	**Montclair**	24
Pad Thai	**Highland Pk**	24
Z P.F. Chang's	**multi.**	20
Z Piccola	**Ocean Twp**	26
Risotto House	**Rutherford**	23
Spanish Tavern	**Mountainside**	22
Trattoria Med.	**Bedminster**	24
Treno	**Westmont**	-

FIREPLACES

Adega Grill	**Newark**	22
Z Amanda's	**Hoboken**	26
Anna's Kitchen	**Middletown**	23
Anton's/Swan	**Lambertville**	22
Arthur's Steak	**N Brunswick**	19
Z Avenue	**Long Branch**	22

Axia Taverna | **Tenafly**	23
Bareli's | **Secaucus**	23
Barrels | **Linwood**	21
🆉 Bernards Inn | **Bernardsville**	27
Berta's | **Wanaque**	22
Biagio's | **Paramus**	17
NEW Biddy O'Malley's | **Northvale**	-
Black Forest Inn | **Stanhope**	23
Black Horse | **Mendham**	18
Black Trumpet | **Spring Lake**	24
Blue Pig | **Cape May**	21
Blvd. Five 72 | **Kenilworth**	25
Braddock's | **Medford**	19
Bruschetta | **Fairfield**	21
Cabin | **Howell**	18
Casona | **Collingswood**	22
🆉 Catherine Lombardi | **New Bruns.**	24
Char | **Raritan**	22
Chickie's/Pete's | **Egg Harbor Twp**	17
Chophouse | **Gibbsboro**	23
Ciao | **Basking Ridge**	21
Clydz | **New Bruns.**	22
Crab's Claw Inn | **Lavallette**	18
Crab Trap | **Somers Point**	21
Cranbury Inn | **Cranbury**	14
Da Filippo's | **Somerville**	24
Dauphin | **Asbury Pk**	22
🆉 David Burke | **Rumson**	25
Delicious Hts. | **Berkeley Hts**	18
Dimora | **Norwood**	24
Dino's | **Harrington Pk**	22
🆉 Ebbitt Room | **Cape May**	26
🆉 Eno Terra | **Kingston**	24
Esty St. | **Park Ridge**	25
Filomena Italiana | **Clementon**	25
Filomena Lake. | **Deptford**	23
Filomena Rustica | **W Berlin**	18
Fire/Oak | **Montvale**	19
🆉 Gables | **Beach Haven**	24
Giumarello | **Westmont**	25
Gladstone | **Gladstone**	21
Grain House | **Basking Ridge**	19
🆉 Grand Cafe | **Morristown**	25
🆉 Grato | **Morris Plains**	22
Harvest Bistro | **Closter**	21
Harvest Moon | **Ringoes**	25

High St. Grill | **Mt Holly**	20
Ho-Ho-Kus Inn | **Ho-Ho-Kus**	21
Huntley Taverne | **Summit**	22
NEW Il Cinghiale | **Little Ferry**	-
Il Michelangelo | **Boonton**	20
Inn at Millrace Pond Restaurant | **Hope**	23
Inn/Sugar Hill | **Mays Landing**	18
Inn of the Hawke Restaurant | **Lambertville**	20
Ivy Inn | **Hasbrouck Hts**	22
NEW Keg/Kitchen | **Westmont**	-
La Campagne | **Cherry Hill**	23
Library IV | **Williamstown**	-
Light Horse | **Jersey City**	22
Lithos | **Livingston**	-
Luciano's | **Rahway**	24
Mad Batter | **Cape May**	23
Main St. | **Princeton**	19
Mastoris | **Bordentown**	19
McLoone's | **multi.**	17
Meyersville Inn | **Gillette**	19
🆉 Milford Oyster | **Milford**	27
Mister C's/Bistro | **Allenhurst**	18
Mohawk House | **Sparta**	22
🆉 Molly Pitcher Inn Restaurant | **Red Bank**	22
Montville Inn | **Montville**	22
Nauvoo Grill | **Fair Haven**	18
Nero's Grille | **Livingston**	18
🆉 Ninety Acres | **Peapack**	25
NEW Pairings | **Cranford**	-
Park Ave. B&G | **Union City**	18
NEW Park West | **Ridgewood**	-
Perryville Inn | **Union Twp**	26
🆉 Peter Shields | **Cape May**	26
Pheasants Landing | **Hillsborough**	15
P.J. Whelihan's | **Medford Lakes**	17
Plantation | **Harvey Cedars**	18
🆉 Pluckemin Inn | **Bedminster**	26
Portobello | **Oakland**	19
Pub | **Pennsauken**	19
🆉 Ram's Head Inn | **Galloway**	24
🆉 Rat's | **Hamilton**	24
Redstone | **Marlton**	21
Remington's | **Manasquan**	21
🆉 River Palm | **Mahwah**	25
Roberto's | **Beach Haven**	21

Rocky Hill Inn | **Rocky Hill**	17
Sallee Tee's | **Monmouth Bch**	18
Salt Creek | **Princeton**	19
Samdan | **Cresskill**	21
Sanzari's | **New Milford**	22
Scarborough Fair | **Sea Girt**	23
NEW Sear House | **Closter**	-
☑ Serenade | **Chatham**	27
Sergeantsville Inn | **Sergeantsville**	24
Settebello | **Morristown**	20
Shanghai Jazz | **Madison**	22
Shipwreck Point | **Pt. Pleas. Bch**	-
Shogun | **Kendall Pk**	21
Silk Road | **Warren**	23
Sirena | **Long Branch**	23
Smithville Inn | **Smithville**	20
Sofia | **Margate**	23
Solaia | **Englewood**	17
Sol-Mar | **Newark**	26
Stage House | **Scotch Plains**	20
☑ Stage Left | **New Bruns.**	27
Steve/Cookie's | **Margate**	25
☑ Stone House | **Warren**	22
Sushi Lounge | **Totowa**	22
Tabor Rd. | **Morris Plains**	21
Grenville | **Bay Hd.**	17
3 West | **Basking Ridge**	23
Trap Rock | **Berkeley Hts**	21
Undici | **Rumson**	22
Union Park | **Cape May**	25
Walpack Inn | **Wallpack**	20
☑ Washington Inn | **Cape May**	28
Windansea | **Highlands**	17
Wine Bar | **Atlantic Highlands**	22
Wolfgang Puck | **A.C.**	23
Yankee Doodle | **Princeton**	13

GREEN/LOCAL/ ORGANIC

Aamantran | **Toms River**	21
Aangan | **Freehold Twp**	23
Akbar | **Edison**	20
Alice's | **Lake Hopatcong**	21
Alps Bistro | **Allentown**	-
Amarone | **Teaneck**	21
☑ Andre's | **Newton**	27
Arturo's | **Midland Pk**	23
☑ A Toute Heure | **Cranford**	26
Bahrs Landing | **Highlands**	17

Baja | **Hoboken**	18
Bella Sogno | **Bradley Bch**	21
☑ Bernards Inn | **Bernardsville**	27
Berta's | **Wanaque**	22
Bibi'z | **Westwood**	-
Bistro 55 | **Rochelle Pk**	19
Bistro/Red Bank | **Red Bank**	21
Bistro/Marino | **Collingswood**	22
Bistro Olé | **Asbury Pk**	23
NEW Blue Morel | **Morristown**	-
Blvd. Five 72 | **Kenilworth**	25
Brothers Moon | **Hopewell**	23
Bruschetta | **Fairfield**	21
Cafe Arugula | **S Orange**	21
☑ Cafe Madison | **Riverside**	22
Cafe Metro | **Denville**	22
☑ Cafe Panache | **Ramsey**	27
Capt'n Ed's | **Pt. Pleas.**	20
☑ Catherine Lombardi | **New Bruns.**	24
☑ Chakra | **Paramus**	20
Circa | **High Bridge**	17
Clydz | **New Bruns.**	22
Copper Fish | **W Cape May**	20
Corso 98 | **Montclair**	22
Daddy O | **Long Beach**	19
Dimora | **Norwood**	24
Dream Cuisine | **Cherry Hill**	27
Due Mari | **New Bruns.**	26
Elevation Burg. | **multi.**	19
☑ Eno Terra | **Kingston**	24
NEW 5 Seasons | **Ridgewood**	-
☑ Frog/Peach | **New Bruns.**	26
☑ Gables | **Beach Haven**	24
Gazelle Café | **Ridgewood**	23
☑ Highlawn Pavilion | **W Orange**	25
Ho-Ho-Kus Inn | **Ho-Ho-Kus**	21
Hummus Elite | **Englewood**	21
Inlet Café | **Highlands**	20
Inn at Millrace Pond Restaurant | **Hope**	23
Java Moon | **Jackson**	22
Kaya's | **Belmar**	24
Kevin's Thyme | **Ho-Ho-Kus**	23
Le Fandy | **Fair Haven**	25
Luke Palladino | **Northfield**	26
Mad Batter | **Cape May**	23
Maritime Parc | **Jersey City**	-
☑ Mattar's Bistro | **Allamuchy**	24

Matt's/Rooster | **Flemington**	26
Meyersville Inn | **Gillette**	19
Mie Thai | **Woodbridge**	24
Nero's Grille | **Livingston**	18
☑ Ninety Acres | **Peapack**	25
One 53 | **Rocky Hill**	23
NEW Pairings | **Cranford**	-
☑ Park/Orchard | **E Rutherford**	23
Park Ave. B&G | **Union City**	18
Peacock Inn Restaurant | **Princeton**	26
☑ Picnic | **Fair Lawn**	27
☑ Rat's | **Hamilton**	24
Red | **Red Bank**	21
Rest. L | **Allendale**	18
☑ Rest. Latour | **Hamburg**	27
Robin's Nest | **Mt Holly**	22
☑ Sapori | **Collingswood**	28
☑ Serenade | **Chatham**	27
Sergeantsville Inn | **Sergeantsville**	24
Ship Inn | **Milford**	17
Soho 33 | **Madison**	18
Sophie's | **Somerset**	24
Spargo's | **Manalapan**	23
☑ Stage Left | **New Bruns.**	27
Stella Marina | **Asbury Pk**	23
NEW St. Eve's | **Ho-Ho-Kus**	-
☑ Stone House | **Warren**	22
Sushi Lounge | **Totowa**	22
3 West | **Basking Ridge**	23
Tim McLoone's | **Asbury Pk**	20
Tisha's | **Cape May**	25
Tre Piani | **Princeton**	20
Uproot | **Warren**	22
Za | **Pennington**	23

HISTORIC PLACES

(Year opened; * building)

1697 | Lincroft Inn* | **Lincroft**	19
1714 | Eno Terra* | **Kingston**	24
1720 | Barnsboro Inn* | **Sewell**	22
1734 | Sergeantsville Inn* | **Sergeantsville**	24
1737 | Stage House* | **Scotch Plains**	20
1742 | Black Horse* | **Mendham**	18
1750 | Cranbury Inn* | **Cranbury**	14
1768 | Grain House* | **Basking Ridge**	19

1770 | Inn at Millrace Pond Restaurant* | **Hope**	23
1770 | Montville Inn* | **Montville**	22
1770 | Rocky Hill Inn* | **Rocky Hill**	17
1785 | Meyersville Inn* | **Gillette**	19
1787 | Smithville Inn* | **Smithville**	20
1796 | Ho-Ho-Kus Inn* | **Ho-Ho-Kus**	21
1799 | Saddle River Inn* | **Saddle River**	28
1800 | Bell's Mansion* | **Stanhope**	15
1800 | Tewksbury Inn* | **Oldwick**	23
1805 | Frenchtown Inn* | **Frenchtown**	23
1811 | Harvest Moon* | **Ringoes**	25
1812 | Perryville Inn* | **Union Twp**	26
1813 | Farnsworth House* | **Bordentown**	22
1818 | Stony Hill Inn* | **Hackensack**	22
1823 | Braddock's* | **Medford**	19
1840 | Inn of the Hawke Restaurant* | **Lambertville**	20
1840 | Milford Oyster* | **Milford**	27
1840 | Washington Inn* | **Cape May**	28
1841 | La Campagne* | **Cherry Hill**	23
1847 | Gladstone* | **Gladstone**	21
1850 | David Burke* | **Rumson**	25
1850 | Delta's* | **New Bruns.**	22
1850 | Light Horse* | **Jersey City**	22
1851 | National Hotel Rest.* | **Frenchtown**	-
1856 | High St. Grill* | **Mt Holly**	20
1856 | Il Michelangelo* | **Boonton**	20
1857 | Old Bay* | **New Bruns.**	19
1858 | Trinity* | **Keyport**	25
1859 | Alps Bistro* | **Allentown**	-
1860 | Ship Inn* | **Milford**	17
1862 | Park Ave. B&G* | **Union City**	18
1863 | Lambertville Station* | **Lambertville**	17

SPECIAL FEATURES

1864 | Renault Winery* | Egg Harbor — 21

1868 | Rick's* | Lambertville — 21

1870 | Edward's Steak* | Jersey City — 23

1870 | Ivy Inn* | Hasbrouck Hts — 22

1879 | Ebbitt Room* | Cape May — 26

1880 | Claude's* | N Wildwood — 27

1880 | 410 Bank St.* | Cape May — 26

1880 | Moonstruck* | Asbury Pk — 25

1882 | Mad Batter* | Cape May — 23

1890 | Gables* | Beach Haven — 24

1890 | Matt's/Rooster* | Flemington — 26

1890 | Red* | Red Bank — 21

1890 | Robin's Nest* | Mt Holly — 22

1890 | Scarborough Fair* | Sea Girt — 23

1890 | Grenville* | Bay Hd. — 17

1890 | Whispers* | Spring Lake — 27

1892 | Black Trumpet* | Spring Lake — 24

1895 | Amanda's* | Hoboken — 26

1895 | Elysian Café* | Hoboken — 21

1897 | Dock's | A.C. — 26

1900 | Athenian Gdn.* | Galloway Twp — 23

1900 | Elements* | Haddon Hts — 23

1903 | Columbia Inn* | Montville — 21

1905 | Casona* | Collingswood — 22

1906 | Onieal's* | Hoboken — 20

1909 | Highlawn Pavilion* | W Orange — 25

1912 | Hobby's | Newark — 24

1912 | Ninety Acres* | Peapack — 25

1917 | Bahrs Landing | Highlands — 17

1920 | Cafe Italiano* | Englewood Cliffs — 19

1920 | Harvey Cedars* | Harvey Cedars — 23

1920 | Ugly Mug* | Cape May — 15

1921 | Chef Vola's | A.C. — 26

1921 | Federici's | Freehold — 21

1922 | Lobster House | Cape May — 20

1924 | Stage Left* | New Bruns. — 27

1925 | Berkeley | S Seaside Pk — 20

1926 | Iberia | Newark — 20

1926 | Spike's | Pt. Pleas. Bch — 22

1927 | Berta's* | Wanaque — 22

1927 | Tony's Baltimore Grill | A.C. — 18

1928 | Molly Pitcher Inn Restaurant* | Red Bank — 22

1928 | Rutt's Hut | Clifton — 21

1929 | Picnic | Fair Lawn — 27

1930 | Anthony's* | Haddon Hts — 24

1930 | Blueplate* | Mullica Hill — ‒

1930 | Clementine's* | Avon-by-Sea — 23

1930 | Pheasants Landing* | Hillsborough — 15

1930 | Tito's* | Morristown — 20

1932 | Hiram's | Fort Lee — 21

1932 | Spanish Tavern | Newark — 22

1933 | Sammy's | Mendham — 23

1935 | Angelo's | A.C. — 21

1936 | Helmers' | Hoboken — 19

1936 | McGovern's | Newark — 18

1936 | Reservoir | Boonton — 23

1936 | Steve/Cookie's* | Margate — 25

1936 | Steve's Sizzling | Carlstadt — ‒

1937 | Kinchley's | Ramsey — 21

1937 | Yankee Doodle | Princeton — 13

1938 | Bell's Tavern | Lambertville — 20

1938 | DeLorenzo's Pizza | Trenton — 24

1938 | Mill/Spring Lake Hts. | Spring Lake Hts — 21

1938 | Solari's | Hackensack — 19

1939 | Holsten's | Bloomfield — 16

1939 | Homestead Inn | Trenton — 22

1939 | White Manna* | Hackensack — 23

1940 | Blackbird* | Collingswood — 24

1940 | La Spiaggia* | Ship Bottom — 24

1941 | Conte's | Princeton — 25

1941 | Walpack Inn* | Wallpack — 20

1942 | Tuzzio's* | Long Branch — 20

1944 | Hot Dog Johnny's | Buttzville — 21

1946 | White House* | A.C. — 26

1946 | White Mana | Jersey City — 17

1947 | Vic's | Bradley Bch — 21

1948 | Luigi's | Ridgefield Pk — ‒

1948 | Tick Tock* | **Clifton**	18
1950 | Main St.* | **Princeton**	19
1951 | Pub | **Pennsauken**	19
1951 | Rod's Steak | **Morristown**	22
1956 | Arthur's Tavern | **Morris Plains**	20
1956 | Eppes Essen | **Livingston**	20
1956 | Manor | **W Orange**	24
1957 | Pete/Elda's | **Neptune City**	22
1959 | Mustache Bill's | **Barnegat Light**	24
1959 | Renato's | **Jersey City**	22
1960 | Hunan Spring* | **Springfield**	18
1960 | Rosie's* | **Randolph**	21
1961 | Mastoris | **Bordentown**	19

HOTEL DINING

Atlantic City Hilton	
Simon Prime | **A.C.**	-
Berkeley Hotel	
Dauphin | **Asbury Pk**	22
Best Western Fairfield	
Cucina Calandra | **Fairfield**	21
Best Western Robert Treat	
Maize | **Newark**	17
Best Western Westfield	
☑ Chez Catherine | **Westfield**	26
Blue Bay Inn	
Copper Canyon | **Atlantic Highlands**	23
Borgata Hotel, Casino & Spa	
Bobby Flay | **A.C.**	25
Fornelletto | **A.C.**	24
☑ Izakaya | **A.C.**	23
☑ Old Homestead | **A.C.**	27
☑ SeaBlue | **A.C.**	26
Tony Luke's | **A.C.**	20
Wolfgang Puck | **A.C.**	23
Bridgewater Marriott	
Tbones Tuscan Steakhouse | **Bridgewater**	22
Caesars on the Boardwalk	
Mia | **A.C.**	26
Carroll Villa Hotel	
Mad Batter | **Cape May**	23
Chelsea Hotel	
Chelsea Prime | **A.C.**	24
Teplitzky's | **A.C.**	18

Congress Hall Hotel	
Blue Pig | **Cape May**	21
Courtyard by Marriott	
Fire/Oak | **Montvale**	19
Crystal Springs Resort	
☑ Rest. Latour | **Hamburg**	27
Daddy O Hotel	
Daddy O | **Long Beach**	19
DoubleTree Mount Laurel	
GG's | **Mt Laurel**	25
Gables Inn	
☑ Gables | **Beach Haven**	24
Golden Nugget Hotel & Casino	
☑ Chart House | **A.C.**	21
Grand Summit Hotel	
Hat Tavern | **Summit**	-
Grand Victorian Hotel	
Black Trumpet | **Spring Lake**	24
Grenville Hotel	
Grenville | **Bay Hd.**	17
Hampton Inn & Suites	
Calandra's/Grill | **Fairfield**	21
Harrah's	
NEW Dos Caminos | **A.C.**	-
Luke Palladino | **A.C.**	26
McCormick/Schmick | **A.C.**	20
Heldrich Hotel	
NEW Daryl | **New Bruns.**	-
Hewitt Wellington Hotel	
☑ Whispers | **Spring Lake**	27
Hilton Parsippany	
☑ Ruth's Chris | **Parsippany**	25
Hyatt Regency Jersey City	
Vu | **Jersey City**	16
Inn at Millrace Pond	
Inn at Millrace Pond Restaurant | **Hope**	23
Lambertville House Hotel	
Caffe Galleria | **Lambertville**	21
Macomber, Hotel	
Union Park | **Cape May**	25
Madison Hotel	
NEW GK's Red Dog | **Morristown**	-
Rod's Steak | **Morristown**	22
Molly Pitcher Inn	
☑ Molly Pitcher Inn Restaurant | **Red Bank**	22

Nassau Inn
   Yankee Doodle | **Princeton**   13

National Hotel
   National Hotel Rest. | –
   Frenchtown

Natirar Resort & Spa
   Z Ninety Acres | **Peapack**   25

Ocean Club Condos
   Girasole | **A.C.**   26

Olde Mill Inn
   Grain House | **Basking Ridge**   19

Peacock Inn
   Peacock Inn Restaurant | 26
   Princeton

Quarter at the Tropicana
   Carmine's | **A.C.**   21
   Cuba Libre | **A.C.**   21
   Z P.F. Chang's | **A.C.**   20
   Z Red Square | **A.C.**   21
   Palm | **A.C.**   25

Resorts Casino & Hotel
   Z Capriccio | **A.C.**   25
   Gallagher's | **A.C.**   22

Revel
   NEW Breakfast Room | **A.C.**   –
   NEW Mussel Bar | **A.C.**   –
   NEW O Bistro | **A.C.**   –

Sheraton Atlantic City
   Tun Tavern | **A.C.**   18

Showboat Casino
   NEW Scarduzio's | **A.C.**   –

Tropicana Casino & Resort
   Fin | **A.C.**   25

Trump Taj Mahal
   Z Il Mulino | **A.C.**   27

Virginia Hotel
   Z Ebbitt Room | **Cape May**   26

Westin Governor Morris
   NEW Blue Morel | **Morristown**   –

Westin Jersey City Newport
   Fire/Oak | **Jersey City**   19

Westminster Hotel
   Strip House | **Livingston**   25

W Hotel
   Zylo | **Hoboken**   21

JACKET REQUIRED

Z Manor | **W Orange**   24
Z Molly Pitcher Inn Restaurant | 22
Red Bank

LATE DINING

(Weekday closing hour)

Barnacle Bill's | 2 AM | **Rumson**   22
Benny Tudino's | 12:45 AM | 22
Hoboken
Bibi'z | 12 AM | **Westwood**   –
NEW Blind Boar | 2 AM | –
Norwood
Brickwall Tavern | 1 AM | 18
Asbury Pk
Chickie's/Pete's | varies | **multi.**   17
Clydz | 1:30 AM | **New Bruns.**   22
Danny's | 1 AM | **Red Bank**   20
Dong Bang Grill | 12 AM | 22
Fort Lee
Farnsworth House | varies | 22
Bordentown
Gam Mee Ok | 24 hrs. | **Fort Lee**   21
Gusto Grill | 2 AM | **E Brunswick**   19
Ibby's | 12 AM | **Jersey City**   22
Iberia | 1:30 AM | **Newark**   20
Irish Pub | 24 hrs. | **A.C.**   18
Iron Hill Brewery | 1 AM | 20
Maple Shade
Java Moon | 12 AM | **Newark**   22
NEW Keg/Kitchen | 2 AM | –
Westmont
NEW Khloe Bistrot | 12 AM | –
Fort Lee
Kinchley's | 12 AM | **Ramsey**   21
LITM | varies | **Jersey City**   14
Lucky Bones | 1 AM | **Cape May**   20
Mastoris | 1 AM | **Bordentown**   19
Z Mattar's Bistro | 12 AM | 24
Allamuchy
McGovern's | 12 AM | **Newark**   18
NEW Mussel Bar | varies | **A.C.**   –
NEW O Bistro | 1 AM | **A.C.**   –
Onieal's | varies | **Hoboken**   20
Orange Squirrel | 1 AM | 22
Bloomfield
Pete/Elda's | 12 AM | 22
Neptune City
NEW Pilsener Haus | varies | –
Hoboken
P.J. Whelihan's | varies | **multi.**   17
Renato's | 12 AM | **Jersey City**   22
Sage Diner | 1 AM | **Mt Laurel**   14
Santorini | 12 AM | **Fort Lee**   21
Skylark | 1 AM | **Edison**   22
Sol-Mar | 1 AM | **Newark**   26

So Moon Nan Jip | 3 AM | **Palisades Pk** | 24

Surf Taco | 12 AM | **Jackson** | 21

WindMill | varies | **multi.** | 19

Tick Tock | 24 hrs. | **Clifton** | 18

Tony Luke's | varies | **multi.** | 20

Tony's Baltimore Grill | 3 AM | **A.C.** | 18

Trinity | varies | **Hoboken** | 18

Tun Tavern | varies | **A.C.** | 18

Ugly Mug | 2 AM | **Cape May** | 15

Ventura's | 1 AM | **Margate** | 18

Victor's Pub | varies | **Camden** | ‑

Vu | varies | **Jersey City** | 16

White Mana | 24 hrs. | **Jersey City** | 17

White Manna | 12 AM | **Hackensack** | 23

Zen Zen | 12 AM | **Fairview** | 21

MEET FOR A DRINK

Adega Grill | **Newark** | 22

Amelia's | **Jersey City** | 19

NEW Aqua Blu | **Toms River** | ‑

Arturo's | **Midland Pk** | 23

Assembly | **Englewood Cliffs** | 16

Atlantic B&G | **S Seaside Pk** | 26

Z Avenue | **Long Branch** | 22

Bahama Breeze | **Wayne** | 17

Bar Cara | **Bloomfield** | 20

Barnacle Bill's | **Rumson** | 22

Basil T's | **Red Bank** | 20

Bell's Tavern | **Lambertville** | 20

Biagio's | **Paramus** | 17

Bibi'z | **Westwood** | ‑

Bicycle Club | **Englewood Cliffs** | 14

NEW Biddy O'Malley's | **Northvale** | ‑

Bin 14 | **Hoboken** | 22

Bistro 55 | **Rochelle Pk** | 19

Black Horse | **Mendham** | 18

NEW Blind Boar | **Norwood** | ‑

NEW Blue Morel | **Morristown** | ‑

Blue Pig | **Cape May** | 21

Bonefish Grill | **Deptford** | 21

Bottagra | **Hawthorne** | 20

Brass Rail | **Hoboken** | 19

Brickwall Tavern | **Asbury Pk** | 18

NEW Bushido | **Cliffside Pk** | ‑

Cassie's | **Englewood** | 18

Cenzino | **Oakland** | 24

Z Chakra | **Paramus** | 20

Charley's | **Long Branch** | 18

Char | **Raritan** | 22

Chelsea Prime | **A.C.** | 24

Chickie's/Pete's | **Bordentown** | 17

Chilangos | **Highlands** | 21

Circa | **High Bridge** | 17

Clydz | **New Bruns.** | 22

Continental | **A.C.** | 23

Copper Canyon | **Atlantic Highlands** | 23

Crab's Claw Inn | **Lavallette** | 18

NEW Cubacan | **Asbury Pk** | ‑

Cuba Libre | **A.C.** | 21

Cucharamama | **Hoboken** | 26

Daddy O | **Long Beach** | 19

Danny's | **Red Bank** | 20

NEW Daryl | **New Bruns.** | ‑

Z David Burke | **Rumson** | 25

Delicious Hts. | **Berkeley Hts** | 18

Z Dino/Harry's | **Hoboken** | 27

NEW Dos Caminos | **A.C.** | ‑

Due Mari | **New Bruns.** | 26

Edward's Steak | **Jersey City** | 23

Egan/Sons | **W Orange** | 19

Elysian Café | **Hoboken** | 21

Espo's | **Raritan** | 23

Fire/Oak | **Jersey City** | 19

NEW Firecreek | **Voorhees** | ‑

NEW GK's Red Dog | **Morristown** | ‑

Gladstone | **Gladstone** | 21

Hat Tavern | **Summit** | ‑

Helmers' | **Hoboken** | 19

Hoboken B&G | **Hoboken** | 19

Z Hotoke | **New Bruns.** | 20

Huntley Taverne | **Summit** | 22

Inlet Café | **Highlands** | 20

Inn of the Hawke Restaurant | **Lambertville** | 20

Irish Pub | **A.C.** | 18

Iron Hill Brewery | **Maple Shade** | 20

Z Izakaya | **A.C.** | 23

NEW Keg/Kitchen | **Westmont** | ‑

Langosta | **Asbury Pk** | 22

Light Horse | **Jersey City** | 22

LITM | **Jersey City** | 14

Locale | **Closter** | 20

Lola's | **Hoboken** | 18

Los Amigos | **multi.** | 23

Luciano's | **Rahway**	24
Madison B&G | **Hoboken**	19
Marco/Pepe | **Jersey City**	22
Maritime Parc | **Jersey City**	-
Martini Bistro | **Millburn**	19
Martini 494 | **Newark**	-
Martino's | **Somerville**	22
McCormick/Schmick | **Cherry Hill**	20
McLoone's | **Sea Bright**	17
Mediterra | **Princeton**	20
Metropolitan Cafe | **Freehold**	21
Mia | **A.C.**	26
Mister C's/Bistro | **Allenhurst**	18
NEW MK Valencia | **Ridgefield Pk**	-
Mohawk House | **Sparta**	22
Mompou | **Newark**	23
NEW MoonShine | **Millburn**	-
NEW Mussel Bar | **A.C.**	-
National Hotel Rest. | **Frenchtown**	-
NEW Nico | **Newark**	-
NEW O Bistro | **A.C.**	-
Oddfellows | **Hoboken**	18
Old Bay | **New Bruns.**	19
Old Man Rafferty's | **multi.**	18
One 53 | **Rocky Hill**	23
Onieal's | **Hoboken**	20
Orange Squirrel | **Bloomfield**	22
NEW Osteria Morini | **Bernardsville**	-
Park Ave. B&G | **Union City**	18
NEW Park West | **Ridgewood**	-
NEW Pilsener Haus | **Hoboken**	-
Pine Tavern | **Old Bridge**	20
P.J. Whelihan's | **multi.**	17
Plantation | **Harvey Cedars**	18
Z Pluckemin Inn | **Bedminster**	26
Z Porto Leggero | **Jersey City**	26
Quays | **Hoboken**	18
Quiet Man | **Dover**	22
Rare | **Little Falls**	24
Redstone | **Marlton**	21
Rocky Hill Inn | **Rocky Hill**	17
Rod's Olde Irish | **Sea Girt**	18
Roots Steak | **Summit**	26
Rumba Cubana/Cafe | **N Bergen**	23
Sallee Tee's | **Monmouth Bch**	18
Salt Creek | **Rumson**	19
NEW Sear House | **Closter**	-
Settimo Cielo | **Trenton**	23
Ship Inn | **Milford**	17
Sirena | **Long Branch**	23
Sofia | **Margate**	23
Son Cubano | **W New York**	-
Z Stage Left | **New Bruns.**	27
Stella Marina | **Asbury Pk**	23
Z Stone House | **Warren**	22
Sushi Lounge | **multi.**	22
Tabor Rd. | **Morris Plains**	21
Teak | **Red Bank**	21
Terra Nova | **Sewell**	-
Tewksbury Inn | **Oldwick**	23
Tortilla Press | **Merchantville**	24
Toscano | **Bordentown**	22
Trap Rock | **Berkeley Hts**	21
Treno | **Westmont**	-
Trinity | **Keyport**	25
Trinity | **Hoboken**	18
Trinity/Pope | **Asbury Pk**	21
Triumph Brew. | **Princeton**	16
Tun Tavern | **A.C.**	18
27 Mix | **Newark**	21
Ugly Mug | **Cape May**	15
Undici | **Rumson**	22
Uproot | **Warren**	22
NEW Upstairs | **Upper Montclair**	-
NEW Ursino | **Union**	-
Verve | **Somerville**	23
Victor's Pub | **Camden**	-
Vine | **Basking Ridge**	23
Vu | **Jersey City**	16
Z Waterside | **N Bergen**	21
Wicked Wolf | **Hoboken**	19
Windansea | **Highlands**	17
Wine Bar | **Atlantic Highlands**	22
Witherspoon | **Princeton**	21
Wolfgang Puck | **A.C.**	23
Yankee Doodle | **Princeton**	13

MICROBREWERIES

Basil T's | **Red Bank**	20
Egan/Sons | **multi.**	19
Iron Hill Brewery | **Maple Shade**	20
Ship Inn | **Milford**	17
Trap Rock | **Berkeley Hts**	21
Triumph Brew. | **Princeton**	16
Tun Tavern | **A.C.**	18

OFFBEAT

Aangan | **Freehold Twp**	23
NEW Adara | **Montclair**	-
Ali Baba | **Hoboken**	19
Ariel's | **Englewood**	20
Augustino's | **Hoboken**	26
Z Baumgart's | **multi.**	19
Belmont Tavern | **Belleville**	23
Beyti Kebab | **Union City**	21
NEW Blind Boar | **Norwood**	-
Blue Danube | **Trenton**	22
NEW Brick Lane Curry | **multi.**	-
NEW Bushido | **Cliffside Pk**	-
Z Chef Vola's | **A.C.**	26
Clydz | **New Bruns.**	22
Cuban Pete's | **Montclair**	19
DiPalma Brothers | **N Bergen**	21
El Mesón Café | **Freehold**	24
Fedora Café | **Lawrenceville**	20
Flirt Sushi | **Allendale**	23
Garlic Rose | **multi.**	20
Hummus Elite | **Englewood**	21
NEW JBJ Soul Kitchen | **Red Bank**	-
Kairo | **New Bruns.**	-
NEW Khloe Bistrot | **Fort Lee**	-
Kinara | **Edgewater**	22
LITM | **Jersey City**	14
Magic Pot | **Edgewater**	18
Makeda | **New Bruns.**	24
Manon | **Lambertville**	25
Meemah | **Edison**	25
Mehndi | **Morristown**	24
Mesob | **Montclair**	24
Minado | **multi.**	20
Ming | **Edison**	24
Namaskaar | **Englewood**	20
Negeen | **Summit**	18
Nifty Fifty's | **Turnersville**	19
Oddfellows | **Hoboken**	18
Oh! Calamares | **Kearny**	-
Orange Squirrel | **Bloomfield**	22
Pamir | **Morristown**	22
Penang | **Edison**	22
Pop Shop | **Collingswood**	20
Prime/Beyond | **Fort Lee**	-
Pub | **Pennsauken**	19
Risotto House | **Rutherford**	23
Royal Warsaw | **Elmwood Pk**	23
Rumba Cubana/Cafe | **N Bergen**	23

Sammy's | **Mendham**	23
Satis | **Jersey City**	-
Shanghai Jazz | **Madison**	22
Skylark | **Edison**	22
Sublime | **Gladstone**	20
Sushi X | **Ridgewood**	21
Tim Schafer's | **Morristown**	23
Trinity | **Keyport**	25
NEW Upstairs | **Upper Montclair**	-
Vincentown Diner | **Vincentown**	20

OUTDOOR DINING

(G=garden; P=patio; S=sidewalk; T=terrace)

Alice's | T | **Lake Hopatcong**	21
Amelia's | S | **Jersey City**	19
Anthony David's | S | **Hoboken**	25
NEW Aqua Blu | P | **Toms River**	-
Arturo's | P | **Maplewood**	24
Atlantic B&G | P | **S Seaside Pk**	26
Z Avenue | T | **Long Branch**	22
Avon Pavilion | T | **Avon-by-Sea**	19
Axelsson's | G | **Cape May**	23
NEW Baia | T | **Somers Point**	-
Bamboo Leaf | S | **Bradley Bch**	22
Bell's Mansion | G | **Stanhope**	15
Z Bernards Inn | T | **Bernardsville**	27
Bin 14 | S | **Hoboken**	22
Z Blue Point | P | **Princeton**	26
Bobby Chez | P | **Margate**	24
Brothers Moon | S | **Hopewell**	23
Café Gallery | T | **Burlington**	20
Z Cafe Matisse | G | **Rutherford**	27
Caffe Aldo | P | **Cherry Hill**	24
Cuban Pete's | P | **Montclair**	19
Cucharamama | S | **Hoboken**	26
Danny's | S | **Red Bank**	20
Diving Horse | P | **Avalon**	24
Elysian Café | S | **Hoboken**	21
NEW Firecreek | P, S | **Voorhees**	-
Frenchtown Inn | P | **Frenchtown**	23
Z Frog/Peach | P | **New Bruns.**	26
Z Gables | P | **Beach Haven**	24
Girasole | P | **A.C.**	26
Girasole | P | **Bound Brook**	26
Giumarello | P | **Westmont**	25
Z Grand Cafe | P | **Morristown**	25
Hamilton's | P | **Lambertville**	26

Z Highlawn Pavilion | P | **W Orange** — 25

Ho-Ho-Kus Inn | P | **Ho-Ho-Kus** — 21

India/Hudson | S | **Hoboken** — 21

Inn of the Hawke Restaurant | P | **Lambertville** — 20

Kitchen Consigliere | P | **Collingswood** — -

Klein's | P, T | **Belmar** — 19

La Campagne | P | **Cherry Hill** — 23

NEW La Fontana Coast | P | **Sea Isle City** — -

Z Latour | S | **Ridgewood** — 26

Le Jardin | P, T | **Edgewater** — 20

Z Le Rendez-Vous | S | **Kenilworth** — 27

Liberty House | T | **Jersey City** — 20

Lilly's/Canal | P | **Lambertville** — 21

Maritime Parc | P | **Jersey City** — -

Matisse | T | **Belmar** — 22

Mexican Food | P | **Marlton** — 20

Mill/Spring Lake Hts. | T | **Spring Lake Hts** — 21

Z Moonstruck | T | **Asbury Pk** — 25

NEW Nico | S | **Newark** — -

Z Ninety Acres | G, P | **Peapack** — 25

Nomad Pizza | S | **Hopewell** — 26

Perryville Inn | P | **Union Twp** — 26

Z Peter Shields | T | **Cape May** — 26

NEW Pilsener Haus | G, P | **Hoboken** — -

Quays | S | **Hoboken** — 18

Z Rat's | T | **Hamilton** — 24

Z Raven/Peach | P | **Fair Haven** — 24

Rebecca's | P | **Edgewater** — 23

Robin's Nest | P, T | **Mt Holly** — 22

Robongi | S | **Hoboken** — 24

Z Ruth's Chris | S | **Weehawken** — 25

Santorini | P | **Fort Lee** — 21

Shipwreck Grill | T | **Brielle** — 24

Sirena | T | **Long Branch** — 23

Sofia | G, P, T | **Margate** — 23

Stage House | G | **Scotch Plains** — 20

Z Stage Left | P | **New Bruns.** — 27

Stella Marina | P | **Asbury Pk** — 23

Z Stone House | P | **Warren** — 22

Tisha's | P | **Cape May** — 25

Trinity | S | **Hoboken** — 18

Varka | P | **Ramsey** — 26

Village Green | S | **Ridgewood** — 24

Z Waterside | P | **N Bergen** — 21

Windansea | T | **Highlands** — 17

Za | G, P | **Pennington** — 23

Zafra | P | **Hoboken** — 23

PEOPLE-WATCHING

Z Bernards Inn | **Bernardsville** — 27

Bicycle Club | **Englewood Cliffs** — 14

Bin 14 | **Hoboken** — 22

Bistro 55 | **Rochelle Pk** — 19

Bistro/Marino | **Collingswood** — 22

Bobby Flay | **A.C.** — 25

Brio | **Cherry Hill** — 19

Z Buddakan | **A.C.** — 26

Z Cafe Madison | **Riverside** — 22

Caffe Aldo | **Cherry Hill** — 24

Z Chart House | **Weehawken** — 21

Chickie's/Pete's | **Bordentown** — 17

Clydz | **New Bruns.** — 22

Continental | **A.C.** — 23

NEW Cubacan | **Asbury Pk** — -

Cuba Libre | **A.C.** — 21

Cucharamama | **Hoboken** — 26

Daddy O | **Long Beach** — 19

NEW Daryl | **New Bruns.** — -

Delta's | **New Bruns.** — 22

Z Dino/Harry's | **Hoboken** — 27

Dream Cuisine | **Cherry Hill** — 27

Eccola | **Parsippany** — 23

Egan/Sons | **W Orange** — 19

Elysian Café | **Hoboken** — 21

Fire/Oak | **multi.** — 19

NEW Firecreek | **Voorhees** — -

Grissini | **Englewood Cliffs** — 22

Hoboken B&G | **Hoboken** — 19

Z Hotoke | **New Bruns.** — 20

Huntley Taverne | **Summit** — 22

IndeBlue | **Collingswood** — 25

Kitchen Consigliere | **Collingswood** — -

Langosta | **Asbury Pk** — 22

Light Horse | **Jersey City** — 22

LITM | **Jersey City** — 14

Lu Nello | **Cedar Grove** — 25

Makeda | **New Bruns.** — 24

Marco/Pepe | **Jersey City** — 22

Martini Bistro | **Millburn** — 19

Martini 494 | **Newark** — -

McCormick/Schmick | **Cherry Hill** — 20

Mélange | **Haddonfield**	25
Mia | **A.C.**	26
NEW MK Valencia | **Ridgefield Pk**	-
Z Molly Pitcher Inn Restaurant | **Red Bank**	22
Mompou | **Newark**	23
NEW MoonShine | **Millburn**	-
NEW O Bistro | **A.C.**	-
NEW Osteria/Fiamma | **Ridgewood**	-
Park Ave. B&G | **Union City**	18
Peacock Inn Restaurant | **Princeton**	26
Plan B | **Asbury Pk**	24
Z Pluckemin Inn | **Bedminster**	26
Ponzio's | **Cherry Hill**	19
Pop Shop | **Collingswood**	20
Pub | **Pennsauken**	19
Quays | **Hoboken**	18
NEW Ralic's Steak | **Haddonfield**	-
Rumba Cubana/Cafe | **N Bergen**	23
Sabor | **N Bergen**	22
Salt Creek | **Rumson**	19
Sammy's | **Mendham**	23
Son Cubano | **W New York**	-
Tabor Rd. | **Morris Plains**	21
Tapas/Espana | **N Bergen**	22
Teak | **Red Bank**	21
Terra Nova | **Sewell**	-
3 West | **Basking Ridge**	23
Treno | **Westmont**	-
Trinity | **Hoboken**	18
27 Mix | **Newark**	21
Undici | **Rumson**	22
Victor's Pub | **Camden**	-
Wicked Wolf | **Hoboken**	19
Witherspoon | **Princeton**	21
Wolfgang Puck | **A.C.**	23
NEW Zeppoli | **Collingswood**	-

POWER SCENES

Z Basilico | **Millburn**	23
Z Bernards Inn | **Bernardsville**	27
Blackbird | **Collingswood**	24
NEW Blue Morel | **Morristown**	-
Bobby Flay | **A.C.**	25
Caffe Aldo | **Cherry Hill**	24
Casa Dante | **Jersey City**	24

Z Catherine Lombardi | **New Bruns.**	24
Z Chakra | **Paramus**	20
Z Chez Catherine | **Westfield**	26
Cuba Libre | **A.C.**	21
NEW Daryl | **New Bruns.**	-
Z David Burke | **Rumson**	25
Edward's Steak | **Jersey City**	23
Z Fascino | **Montclair**	26
NEW Firecreek | **Voorhees**	-
410 Bank St. | **Cape May**	26
Gallagher's | **A.C.**	22
Grain House | **Basking Ridge**	19
Z Grand Cafe | **Morristown**	25
Hamilton/Ward | **Paterson**	23
Z Il Mondo | **Madison**	26
McCormick/Schmick | **Cherry Hill**	20
McLoone's | **Sea Bright**	17
Z Morton's | **multi.**	25
NEW Nico | **Newark**	-
Z Ninety Acres | **Peapack**	25
Z Old Homestead | **A.C.**	27
Peacock Inn Restaurant | **Princeton**	26
Phillips Seafood | **A.C.**	20
Ponzio's | **Cherry Hill**	19
Z Porto Leggero | **Jersey City**	26
NEW Ralic's Steak | **Haddonfield**	-
Redstone | **Marlton**	21
Z Rest. Latour | **Hamburg**	27
Z Rist./Benito | **Union**	26
Roots Steak | **Summit**	26
Z Saddle River Inn | **Saddle River**	28
Z Scalini Fedeli | **Chatham**	27
Z SeaBlue | **A.C.**	26
Z Serenade | **Chatham**	27
Settimo Cielo | **Trenton**	23
Solari's | **Hackensack**	19
Stony Hill Inn | **Hackensack**	22
Undici | **Rumson**	22
Z Washington Inn | **Cape May**	28
William Douglas | **Cherry Hill**	25
Wolfgang Puck | **A.C.**	23

PRIVATE ROOMS

(Restaurants charge less at off times; call for capacity)

Alice's | **Lake Hopatcong**	21

🛛 Amanda's | **Hoboken**	26	
🛛 Andre's | **Newton**	27	
Antonia's | **N Bergen**	20	
Arturo's | **Midland Pk**	23	
Barone's/Villa Barone/Tuscan | **Moorestown**	22	
🛛 Bernards Inn | **Bernardsville**	27	
Bistro Olé | **Asbury Pk**	23	
Black Duck | **W Cape May**	26	
Black Forest Inn | **Stanhope**	23	
NEW Blue Morel | **Morristown**	-	
Blvd. Five 72 | **Kenilworth**	25	
🛛 Buddakan | **A.C.**	26	
🛛 Cafe Matisse | **Rutherford**	27	
🛛 Cafe Panache | **Ramsey**	27	
Caffe Aldo | **Cherry Hill**	24	
Cenzino | **Oakland**	24	
🛛 Chakra | **Paramus**	20	
Chelsea Prime | **A.C.**	24	
🛛 Chez Catherine | **Westfield**	26	
Chez Elena Wu | **Voorhees**	22	
Chophouse | **Gibbsboro**	23	
NEW Daryl | **New Bruns.**	-	
Dimora | **Norwood**	24	
Edward's Steak | **Jersey City**	23	
Charrito's/El Charro | **Weehawken**	22	
🛛 Elements | **Princeton**	26	
🛛 Eno Terra | **Kingston**	24	
🛛 Fascino | **Montclair**	26	
Fiorino | **Summit**	24	
Frenchtown Inn | **Frenchtown**	23	
🛛 Frog/Peach | **New Bruns.**	26	
🛛 Gables | **Beach Haven**	24	
Giumarello | **Westmont**	25	
🛛 Grand Cafe | **Morristown**	25	
Hamilton's | **Lambertville**	26	
Harvest Bistro | **Closter**	21	
🛛 Highlawn Pavilion | **W Orange**	25	
Ho-Ho-Kus Inn | **Ho-Ho-Kus**	21	
Iberia | **Newark**	20	
🛛 Il Capriccio | **Whippany**	25	
Il Villaggio | **Carlstadt**	24	
Inn at Millrace Pond Restaurant | **Hope**	23	
Le Jardin | **Edgewater**	20	
Liberty House | **Jersey City**	20	
Lithos | **Livingston**	-	

Luciano's | **Rahway**	24	
Madeleine's | **Northvale**	25	
🛛 Manor | **W Orange**	24	
Maritime Parc | **Jersey City**	-	
🛛 Mattar's Bistro | **Allamuchy**	24	
Mediterra | **Princeton**	20	
Mehndi | **Morristown**	24	
Montville Inn | **Montville**	22	
Nauvoo Grill | **Fair Haven**	18	
🛛 Nicholas | **Red Bank**	29	
NEW Nico | **Newark**	-	
🛛 Ninety Acres | **Peapack**	25	
Oceanos | **Fair Lawn**	23	
NEW Pairings | **Cranford**	-	
Perryville Inn | **Union Twp**	26	
🛛 Pluckemin Inn | **Bedminster**	26	
🛛 Porto Leggero | **Jersey City**	26	
Pub | **Pennsauken**	19	
Rare | **Little Falls**	24	
🛛 Rest. Latour | **Hamburg**	27	
🛛 River Palm | **multi.**	25	
🛛 Saddle River Inn | **Saddle River**	28	
🛛 Serenade | **Chatham**	27	
Stage House | **Scotch Plains**	20	
🛛 Stage Left | **New Bruns.**	27	
🛛 Stone House | **Warren**	22	
Stony Hill Inn | **Hackensack**	22	
Tomatoes | **Margate**	25	
Villa Amalfi | **Cliffside Pk**	23	
🛛 Washington Inn | **Cape May**	28	
🛛 Waterside | **N Bergen**	21	

PRIX FIXE MENUS

(Call for prices and times)

NEW Adara | **Montclair**	-	
🛛 Amanda's | **Hoboken**	26	
🛛 Andre's | **Newton**	27	
Arturo's | **Maplewood**	24	
🛛 Bernards Inn | **Bernardsville**	27	
NEW Blind Boar | **Norwood**	-	
🛛 Cafe Matisse | **Rutherford**	27	
🛛 Cafe Panache | **Ramsey**	27	
🛛 Chez Catherine | **Westfield**	26	
🛛 David Burke | **Rumson**	25	
Dream Cuisine | **Cherry Hill**	27	
🛛 Drew's Bayshore | **Keyport**	27	
Eccola | **Parsippany**	23	
Edward's Steak | **Jersey City**	23	
Esty St. | **Park Ridge**	25	

⦾ Fascino | **Montclair**	26
Filomena Italiana | **Clementon**	25
⦾ Frog/Peach | **New Bruns.**	26
Fuji | **Haddonfield**	25
⦾ Gables | **Beach Haven**	24
Girasole | **A.C.**	26
⦾ Highlawn Pavilion | **W Orange**	25
J&K Steak | **multi.**	-
Komegashi | **Jersey City**	22
⦾ Latour | **Ridgewood**	26
Le Fandy | **Fair Haven**	25
Liberty House | **Jersey City**	20
Madeleine's | **Northvale**	25
Manon | **Lambertville**	25
Mikado | **multi.**	23
⦾ Nicholas | **Red Bank**	29
Norma's | **Cherry Hill**	22
Nunzio | **Collingswood**	24
Oliver a Bistro | **Bordentown**	27
Perryville Inn | **Union Twp**	26
⦾ Pluckemin Inn | **Bedminster**	26
⦾ Rat's | **Hamilton**	24
⦾ Rest. Latour | **Hamburg**	27
Rocca | **Glen Rock**	24
⦾ Rosemary/Sage | **Riverdale**	26
⦾ Sapori | **Collingswood**	28
⦾ Scalini Fedeli | **Chatham**	27
⦾ Serenade | **Chatham**	27
⦾ Stage Left | **New Bruns.**	27
⦾ Stone House | **Warren**	22
Sumo | **Wall**	25
Verjus | **Maplewood**	25
Village Green | **Ridgewood**	24
Wasabi | **Somerville**	24

QUICK BITES

Aby's | **Matawan**	20
Alchemist/Barrister | **Princeton**	16
Ariel's | **Englewood**	20
Blueplate | **Mullica Hill**	-
Bobby Chez | **multi.**	24
Bobby's | **Eatontown**	21
NEW Breakfast Room | **A.C.**	-
Cassie's | **Englewood**	18
Chickie's/Pete's | **Bordentown**	17
Continental | **A.C.**	23
Cubby's BBQ | **Hackensack**	19
Dauphin | **Asbury Pk**	22

DeLorenzo's Pizza | **Trenton**	24
⦾ DeLorenzo's/Pies | **Robbinsville**	27
Egan/Sons | **W Orange**	19
El Caney | **Bergenfield**	-
Fishery | **S Amboy**	20
⦾ Five Guys | **Mount Ephraim**	21
Franco's Metro | **Fort Lee**	19
Full Moon | **Lambertville**	19
Grub Hut | **Manville**	21
Hiram's | **Fort Lee**	21
Hobby's | **Newark**	24
Holsten's | **Bloomfield**	16
Hummus Elite | **Englewood**	21
Ibby's | **multi.**	22
Irish Pub | **A.C.**	18
Jack's | **Westwood**	20
Jerry/Harvey's | **Marlboro**	18
Jimmy Buff's | **E Hanover**	20
Kairo | **New Bruns.**	-
Kibitz Room | **Cherry Hill**	23
Kilkenny Ale | **Newark**	18
Kinchley's | **Ramsey**	21
Little Food Cafe | **multi.**	23
Locale | **Closter**	20
Mastoris | **Bordentown**	19
McGovern's | **Newark**	18
Mexican Food | **Marlton**	20
Mustache Bill's | **Barnegat Light**	24
Nana's Deli | **Livingston**	23
Napoli's Pizza | **Hoboken**	25
Nha Trang Pl. | **Jersey City**	23
Nifty Fifty's | **multi.**	19
Pic-Nic | **E Newark**	21
Ponzio's | **Cherry Hill**	19
Pop's Garage | **Asbury Pk**	22
Pop Shop | **Collingswood**	20
Raymond's | **Montclair**	21
Renato's | **Jersey City**	22
Rolling Pin | **Westwood**	23
Rutt's Hut | **Clifton**	21
Sage Diner | **Mt Laurel**	14
Skylark | **Edison**	22
Smashburger | **multi.**	19
Takara | **Oakhurst**	20
Taqueria Downtown | **Jersey City**	24
WindMill | **multi.**	19
Tick Tock | **Clifton**	18

Tito's | **multi.**	20
Toast | **Montclair**	22
Tony Luke's | **A.C.**	20
Tortilla Press | **Merchantville**	24
Trinity | **Hoboken**	18
NEW Urban Table | **Morristown**	-
Victor's Pub | **Camden**	-
White Mana | **Jersey City**	17
White Manna | **Hackensack**	23
Windansea | **Highlands**	17
Witherspoon | **Princeton**	21
Zinburger | **Clifton**	-

QUIET CONVERSATION

Amarone | **Teaneck**	21
Biagio's | **Paramus**	17
Blackbird | **Collingswood**	24
Black Trumpet | **Spring Lake**	24
NEW Blue Morel | **Morristown**	-
Braddock's | **Medford**	19
BV Tuscany | **Teaneck**	23
Z Cafe Madison | **Riverside**	22
Chao Phaya | **multi.**	22
Z Chef's Table | **Franklin Lakes**	28
Z Chez Catherine | **Westfield**	26
Christopher | **Cherry Hill**	-
Corso 98 | **Montclair**	22
Davia | **Fair Lawn**	20
Dino's | **Harrington Pk**	22
Z Elements | **Princeton**	26
Etc. Steak | **Teaneck**	25
Farnsworth House | **Bordentown**	22
55 Main | **Flemington**	22
Fiorino | **Summit**	24
Fontana/Trevi | **Leonia**	23
Franco's Metro | **Fort Lee**	19
Frenchtown Inn | **Frenchtown**	23
Gianna's | **Carlstadt**	20
Giumarello | **Westmont**	25
Z Il Capriccio | **Whippany**	25
NEW Il Cinghiale | **Little Ferry**	-
Inn/Sugar Hill | **Mays Landing**	18
NEW Khloe Bistrot | **Fort Lee**	-
Kinara | **Edgewater**	22
Krave Café | **Newton**	24
La Strada | **Randolph**	23
Z Latour | **Ridgewood**	26
Locale | **Closter**	20

Luciano's | **Rahway**	24
Luigi's | **Ridgefield Pk**	-
Melting Pot | **Westwood**	19
Meyersville Inn | **Gillette**	19
Z Molly Pitcher Inn Restaurant | **Red Bank**	22
Namaskaar | **Englewood**	20
NEW Nico | **Newark**	-
NEW Ohana Grill | **Lavallette**	-
Peacock Inn Restaurant | **Princeton**	26
Z Peter Shields | **Cape May**	26
Z Pluckemin Inn | **Bedminster**	26
Quays | **Hoboken**	18
Z Rat's | **Hamilton**	24
Renato's | **Jersey City**	22
Z Rest. Latour | **Hamburg**	27
Roberto's II | **Edgewater**	21
Rocky Hill Inn | **Rocky Hill**	17
Z Saddle River Inn | **Saddle River**	28
Segovia Steak | **Little Ferry**	23
Sergeantsville Inn | **Sergeantsville**	24
Settebello | **Morristown**	20
Settimo Cielo | **Trenton**	23
Sirin | **Morristown**	21
Smithville Inn | **Smithville**	20
Solari's | **Hackensack**	19
Sorrento | **E Rutherford**	24
Z Stone House | **Warren**	22
Stony Hill Inn | **Hackensack**	22
Tbones Tuscan Steakhouse | **Bridgewater**	22
Tewksbury Inn | **Oldwick**	23
Tony/Caneca | **Newark**	23
Très Yan & Wu | **Mt Laurel**	23
Umeya | **Cresskill**	23
Vasili's | **Teaneck**	21
Verjus | **Maplewood**	25
Villa Amalfi | **Cliffside Pk**	23
Village Green | **Ridgewood**	24
Z Whispers | **Spring Lake**	27
William Douglas | **Cherry Hill**	25

RAW BARS

Akai | **Englewood**	24
NEW Aqua Blu | **Toms River**	-
Z Avenue | **Long Branch**	22
Bahrs Landing | **Highlands**	17

Berkeley | **S Seaside Pk**	20
NEW Blue Morel | **Morristown**	–
Z Blue Point | **Princeton**	26
Bobby Flay | **A.C.**	25
Caffe Aldo | **Cherry Hill**	24
Char | **Raritan**	22
Costanera | **Montclair**	24
Crab Trap | **Somers Point**	21
Dock's | **A.C.**	26
Edward's Steak | **Jersey City**	23
Fin | **A.C.**	25
Fin Raw Bar | **Montclair**	–
Fishery | **S Amboy**	20
NEW GK's Red Dog | **Morristown**	–
Hamilton/Ward | **Paterson**	23
Harvest Bistro | **Closter**	21
Harvey Cedars | **Beach Haven**	23
Z Il Capriccio | **Whippany**	25
Klein's | **Belmar**	19
La Focaccia | **Summit**	23
La Griglia | **Kenilworth**	23
Z Legal Sea Foods | **multi.**	21
Liberty House | **Jersey City**	20
Limani | **Westfield**	24
Little Tuna | **Haddonfield**	23
Lobster House | **Cape May**	20
LouCás | **Edison**	23
Maritime Parc | **Jersey City**	–
Martini Bistro | **Millburn**	19
McCormick/Schmick | **Hackensack**	20
McLoone's | **multi.**	17
Nero's Grille | **Livingston**	18
Nikko | **Whippany**	24
Oceanos | **Fair Lawn**	23
NEW Ohana Grill | **Lavallette**	–
Z Old Homestead | **A.C.**	27
Park Steak | **Park Ridge**	23
NEW Park West | **Ridgewood**	–
Pino's | **Marlboro**	21
Plantation | **Harvey Cedars**	18
Portobello | **Oakland**	19
Rare | **Little Falls**	24
Red's Lobster | **Pt. Pleas. Bch**	24
Rest. L | **Allendale**	18
Rooney's | **Long Branch**	19
Rosie's | **Randolph**	21
NEW Scarduzio's | **A.C.**	–
Shipwreck Grill | **Brielle**	24

Sofia | **Margate**	23
Solaia | **Englewood**	17
Spike's | **Pt. Pleas. Bch**	22
Stage House | **Scotch Plains**	20
Stella Marina | **Asbury Pk**	23
Steve/Cookie's | **Margate**	25
Sumo | **Wall**	25
3 Forty Grill | **Hoboken**	20
Varka | **Ramsey**	26
Z Waterside | **N Bergen**	21
NEW Wayne Steak | **Wayne**	–

ROMANTIC PLACES

Acquaviva/Fonti | **Westfield**	22
Z Amanda's | **Hoboken**	26
Z Andre's | **Newton**	27
Anton's/Swan | **Lambertville**	22
Atlantic B&G | **S Seaside Pk**	26
Z Avenue | **Long Branch**	22
Bell's Mansion | **Stanhope**	15
Z Bernards Inn | **Bernardsville**	27
Black Trumpet | **Spring Lake**	24
NEW Blue Morel | **Morristown**	–
Blueplate | **Mullica Hill**	–
Z Cafe Madison | **Riverside**	22
Z Cafe Matisse | **Rutherford**	27
Cara Mia | **Millburn**	–
Z Catherine Lombardi | **New Bruns.**	24
Z Chakra | **Paramus**	20
Claude's | **N Wildwood**	27
Z CulinAriane | **Montclair**	27
Z David Burke | **Rumson**	25
Z Ebbitt Room | **Cape May**	26
Z Elements | **Princeton**	26
Z Eno Terra | **Kingston**	24
Esty St. | **Park Ridge**	25
55 Main | **Flemington**	22
Flirt Sushi | **Allendale**	23
Frenchtown Inn | **Frenchtown**	23
Z Frog/Peach | **New Bruns.**	26
Fuji | **Haddonfield**	25
Z Gables | **Beach Haven**	24
Giumarello | **Westmont**	25
Gladstone | **Gladstone**	21
Z Grand Cafe | **Morristown**	25
Harvest Bistro | **Closter**	21
Harvest Moon | **Ringoes**	25
Z Highlawn Pavilion | **W Orange**	25

Ho-Ho-Kus Inn | **Ho-Ho-Kus**	21
Huntley Taverne | **Summit**	22
☑ Il Capriccio | **Whippany**	25
Il Villaggio | **Carlstadt**	24
Inn at Millrace Pond Restaurant | **Hope**	23
Ivy Inn | **Hasbrouck Hts**	22
Jose's Cantina | **multi.**	19
Komegashi | **Jersey City**	22
Krave Café | **Newton**	24
La Cipollina | **Freehold**	22
Langosta | **Asbury Pk**	22
☑ Latour | **Ridgewood**	26
Le Jardin | **Edgewater**	20
☑ Le Rendez-Vous | **Kenilworth**	27
Liberty House | **Jersey City**	20
Lola's | **Hoboken**	18
☑ Lorena's | **Maplewood**	28
☑ Manor | **W Orange**	24
Maritime Parc | **Jersey City**	-
NEW Marlene Mangia Bene | **Woodbury**	-
Matisse | **Belmar**	22
Mehndi | **Morristown**	24
Melting Pot | **Westwood**	19
Mia | **A.C.**	26
Ming | **Morristown**	24
NEW MK Valencia | **Ridgefield Pk**	-
☑ Molly Pitcher Inn Restaurant | **Red Bank**	22
Mompou | **Newark**	23
NEW MoonShine | **Millburn**	-
☑ Ninety Acres | **Peapack**	25
Park Ave. B&G | **Union City**	18
Peacock Inn Restaurant | **Princeton**	26
Perryville Inn | **Union Twp**	26
☑ Peter Shields | **Cape May**	26
Pino's | **Marlboro**	21
☑ Pluckemin Inn | **Bedminster**	26
Pointé | **Jersey City**	21
NEW Ralic's Steak | **Haddonfield**	-
☑ Ram's Head Inn | **Galloway**	24
☑ Rat's | **Hamilton**	24
☑ Raven/Peach | **Fair Haven**	24
Rebecca's | **Edgewater**	23
☑ Rest. Latour | **Hamburg**	27
Rod's Steak | **Morristown**	22

☑ Saddle River Inn | **Saddle River**	28
☑ Scalini Fedeli | **Chatham**	27
Scarborough Fair | **Sea Girt**	23
☑ SeaBlue | **A.C.**	26
NEW Sear House | **Closter**	-
☑ Serenade | **Chatham**	27
Sergeantsville Inn | **Sergeantsville**	24
Sette | **Bernardsville**	24
Sirena | **Long Branch**	23
Son Cubano | **W New York**	-
☑ Stone House | **Warren**	22
Stony Hill Inn | **Hackensack**	22
Taka | **Asbury Pk**	25
Tewksbury Inn | **Oldwick**	23
Grenville | **Bay Hd.**	17
NEW Ursino | **Union**	-
Vu | **Jersey City**	16
☑ Washington Inn | **Cape May**	28
☑ Waterside | **N Bergen**	21
☑ Whispers | **Spring Lake**	27
Wine Bar | **Atlantic Highlands**	22
Za | **Pennington**	23

SENIOR APPEAL

Armando's | **Fort Lee**	19
Armando's Tuscan | **River Vale**	20
Athenian Gdn. | **Galloway Twp**	23
Bahrs Landing | **Highlands**	17
Berkeley | **S Seaside Pk**	20
Bistro/Marino | **Collingswood**	22
NEW Blind Boar | **Norwood**	-
Blueplate | **Mullica Hill**	-
Bonefish Grill | **Deptford**	21
Brio | **Cherry Hill**	19
Café Azzurro | **Peapack**	24
☑ Cafe Madison | **Riverside**	22
Capt'n Ed's | **Pt. Pleas.**	20
Carmine's | **A.C.**	21
Casa Dante | **Jersey City**	24
☑ Catherine Lombardi | **New Bruns.**	24
Chophouse | **Gibbsboro**	23
Christopher | **Cherry Hill**	-
Crab Trap | **Somers Point**	21
Davia | **Fair Lawn**	20
DiPalma Brothers | **N Bergen**	21
Don Pepe | **multi.**	22
Don Pepe's Steak | **Pine Brook**	22

NEW Duck King | **Edgewater**	–
E & V | **Paterson**	23
Edward's Steak | **Jersey City**	23
El Cid | **Paramus**	22
Eppes Essen | **Livingston**	20
55 Main | **Flemington**	22
Z Fornos/Spain | **Newark**	24
Franco's Metro | **Fort Lee**	19
Gallagher's | **A.C.**	22
NEW GK's Red Dog | **Morristown**	–
Z Grand Cafe | **Morristown**	25
Helmers' | **Hoboken**	19
Z Highlawn Pavilion | **W Orange**	25
Hiram's | **Fort Lee**	21
Hobby's | **Newark**	24
Ho-Ho-Kus Inn | **Ho-Ho-Kus**	21
Holsten's | **Bloomfield**	16
Iberia | **Newark**	20
Z Il Capriccio | **Whippany**	25
NEW Il Cinghiale | **Little Ferry**	–
Il Fiore | **Collingswood**	26
Il Villaggio | **Carlstadt**	24
In Napoli | **Fort Lee**	17
Ivy Inn | **Hasbrouck Hts**	22
Java Moon | **Jackson**	22
Joe Pesce | **Collingswood**	24
Kibitz Room | **Cherry Hill**	23
Klein's | **Belmar**	19
Krave Café | **Newton**	24
Kuzina/Sofia | **Cherry Hill**	22
Z Legal Sea Foods | **Short Hills**	21
Little Tuna | **Haddonfield**	23
Lobster House | **Cape May**	20
Lotus Cafe | **Hackensack**	23
LouCás | **Edison**	23
Luigi's | **Ridgefield Pk**	–
Madeleine's | **Northvale**	25
Z Manor | **W Orange**	24
NEW Marlene Mangia Bene | **Woodbury**	–
McCormick/Schmick | **multi.**	20
Mesón Madrid | **Palisades Pk**	18
Meyersville Inn | **Gillette**	19
Mill/Spring Lake Hts. | **Spring Lake Hts**	21
Nifty Fifty's | **multi.**	19
Oceanos | **Fair Lawn**	23
Octopus's Gdn. | **West Creek**	22
Patsy's | **Fairview**	23
Pete/Elda's | **Neptune City**	22
Pop Shop | **Collingswood**	20
Portobello | **Oakland**	19
Portuguese Manor | **Perth Amboy**	19
Pub | **Pennsauken**	19
NEW Ralic's Steak | **Haddonfield**	–
Renato's | **Jersey City**	22
Rio Rodizio | **Union**	20
Z Rist./Benito | **Union**	26
Roberto's II | **Edgewater**	21
Rod's Steak | **Morristown**	22
Z SeaBlue | **A.C.**	26
Segovia Steak | **Little Ferry**	23
Smithville Inn | **Smithville**	20
Solari's | **Hackensack**	19
Spain | **Newark**	24
Spanish Tavern | **multi.**	22
Z Stone House | **Warren**	22
Stony Hill Inn | **Hackensack**	22
Grenville | **Bay Hd.**	17
WindMill | **multi.**	19
Très Yan & Wu | **Mt Laurel**	23
Varka | **Ramsey**	26
Verjus | **Maplewood**	25
Villa Amalfi | **Cliffside Pk**	23
Villa Vittoria | **Brick**	23
William Douglas | **Cherry Hill**	25
Wolfgang Puck | **A.C.**	23

SINGLES SCENES

Adega Grill | **Newark**	22
Alice's | **Lake Hopatcong**	21
Atlantic B&G | **S Seaside Pk**	26
Z Avenue | **Long Branch**	22
Bahama Breeze | **Wayne**	17
Biagio's | **Paramus**	17
Bibi'z | **Westwood**	–
Bicycle Club | **Englewood Cliffs**	14
Bin 14 | **Hoboken**	22
Bistro 55 | **Rochelle Pk**	19
Blue Pig | **Cape May**	21
Brass Rail | **Hoboken**	19
Brickwall Tavern | **Asbury Pk**	18
Brooklyn's Pizza | **Ridgewood**	22
Bruschetta | **Fairfield**	21
Z Buddakan | **A.C.**	26
Cenzino | **Oakland**	24
Z Chakra | **Paramus**	20

Char | **Raritan**	22
Chickie's/Pete's | **Bordentown**	17
Ciao | **Basking Ridge**	21
Circa | **High Bridge**	17
Clydz | **New Bruns.**	22
Continental | **A.C.**	23
Copper Canyon | **Atlantic Highlands**	23
Cuba Libre | **A.C.**	21
Cucharamama | **Hoboken**	26
NEW Daryl | **New Bruns.**	-
Delicious Hts. | **Berkeley Hts**	18
Egan/Sons | **W Orange**	19
Fire/Oak | **multi.**	19
Fleming's | **Edgewater**	23
Grissini | **Englewood Cliffs**	22
Gusto Grill | **E Brunswick**	19
Hat Tavern | **Summit**	-
Hoboken B&G | **Hoboken**	19
Huntley Taverne | **Summit**	22
Inlet Café | **Highlands**	20
Langosta | **Asbury Pk**	22
Light Horse | **Jersey City**	22
Luke Palladino | **A.C.**	26
Madison B&G | **Hoboken**	19
Martini Bistro | **Millburn**	19
McLoone's | **Sea Bright**	17
Metropolitan Cafe | **Freehold**	21
Mia | **A.C.**	26
Mill/Spring Lake Hts. | **Spring Lake Hts**	21
NEW MK Valencia | **Ridgefield Pk**	-
Mompou | **Newark**	23
Old Man Rafferty's | **multi.**	18
Orange Squirrel | **Bloomfield**	22
Park Ave. B&G | **Union City**	18
NEW Pilsener Haus | **Hoboken**	-
P.J. Whelihan's | **multi.**	17
Plantation | **Harvey Cedars**	18
Quays | **Hoboken**	18
Quiet Man | **Dover**	22
Red | **Red Bank**	21
Redstone | **Marlton**	21
Rest. L | **Allendale**	18
Rooney's | **Long Branch**	19
Sabor | **N Bergen**	22
Sage | **Ventnor**	25
Sallee Tee's | **Monmouth Bch**	18

Salt Creek | **multi.**	19
Shipwreck Grill | **Brielle**	24
Son Cubano | **W New York**	-
Sushi Lounge | **multi.**	22
Tabor Rd. | **Morris Plains**	21
Teak | **Red Bank**	21
3 Forty Grill | **Hoboken**	20
3 West | **Basking Ridge**	23
Tomatoes | **Margate**	25
Trap Rock | **Berkeley Hts**	21
Trinity | **Hoboken**	18
Ugly Mug | **Cape May**	15
Verve | **Somerville**	23
Z Waterside | **N Bergen**	21
Wicked Wolf | **Hoboken**	19
Windansea | **Highlands**	17
Witherspoon | **Princeton**	21

SLEEPERS

(Good food, but little known)

Aligado | **Hazlet**	24
Assaggini/Roma | **Newark**	24
BV Tuscany | **Teaneck**	23
Cafe Loren | **Avalon**	25
Chateau/Spain | **Newark**	23
Chelsea Prime | **A.C.**	24
Claude's | **N Wildwood**	27
D&L BBQ | **Bradley Bch**	24
Dream Cuisine | **Cherry Hill**	27
Etc. Steak | **Teaneck**	25
Filomena Italiana | **Clementon**	25
Filomena Lake. | **Deptford**	23
Fin | **A.C.**	25
GG's | **Mt Laurel**	25
I Gemelli | **S Hackensack**	24
IndeBlue | **Collingswood**	25
Inn at Millrace Pond Restaurant | **Hope**	23
Je's | **Newark**	25
Jose's | **Spring Lake Hts**	23
Kaya's | **Belmar**	24
Konbu | **Manalapan**	26
Krave Café | **Newton**	24
La Locanda | **Voorhees**	28
La Sorrentina | **N Bergen**	24
Lazy Dog Saloon | **Asbury Pk**	23
Little Food Cafe | **multi.**	23
Luigi's | **E Hanover**	26
Manolo's | **Elizabeth**	25
Megu | **multi.**	23

Mi Bandera | **Union City**	24
Nobi | **Toms River**	26
Oliver a Bistro | **Bordentown**	27
Oyako Tso's | **Freehold**	23
Pasquale's | **Edison**	24
Rumba Cubana/Cafe | **multi.**	23
Sakura Spring | **Cherry Hill**	24
Settimo Cielo | **Trenton**	23
Sol-Mar | **Newark**	26
So Moon Nan Jip | **Palisades Pk**	24
Sumo | **Wall**	25
Trattoria Med. | **Bedminster**	24
Três Yan & Wu | **Mt Laurel**	23
Umeya | **Cresskill**	23
William Douglas | **Cherry Hill**	25

SPECIAL OCCASIONS

NEW Adara | **Montclair**	-
Anton's/Swan | **Lambertville**	22
Z Bernards Inn | **Bernardsville**	27
Blackbird | **Collingswood**	24
NEW Blue Morel | **Morristown**	-
Bobby Flay | **A.C.**	25
Brandl | **Belmar**	24
Z Buddakan | **A.C.**	26
Z Cafe Matisse | **Rutherford**	27
Z Cafe Panache | **Ramsey**	27
Cara Mia | **Millburn**	-
Z Chakra | **Paramus**	20
Z Chart House | **Weehawken**	21
Z Chef's Table | **Franklin Lakes**	28
Chengdu 46 | **Clifton**	24
Z Chez Catherine | **Westfield**	26
Cucharamama | **Hoboken**	26
Z CulinAriane | **Montclair**	27
NEW Daryl | **New Bruns.**	-
Z David Burke | **Rumson**	25
Esty St. | **Park Ridge**	25
55 Main | **Flemington**	22
Fiorino | **Summit**	24
Frenchtown Inn | **Frenchtown**	23
Z Frog/Peach | **New Bruns.**	26
Gallagher's | **A.C.**	22
Girasole | **A.C.**	26
Girasole | **Bound Brook**	26
Giumarello | **Westmont**	25
Z Grand Cafe | **Morristown**	25
Harvest Bistro | **Closter**	21
Harvest Moon | **Ringoes**	25

Z Highlawn Pavilion | **W Orange**	25
Ho-Ho-Kus Inn | **Ho-Ho-Kus**	21
Z Hotoke | **New Bruns.**	20
Z Il Capriccio | **Whippany**	25
Il Villaggio | **Carlstadt**	24
Inn at Millrace Pond Restaurant | **Hope**	23
Ivy Inn | **Hasbrouck Hts**	22
La Cipollina | **Freehold**	22
Z Latour | **Ridgewood**	26
Lincroft Inn | **Lincroft**	19
Locale | **Closter**	20
Luciano's | **Rahway**	24
Lu Nello | **Cedar Grove**	25
Madeleine's | **Northvale**	25
Z Manor | **W Orange**	24
Maritime Parc | **Jersey City**	-
Z Mattar's Bistro | **Allamuchy**	24
Mehndi | **Morristown**	24
Mill/Spring Lake Hts. | **Spring Lake Hts**	21
NEW MoonShine | **Millburn**	-
Z Nicholas | **Red Bank**	29
Z Ninety Acres | **Peapack**	25
Nunzio | **Collingswood**	24
NEW Pairings | **Cranford**	-
Peacock Inn Restaurant | **Princeton**	26
Perryville Inn | **Union Twp**	26
Z Peter Shields | **Cape May**	26
Z Piccola | **Ocean Twp**	26
Z Picnic | **Fair Lawn**	27
Z Pluckemin Inn | **Bedminster**	26
Z Ram's Head Inn | **Galloway**	24
Z Rat's | **Hamilton**	24
Z Raven/Peach | **Fair Haven**	24
Rebecca's | **Edgewater**	23
Z Rest. Latour | **Hamburg**	27
Z Resto | **Madison**	25
River Palm | **multi.**	25
Rod's Steak | **Morristown**	22
Roots Steak | **Summit**	26
Z Saddle River Inn | **Saddle River**	28
Z Scalini Fedeli | **Chatham**	27
Scarborough Fair | **Sea Girt**	23
Z SeaBlue | **A.C.**	26
NEW Sear House | **Closter**	-
Z Serenade | **Chatham**	27

Shanghai Jazz | **Madison**	22
Son Cubano | **W New York**	-
Stage House | **Scotch Plains**	20
☑ Stage Left | **New Bruns.**	27
☑ Stone House | **Warren**	22
Stony Hill Inn | **Hackensack**	22
Palm | **A.C.**	25
3 West | **Basking Ridge**	23
Trinity | **Keyport**	25
Villa Amalfi | **Cliffside Pk**	23
☑ Washington Inn | **Cape May**	28
William Douglas | **Cherry Hill**	25
Wolfgang Puck | **A.C.**	23

TASTING MENUS

NEW Adara | **Montclair**	-
Arturo's | **Maplewood**	24
☑ Bernards Inn | **Bernardsville**	27
Bienvenue | **Red Bank**	22
Blvd. Five 72 | **Kenilworth**	25
☑ Cafe Matisse | **Rutherford**	27
☑ Cafe Panache | **Ramsey**	27
☑ Chez Catherine | **Westfield**	26
Cuba Libre | **A.C.**	21
Da Filippo's | **Somerville**	24
Dauphin | **Asbury Pk**	22
Due Mari | **New Bruns.**	26
☑ Ebbitt Room | **Cape May**	26
☑ Elements | **Princeton**	26
Etc. Steak | **Teaneck**	25
☑ Fascino | **Montclair**	26
☑ Frog/Peach | **New Bruns.**	26
Fuji | **Haddonfield**	25
☑ Gables | **Beach Haven**	24
Komegashi | **Jersey City**	22
Kuzina/Sofia | **Cherry Hill**	22
La Campagne | **Cherry Hill**	23
La Cipollina | **Freehold**	22
☑ Latour | **Ridgewood**	26
☑ Le Rendez-Vous | **Kenilworth**	27
Limani | **Westfield**	24
☑ Nicholas | **Red Bank**	29
☑ Ninety Acres | **Peapack**	25
Norma's | **Cherry Hill**	22
Nunzio | **Collingswood**	24
NEW Pairings | **Cranford**	-
Peacock Inn Restaurant | **Princeton**	26
Perryville Inn | **Union Twp**	26

☑ Pluckemin Inn | **Bedminster**	26
☑ Rest. Latour | **Hamburg**	27
☑ Rosemary/Sage | **Riverdale**	26
☑ Serenade | **Chatham**	27
Spargo's | **Manalapan**	23
☑ Stage Left | **New Bruns.**	27
NEW Ursino | **Union**	-
Village Green | **Ridgewood**	24
Vine | **Basking Ridge**	23

TRENDY

NEW Adara | **Montclair**	-
Alice's | **Lake Hopatcong**	21
Aozora | **Montclair**	24
Atlantic B&G | **S Seaside Pk**	26
☑ A Toute Heure | **Cranford**	26
Bar Cara | **Bloomfield**	20
Bibi'z | **Westwood**	-
Bin 14 | **Hoboken**	22
Bistro 55 | **Rochelle Pk**	19
Blu | **Montclair**	25
Blue Bottle | **Hopewell**	26
Bobby Flay | **A.C.**	25
Blvd. Five 72 | **Kenilworth**	25
☑ Buddakan | **A.C.**	26
☑ Cafe Matisse | **Rutherford**	27
☑ Chakra | **Paramus**	20
Char | **Raritan**	22
Clydz | **New Bruns.**	22
Continental | **A.C.**	23
Cuba Libre | **A.C.**	21
Cubanu | **Rahway**	21
Cucharamama | **Hoboken**	26
Daddy O | **Long Beach**	19
NEW Daryl | **New Bruns.**	-
☑ David Burke | **Rumson**	25
☑ Dino/Harry's | **Hoboken**	27
☑ Drew's Bayshore | **Keyport**	27
☑ Fascino | **Montclair**	26
Fin | **A.C.**	25
Fin Raw Bar | **Montclair**	-
Fire/Oak | **multi.**	19
NEW Firecreek | **Voorhees**	-
NEW 5 Seasons | **Ridgewood**	-
Flirt Sushi | **Allendale**	23
Girasole | **Bound Brook**	26
☑ Hotoke | **New Bruns.**	20
Hummus Elite | **Englewood**	21
Iron Hill Brewery | **Maple Shade**	20

NEW Keg/Kitchen | **Westmont**	–	Shanghai Jazz | **Madison**	22
NEW Khloe Bistrot | **Fort Lee**	–	Z Shumi | **Somerville**	28
Komegashi | **Jersey City**	22	Sirena | **Long Branch**	23
Labrador | **Normandy Bch**	25	Skylark | **Edison**	22
Langosta | **Asbury Pk**	22	Son Cubano | **W New York**	–
Lemongrass | **Morris Plains**	–	Steakhouse 85 | **New Bruns.**	26
NEW Levant Grille | **Englewood**	–	Stella Marina | **Asbury Pk**	23
Light Horse | **Jersey City**	22	Steve/Cookie's | **Margate**	25
LITM | **Jersey City**	14	NEW St. Eve's | **Ho-Ho-Kus**	–
Z Lorena's | **Maplewood**	28	Sushi Lounge | **multi.**	22
Luce | **Caldwell**	22	Sushi X | **Ridgewood**	21
Makeda | **New Bruns.**	24	Taj Mahal | **Jersey City**	–
Mantra | **Paramus**	22	Taverna Mykonos | **Elmwood Pk**	25
Marco/Pepe | **Jersey City**	22	Teak | **Red Bank**	21
Maritime Parc | **Jersey City**	–	Terra Nova | **Sewell**	–
Martini 494 | **Newark**	–	Theresa's | **Westfield**	22
Mehndi | **Morristown**	24	3 Forty Grill | **Hoboken**	20
Mélange | **Haddonfield**	25	3 West | **Basking Ridge**	23
Metropolitan Cafe | **Freehold**	21	Trap Rock | **Berkeley Hts**	21
Mia | **A.C.**	26	Treno | **Westmont**	–
NEW MK Valencia | **Ridgefield Pk**	–	Tre Piani | **Princeton**	20
Mompou | **Newark**	23	Trinity | **Hoboken**	18
NEW MoonShine | **Millburn**	–	Trinity/Pope | **Asbury Pk**	21
NEW Nico | **Newark**	–	Tula | **New Bruns.**	19
Z Ninety Acres | **Peapack**	25	27 Mix | **Newark**	21
Nomad Pizza | **Hopewell**	26	Undici | **Rumson**	22
Z Old Homestead | **A.C.**	27	Uproot | **Warren**	22
Orange Squirrel | **Bloomfield**	22	NEW Upstairs | **Upper Montclair**	–
NEW Osteria/Fiamma | **Ridgewood**	–	NEW Urban Table | **Morristown**	–
NEW Osteria Morini | **Bernardsville**	–	NEW Ursino | **Union**	–
NEW Pairings | **Cranford**	–	Verve | **Somerville**	23
Park Ave. B&G | **Union City**	18	Vincentown Diner | **Vincentown**	20
Z Picnic | **Fair Lawn**	27	Vine | **Basking Ridge**	23
NEW Pilsener Haus | **Hoboken**	–	Vu | **Jersey City**	16
Plan B | **Asbury Pk**	24	Z Waterside | **N Bergen**	21
Pointé | **Jersey City**	21	Wicked Wolf | **Hoboken**	19
Pop's Garage | **Asbury Pk**	22	Witherspoon | **Princeton**	21
Z Rat's | **Hamilton**	24	Wolfgang Puck | **A.C.**	23
Red | **Red Bank**	21	Z Yellow Fin | **Surf City**	27
Z Resto | **Madison**	25	Zafra | **Hoboken**	23
Rob's Bistro | **Madison**	–	Zylo | **Hoboken**	21

VIEWS

Rumba Cubana/Cafe | **N Bergen**	23

Alice's | **Lake Hopatcong**	21
Sabor | **N Bergen**	22
NEW Aqua Blu | **Toms River**	–
Sage | **Ventnor**	25
Atlantic B&G | **S Seaside Pk**	26
Satis | **Jersey City**	–
Z Avenue | **Long Branch**	22
Z SeaBlue | **A.C.**	26
Avon Pavilion | **Avon-by-Sea**	19

Bahrs Landing | **Highlands**	17
NEW Baia | **Somers Point**	-
Barnacle Bill's | **Rumson**	22
Z Baumgart's | **Edgewater**	19
Berkeley | **S Seaside Pk**	20
Z Buddakan | **A.C.**	26
Café Gallery | **Burlington**	20
Z Cafe Matisse | **Rutherford**	27
Z Capriccio | **A.C.**	25
Charley's | **Long Branch**	18
Z Chart House | **Weehawken**	21
Chelsea Prime | **A.C.**	24
Chickie's/Pete's | **Wildwood**	17
Chophouse | **Gibbsboro**	23
Continental | **A.C.**	23
Crab House | **Edgewater**	16
Crab Trap | **Somers Point**	21
NEW Cubacan | **Asbury Pk**	-
NEW Dos Caminos | **A.C.**	-
Charrito's/El Charro | **Weehawken**	22
Frenchtown Inn | **Frenchtown**	23
Greek Taverna | **Edgewater**	20
Hamilton's | **Lambertville**	26
Z Highlawn Pavilion | **W Orange**	25
Hot Dog Johnny's | **Buttzville**	21
Inlet Café | **Highlands**	20
Komegashi | **Jersey City**	22
NEW La Fontana Coast | **Sea Isle City**	-
Lambertville Station | **Lambertville**	17
Langosta | **Asbury Pk**	22
Le Jardin | **Edgewater**	20
Liberty House | **Jersey City**	20
Lilly's/Canal | **Lambertville**	21
Maritime Parc | **Jersey City**	-
Matisse | **Belmar**	22
McLoone's | **multi.**	17
Mesón Madrid | **Palisades Pk**	18
Z Milford Oyster | **Milford**	27
Mill/Spring Lake Hts. | **Spring Lake Hts**	21
Mister C's/Bistro | **Allenhurst**	18
Z Molly Pitcher Inn Restaurant | **Red Bank**	22
Z Moonstruck | **Asbury Pk**	25
Z Ninety Acres | **Peapack**	25
NEW O Bistro | **A.C.**	-
Park Ave. B&G | **Union City**	18
Phillips Seafood | **A.C.**	20
P.J. Whelihan's | **Medford Lakes**	17
Plantation | **Harvey Cedars**	18
Pointé | **Jersey City**	21
Quays | **Hoboken**	18
Z Rat's | **Hamilton**	24
Z Rest. Latour | **Hamburg**	27
Robin's Nest | **Mt Holly**	22
Robongi | **Weehawken**	24
Rooney's | **Long Branch**	19
Z Ruth's Chris | **Weehawken**	25
Z Saddle River Inn | **Saddle River**	28
Sallee Tee's | **Monmouth Bch**	18
Salt Creek | **Rumson**	19
Sawa | **Long Branch**	23
Ship Inn | **Milford**	17
Shipwreck Point | **Pt. Pleas. Bch**	-
Sirena | **Long Branch**	23
Smithville Inn | **Smithville**	20
Sofia | **Margate**	23
Son Cubano | **W New York**	-
Stella Marina | **Asbury Pk**	23
3 Forty Grill | **Hoboken**	20
Tim McLoone's | **Asbury Pk**	20
Trinity | **Hoboken**	18
Union Park | **Cape May**	25
NEW Ursino | **Union**	-
Ventura's | **Margate**	18
Victor's Pub | **Camden**	-
Vu | **Jersey City**	16
Walpack Inn | **Wallpack**	20
Z Waterside | **N Bergen**	21
Wicked Wolf | **Hoboken**	19
Windansea | **Highlands**	17
Zylo | **Hoboken**	21

VISITORS ON EXPENSE ACCOUNT

NEW Adara | **Montclair**	-
Z Avenue | **Long Branch**	22
Z Bernards Inn | **Bernardsville**	27
Bienvenue | **Red Bank**	22
NEW Blue Morel | **Morristown**	-
Bobby Flay | **A.C.**	25
Blvd. Five 72 | **Kenilworth**	25
Brennen's | **Neptune City**	23
Z Buddakan | **A.C.**	26
Cafe Emilia | **Bridgewater**	22

☑ Cafe Madison | **Riverside**	22
☑ Cafe Matisse | **Rutherford**	27
☑ Capriccio | **A.C.**	25
☑ Catherine Lombardi | **New Bruns.**	24
☑ Chakra | **Paramus**	20
Char | **Raritan**	22
Chelsea Prime | **A.C.**	24
☑ Chez Catherine | **Westfield**	26
☑ CulinAriane | **Montclair**	27
☑ David Burke | **Rumson**	25
Esty St. | **Park Ridge**	25
☑ Fascino | **Montclair**	26
☑ Gables | **Beach Haven**	24
Gallagher's | **A.C.**	22
Girasole | **A.C.**	26
☑ Grand Cafe | **Morristown**	25
Grissini | **Englewood Cliffs**	22
Hamilton/Ward | **Paterson**	23
☑ Highlawn Pavilion | **W Orange**	25
☑ Il Capriccio | **Whippany**	25
☑ Il Mulino | **A.C.**	27
Il Villaggio | **Carlstadt**	24
Luke Palladino | **A.C.**	26
Lu Nello | **Cedar Grove**	25
Mantra | **Paramus**	22
Maritime Parc | **Jersey City**	-
McCormick/Schmick | **Cherry Hill**	20
Mia | **A.C.**	26
☑ Morton's | **Hackensack**	25
☑ Nicholas | **Red Bank**	29
☑ Ninety Acres | **Peapack**	25
☑ Old Homestead | **A.C.**	27
Panico's | **New Bruns.**	21
Park Ave. B&G | **Union City**	18
Park Steak | **Park Ridge**	23
☑ Pluckemin Inn | **Bedminster**	26
Portofino | **Tinton Falls**	24
☑ Porto Leggero | **Jersey City**	26
☑ Ram's Head Inn | **Galloway**	24
☑ Rest. Latour | **Hamburg**	27
☑ Rist./Benito | **Union**	26
☑ River Palm | **multi.**	25
Rod's Steak | **Morristown**	22
Roots Steak | **multi.**	26
☑ Ruth's Chris | **Princeton**	25
☑ Scalini Fedeli | **Chatham**	27

☑ SeaBlue | **A.C.**	26
NEW Sear House | **Closter**	-
☑ Serenade | **Chatham**	27
Sirena | **Long Branch**	23
Smoke Chophouse | **Englewood**	23
☑ Stage Left | **New Bruns.**	27
☑ Stone House | **Warren**	22
3 West | **Basking Ridge**	23
Undici | **Rumson**	22
Uproot | **Warren**	22
Varka | **Ramsey**	26
Villa Amalfi | **Cliffside Pk**	23
Vu | **Jersey City**	16
☑ Waterside | **N Bergen**	21
Wolfgang Puck | **A.C.**	23

WARM WELCOME

Alps Bistro | **Allentown**	-
☑ Amanda's | **Hoboken**	26
Angelo's | **A.C.**	21
☑ A Toute Heure | **Cranford**	26
Babylon | **River Edge**	21
Benito's | **Chester**	23
Berta's | **Wanaque**	22
NEW Biddy O'Malley's | **Northvale**	-
Cafe Emilia | **Bridgewater**	22
Casa Giuseppe | **Iselin**	22
Cenzino | **Oakland**	24
☑ Chez Catherine | **Westfield**	26
Cinnamon | **Morris Plains**	23
Corso 98 | **Montclair**	22
Cucharamama | **Hoboken**	26
Da Filippo's | **Somerville**	24
Dai-Kichi | **Upper Montclair**	23
DiPalma Brothers | **N Bergen**	21
Far East Taste | **Eatontown**	23
Fernandes | **Newark**	24
☑ Il Capriccio | **Whippany**	25
NEW Il Cinghiale | **Little Ferry**	-
Labrador | **Normandy Bch**	25
Langosta | **Asbury Pk**	22
☑ Le Rendez-Vous | **Kenilworth**	27
Madeleine's | **Northvale**	25
Nana's Deli | **Livingston**	23
Oceanos | **Fair Lawn**	23
NEW Ohana Grill | **Lavallette**	-
Plan B | **Asbury Pk**	24
Plantation | **Harvey Cedars**	18

Pop's Garage	**Asbury Pk**	22
Quiet Man	**Dover**	22
Risotto House	**Rutherford**	23
🅩 Rist./Benito	**Union**	26
Rod's Olde Irish	**Sea Girt**	18
Sage	**Ventnor**	25
Taqueria Downtown	**Jersey City**	24
Verjus	**Maplewood**	25

WATERSIDE

Alice's	**Lake Hopatcong**	21
NEW Aqua Blu	**Toms River**	-
Atlantic B&G	**S Seaside Pk**	26
🅩 Avenue	**Long Branch**	22
Avon Pavilion	**Avon-by-Sea**	19
Axelsson's	**Cape May**	23
Bahrs Landing	**Highlands**	17
NEW Baia	**Somers Point**	-
Barnacle Bill's	**Rumson**	22
🅩 Baumgart's	**Edgewater**	19
🅩 Capriccio	**A.C.**	25
🅩 Chart House	**Weehawken**	21
Chickie's/Pete's	**Wildwood**	17
Chophouse	**Gibbsboro**	23
Crab House	**Edgewater**	16
Crab Trap	**Somers Point**	21
Fin	**A.C.**	25
Hamilton's	**Lambertville**	26
Hot Dog Johnny's	**Buttzville**	21
Inlet Café	**Highlands**	20
Inn/Sugar Hill	**Mays Landing**	18
It's Greek To Me	**Long Branch**	18
Klein's	**Belmar**	19
Komegashi	**Jersey City**	22
Lambertville Station	**Lambertville**	17
Langosta	**Asbury Pk**	22
Le Jardin	**Edgewater**	20
Liberty House	**Jersey City**	20
Lilly's/Canal	**Lambertville**	21
Maritime Parc	**Jersey City**	-
Matisse	**Belmar**	22
McLoone's	**multi.**	17
Mill/Spring Lake Hts.	**Spring Lake Hts**	21
Mister C's/Bistro	**Allenhurst**	18
🅩 Molly Pitcher Inn Restaurant	**Red Bank**	22
🅩 Peter Shields	**Cape May**	26

Pointé	**Jersey City**	21
Pop's Garage	**Asbury Pk**	22
Quays	**Hoboken**	18
Red's Lobster	**Pt. Pleas. Bch**	24
Robin's Nest	**Mt Holly**	22
Robongi	**Weehawken**	24
Rooney's	**Long Branch**	19
Sallee Tee's	**Monmouth Bch**	18
Sirena	**Long Branch**	23
Stella Marina	**Asbury Pk**	23
Teplitzky's	**A.C.**	18
3 Forty Grill	**Hoboken**	20
Tim McLoone's	**Asbury Pk**	20
Trinity	**Hoboken**	18
Union Park	**Cape May**	25
NEW Ursino	**Union**	-
Ventura's	**Margate**	18
Victor's Pub	**Camden**	-
Vu	**Jersey City**	16
🅩 Waterside	**N Bergen**	21
White Manna	**Hackensack**	23
Wicked Wolf	**Hoboken**	19
Windansea	**Highlands**	17

WINNING WINE LISTS

🅩 Bernards Inn	**Bernardsville**	27
Berta's	**Wanaque**	22
Bin 14	**Hoboken**	22
Black Forest Inn	**Stanhope**	23
NEW Blue Morel	**Morristown**	-
Bobby Flay	**A.C.**	25
Brass Rail	**Hoboken**	19
🅩 Cafe Madison	**Riverside**	22
🅩 Catherine Lombardi	**New Bruns.**	24
🅩 Chakra	**Paramus**	20
Chengdu 46	**Clifton**	24
Court St.	**Hoboken**	22
Crab's Claw Inn	**Lavallette**	18
Cucharamama	**Hoboken**	26
NEW Daryl	**New Bruns.**	-
🅩 David Burke	**Rumson**	25
Due Mari	**New Bruns.**	26
Edward's Steak	**Jersey City**	23
Esty St.	**Park Ridge**	25
Fin	**A.C.**	25
🅩 Frog/Peach	**New Bruns.**	26
Gladstone	**Gladstone**	21
Hamilton/Ward	**Paterson**	23

SPECIAL FEATURES

Wine Vintage Chart

This chart is based on a 30-point scale. The ratings (by U. of South Carolina law professor **Howard Stravitz**) reflect vintage quality and the wine's readiness to drink. A dash means the wine is past its peak or too young to rate. Loire ratings are for dry whites.

Whites	95	96	97	98	99	00	01	02	03	04	05	06	07	08	09	10
France:																
Alsace	24	23	23	25	23	25	26	22	21	22	23	21	26	26	23	26
Burgundy	27	26	22	21	24	24	23	27	23	26	26	25	26	25	25	–
Loire Valley	–	–	–	–	–	–	–	25	20	22	27	23	24	24	24	25
Champagne	26	27	24	25	25	25	21	26	21	–	–	–	–	–	–	–
Sauternes	21	23	25	23	24	24	29	24	26	21	26	25	27	24	27	–
California:																
Chardonnay	–	–	–	–	22	21	24	25	22	26	29	24	27	23	27	–
Sauvignon Blanc	–	–	–	–	–	–	–	–	–	25	24	27	25	24	25	–
Austria:																
Grüner V./Riesl.	22	–	25	22	26	22	23	25	25	24	23	26	25	24	25	–
Germany:	22	26	22	25	24	–	29	25	26	27	28	26	26	26	26	–

Reds	95	96	97	98	99	00	01	02	03	04	05	06	07	08	09	
France:																
Bordeaux	25	25	24	25	24	29	26	24	26	25	28	24	24	25	27	–
Burgundy	26	27	25	24	27	22	23	25	25	23	28	24	24	25	27	–
Rhône	26	22	23	27	26	27	26	–	26	25	27	25	26	23	27	–
Beaujolais	–	–	–	–	–	–	–	–	–	–	27	25	24	23	28	25
California:																
Cab./Merlot	27	24	28	23	25	–	27	26	25	24	26	24	27	26	25	–
Pinot Noir	–	–	–	–	–	–	26	25	24	25	26	24	27	24	26	–
Zinfandel	–	–	–	–	–	–	25	24	26	24	23	21	26	23	25	–
Oregon:																
Pinot Noir	–	–	–	–	–	–	–	26	24	25	24	25	24	27	24	–
Italy:																
Tuscany	25	24	29	24	27	24	27	–	24	27	25	26	25	24	–	–
Piedmont	21	27	26	25	26	28	27	–	24	27	26	26	27	26	–	–
Spain:																
Rioja	26	24	25	22	25	24	28	–	23	27	26	24	24	25	26	–
Ribera del Duero/ Priorat	25	26	24	25	25	24	27	–	24	27	26	24	25	27	–	–
Australia:																
Shiraz/Cab.	23	25	24	26	24	24	26	26	25	25	26	21	23	26	24	–
Chile:	–	–	–	–	24	22	25	23	24	24	27	25	24	26	24	–
Argentina:																
Malbec	–	–	–	–	–	–	–	–	25	26	27	26	26	25	–	

Vote at zagat.com

ZAGAT
New Jersey Map

Google

Wanaque
Reservoir

Ramapo
Mountain

Map data ©2012 Google

Most Popular Restaurants

Map coordinates follow each name. For chains, only flagship or central locations are plotted. Sections A-G show the northern half of the state (see adjacent map). Sections H-O show the southern half of the state (see reverse side of the map).

1. Nicholas (I-6)
2. Cheesecake Factory† (D-4, J-5, K-3)
3. River Palm (A-5, E-7, D-6)
4. Cafe Panache (B-6)
5. Highlawn Pavilion (E-5)
6. Five Guys† (D-6, K-2, K-5)
7. Ruth's Chris† (F-6, E-3, I-4)
8. P.F. Chang's† (F-7, K-3, M-4)
9. Scalini Fedeli (F-3)
10. Saddle River Inn (B-6)
11. Cafe Matisse (E-6)
12. Amanda's (F-6)
13. Serenade (F-3)
14. Bernards Inn (G-2)
15. Legal Sea Foods (D-6, F-3)
16. Frog and the Peach (I-5)
17. Latour (C-6)
18. CulinAriane (E-5)
19. Lorena's (G-4)
20. Varka (B-5)
21. Origin (F-2, H-4)
22. Pluckemin Inn (H-4)
23. Moonstruck (J-6)
24. Fascino (E-5)
25. Avenue (I-6)
26. Baumgart's Café† (D-7, E-4, E-7)
27. Morton's Steak (D-6, M-4)
28. Ninety Acres (G-1)
29. Il Mondo Vecchio (F-3)
30. David Burke (I-6)
31. Osteria Giotto (E-5)
32. Fornos of Spain (G-5)
33. Chef's Table (B-5)
34. Blue Point (I-4)
35. Park & Orchard (E-6)
36. Basilico (G-4)
37. Chart House (F-7, M-4)
38. McCormick & Schmick's† (D-6, H-4, K-3)
39. Huntley Taverne (G-4)
40. Bay Ave. Trattoria (I-6)
41. A Toute Heure (H-5)
42. Chef Vola's (M-4)
43. Rat's (I-4)
44. Arthur's Tavern (F-6)
45. 410 Bank St. (O-3)
46. Elements (I-4)
47. Manor (E-4)
48. Buddakan (M-4)
49. It's Greek To Me† (C-6, F-6, I-6)
50. Due Mari (H-5)

† Indicates multiple branches